CRUCIFORM SCRIPTURE

CRUCIFORM SCRIPTURE

Cross, Participation, and Mission

Essays from Matthew to Revelation in Honor of Michael J. Gorman

EDITED BY

*Christopher W. Skinner, Nijay K. Gupta,
Andy Johnson & Drew J. Strait*

WILLIAM B. EERDMANS PUBLISHING COMPANY
GRAND RAPIDS, MICHIGAN

Wm. B. Eerdmans Publishing Co.
4035 Park East Court SE, Grand Rapids, Michigan 49546
www.eerdmans.com

© 2021 Christopher W. Skinner, Nijay K. Gupta, Andy Johnson, Drew J. Strait
All rights reserved
Published 2020

ISBN 978-0-8028-7637-9

Library of Congress Cataloging-in-Publication Data

Names: Gupta, Nijay K., editor. | Johnson, Andy, 1960– editor. | Skinner, Christopher W., editor. | Strait, Drew J., editor. | Gorman, Michael J., 1955– honouree.
Title: Cruciform scripture : cross, participation, and mission / edited by Christopher W. Skinner, Nijay K. Gupta, Andy Johnson & Drew J. Strait.
Description: Grand Rapids, Michigan : William B. Eerdmans Publishing Company, 2021. | Includes bibliographical references and index. | Summary: "A collection of essays that build upon and honor the work of Michael Gorman"—Provided by publisher.
Identifiers: LCCN 2020012148 | ISBN 9780802876379 (paperback)
Subjects: LCSH: Jesus Christ—Crucifixion—Biblical teaching. | Bible. New Testament—Criticism, interpretation, etc.
Classification: LCC BT453 .C777 2020 | DDC 232.96/3—dc23
LC record available at https://lccn.loc.gov/2020012148

Unless otherwise noted, quotations of the Bible are taken from the New Revised Standard Version of the Bible

Contents

Editors' Preface	ix
Abbreviations	xi
Introduction	xv
Brent Laytham and Pat Fosarelli	

PART ONE: THE CROSS AND THE CRUCIFORM LIFE

1.	Matthew, the Cross, and the Cruciform Life	3
	Rebekah Eklund	
2.	The Crucified One: Jesus's Death and Discipleship in the Gospel of Mark	22
	Richard B. Hays	
3.	Luke and the Cross: A Vision of Crucicentric Discipleship	37
	Frank E. Dicken	
4.	The Johannine Cross as Revelation of the Father: Finding a Cruciform God in the Fourth Gospel	56
	Christopher W. Skinner	
5.	Cruciformity and the Believer's Governing Faculties: Rethinking Ἡγέομαι in Philippians	72
	Nijay K. Gupta	

PART TWO: PARTICIPATION IN CHRIST, ONE WITH GOD

6.	Grasping and Being Grasped: Gift and Agency in Paul	89
	Stephen E. Fowl	

CONTENTS

7. Baptized into Christ: Romans 6:3–4—*the* Text on Baptism and Participation 106
   Klyne Snodgrass

8. The Holy Spirit, Justification, and Participation in the Divine Life in Galatians 123
   Ben C. Blackwell

9. Participation in Christ in 1 Peter 144
   Dennis R. Edwards

PART THREE: BECOMING THE GOSPEL IN MISSION

10. "Follow Me": The Mandate for Mission in the Gospel of John 163
    Sherri Brown

11. An Alternative Global Imaginary: Imperial Rome's *Pax Romana* and Luke's "Counter-Violent" *Missio Dei* 184
    Drew J. Strait

12. The Past, Present, and Future of Bodily Resurrection as Salvation: Christ, Church, and Cosmos 207
    Andy Johnson

13. Mother Zion Rejoices: Psalm 87 as a Missing Link in Galatians 4 225
    N. T. Wright

14. Citizenship and Empire: A Missional Engagement with Ephesians 240
    Sylvia C. Keesmaat

15. Following the Lamb Wherever He Goes: Missional Ecclesiology in Revelation 7 and 14:1–5 260
    Dean Flemming

Epilogue 279

Dr. Michael J. Gorman: Cursus Vitae 281

Contributors 295

Index of Modern Authors 297

Index of Scripture and Other Ancient Texts 303

.... Editors' Preface

Although Michael Gorman began his publishing career almost twenty years earlier, it was the 2001 release of his first Eerdmans book, *Cruciformity: Paul's Narrative Spirituality of the Cross*, that gave him a seat at the table among those shaping the direction of Pauline studies. Today, it is clear that Mike has made the most of his seat at that table. But he has not just influenced various aspects of Pauline studies; he has also made significant contributions in other related areas, such as atonement theology and theological and missional hermeneutics. In addition, over the last decade or so he has produced noteworthy volumes on the Fourth Gospel and Revelation. But *Cruciformity* remains the catalyst that propelled and shaped the main lines of Mike's subsequent scholarly trajectory. Already in that volume, whose focus was on the cross and the cruciform life, were the seeds of what would develop into what Mike would later call an accidental trilogy.[1] In a subsequent Eerdmans book in 2009, *Inhabiting the Cruciform God: Kenosis, Justification, and Theosis in Paul's Narrative Soteriology*, he would go on to develop in more detail the theme of participation in Christ as sharing in the life of the Triune God. Six years later, in 2015, Mike released the third Eerdmans volume of this accidental trilogy entitled *Becoming the Gospel: Paul, Participation, and Mission*. There he emphasized in detail that the cruciform life of participation in Christ, in which one was becoming more like God, was inherently missional in nature because the nature of the Triune God was inherently missional.

As we were trying to decide how to structure this volume of essays, the respective themes of this accidental trilogy suggested a three-part structure. In Part One, contributors focus their essays on the cross and the cruciform life. The focus of Part Two is on participation in Christ as sharing in the life of the Triune God. Finally, in Part Three, the essays develop missional aspects

---

1. *Becoming the Gospel: Paul, Participation, and Mission* (Grand Rapids: Eerdmans, 2015), 2–3.

of a variety of biblical texts. As in Mike's own work, even as they focus on one of these themes, some of the contributors incorporate aspects of the themes from the other two parts of the volume. The contributors were not given the task of dialoguing with Mike's published work directly—although many do, and others cite his work often. Rather, their task was to produce an essay that would fit the theme of one of the parts of the volume. In addition to these essays, the volume contains a brief introduction, written by two of Mike's colleagues at St. Mary's Seminary & University, sketching the impact of his academic work and teaching. It closes with an even briefer epilogue in which Mike's three children pay tribute to their dad.

We are grateful to Eerdmans for agreeing to help us honor our friend and colleague in this way. We are particularly indebted to Michael Thomson and Trevor Thompson. Before moving on from Eerdmans, Michael helped us launch this project and then handed it off to Trevor, who has been a constant source of encouragement and support in bringing the volume to completion. We offer these essays to Mike in the sincere hope that they will honor his life, teaching, and scholarship appropriately. But even more so, we offer them to other scholars, students, and pastors with the hope that they will aid in shaping the whole church into "colonies of cruciformity"[2] who participate in Christ and thereby become more like the missional God revealed on the cross.

Nijay Gupta, Andy Johnson,
Chris Skinner, and Drew Strait

---

2. Mike's phrase from, among other places, *Cruciformity: Paul's Narrative Spirituality of the Cross* (Grand Rapids: Eerdmans, 2001), 349.

Abbreviations

AB	Anchor Bible
AcBib	Academia Biblica
ACCS	Ancient Christian Commentary on Scripture
ACW	Ancient Christian Writers
AJEC	Ancient Judaism and Early Christianity
AJP	*American Journal of Philology*
AnBib	Analecta Biblica
ANQ	*Andover Newton Quarterly*
ANTC	Abingdon New Testament Commentaries
AThR	*Anglican Theological Review*
BDAG	Walter Bauer et al. *A Greek-English Lexicon of the New Testament and Other Early Christian Literature*. 3rd ed. Revised and edited by Frederick William Danker. Chicago: University of Chicago Press, 2000.
BETL	Bibliotheca Ephemeridum Theologicarum Lovaniensium
BGBE	Beiträge zur Geschichte der biblischen Exegese
Bib	*Biblica*
BibInt	*Biblical Interpretation*
BibInt	Biblical Interpretation Series
BNTC	Black's New Testament Commentaries
BSac	*Bibliotheca Sacra*
BTS	Biblical Tools and Studies
BZNW	Beihefte zur Zeitschrift fur die neutestamentliche Wissenschaft
CBET	Contributions to Biblical Exegesis and Theology
ChrCent	*Christian Century*
ClQ	*Classical Quarterly*
ConBNT	Coniectanea Biblica: New Testament Series
CurBR	*Currents in Biblical Research*
ECL	Early Christianity and Its Literature
EKKNT	Evangelisch-katholischer Kommentar zum Neuen Testament

ESV	English Standard Version
EvQ	*Evangelical Quarterly*
ExAud	*Ex Auditu*
ExpTim	*Expository Times*
HBT	Horizons in Biblical Theology
HNTC	Harper's New Testament Commentaries
HTR	Harvard Theological Review
ICC	International Critical Commentary
Int	*Interpretation*
JBL	*Journal of Biblical Literature*
JETS	*Journal of the Evangelical Theological Society*
JMTh	*Journal of Moral Theology*
JRS	*Journal of Roman Studies*
JSNT	*Journal for the Study of the New Testament*
JSNTSup	Journal for the Study of the New Testament Supplement Series
JSOTSup	Journal for the Study of the Old Testament Supplement Series
JSPL	*Journal for the Study of Paul and His Letters*
JTI	*Journal of Theological Interpretation*
KJV	King James Version
L&N	Louw, Johannes P., and Eugene A. Nida, eds. *Greek-English Lexicon of the New Testament: Based on Semantic Domains*. 2nd ed. New York: United Bible Societies, 1989
LCC	Library of Christian Classics
LNTS	Library of New Testament Studies
LW	*Luther's Works*, American Edition
LXX	Septuagint
MT	Masoretic Text
NABRE	New American Bible Revised Edition
NCB	New Century Bible
Neot	*Neotestamentica*
NET	New English Translation
NETS	New English Translation of the Septuagint
NIB	*The New Interpreter's Bible*. Edited by Leander E. Keck. 12 vols. Nashville: Abingdon, 1994–2004
NICNT	New International Commentary on the New Testament
NIDB	*New Interpreter's Dictionary of the Bible.* Edited by Katherine Doob Sakenfield. 5 vols. Nashville: Abingdon, 2006–2009
NIGTC	New International Greek Testament Commentary
NIV	New International Version

NovT	*Novum Testamentum*
NovTSup	Supplements to Novum Testamentum
NPNF2	*Nicene and Post-Nicene Fathers*, Series 2
NRSV	New Revised Standard Version
NSBT	New Studies in Biblical Theology
NT	New Testament
NTD	Das Neue Testament Deutsch
NTG	New Testament Guides
NTL	New Testament Library
NTOA	Novum Testamentum et Orbis Antiquus
NTS	*New Testament Studies*
OT	Old Testament
OTP	*Old Testament Pseudepigrapha*. Edited by James H. Charlesworth. 2 vols. New York: Doubleday, 1983, 1985
ProEccl	*Pro Ecclesia*
PRSt	*Perspectives in Religious Studies*
PSB	*Princeton Seminary Bulletin*
RB	*Revue biblique*
RelSRev	*Religious Studies Review*
RevExp	*Review and Expositor*
RIC	Roman Imperial Coinage
RNT	Regensburger Neues Testament
RRC	Coinage of the Roman Republic
RSV	Revised Standard Version
RTR	*Reformed Theological Review*
SBL	Society of Biblical Literature
SCJR	*Studies in Christian-Jewish Relations*
SHBC	Smyth & Helwys Bible Commentary
SNTSMS	Society of New Testament Studies Monograph Series
SNTSU	Studien zum Neuen Testament und seiner Umwelt
SP	Sacra Pagina
ST	*Studia Theologica*
THNTC	Two Horizons New Testament Commentary
ThTo	*Theology Today*
TOTC	Tyndale Old Testament Commentaries
TTCT	T & T Clark Theology
VE	*Vox Evangelica*
VT	*Vetus Testamentum*
WBC	Word Biblical Commentary

ABBREVIATIONS

WEC	Wycliffe Exegetical Commentary
WTJ	*Westminster Theological Journal*
WUNT	Wissenschaftliche Untersuchungen zum Neuen Testament
ZNW	*Zeitschrift für die neutestamentliche Wissenschaft und die Kunde der älteren Kirche*

.... Introduction

Brent Laytham and Pat Fosarelli

Just as the apostle Paul was a zealous student of Scripture, teacher of the gospel, and servant of the church, so is his student Michael J. Gorman—consummate scholar, extraordinary teacher, and faithful churchman. And though Mike's scholarship, teaching, and service can be conceptualized independently, they actually coalesce with and amplify one another; we might venture to say that his research/*meletē*, instruction/*didaskalia*, and churchmanship/*diakonia* participate in one another, just as each activity participates in his "work of faith and labor of love and steadfastness of hope in our Lord Jesus Christ" (1 Thess 1:3). Most readers of this volume will already be quite familiar with Mike's scholarship and will have some sense of its overall importance to the field of biblical studies. In addition, the copious number of times his numerous works are referred to—and at times engaged directly—in the essays that follow offer ample testimony to the impact of his scholarship in academic circles. The extraordinary impact of Mike's teaching and service, however, will be less well known to most readers. Hence, this introduction will focus only briefly on the substance and significance of Mike's scholarship, and then more substantially on the quality and impact of Mike's teaching and service.

Mike Gorman is a consummate scholar of Scripture who has significantly shaped the agenda for Pauline studies in the twenty-first century. His work on Paul has made cruciformity, participation, and mission inescapable themes for understanding the apostle of the crucified Lord. His books on Revelation, the Gospel of John, and atonement have shown that those same themes are equally essential for reading the rest of the New Testament responsibly. Mike's stature in biblical studies was doubly recognized in 2012, by his peers with his election into the prestigious Studiorum Novi Testamenti Societas (Society for New Testament Studies), and by St. Mary's Seminary & University with his appointment as the Raymond E. Brown Chair in Biblical Studies and Theology.

The true measure of his contribution, however, may be that the very books which scholars praise as pioneering, profound, and rigorous are widely read by pastors and laity because they are accessible, stimulating, and practical. I (Brent) attended an ecumenical gathering in 2012 that included a workshop on how congregations can partner with local and state agencies to offer victim-offender reconciliation programs. The workshop leader was a lay person with a master's degree in social work; he read theology avidly but had no formal theological education. Nonetheless, this presenter extensively grounded both the rationale *for* and the shape *of* victim-offender reconciliation programs in Mike's work on cruciformity and participation. The perennial phenomenon this anecdote illustrates led to Mike's selection as a Henry Luce III Fellow in the category of Bible and the church (2015), a project that culminated in *Abide and Go: Missional Theosis in the Gospel of John*.[1]

All of this means that Mike's scholarship is not just a great source *for* powerful teaching; it is already a powerful form *of* great teaching. Which brings us to Mike Gorman the master teacher. I (Pat) am a physician and a practical theologian, and I would have never been the latter had it not been for Mike Gorman. In the fall of 1992, I had been a physician for fifteen years on the pediatrics faculty at the Johns Hopkins School of Medicine. I came to study at St. Mary's Ecumenical Institute because I believed that I would be a better physician if I knew more about the spiritual dimensions of the human person, something which had not been part of the medical school curriculum. I thought I would be a brief sojourner at the Ecumenical Institute, but meeting—and more importantly being taught by—Mike Gorman changed all that. He simply was the best teacher I had ever had . . . period. He took an interest in my studies, encouraging me to complete a degree in theology. After that was accomplished, and because he knew that my heart was always in the practical rather than the theoretical, he further encouraged me to pursue a doctorate in ministry. And, after that was accomplished, because he knew that I wanted to bring science and theology, especially medicine and ministry, together, he recruited me to do that work—for the good of the church—in St. Mary's Ecumenical Institute. As my teacher, Mike "exegeted" not only Pauline texts but my passions and aspirations, all in service to the church.

For nearly thirty years, Mike Gorman has been a superlative classroom teacher in both academic divisions of St. Mary's Seminary & University: the School of Theology and the Ecumenical Institute. He has extraordinary versatility in his teaching, which began with a course in early church history (taught as an adjunct) and has ranged from virtually every conceivable New Testament

---

1. Michael J. Gorman, *Abide and Go: Missional Theosis in the Gospel of John* (Eugene, OR: Cascade, 2018).

Introduction

course, through theological ethics, to spirituality, and even preaching. A recent (January 2019) intensive exemplified Mike's educational versatility and vision: he retooled an earlier course in order to offer "Taizé: Community, Spirituality, Theology" and co-taught it with a systematic theologian (his son, Rev. Dr. Mark Gorman) and Brother John of Taizé.

Like the subtitle of his edited introduction to *Scripture and Its Interpretation*, Mike's teaching is ecumenical and global. In Baltimore, he teaches a classroom of Catholic seminarians in the afternoon, and that same evening, in that same classroom, he teaches men and women who run the gamut from Catholic and Orthodox to mainline Protestants to nondenominational and Unitarian. Globally, Mike has taught students in Canada, the Democratic Republic of Congo, England, Cameroon, and New Zealand. For the last group, however, Mike did not travel to the Global South as he had originally planned. Due to unforeseen circumstances, Mike taught using a virtual communications platform, which he has done many times before. This willingness to adapt old pedagogies and adopt new ones is a reminder that Mike is a master teacher in part because he is a constant learner, not only in his scholarly research, but also in the best practices of teaching. For this reason, most of his faculty colleagues can testify that Mike has taught them to be better teachers. (And when faculty colleagues fall short of Mike's high standards, we have never seen him withhold respect by subtly or overtly treating that individual as anything other than a valued member of the faculty.)

Given that Mike was a full-time dean for eighteen years (1993–2012), his scholarly output appears prodigiously productive. But perhaps his teaching is even more prodigious, as he has taught at least 128 different courses at St. Mary's, not to mention myriad independent studies, theses directed, and Greek reading seminars. At the same time, he has led a weekly Bible study in his home (for thirty years) and taught in local congregations (his own and many others) and at judicatory and national gatherings; in fall 2018 he offered a ten-week survey of the New Testament to two dozen local congregations, with several hundred laity joining virtually. Clearly, the classroom is Mike's true home. And the extraordinary thing is not his stamina in doing this; rather, it is his superlative ability to make the same class academically rigorous and spiritually soul-searching; it is his capacity to bring out the best in students of every ability, and indeed not just to draw from them their best intellectual work, but—as many students report—to deepen their desire to become better persons. Of course, Mike hasn't always been able to elicit his students' best work (any more than Jesus the master teacher could). When a student has performed miserably, Mike always "speaks the truth in love" (Eph 4:15), neither sugar-coating the student's deficiencies nor robbing that student of dignity and the hope that things could improve.

Thus, there are two common themes resounding in Mike's course evaluations over the two decades we have been reading them: Mike is the best teacher I've ever had; Mike's teaching inspires me to be a better person. But Mike's teaching—Pauline as it inevitably is—has shaped student imagination even more deeply than that. So students regularly report that Mike's teaching deepened their *love* of God and Scripture, that it enlivened their *joy* in discipleship, and that Mike's teaching manifested profound qualities of *patience*, *kindness*, *gentleness*, and *generosity*. Not surprisingly, Mike's students are intuitively describing his teaching in the vocabulary of the fruit of the Spirit (Gal 5:22–23).

Mike used John's paradoxical imperative to title his study of missional theosis in that gospel—*Abide and Go*. Mike argues that *abide* and *go* are not mutually exclusive commands but are rather the centripetal and centrifugal sides of the same gospel coin. We bear that in mind when considering Mike's own life and career, which might appear to have emphasized abide at the expense of go. Born in Fort Meade, Maryland, living most of his life in the vicinity of Baltimore and working most of his career at St. Mary's Seminary & University, Mike seems to have incarnated the wisdom of Baltimore jazz legend Ethel Ennis, who once quipped: "You don't have to move on to move up." Though we consider that Ennis was right to contest the popular idea that success requires moving on to bigger places or better opportunities, we also recognize that imitating Ethel Ennis was not what Michael Gorman had in mind. His consummate scholarship, extraordinary teaching, and faithful service to the church have all been his attempt to have the same mind that was in Christ Jesus (Phil 2:5).

PART ONE

The Cross and the Cruciform Life

Chapter 1

Matthew, the Cross, and the Cruciform Life

Rebekah Eklund

Michael Gorman has given us a promising new lens through which to view the New Testament texts, one not of a crucified God but of a cruciform God.[1] This theme emerges most clearly in the writings of the apostle Paul, who spent his apostolic career wrestling with the significance of Jesus's death and resurrection for the Christian life—and indeed, for the whole cosmos. In the gospels, given their narrative character, one may perceive this theme mostly in retrospect. Nonetheless, to borrow a phrase from Richard Hays, the gospels themselves encourage us to read and reread them "in light of the resurrection."[2] Mark's Gospel is perhaps the starkest example of this, since he leaves his entire narrative hanging on a note of fear and surprise, with the women fleeing the empty tomb—prompting the readers to return to the beginning and read it again as *their* story.[3] But one may also see Matthew's Gospel as a text meant to be read in light of its ending, which neatly bookends its beginning with the theme of Jesus as God *with us*, "even to the end of the age" (Matt 1:23; 28:20).

I have chosen to explore Matthew, then, precisely because of its apparent

---

1. Michael J. Gorman, *Cruciformity: Paul's Narrative Spirituality of the Cross* (Grand Rapids: Eerdmans, 2001), 17.
2. Richard B. Hays, "Reading Scripture in Light of the Resurrection," in *The Art of Reading Scripture*, ed. Ellen F. Davis and Richard B. Hays (Grand Rapids: Eerdmans, 2003), 216–38.
3. Joel Marcus, *Mark 8–16*, AB 27A (New Haven: Yale University Press, 2009), 1096.

dearth of explicit references to cruciformity, theosis, and the new covenant.[4] I will begin by wondering if Matthew is less interested in a *new* covenant than in the fulfillment and perfection of *the* covenant. I will then argue that the "Gormanian" theme of "taking up the cross" pervades Matthew's Gospel and resonates deeply with one very central (if unexpected) text: the Beatitudes. Finally, I will suggest that the climax of Matthew's story (the empty tomb and the risen Jesus) focuses our attention on God both as cruciform and as resurrecting—as the One with life-giving and death-defeating power.

The (Not-So-New) New Covenant

In *The Death of the Messiah*, Gorman develops a "new covenant" model of atonement, a model he takes to be true to all the New Testament writers. Of course, of the three Last Supper texts in which Jesus identifies the Passover cup as his blood of the (new) covenant, only Luke includes the word "new," but Gorman suggests that he is likely making explicit what Mark and Matthew left implicit.[5] He sees Jeremiah's new covenant, among other Old Testament promises, underlying all three texts.

Matthew is certainly aware of Jer 31; he uses a quotation from it to illuminate the grief of the Bethlehem mothers over the slaughter of their innocent children, linking their lament to Rachel's inconsolable grief over the loss of her children. In Jeremiah's context, Rachel weeps for all the children of Israel who have been carried away into exile (Jer 31:15//Jer 38:15 LXX; Matt 2:18). Matthew's opening chapters are replete with imagery of both exodus and exile, suggesting that his use of Jer 31 (and its exilic resonances) is not incidental; the theme of Israel's restoration and return from exile is central to his gospel and his understanding of Jesus's mission.

So it seems likely that Jer 31 is one of the texts he has in mind when he

---

4. Michael Gorman's work has profoundly shaped and informed me as a pastor and a New Testament scholar, so I offer these thoughts out of gratitude to him in the hopes that they may extend his insights into another context.

5. Michael J. Gorman, *The Death of the Messiah and the Birth of the New Covenant: A (Not So) New Model of the Atonement* (Eugene, OR: Cascade, 2014), 14. In Matt 26:28, the more probable reading "the covenant" appears in P37, likely in P45, Sinaiticus, Vaticanus, L, Z, Θ, etc. The variant "the new covenant" appears in Alexandrinus, C (Ephraemi Rescriptus), D (Bezae Cantabrigiensis), K (Byzantine text type), W, Γ, Δ, etc. The word "new" was likely added to align Matthew's text with Luke 22:20 or 1 Cor 11:25. Gorman himself notes that there are only hints of this model in Matthew, devoting only about a page and a half to the theme of "cross and new covenant in Matthew"; by contrast Luke-Acts gets six pages (Gorman, *The Death of the Messiah*, 36–37).

describes Jesus's blood in covenantal terms. But does this mean that Matthew thinks of Jesus's covenant as new? There are, to be sure, elements of newness to Jeremiah's new covenant: namely, that God will put the law directly into their hearts (Jer 31:33–34), a theme that accords quite well with Jesus's emphasis on the heart in the Sermon on the Mount. But it is not a covenant that differs in kind in other ways from those that preceded it; it still involves the Mosaic law and is still made with the same people: the houses of Israel and Judah. On Jeremiah's terms, then, it operates more as a renewed covenant than a new (read: different) one.

Likewise, Matthew's understanding of the "new covenant" community which follows Jesus still involves the Mosaic law, as it is interpreted by Jesus's authoritative teaching (Matt 5:17–48; see also 19:3–9, 16–22; 22:34–40), and is still *initially* offered to the same people of God: the lost sheep of the house of Israel (15:24). Hints of gentile inclusion appear as early as the genealogy, peek out again in Jesus's encounter with the Canaanite woman, and come to fruition in the Great Commission. But for Matthew, on the whole, practices like forgiveness, deeds of mercy, and caring for the poor and weak do not seem to be practices that result from the new covenant established by Jesus's death as much as they were *already* practices described in the law of the "old" covenant. Jesus seems to assume that his (Jewish) listeners are already engaged in many of these central Jewish practices (as in 6:2–18). Of course, he interprets these actions to his followers, loosening some and tightening others, but none of them are wholly new. Perhaps, then, Matthew's covenant theme can remind us, as Gorman himself does in the subtitle to one of his books—*A (Not So) New Model of the Atonement*—that the new covenant is not so new after all, at least not for the evangelist.

Taking Up the Cross

Gorman's theme of cruciformity certainly coheres deeply with Matthew's ethos. Hints of Matthew's emphasis on the way of Jesus as costly, self-giving service appear in chapter one: in two foremothers of Jesus—Rahab, who hides the spies at significant risk to herself; and Ruth, who shows loving and sacrificial *ḥesed* to Naomi—and in Jesus's earthly father Joseph, who risks social disgrace (no small matter in his culture) by taking a shamefully pregnant woman as his wife. Further clues appear in the temptation narrative in chapter four, when Jesus rejects the tempter's offers of political, military, and religious power, presaging his refusal to exercise his right to call down legions of angels for protection when he is arrested (Matt 4:1–11; 26:53).

Two additional themes about the way of the cross emerge as we advance through Matthew's narrative: persecution and renunciation. A cruciform life, writes Matthew, is a persecuted life. The followers of Jesus will be hated and persecuted because of Jesus's name, just as Jesus himself was hated, reviled, and persecuted (Matt 5:10–12; 10:22). They will conform to this aspect of Jesus's life, whether they like it or not. As Gorman writes, the followers of Jesus can expect to participate in Jesus's fate: "his rejection, suffering, and death."[6] In the slender evidence that we can glean from Matthew's Gospel about his community, this appears to be the case for the followers of Jesus to whom Matthew writes. They do not need a warning that they will be hated; they already experience this for themselves.

By the time Matthew composed his gospel, presumably in the 70s or 80s CE, Jerusalem had been captured by the Romans and the temple destroyed, displacing Jewish Christians (perhaps even some members of Matthew's eventual community) along with their fellow Jews.[7] Nero's recent persecution of Christians in Rome surely meant Christians were keeping a wary eye on the local Roman rulers. And tensions were rising between Jews who worshiped Jesus and Jews who did not. Jesus's predictions, then, function not as warnings but as encouragement to remain steadfast, since they are following in his footsteps. Indeed, their very suffering is the mark of their faithfulness to their Lord.

Likewise, throughout history, Christians have claimed their suffering as the mark of their faithfulness, sometimes even over against other Christians, as when Reformers and Anabaptists alike pointed to their own suffering at the hands of other Christians as the sign of their true faith. John Calvin (who was confident that he was suffering for the sake of Christ) firmly rejected the idea that the Anabaptists were being persecuted for righteousness, saying that they suffered instead for their errors.[8] One is not a martyr, he wrote tartly, if one "suffers persecution for his own fault."[9] Roman Catholics likewise protested that the Protestants were suffering for their heresy, not for their faith.

---

6. Gorman, *The Death of the Messiah*, 98.

7. Carol Bakker Wilson points out that food insecurity (to use a modern term) was widespread in the first-century Roman Empire and that the Jewish-Roman War likely further disrupted food supplies, perhaps even for Antiochene Christians (*For I Was Hungry and You Gave Me Food: Pragmatics of Food Access in the Gospel of Matthew* [Eugene, OR: Pickwick, 2014], 5–11, 80).

8. John Calvin, *Sermons on the Beatitudes: Five Sermons from the Gospel Harmony, Delivered in Geneva in 1560* (Carlisle, PA: Banner of Truth Trust, 2006), 60–61.

9. John Calvin, *A Harmony of the Gospels Matthew, Mark and Luke*, trans. A. W. Morrison, ed. David W. Torrance and Thomas F. Torrance (Grand Rapids: Eerdmans, 1972), 1:173.

This should give us pause. At least, it should remind us that it is not always straightforward to judge whether Christian suffering is a result of cruciformity or some other cause.

Whether hatred and persecution are likewise the marks of a contemporary Christian's faithfulness is an even more complicated question. Western Christians rarely suffer and die for their faith in Jesus, whereas Christians elsewhere in the world fit more closely into Matthew's model. One need only think of the shocking plight of Syrian, Palestinian, and Nigerian Christians (among others) to recognize that some contemporary Christians are losing their homes, livelihoods, and lives for their commitment to Christ.

Matthew's theme of renunciation likewise raises uncomfortable questions for wealthy Christians of any era. Matthew writes straightforwardly that taking up the cross and following Jesus will entail leaving one's family, renouncing one's possessions, having no home and nowhere soft to sleep, and loving Jesus more than one's relatives, one's livelihood, and even one's own life (Matt 8:18–22; 10:37–39; 16:24–26; 19:16–30). Conversely, Jesus insists in Matthew that his cross is a light burden to bear, but this reassurance appears to be less about the costly demands of discipleship and more about Jesus's interpretation of the requirements of the Mosaic law (11:30; cf. 23:4).

Suffering as the Way of the Cross

Like Matthew, Paul expects "that all believers will likely endure suffering."[10] Indeed, in one letter Paul names suffering with Christ as a prerequisite for being glorified with him (Rom 8:17).[11] It is hard to say how much this expectation arises from the sociopolitical contexts of Matthew and Paul, respectively. In the first century, whether in Antioch or in Asia Minor, Christians could expect suffering from all sides—from Jews who saw them as blasphemers, perhaps from Jewish Christians who objected to law-breaking gentiles, from local Roman rulers and sometimes from Caesar himself, and from pagan neighbors who often misunderstood or distrusted Christian customs.[12]

Today the church's split from Judaism is complete and a painful reversal has ensued—Jews no longer persecute Christians, but Christians have been harsh persecutors of Jews. In many countries in the world, including the United

---

10. Gorman, *Cruciformity*, 301.
11. Gorman, *Cruciformity*, 326.
12. Joseph Walsh, ed., *What Would You Die For? Perpetua's Passion* (Baltimore: Apprentice House, 2006), 25–47.

States, Christians do not suffer for their faith at the hands of the government or in any significant way at the hands of their neighbors. It is possible that disdain and mistrust of American Christians is rising in the current heated political climate, but it is rare for such social pressure to result in the loss of a job or a home.[13] And while following the earthly Jesus in his itinerant ministry led the disciples to leave behind families, job securities, and fixed addresses, relatively few Christians today take such radical steps in order to follow the risen Lord—aside, perhaps, from some missionaries. And Christians who flee as refugees from war-torn homelands are not *voluntarily* taking up the cross; they model in a far more painful way the cost of following Jesus in a hostile environment.

This suggests a certain nuance in the theme of cruciformity when comparing our social context to Matthew's. Gorman acknowledges that power and privilege are relative, and he is careful to say that cruciformity must be freely chosen and "can never be imposed 'top-down.'"[14] But what shall we say about a cruciformity that is *not* freely chosen, but that is imposed from without, even when it results from one's refusal to renounce faith in Christ? The Christian schoolgirls (alongside a smaller group of Muslim girls) kidnapped by the Islamic militant group Boko Haram did not freely choose to give of themselves in love. Nonetheless, might we say that they are being "persecuted for the sake of righteousness" (Matt 5:10), or that they are treading the sorrowful way of the cross? Or is their suffering simply a deep injustice and affront to the God who protects the powerless and sides with the oppressed? Matthew's Gospel does not give us the answer to this dilemma—but it does have harsh words for anyone who causes a little one to stumble (18:1–7).

The Son of Man

A turning point in Matthew's Gospel occurs when Jesus begins to predict that he must suffer, die, and be raised from the dead. To be certain that the disciples do not miss the importance of this declaration, he issues it three times. The second two announcements introduce the theme of Jesus as the Son of Man. Matthew's use of the Son of Man title ties together two key Matthean themes: Jesus's service and suffering (Matt 8:20; 12:40; 17:12, 22; 20:18, 28); and his

---

13. On false perceptions of discrimination among white American evangelical Christians, see Cheryl Cornish, "What Kind of Righteousness? What Kind of Blessing?," *The Yale ISM Review* 4 (2018): http://ismreview.yale.edu/article/what-kind-of-righteousness-what-kind-of-blessing/#_ednref3.

14. Gorman, *Cruciformity*, 378.

hidden status as the judge who has the authority to forgive sins and will come again in power and glory to judge the earth (9:6; 10:23; 13:41; 16:27–28; 19:28; 24:27, 29–31, 37–44; 25:31).

The threefold declaration of the necessity of Jesus's suffering and death in the latter half of Matthew's Gospel echoes the themes of the temptation narrative by indicating again Jesus's refusal to use power to achieve his aims or to avoid his death, choosing instead the path of apparent weakness and defeat. The first passion prediction gives rise to the sharp rebuke of Peter ("Get behind me, Satan!"); as with the temptation, Matthew links renunciation of power with God's will and the avoidance of suffering with the devil (Matt 16:21–23). An observation that the disciples are greatly distressed follows the second passion prediction (17:22–23); they still have not understood. Immediately after the third passion prediction, the mother of the sons of Zebedee represents the continued failure of Jesus's followers to grasp the way of the cross when she asks for her sons to have places of honor in the kingdom (20:17–23). She, like the disciples, has correctly perceived at least some aspect of Jesus's status and power (he has access to the Father) but has misunderstood the mode of that status and power (it operates not through the usual signs of glory, but through the bitter cup of suffering).

The other ten disciples are indignant, but they are upset not because James and John have so radically misunderstood the way of the cross, but because they are angry at the idea of the two brothers selfishly asking for the places of honor in the kingdom that all of them would quite like to have. Jesus takes this opportunity to give his clearest teaching yet about what the way of the cross, his manner of discipleship, entails: not to lord it over one another, but to serve one another—not to seek to become great, but to strive instead to be the least. Jesus himself models what this looks like: "just as the Son of Man came not to be served but to serve, and to give his life a ransom for many" (Matt 20:28; see also 23:11–12).

This theme reaches its height (or its depth, as it were) at Jesus's crucifixion when Jesus's apparent humiliation is, for those with ears to hear, his exaltation as Israel's true king and God's Messiah. The soldiers perform an ironic enthronement ceremony, which they take to be mockery, but which Matthew's readers know enacts the truth (Matt 27:27–31). By humiliating Jesus, Rome has unwittingly exalted him; the Roman Empire has not defeated Jesus but enacted his enthronement as Israel's true king and foreshadowed his rightful place in the heavenly throne room, when he will have *all* authority, *all* power (ἐξουσία) both in heaven and on earth (28:18). The marks of his kingship foreshadow an aspect of Jesus's power that coheres most closely not with the cross but with the resurrection: his future role as the heavenly Son of Man who will rule over all the nations and who will serve as the judge of all the earth.

Gorman observes that the theme of cruciformity does not exclude God's rightful power to judge and to punish injustice and indeed that Paul expects that God will do so (1 Cor 15).[15] It is worth dwelling on this theme a bit longer in relation to Matthew's theme of Jesus as the Son of Man alongside the Matthean parables of judgment (Matt 13:24-30, 36-43, 47-50; 21:33-46; 25:1-13, 31-46). The function of the judgment parables is *not* to encourage Matthew's readers to exercise judgment on one another (as the parables of the wheat and tares makes clear) or to fear God's wrath, but rather to exhort them to lives of faithfulness modeled by Jesus and characterized precisely by self-giving service: acts of mercy and help for the poor (25:31-46), evangelistic witness to their risen Lord (28:5-7, 19), and unwavering obedience to Jesus's teaching (28:20). But these parables also claim that the risen Jesus, as the Son of Man in all his glory, will come in power. At that time Christ's power will not be veiled in weakness or defeat but will be made manifest before all the nations (as in Phil 2:10-11, when every knee bends before the exalted Christ and confesses him as Lord).

So the mode of God's power in Matthew's Gospel looks definitively cruciform: power in weakness, in service, in self-giving love, in kenosis, in the refusal to wield even one's rightful power.[16] But it also includes an uncompromising warning that Jesus will return to punish the wicked and unrepentant, to hold to account those who ignore the poor, to banish into the outer darkness those who reject the Son and the Father who sent him. It is both a cruciform power and a resurrecting power—the power of the God of Israel who makes both weal and woe (Isa 45:7).

The suggestion that Matthew argues for the importance of "the obedience of faith" (to borrow a Pauline phrase) raises another question in relation to Gorman's work. Is Matthew more interested in the imitation of Christ or in participation in Christ?

Imitation or Participation?

In *Cruciformity*, Gorman writes that the category of the imitation of Christ is inadequate because it fails to describe fully what happens to followers of Christ, who do not merely imitate Christ but are transformed from glory to

---

15. Michael J. Gorman, *Inhabiting the Cruciform God: Kenosis, Justification, and Theosis in Paul's Narrative Soteriology* (Grand Rapids: Eerdmans, 2009), 158.
16. Gorman, *Inhabiting the Cruciform God*, 34.

glory.[17] In Paul's letters, the followers of Christ are caught up in a process that Gorman describes as theosis, or "transformative participation in the kenotic, cruciform character and life of God through Spirit-enabled conformity to the incarnate, crucified, and resurrected/glorified Christ, who is the image of God."[18] Gorman enlists Douglas Campbell to argue against the category of the *imitatio Christi*: "God is not asking [believers] . . . to imitate Christ—perhaps an impossible task—so much as *to inhabit or to indwell him* . . . the Spirit of God is actively reshaping the Christian into the likeness of Christ."[19]

These are, of course, apt descriptions of the apostle Paul. Matthew, on the other hand, uses explicit language neither of imitation nor of participation. Still, he seems relatively comfortable with the idea of the disciples imitating Christ's model (see again Matt 20:25-28). Perhaps this should come as no surprise. The evangelist does not share Paul's discomfort with the link between righteousness and "good works" or the "good fruit" of praying, fasting, almsgiving, forgiving the debts and offenses of others, and helping the poor (5:16-20; 6:1-18; 7:17-20, 24-27; 25:31-46). Indeed, in a twist that startles everyone involved in the parable of the sheep and the goats, it is the *poor* who unknowingly embody Christ (who unknowingly participate in Christ?), *not* the faithful who give them water, food, clothing, shelter, and company. Thus, Matthew's only "participatory" parable displays the poor, sick, hungry, and imprisoned as sharing in Christ's identity not through God's power or even through their faith in Christ, but simply through their low social status—through, in fact, their suffering.

Gorman proposes that for Paul, "cruciformity cannot be attributed to human effort" but is the "power at work within him" and in the church communities.[20] Can the same be said of Matthew, who seems to place a great deal of emphasis on the necessity of human actions and effort? One way to answer this question is to return to the theme of reading in light of the resurrection. From the very beginning of Matthew's Gospel, the readers are in on the secret: Jesus is the Messiah and the Son of God, the fulfillment of God's promises to David and Abraham (Matt 1:1). The same Jesus who demands perfection (5:48) is also God-with-them and the risen Lord who promises to be with them, even to the end of the age. This suggests that the disciples are not expected to strive to fulfill the serious demands of (say) the Sermon on the Mount on their own power.

17. Gorman, *Cruciformity*, 48.
18. Gorman, *Inhabiting the Cruciform God*, 125.
19. Gorman, *Inhabiting the Cruciform God*, 71, quoting Douglas A. Campbell, *The Quest for Paul's Gospel* (London: T & T Clark, 2005), 93, emphasis added by Gorman.
20. Gorman, *Cruciformity*, 49.

Because the Sermon is often a flashpoint in debates over divine and human agency, it offers a good case study for this question and for the theme of cruciformity in general in Matthew. I will focus on one small but significant piece of the Sermon, the Beatitudes (Matt 5:1–12). Dale Allison notes that the crowds who hear the Beatitudes are "those who have already been healed by Jesus" (4:23–25). He uses this detail to argue, "So grace comes before task, succor before demand, healing before imperative. The first act of the Messiah is not the imposition of his commandments but the giving of himself.... The Beatitudes, then, depict the future as a gift."[21] Indeed, this is an apt summary of how many interpreters throughout history understood the Beatitudes (and the Sermon as a whole). Grace precedes demand, but this does not mean there is *no* demand involved. This understanding of the Beatitudes indicates the necessity of grace-enabled human action—a description even the apostle Paul might find acceptable (Rom 1:5; 16:26; Gal 5:6)! Recall the delightfully paradoxical statements in Paul's letter to the Philippians: "Therefore, my beloved, just as you have always obeyed me, not only in my presence, but much more now in my absence, work out your own salvation with fear and trembling; for it is God who is at work in you, enabling you both to will and to work for his good pleasure" (Phil 2:12–13; see also 3:13).

The Beatitudes as the Way of the Cross

The earlier reference to the eighth blessing on the persecuted (Matt 5:10–12) has already suggested the Beatitudes as a possible resource for exploring the way of the cross in Matthew. To be sure, the Beatitudes may not immediately appear to be the most obvious place to turn for a cruciform ethic. But Gorman has astutely pointed out that Paul's description of his suffering on behalf of Christ in 1 Cor 4:8–13 echoes Matthew's Beatitudes (as well as the "enemy love" teachings in Matt 5:43–44 and Luke 6:28, 32, 36). Several phrases are especially resonant: "for the sake of Christ," "hungry and thirsty," "poor," "reviled," "slandered." Furthermore, a brief tour through the history of interpretation reveals just how many interpreters have connected the Beatitudes to the way of the cross. To explore this somewhat surprising theme, we will visit first a ninth-century Benedictine monk, followed by two twentieth-century preachers on Good Friday, a Reformer in Geneva and his heir in Germany, the

---

21. Dale Allison, *Studies in Matthew: Interpretation Past and Present* (Grand Rapids: Baker Academic, 2005), 198. See also Dale Allison, *The Sermon on the Mount: Inspiring the Moral Imagination* (New York: Crossroad, 1999), 9.

Byzantine liturgy, and finally one of the great twentieth-century theological readers of Scripture.

A Cruciform Text

We turn first to a ninth-century Benedictine monastery, where monk Hrabanus Maurus (780–856) composed *De laudibus sanctae crucis* ("Veneration of the Holy Cross"), in which one of the illuminated prose poems displayed the Beatitudes in a cruciform arrangement. The first two beatitudes form the bottom half of the cross's vertical beam; the next four are the horizontal crossbar; and the final two comprise the top half of the vertical beam.[22] The Beatitudes are thus depicted quite literally as the way of the cross in cruciform shape. They also ascend, with the first beatitude at the lowest point of the cross and the eighth at the highest point. This ascent not only indicates Maurus's indebtedness to his predecessors, who described the Beatitudes as steps of ascent toward God, but it also hints at the rising up of the resurrection. For Maurus as for other medieval thinkers, the Beatitudes were embodied perfectly by Christ; and they were also the way of life that Christ intended for all his followers, via the *imitatio Christi* and with the help of the Spirit.

The Last Words and the Beatitudes

From there we fast-forward in history to two twentieth-century American preachers who conceived of a different possible relationship between the Beatitudes and the cross. Fulton Sheen and George Barrett both correlated each of the first seven beatitudes with one of Christ's seven last words from the cross.[23] When Barrett describes the relationship between the two texts, he makes explicit what Maurus illuminated visually: the Beatitudes can only be understood "in the light of the cross" and in the way that their teaching is "fulfilled by the cross."[24] Indeed, Barrett claims, "The closer we come to living

---

22. PL 107 col. 822; see Brigitta Stoll, *De Virtute in Virtutem: zur Auslegungs- und Wirkungsgeschichte der Bergpredigt in Kommentaren, Predigten und hagiographischer Literatur von der Merowingerzeit bis um 1200*, BGBE 30 (Tübingen: Mohr/Siebeck, 1988), 140, 156. A digitized copy is available via the website of the Bibliothèque Nationale de France at https://gallica.bnf.fr/ark:/12148/btv1b8490076p/f46.image.r=.langEN.

23. Fulton J. Sheen, *The Cross and the Beatitudes* (Garden City, NY: Garden City Books, 1937, 1952); George W. Barrett, *Christ's Keys to Happiness* (New York: The World Publishing Company, 1970).

24. Barrett, *Christ's Keys*, 15.

by the Beatitudes the more risk we run of finding ourselves nailed to a cross."[25] This points to the eighth beatitude, which is left out of the seven-part scheme, not because it is irrelevant but because it is typically seen as the fulfillment or even result of the first seven beatitudes. Thus, the eighth beatitude correlates not to any particular last word but to the crucifixion itself, the ultimate symbol of Jesus's persecution and rejection.

Both Sheen and Barrett follow the traditional order of the seven last words, and both reorder the Beatitudes in their (sometimes creative) efforts to find correspondences between them. They overlap only twice in their pairings: the second word ("Today you will be with me in Paradise") links to the blessing on the merciful, with mercy construed as God's pardon of the repentant thief. The fifth word ("I thirst") is, sensibly enough, connected to the blessing on those who hunger and thirst for righteousness. Other pairings prompt interesting reflections, such as Barrett's connections from "Father, forgive" to the peacemakers (with reference both to Vietnam and racial unrest—Barrett was writing in 1970) and from "My God, my God, why have you forsaken me?" to the mourners (with reference to Vietnam and to the death of Martin Luther King Jr.). Sheen chooses different resonances for both beatitudes by linking "It is finished" with the peacemakers (narrating peace as "peace with God," or the completion of atonement), and "Into your hands" with mourning (focusing on the promise "they shall be comforted").

Whatever one makes of these pairings, they illuminate both preachers' conviction that the Beatitudes were an integral part of the way of the cross.

The School of the Cross

They were not alone in this belief. They had a predecessor four centuries earlier in Reformer John Calvin, for whom the Beatitudes were "the school of the cross." For Calvin, Christ taught the Beatitudes primarily in order to accustom his followers to bear the cross.[26] By the time Calvin began to preach on the Beatitudes, toward the end of his life, he was gravely ill, suffering from a variety of painful maladies including migraines and kidney stones.[27] During Calvin's ministry, many of his fellow French Protestants had been arrested, some executed, and many had been forced to flee, as Calvin himself had. So

---

25. Barrett, *Christ's Keys*, 17.
26. Calvin, *Harmony of the Gospels*, 169.
27. Chad Quaintance, "The Blessed Life: Theological Interpretation and Use of the Beatitudes by Augustine, Calvin and Barth" (ProQuest Archive, 2003), 156n69.

Matthew, the Cross, and the Cruciform Life

when Calvin writes that each beatitude "calls us to some form of pain,"[28] and when he calls the Beatitudes Christ's school of the cross, like all preachers he may have been speaking to himself as much as to his congregation.[29]

Centuries later, Dietrich Bonhoeffer (1906-1945) followed in Calvin's footsteps by framing his discussion of the Beatitudes around the way of the cross and the costly call to discipleship.[30] He distinguished sharply between the disciples and the crowds, the two audiences indicated in Matt 5:1. For Bonhoeffer, the Beatitudes are decidedly not describing the crowds, because the crowds have not left everything behind in order to follow Christ. Instead, the Beatitudes describe the disciples, who *have* left everything to follow Jesus (as in Matt 8:18-22; 10:37-39; 16:24-26; 19:16-30) and have thus become "the poorest of the poor, the sorest afflicted, and the hungriest of the hungry" (105). Yet for Bonhoeffer they are blessed not because of their privation or even their act of renunciation, since neither privation nor renunciation are "blessed in themselves" (106). Instead, the disciples are blessed because of "the call and the promise of Jesus." In Bonhoeffer's view, the disciples do not need to seek out suffering or find ways to practice self-giving; suffering will naturally come their way as they try to follow Christ (109). (One can imagine Bonhoeffer thinking of his own context as he writes these words!) But there are ways in which they actively follow in Christ's footsteps. As the merciful (5:7), they emulate their Lord by seeking out the company of the sick and downtrodden, the publicans and sinners (111). And, as the peacemakers (5:9), they "renounce all violence and tumult" (112).

Ultimately, for Bonhoeffer, there is only one place on earth where a person who represents all the Beatitudes may be found, and that is "on the cross at Golgotha" (114). Only Jesus can fulfill all the Beatitudes; the disciples reflect them only in a subsidiary way since "the fellowship of the Beatitudes is the fellowship of the Crucified" (114). But Bonhoeffer does not end his meditations on the Beatitudes at the foot of the cross. Instead, he concludes it in the halls of

---

28. Quaintance, "The Blessed Life," 159.

29. More than a century later, Jeremiah Burroughs, a Puritan Reformer in England, will also describe the Beatitudes as a school in which Christ's first lesson ("the ABC of a Christian") is the self-denial of the cross (*The Saints' Happiness* [Edinburgh: James Nichol, 1867; Orlando: Soli Deo Gloria, 1988, 1992], 80).

30. Dietrich Bonhoeffer, *The Cost of Discipleship* (SCM, 1959; New York: Simon & Schuster, 1995), 91. Hereafter, page references are given in parentheses in the text. Gorman acknowledges his deep indebtedness to Bonhoeffer's *Discipleship* in both *Cruciformity* (385-86) and *Inhabiting the Cruciform God* (168). For a discussion of Bonhoeffer's understanding of discipleship as kenosis in the later chapters of *Discipleship*, see Gorman, *Inhabiting the Cruciform God*, 168-70.

heavenly joy, when "with his own hand God wipes away the tears from the eyes of those who had mourned upon earth" and "feeds the hungry at his Banquet" (114). In this way, Bonhoeffer highlights one last, centrally important feature of the Beatitudes: their eschatological setting. They point not only to an earthly way of life for the Christian community, but they also point forward to their heavenly fulfillment in the kingdom of heaven: the consolation of the saints, the inheritance of the new creation, the fullness of the heavenly banquet, the wideness of God's mercy, the vision of God, and the glorious freedom of the children of God (to merge a Pauline phrase with a Matthean one).

Beatitudes as Theosis

Orthodox writers also tend to locate the Beatitudes eschatologically. Orthodox writer Vigen Guroian points out that the Beatitudes occur in two key places in Byzantine liturgy: in the Lesser Entrance (the procession of the gospel into the sanctuary) and in the rite of burial.[31] For Guroian, these liturgical placements highlight the eschatological character of the Beatitudes and their role in the process of theosis. He writes, "In this sacramental and liturgical context, the Beatitudes are ethically compelling... because they are attributes of the person in whom the reign of God is present and being inaugurated.... [T]hey are *what* Christians participate *in* and *become* when they bind themselves to Christ by baptism and gather as one body in eucharistic assembly."[32]

This emphasis can be traced back to the fourth-century thinker Gregory of Nyssa. For Gregory, as one ascends the "ladder" of the Beatitudes, living more fully into them, one becomes more like God, as God's image is progressively restored.[33] For Gregory the Beatitudes are part of the means by which God washes away the stain of sin that disfigures the beauty of the original image of God in humanity. Because "the end of the life of virtue is to become like to God [ἡ πρὸς τὸ Θεῖον ὁμοίωσις]," participation in the Beatitudes means striving toward the ultimate *telos* or end of all the virtues, which is Godlikeness.[34]

Moreover, the Beatitudes' appearance in the Byzantine rite of burial high-

---

31. Vigen Guroian, "Liturgy and the Lost Eschatological Vision of Christian Ethics," *Annual of the Society of Christian Ethics* 20 (2000): 227, 236–37.

32. Guroian, "Liturgy and the Lost Eschatological Vision," 236.

33. Gregory of Nyssa, *The Lord's Prayer; The Beatitudes*, ACW 18, trans. Hilda C. Graef (Mahwah, NJ: Paulist Press, 1954), 131, 148.

34. Gregory of Nyssa, *The Lord's Prayer; The Beatitudes*, 89. For more on Gregory's understanding of the beatitudes, see Rebekah Eklund, "Blessed Are the Image-Bearers: Gregory of Nyssa and the Beatitudes," *AThR* 99 (2017): 729–40.

Matthew, the Cross, and the Cruciform Life

lights even more strongly their eschatological character. This eschatological connection is also made in Catholic liturgy, via the All Saints' service, where the Beatitudes are the gospel reading and Rev 7 (the "adoration of the Lamb") is the New Testament lesson. This also explains why the Beatitudes appear in personified form in the Ghent altarpiece, where they are depicted as a variety of worshipers approaching the heavenly throne room to worship the slain Lamb, portraying visually the overlap between the Beatitudes, the cross (by way of the crucified and risen Lamb), and the eschaton.[35]

This is the clearest case yet that an aspect of Matthew's Gospel *might* be construed as participation rather than imitation. Nonetheless, it is hard to say that this theme originates with Matthew himself, or with the gospel text. Instead, authorization for this reading derives from an Orthodox use of the text, which is not surprising since Orthodox theology relies so thoroughly on the theme of theosis that animates Gorman's work. Still, it rightly perceives the eschatological character of the Beatitudes, which is evident from their placement in Matthew's text shortly following Jesus's announcement that "the kingdom of heaven has come near" (Matt 4:17) and from the repetition of the reward "theirs is the kingdom of heaven" (5:3, 10) that encloses the Beatitudes.

The connection between theosis and eschatology also helps to remind us of the eschatological character of the cross itself in Matthew. As Jesus is dying on the cross, the sun darkens—an apocalyptic sign of the "day of the Lord" (Matt 27:45). At the moment of his death, more eschatological signs indicate the apocalyptic nature of the event—the ripping of the temple curtain, an earthquake, and the raising of the saints from their tombs (27:51–53). Another earthquake accompanies the angelic visitor to the empty tomb (28:2). In this way, not only the theme of theosis but also Matthew's Gospel itself can remind us that cruciformity is eschatological—a way of life made possible by the dawning and inbreaking of the kingdom, and one that seeks to mirror this kingdom, toward which it eagerly reaches.

Our final interpreter (and a few of his like-minded companions) understood the Beatitudes (and other aspects of Matthew's Gospel) not as theosis per se but as kenosis.

Beatitudes as Descent and Ascent

This final stop on our tour brings us back to a Protestant thinker, to the first half of the twentieth century, and to one of its most prominent and prodigious

---

35. Images and fuller explanation available at https://thevcs org/blessed.

readers of Scripture. Karl Barth specifically identifies six of the eight Beatitudes under the heading of Christ's kenosis, or self-emptying (Phil 2:6-11). (Somewhat oddly, he omits the blessings on the pure in heart and the peacemakers.) He sees the Beatitudes as part of Christ's exhortation to "lowliness of mind" or humility (ταπεινοφροσύνη), an echo of the line that precedes Paul's "hymn" of kenosis: "Do nothing from selfish ambition or conceit, but in humility [ταπεινοφροσύνη] regard others as better than yourselves" (Phil 2:3). Barth describes ταπεινοφροσύνη as the natural way of the children of God, since it is both "the reflection of His own being" and a way made possible by Christ.[36]

In this way, Barth enlists both imitation language ("the reflection of His own being") and participatory language ("a way made possible by Christ"). The Beatitudes are thus a way of taking up Christ's example, of *imaging* Christ, and (paradoxically) a way of life enabled by being already *in* Christ. Perhaps Barth does not resolve the tension between imitation of and participation in Christ, but he does suggest that they may not be mutually exclusive, just as human effort and divine enablement often mysteriously work together (with divine grace being always prior).

A handful of other writers, both before and after Barth, have also understood the Beatitudes as a kind of kenosis.[37] Earlier, I alluded to the common premodern understanding of the Beatitudes as steps of ascent toward God. A handful of writers turn this model literally upside down by depicting the Beatitudes instead as a descent—indeed, like Barth, as a kenosis, or a path of humiliation that ends up, paradoxically, in exaltation. J. P. Lange, for example, writes that the point of the Beatitudes was not to enrich their hearers "but to make them all the poorer." He goes on to describe the Beatitudes as "the apparent descent, and the actual ascent of souls"; they paradoxically indicate both "deepening humiliation" and "deepening exaltation."[38]

It is an unexpected source who provides the clearest picture of this re-

36. Karl Barth, *Church Dogmatics* IV/1, trans. G. W. Bromiley, ed. G. W. Bromiley and T. F. Torrance (Peabody, MA: Hendrickson, 1958, 2004), 191.

37. Several other thinkers have linked the first beatitude ("Blessed are the poor in spirit") with kenosis. Gregory of Nyssa did so, citing 2 Cor 8:9 and Phil 2:5-7 (*Lord's Prayer*, 90-91). See also Nicholas Cabasilas, *The Life in Christ*, trans. Carmino J. deCatanzaro (Yonkers, NY: St. Vladimir's Seminary Press, 1974), 176, 178. Poverty of spirit as kenosis appears in the seventeenth-century Puritan preacher Jeremiah Burroughs, in the early twentieth century via missionary Stanley Jones and Anglican bishop Charles Gore, in Johann Baptiste Metz's little book *Poverty of Spirit* (which is wholly devoted to the theme of kenosis), and in the present day in the work of Reformed theologian George Hunsinger, Orthodox theologian Liviu Barbu, and Capuchin-Franciscan priest Michael Crosby.

38. John Peter Lange, *The Gospel According to Matthew*, vol. 16 of *A Commentary on the*

versal: Billy Graham's associate Sherwood Wirt. In Wirt's book *Magnificent Promise: A Fresh View of the Beatitudes from the Cross*, he rejects the idea that the Beatitudes depict the "ideal life," as so many Christian writers before him termed them. Instead, he insisted that the Beatitudes depict the *crucified* life. All the Beatitudes are descriptions of Christ, and "Jesus's life . . . derives its full meaning from the Cross."[39] By implication, then, when Jesus's followers take up the Beatitudes into their own lives, they take up the cross. For Wirt, then, the Beatitudes are a descent, not an ascent: "The way of the Cross is the way to God, but it is not a way up, it is a way down" (9). He gives a number of examples of this principle from Scripture, including Abraham, who "went to God with absolutely nothing" and Moses, "probably the most unpromising prospect for leadership that a people ever had." But the supreme example, of course, is Christ,

> who, though he was in the form of God,
> did not regard equality with God
> as something to be exploited,
> but emptied himself,
> taking the form of a slave,
> being born in human likeness.
> And being found in human form,
> he humbled himself
> and became obedient to the point of death—
> even death on a cross. (Phil 2:6–8; Wirt, 10–12)

Wirt connects each beatitude specifically to some aspect of the cross. Poverty of spirit, for example, is "the cry of dereliction from the Cross"; it signals the way to Calvary (2). Hunger and thirst are not about striving, but about emptiness; like Barrett and Sheen, Wirt relates this beatitude to Jesus's cry from the cross, "I thirst!" (47–48). Hungering and thirsting is in fact a kind of crucifixion of our selves, a painful renunciation of our selves (52–54). Likewise purity of heart is obtained by taking up the cross and being crucified with Christ (80–81). The eighth beatitude is a prediction of Christ's sufferings; this

---

Holy Scriptures: Critical, Doctrinal, and Homiletical, with Special Reference to Ministers and Students, 12th ed., trans. Philip Schaff (New York: Charles Scribner's Sons, 1884), 105, 106.

39. Sherwood E. Wirt, *Magnificent Promise: A Fresh View of the Beatitudes from the Cross* (Chicago: Moody Press, 1964), preface (no page), 63, 97. Hereafter, page references are given in parentheses in the text.

beatitude, like all the others before it, "lights the way to the Cross of Calvary," and the promise of the kingdom is the promise of resurrection joy (111, 129).

A Cruciform God—and a Resurrecting God

The promise of resurrection joy brings us to our final theme. At the start of this essay, I referred to reading Matthew in light of the resurrection. Should Matthew be read in light of the resurrection or in light of the cross? To be sure, cross and resurrection are inextricably connected. When Paul talks about the cross, he always means death *and* resurrection. There is no shorthand way of remembering this without inventing utterly awkward phrases (cruci-resurrect-iformity?).

Yet I would like to pause and return once more to the theme of new covenant and atonement in relation to Matthew's Gospel and the resurrection. In Matthew, Jesus's humiliation, his willing death on the cross, is not the end of the story. God does not leave Jesus in the tomb. His death is not the completion of God's work. Instead, the heart of Matthew is the angel's message to the astonished, trembling women, "He is not here; for he has been raised, as he said" (Matt 28:6). That Jesus dies is absolutely crucial for Matthew; his blood establishes God's covenant for the forgiveness of sins and, on Gorman's terms, makes possible a new covenant community of Jews and Gentiles, a forgiven and forgiving people. But the good news, the *really* good news, is that the God of Israel raised Jesus from the dead.

This means that, for Matthew, the covenant community itself, as important as it is, has a secondary or penultimate status in relation to the return of the Son of Man and the full arrival of the now-dawning kingdom of God. The covenant community is a foretaste of the kingdom of heaven. It is a way of life pointing forward and beyond itself. In Matthew, Jesus repeatedly exhorts his followers to be alert for the coming of the Son of Man (Matt 24:42–51; 25:1–30). Staying alert and watchfully awaiting the return of Christ in glory appears to be one of the primary tasks of this new covenant community, which makes it an eschatological community, living in-between the times, a sign of what is yet to come.

Conclusion

Gorman writes that to understand Paul, we need "to see the connection between (1) the *living Lord* who resides in and among believers, (2) the *suffering Messiah* who gave himself on the cross in non-retaliatory love, and (3) the *teaching Jesus* who spoke the words of non-retaliation echoed in texts like Romans 12 and 1 Corinthians 4."[40] Substitute Rom 12 and 1 Cor 4 for Matt 5–7, and that could be a summary of the Great Commission. I do not think, then, that Michael Gorman and the evangelist Matthew are too far apart, and I humbly hope that this essay may have showed the places where they are close indeed.

---

40. Gorman, *Inhabiting the Cruciform God*, 152.

Chapter 2

The Crucified One:
Jesus's Death and Discipleship in the Gospel of Mark

Richard B. Hays

What role does the cross play in the Gospel of Mark? Many readers of Mark's narrative would assume that the cross is a heavily emphasized theme in Mark's distinctive telling of the story of Jesus. Yet if we focus on actual incidence of words, it is surprising to discover that the word σταυρός ("cross") appears only four times in the text: once in the middle of the story (Mark 8:34), and three times in the passion narrative (15:21, 30, 32). The instances of the verb σταυρόω ("crucify") are also concentrated almost entirely in the passion narrative (in various forms eight times in 15:12-32), with just one other occurrence, in the gospel's closing scene (16:6). What are we to make of these statistics about word usage? Does Mark's sparing use of these terms suggest that the cross is to be understood not as a theologically laden term but simply as a realistic narrative detail in the depiction of Jesus's execution under the Roman governor Pontius Pilate?

It will be the burden of this essay to suggest, on the contrary, that Mark's few explicit references to the cross, which appear at crucial moments in the structure of the story, play a key role within a network of narrative elements that focus on the death of Jesus. Mark portrays the cross both as the singular redemptive event through which Jesus gives his life as "a ransom for many" (10:45) and as a definitive pattern for the life of discipleship to which his followers are called.[1] We begin with a simple survey of the passages in which the words "cross" and "crucify" do explicitly appear.

---

1. In this way, the message of Mark's Gospel parallels the "narrative spirituality of the

The Crucified One

Occurrences of "Cross" and "Crucify" in Mark

The first reference to the cross in this gospel appears in Jesus's response to Peter's confession at Caesarea Philippi that Jesus is the Messiah (ὁ χριστός, Mark 8:29). In contrast to Matthew's narrative, in which Jesus greets this confession with effusive approval (Matt 16:17–19), Mark depicts Jesus as receiving Peter's words with stern caution: "And he *rebuked* them (ἐπετίμησεν αὐτοῖς) in order that they should tell no one about him" (my translation). He then begins to offer his disciples a sobering prophecy about his own destiny: to suffer, to be rejected by the elders, chief priests, and scribes, to be killed, and to rise after three days. Peter protests, leading Jesus to rebuke him in even harsher terms as "Satan" (Mark 8:31–33). In light of this collision of visions for Jesus's future, Jesus turns to the other disciples and a larger crowd and offers a daunting programmatic challenge: "If any want to become my followers, let them deny themselves and take up their cross (ἀράτω τὸν σταυρὸν) and follow me.[2] For those who want to save their life will lose it, and those who lose their life for my sake, and for the sake of the gospel, will save it" (8:34–35).

This confrontation at Caesarea Philippi marks the pivot point at the center of Mark's narrative. Heretofore, Jesus has appeared chiefly as a powerful wonderworker and healer. But from this point onward, he moves resolutely toward his own death at the hands of the Jerusalem authorities and their Roman ruler. It is precisely at this point that mention of the cross first appears in the story. Strikingly "the cross" appears not in Jesus's prediction of his *own* passion, but in his summons to all who want to follow him. It is *they* who will have to take up the cross. At one level, this could be understood as a simple warning to potential disciples that they are joining a risky revolutionary movement: they might literally face the prospect of being killed by the Roman overlords if they choose to ally themselves with Jesus's proclamation of the kingdom of God. (How else could "take up the cross" be understood by hearers at this point in the story?) At another level, however, on a second reading of Mark's

---

cross" that Michael Gorman has compellingly described in the letters of Paul (Michael J. Gorman, *Cruciformity: Paul's Narrative Spirituality of the Cross* [Grand Rapids: Eerdmans, 2001]). The concluding section of the present essay, however, will suggest some differences between the theologies of Mark and Paul with respect to this central theological theme. This essay is dedicated to Mike Gorman, with appreciation and gratitude for his friendship and for his important scholarly work of elucidating the theme of cruciformity in the New Testament.

2. The subsequent repetition of this command, found in some manuscripts at Mark 10:21, is almost certainly a later scribal addition.

Gospel, this initial reference to "the cross" comes into focus as a metaphor: it signals the necessity of costly sacrifice for those who want to be Jesus's followers. It is, of course, this latter sense that has predominated in the history of interpretation.

In any case, because of its prominent placement here at the dramatic turning point of Mark's story, the cross looms large as a symbol for Jesus's own mission and destiny, as well as for the destiny of his followers. All of this gospel's subsequent references to suffering, sacrifice, and death find their place as specifications of this central symbolic image. And Jesus's emphatic teaching about the cross darkly foreshadows his own unfolding fate.

The other three instances of the noun σταυρός appear close together in Mark 15, in the actual account of Jesus's crucifixion. Mark introduces an otherwise unknown character, Simon of Cyrene, who is conscripted by the Roman soldiers to carry Jesus's cross (ἵνα ἄρῃ τὸν σταυρὸν αὐτοῦ, Mark 15:21) to the place of execution at Golgotha. The phrasing here strikingly echoes Jesus's earlier call to "take up" the cross (ἀράτω τὸν σταυρὸν, 8:34). In this instance, however, Simon has clearly not voluntarily chosen the task of bearing the cross; he has been forcibly compelled by the soldiers. This small, and seemingly otherwise inconsequential, narrative detail teases the reader's imagination. If this vignette holds some mysterious spiritual significance, Mark (characteristically) leaves it to the reader to puzzle it out.[3] Should we conclude that taking up the cross in a metaphorical sense may be a burden thrust upon us—as it was imposed on Simon of Cyrene—rather than freely elected? That is a possible inference, but Mark's concise narration offers no comment on such questions.

The two remaining occurrences of the noun σταυρός entail no such ambiguity. The chief priests and scribes join with a crowd of passersby in taunting the crucified Jesus, derisively challenging him to save himself and prove that he is the Messiah, the King of Israel, by coming down from the cross (Mark 15:30, 32). The irony of their mockery is deep: the reader of this gospel recognizes that Jesus, by enduring the cross, is saving *others*; counterintuitively, his identity as Messiah is most fully disclosed not in his mighty acts but precisely in his death on the cross. The taunters perceive the cross as a literal wooden instrument of torture and death. But Mark's larger message is that the cross, understood as a signifier for Jesus's giving his life as a ransom for many (10:45), is the instrument of mercy and life. Mark explains none of this, but his story has prepared the reader to see the crucifixion of Jesus as the

---

3. On Mark's distinctive style of veiled, indirect suggestion, see Richard B. Hays, *Echoes of Scripture in the Gospels* (Waco: Baylor University Press, 2016), 97–103.

The Crucified One

initiating event of the new covenant, in which his body and blood are given "for many" (14:22–25).

Mark's uses of the verb σταυρόω are clustered almost exclusively within just a few sentences in his bleak, unadorned account of Jesus's execution (Mark 15:12–32). The crowd (incited, Mark tells us, by the chief priests) twice cries out, "Crucify him," and Pilate, acceding to their clamor, "handed him over to be crucified" (15:13–15). The soldiers, after mocking him sarcastically as "King of the Jews," beating him and spitting on him, "led him out to crucify him" (15:20). Then they carried out the execution. In contrast to later elaborate Christian devotional meditations on the crucifixion, Mark provides no gory description of the details. With measured narrative restraint, he simply writes, "and they crucified him" at nine o'clock in the morning (15:24–25). He also mentions that two bandits were crucified alongside him, and that even they, astonishingly, joined in the crowd's mockery (15:27, 32). And that is all.

The severe economy of Mark's narration etches these images indelibly on the reader's mind. All the uses of σταυρός and σταυρόω (including συνεσταυρωμένοι in Mark 15:32) in Mark's passion narrative are straightforwardly literal references to the physical reality of Jesus's cruel death on a wooden stake.[4] Mark offers no theological reflection on these terms, no elaboration or explanation of the significance of this grim and shameful execution.[5] Whatever interpretation may be given to the cross must be informed by the meaning-laden clues planted earlier in the story, particularly, as we have noted, Jesus's interpretation of his impending death as an act of servanthood and "ransom for many" (10:42–45), and his symbolic anticipation, at his final supper with his followers, of his own death as an act of covenant inauguration (14:22–25). These clues are supplemented in Mark's passion narrative by several allusions to texts from Israel's Scripture, including most prominently Jesus's dying words, the cry of derelection drawn from Ps 22:1, the prayer of a righteous sufferer who

---

4. Paul, of course, uses the compound verb συσταυρόω in a metaphorical sense to describe the putting to death of the old self in the believer's mysterious union with Christ (Rom 6:6; Gal 2:19). There is no hint of such a theologically laden sense here in Mark 15:32. For studies of the terrible physical realities of the Roman punishment of death by crucifixion, see Martin Hengel, *Crucifixion in the Ancient World and the Folly of the Message of the Cross* (Philadelphia: Fortress, 1977); Gunnar Samuelsson, *Crucifixion in Antiquity: An Inquiry into the Background and Significance of the New Testament Terminology of Crucifixion*, WUNT 2/310 (Tübingen: Mohr Siebeck, 2010); John Granger Cook, *Crucifixion in the Mediterranean World*, WUNT 327 (Tübingen: Mohr Siebeck, 2014).

5. For a searching theological exploration of the meaning and salvific efficacy of Jesus's crucifixion, see Fleming Rutledge, *The Crucifixion: Understanding the Death of Jesus Christ* (Grand Rapids: Eerdmans, 2015).

cries out in pain and abandonment yet hopes ultimately to be vindicated and to offer praise and thanksgiving "in the midst of the congregation" to the God who "rules over the nations."⁶

Narrative Anticipations of the Cross in Mark

When we read back over Mark's whole narrative, we can recognize that the story contains pervasive foreshadowing of Jesus's crucifixion, even where the terms σταυρός and σταυρόω do not appear. Or, to speak more precisely, the story contains anticipations of Jesus's *violent death*; it is only in Mark 15 that we learn of the specific form that death was to take.

The warning signals begin appearing already in Mark's opening scenes. In the opening chapter of this gospel, Mark tells the reader that Jesus began his public proclamation of the kingdom of God "after John was arrested" (παραδοθῆναι, Mark 1:14).⁷ John has been prophesying the imminent coming of a more powerful figure who will bring God's Spirit to Israel; Mark tells us that when John baptized Jesus, the Spirit descended upon him. And then almost immediately we learn that John has been arrested by the authorities as a troublemaker. This is surely an ominous event for Jesus himself. The reader's sense of foreboding is amplified a little later in the story by Mark's uncharacteristically detailed account of John's imprisonment and beheading by Herod (6:14–29), an alarming development that causes Jesus to withdraw temporarily with his disciples to the desert to "rest for a little while" (6:30–32, my translation). John's execution and burial prefigure Jesus's own fate.

The foreshadowing of Jesus's impending death recurs like the persistent tolling of a bell in the first half of Mark's narrative. In response to the question about why his disciples do not fast, Jesus darkly alludes to the violent end he expects to meet: they will fast "when the bridegroom is taken away from them" (ὅταν ἀπαρθῇ ἀπ' αὐτῶν ὁ νυμφίος, Mark 2:20). The passive verb ἀπαρθῇ does not necessarily indicate a violent snatching away, but on a retrospective reading of the entire story, its grim overtones cannot be overlooked. Lest we be oblivious to the ominous hints in the opening scenes of the narrative, Mark concludes his first cycle of unsettling controversy stories (2:1–3:6)

---

6. For more extensive discussion of the significance of Ps 22 in Mark's passion narrative, see Joel Marcus, *The Way of the Lord: Christological Exegesis of the Old Testament in the Gospel of Mark* (Louisville: Westminster John Knox, 1992), 172–86; Hays, *Echoes of Scripture in the Gospels*, 78–86.

7. We shall return later to the question of the significance of the verb παραδοθῆναι. It means literally "handed over."

The Crucified One

with an explicit statement that the Pharisees have begun to conspire with the Herodians (!)[8] to determine how to "destroy him" (ὅπως αὐτὸν ἀπολέσωσιν, 3:6). From this point onward, there can be little doubt about the eventual outcome of the story. The point is reinforced even by Mark's simple roll call of the followers that Jesus summoned and appointed as apostles; the list climaxes by naming "Judas Iscariot, who betrayed him" (3:19).

As the story reaches its midpoint, the tolling of the bell grows ever louder. The narrative block that runs from Mark 8:22 to 10:52—bookended by two accounts of the healing of a blind man (8:22–26 and 10:46–52)—is structured around Jesus's three explicit predictions of his passion and resurrection (8:31; 9:31; 10:32–34).[9] The third and last of these is the most emphatically detailed:

> See, we are going up to Jerusalem, and the Son of Man will be handed over to the chief priests and the scribes, and they will condemn him to death; then they will hand him over to the Gentiles; they will mock him, and spit upon him, and flog him, and kill him; and after three days he will rise again. (10:33–34)

In each case, however, the disciples resist or fail to comprehend what Jesus is saying about his own vocation and destiny, and in each case their incomprehension is followed immediately by corrective teaching about the costly nature of discipleship (Mark 8:34–9:1; 9:33–37; 10:35–45).[10] This central block of material stands at the heart of Mark's message. We shall return later to consider its significance for understanding the relationship between Jesus's crucifixion and Mark's portrayal of the vocation of Jesus's followers. At this point, we merely observe that Mark, by the middle of his narrative, has moved from subtly hinting at Jesus's impending death to explicitly announcing its inevitability. Jesus's corrective teaching after the third and final announcement culminates in a lapidary explanation for that necessity: "The Son of Man came not to be served but to serve, *and to give his life a ransom for many*" (10:45).

---

8. This unlikely, and in this case dangerous, alliance is again identified in Jesus's warning to the disciples to "beware of the leaven of the Pharisees and the leaven of Herod" (8:15, my translation) and in the joint delegation of Pharisees and Herodians who are sent to pose a political trap by asking Jesus whether it is lawful to pay taxes to Caesar (12:13–17).

9. These texts are often described simply as "passion predictions"; that designation, while not incorrect, overlooks the fact that all three passages also anticipate Jesus's resurrection.

10. On the implications of this threefold corrective narrative structure, see Richard B. Hays, *The Moral Vision of the New Testament: Community, Cross, New Creation* (San Francisco: HarperSanFrancisco, 1996), 80–82.

It is not only in these three passion/resurrection predictions that Mark points the reader forward to the crucifixion; the story repeatedly reminds us, in ways direct and indirect, that Jesus's path is leading toward the cross. In response to the disciples' question about why the scribes say Elijah must come first, Jesus replies with a riddling rhetorical question: "How then is it written about the Son of Man, that he is to go through many sufferings and be treated with contempt?" He then adds that "Elijah has come, and they did to him whatever they pleased, as it is written about him" (Mark 9:11-13). Even if the disciples fail to get the point, readers of Mark's Gospel can hardly fail to recall the gruesome death of John the Baptist a little earlier in the story. Once again, this link between the prophesied suffering of the Son of Man and the already narrated death of John foreshadows what will happen to Jesus.

In response to the clueless request of the sons of Zebedee to be given positions of prominence in eschatological glory, Jesus penetratingly asks whether they will be able to drink the cup that he is to drink or to be baptized with the baptism he is to undergo (Mark 9:38). That question hangs in the air until we come to Jesus's agonized prayer in the Garden of Gethsemane, when he urgently prays that if possible, the Father would "remove this cup" from him (14:36). That urgent intercession removes any possible ambiguity from his earlier response to James and John: the "cup" that he is to drink is his divinely ordained suffering on the cross. This is an excellent example of the necessity of reading the whole story retrospectively in light of its ending; the earlier details and clues come into focus only on a second reading.

Dramatic tension continues to escalate following Jesus's entry to the city of Jerusalem. After his provocative act of driving the merchants and money changers out of the temple, "the chief priests and the scribes" join the coalition of enemies who are seeking to destroy him (Mark 11:18). In response to their subsequent interrogation about the source of his authority, he tells the parable of the wicked tenants who plot to murder the "beloved son" of the vineyard owner (12:1-12). The parable is a transparent allegory about the pervasive and violent resistance of Israel's religious authorities to God's prophets, culminating in their malevolent response to Jesus himself.[11] The chief priests, scribes,

---

11. That Jesus himself is to be identified as the "beloved son" of the parable should be especially clear to readers who recall Mark's earlier account of the transfiguration, in which a voice from heaven declares, "This is my Son, the Beloved" (Mark 9:7). For discussion of this theme in Mark, see Hays, *Echoes of Scripture in the Gospels*, 40-42.

and elders, to whom the parable is told (11:27; 12:1), being no fools, recognize that they are the targets of its prophetic critique. Ironically, this recognition merely intensifies their determination to do away with him, thereby ensuring that the parable will come true (12:12): the Beloved Son will in fact be seized and killed (12:7–8). Hence also Jesus will fulfill the destiny prefigured in Ps 118:22; he will become "the stone that the builders rejected."

As Passover approaches, the ominous tolling of the bell becomes nearly deafening. Mark bluntly reminds readers once again of the hostile plans of Jesus's adversaries: "The chief priests and the scribes were looking for a way to arrest Jesus by stealth and kill him" (Mark 14:1). And the story continues to provide indications that Jesus knows full well where events are leading. An unnamed woman intrudes on a dinner party at Bethany and pours costly oil on Jesus's head, a surprising act that might be interpreted as a prophetic act of kingly/messianic anointing. Some bystanders grumble that this is a waste of resources that might have been put to better use; however, Jesus gives it a different interpretation: "She has done what she could; she has anointed my body beforehand for its burial" (14:8).

The same theme of foreboding looms over Jesus's final Passover meal with his disciples. He abruptly announces in the midst of the dinner that one of his companions will betray him; further, even though he declares that this will happen "as it is written," he pronounces a word of woe upon the one who is to be the agent of that betrayal (Mark 14:17–21). Of course, readers of this gospel have already learned of Judas's plans to be precisely that agent (14:10–11). As the meal continues, Jesus deepens the tone of solemnity by distributing broken bread and sharing a cup of wine as signifiers of his own body and blood (14:22–25). Finally, after the meal, he offers one final prediction of the imminent fate that awaits him by quoting from the prophet Zechariah: "I will strike the shepherd, and the sheep will be scattered" (14:27, citing Zech 13:7). From this point onward, the somber events of the passion narrative unfold with a grinding sense of inevitability. Jesus is seized, interrogated, handed over to Pilate, flogged, mocked, and crucified.

The point of this grim survey is simply to demonstrate how artfully Mark has constructed his entire narrative in a way that first foreshadows the cross and ultimately drives inexorably toward it. The actual terms "cross" and "crucifixion" come into play only in chapter 15, but when they do appear, they stand as the culmination and embodiment of the entire structural logic of the narrative. From the day of his baptism, Jesus has been moving toward the cross.

"Handed Over" to Crucifixion

Mark's story startles the reader by insisting that Jesus accomplishes God's saving purpose not by performing some mighty act to subdue God's enemies but rather by submitting himself to human hostility and violence, becoming a passive victim on the cross as a ransom for many. This remarkable theme finds particular expression in Mark's repeated use of the verb παραδίδωμι ("hand over") both to foreshadow and to narrate Jesus's fate. Mark's insistent sounding of this theme is somewhat obscured in English translations that use various different words to render the single Greek verb: "handed over," "delivered," "betrayed," and "arrested," or even "put in prison." These renderings are lexically justifiable interpretations in the contexts where they occur, but for readers who lack access to the Greek text, they conceal Mark's persistent emphasis on the way in which Jesus allows himself to be seized by the forces that crucified him. A survey of Mark's uses of παραδίδωμι will illuminate this aspect of his interpretation of the cross.

The first instance appears near the beginning of Mark's narrative: "Now after John was *handed over* (παραδοθῆναι), Jesus came to Galilee, proclaiming the good news of God" (Mark 1:14). In this case, the NIV, following the KJV, adopts a highly paraphrastic translation ("put in prison"), while NRSV opts for the simpler "arrested."[12] At this point in the narrative, Mark does not explain why or to whom John was "handed over"; the ominous allusive reference seems to presuppose the reader's prior knowledge of the event. Eventually, later in the story, Mark gives a full account of John's imprisonment and execution (6:17-29). In light of this subsequent narrative elaboration, we come to understand that John's being "handed over" to a ruling authority is a prelude to his violent death.

For that reason, when we read that the final name in Mark's list of the apostles whom Jesus called is "Judas Iscariot, who also *handed him over*" (παρέδωκεν, Mark 3:19, my translation), we may anticipate that this description foreshadows for Jesus a fate similar to that of John the Baptist. The translation "Judas Iscariot, who betrayed him" (NRSV, NIV) is not wrong, but it loses Mark's subtle verbal suggestion of a link to the story of the Baptist's demise.

After the turning point of Peter's confession at Caesarea Philippi (Mark 8:27-30), Jesus begins with ever greater urgency to instruct his uncompre-

---

12. In the following discussion of the various renderings of παραδίδωμι, for the sake of simplicity I will focus on a comparison of the NRSV and the NIV, two of the most widely used contemporary English translations.

hending disciples about the death that awaits him in Jerusalem. His words of warning include the prophecy that he is to be *handed over*. Following the transfiguration, as Jesus is passing secretively through Galilee, he teaches the disciples that "the Son of Man is to be betrayed (παραδίδοται) into human hands, and they will kill him, and three days after being killed, he will rise again" (9:31 NRSV). Here the NIV, again following the KJV, chooses to translate the verb as "delivered." In any case, however we may choose to translate it, this is the first instance in which παραδίδωμι is explicitly linked to Jesus's impending death. Jesus repeats this dire prophecy in still more specific terms in 10:33–34. We have already taken note of this passage as a clear dramatic foreshadowing of the crucifixion, but here, on another reading, we particularly note the repeated sounding of the verb παραδίδωμι:

> See, we are going up to Jerusalem, and the Son of Man will be *handed over* (παραδοθήσεται) to the chief priests and the scribes, and they will condemn him to death; then they will *hand him over* (παραδώσουσιν) to the Gentiles; they will mock him, and spit upon him, and flog him, and kill him; and after three days he will rise again.

The double reference to Jesus's being *handed over*[13] to both Jewish and Gentile authorities serves to emphasize the strange passivity of a Messiah who is destined to die on a cross.

When Jesus at last reaches Jerusalem, as Mark begins the transition to the passion narrative, the prophecies begin to come true like dominoes falling, and the references to Jesus's being *handed over* accordingly increase in frequency. Judas begins to play out the role that was already forecast for him: "Then Judas Iscariot, who was one of the twelve, went to the chief priests in order to *hand him over* (παραδοῖ) to them. When they heard it, they were greatly pleased, and promised to give him money. So he began to look for an opportunity to *hand him over* (παραδοῖ)" (Mark 14:10–11; NRSV translates the verb both times as "betray"; the NIV, after rendering παραδοῖ as "betray" in 14:10, for some reason switches back to "hand him over" in 14:11).

In the immediately following account of Jesus's final supper with the disciples, Jesus once again sounds a prophetic anticipation of the terrible handing over that is about to unfold: "And when they had taken their places and were eating, Jesus said, 'Truly I tell you, one of you will *hand me over* (παραδώσει),

---

13. This time so rendered in the NRSV; the NIV translates the first instance as "delivered over," the second as "hand over."

one who is eating with me.... For the Son of Man goes as it is written of him, but woe to that one by whom the Son of Man is *handed over* (παραδίδοται)!'" (Mark 14:18, 21; here both NRSV and NIV employ "betray" to translate both occurrences of the verb).

At the conclusion of Jesus's agonized prayer in the Garden of Gethsemane (Mark 14:32-41), the references to *handing over* shift from ominous premonition to tragic fulfillment. Jesus upbraids his sleepy disciples by announcing that the time has come for the events of his passion to begin:

> "Are you still sleeping and taking your rest? Enough! The hour has come; the Son of Man is *handed over* (παραδίδοται) into the hands of sinners. Get up, let us be going. See, *the one who hands me over* (ὁ παραδιδούς με) is at hand." (14:41-42, my translation)

Judas appears on cue, now identified not only by name (14:43) but also simply by an epithet, "the betrayer" (ὁ παραδιδοὺς αὐτόν = "*the one who handed him over*," 14:44).

In rapid sequence, the prophesied events of the passion play themselves out. Judas hands Jesus over to the chief priests, elders, and scribes. And they in turn pass him along to Pilate:

> "As soon as it was morning, the chief priests held a consultation with the elders and scribes and the whole council. They bound Jesus, led him away, and *handed him over* (παρέδωκεν) to Pilate." (Mark 15:1 NRSV)

Pilate, recognizing that "it was out of jealousy that the chief priests had *handed him over* (παραδεδώκεισαν αὐτὸν)" (15:10), tries to forestall the inevitable climax of these events but at last relents: "After flogging Jesus, he *handed him over* (παρέδωκεν) to be crucified" (15:15). With that conclusive cadence, the long-deferred linkage of *handing over* to the grim reality of crucifixion is at last completed.

In sum, ever since the brief allusion to John's being "handed over" in the opening verses of this gospel, Mark has placed repeated signposts that Jesus will be finally *handed over* to death on a cross. This repeated foreshadowing emphasizes that Jesus, the Messiah of Israel, relinquishing the awe-inspiring power that enabled him to heal the sick and still the wind and sea, will submit himself to be seized and crucified by fearful and angry authorities. In being *handed over* to be crucified, he will fulfill the will of God by becoming the servant who surrenders his life for many. The cross is therefore not an unexpected horrible accident; it is the consummate enactment of God's inscrutable redeeming will. But that is not the end of the story; in Mark's Gospel, the cross also defines a pattern of obedience for all those who will follow Jesus.

The Cross as a Paradigm for Discipleship

Mark repeatedly describes discipleship as an act of *following* Jesus. In the beginning of Mark's narrative, the verb ἀκολουθέω ("follow") appears to refer to the literal act of leaving other occupations behind and joining Jesus on the road as he walks about Galilee. This simple literal sense is the most obvious meaning of the summons, "Follow me," that Jesus issues to the fishermen Simon, Andrew, James, and John, who drop their nets and follow after him (Mark 1:16–20). Likewise, when we read that Levi son of Alphaeus left his post at the tax booth and "got up and followed him" (2:14), it seems that the verb "follow" refers to Levi's physical action of standing on his feet and trailing after a peripatetic Jesus.

The obvious metaphorical potential of the act of following, however, rises to the surface in Jesus's pivotal teaching to the crowds and to his disciples after his first passion prediction (Mark 8:31): "If any want to become my followers, let them deny themselves and take up their cross and follow me" (8:34). From this point onward, it becomes increasingly clear that to *follow* Jesus will entail costly personal sacrifice and a choice to pattern one's life after a teacher who has just predicted that he will suffer and be killed.

This saying of Jesus, placed at the dramatic center of Mark's narrative, hangs over the rest of the story and informs our reading of subsequent incidents and dialogues. Peter, hearing Jesus's teaching about the difficulty of entering the kingdom of God (Mark 10:23–27), offers a self-justifying response: "Look, we have left everything and *followed* you." Jesus's reply makes it clear that those who followed him as Peter has done will receive "a hundredfold" reward, but that this reward will come "with persecutions" (10:28–31)—a distinctive Markan inflection of this saying; the Synoptic parallels in Matt 19:27–30 and Luke 18:28–30 lack the reference to persecutions. Immediately following this exchange, we learn from Mark that those who were following Jesus on the road to Jerusalem were both amazed and afraid—perhaps because of the sobering teachings that Jesus has offered about the fate that awaits him there, a teaching that he immediately reiterates (Mark 10:32–34).

James and John, seemingly oblivious to what Jesus has been saying, request places of honor when Jesus comes into his glory. But he sets them straight by explaining that whoever wishes to be great must be "slave of all," and he articulates the meaning of such slavery by pointing to the death he is about to die as "a ransom for many" (Mark 10:35-45). By this point in the narrative, it becomes evident that Jesus's death is not simply his own destiny and not simply a vicarious sacrifice; rather, it is also an example to be followed in some way, a template for the sacrificial self-giving that he asks of those who follow him.

This call to follow Jesus in the way of costly self-surrender comes to a climax in the apocalyptic discourse of Mark 13, as Jesus directly foretells what will happen to his followers in the future:

> As for yourselves, beware; for they will *hand you over* (παραδώσουσιν) to councils; and you will be beaten in synagogues; and you will stand before governors and kings because of me, as a testimony to them. . . . When they bring you to trial and *hand you over* (παραδίδοντες), do not worry beforehand about what you are to say; but say whatever is given you at that time, for it is not you who speak, but the Holy Spirit. Brother will *hand over* (παραδώσει) brother to death, and a father his child, and children will rise against parents and have them put to death; and you will be hated by all because of my name. But the one who endures to the end will be saved. (13:9-13)[14]

In this stark prophecy about the troubles that will face the disciples in the future, Jesus three times uses παραδίδωμι—the same ominous verb that Mark repeatedly uses to portend the "handing over" of Jesus to crucifixion. Anyone following Mark's narrative closely will recognize that the disciples are being called to follow in Jesus's footsteps in a way that may lead them also to the cross, just as Jesus had declared in his decisive call to all who would follow him (8:34). The full force of Jesus's warning in 13:9-13 comes into focus when we perceive what it means, within Mark's narrative world, to be "handed over" to councils: those who are *handed over* must await the prospect of crucifixion.

Thus, as we trace the logic of Mark's narrative portrayal of discipleship, we cannot avoid the conclusion that Mark presents the cross as a *paradigm* for obedience. To become a disciple of Jesus is to undertake the vocation of patterning one's life after his own cross-shaped life and death.[15] In this sense,

---

14. This is the NRSV translation, except that I have substituted "hand over" for "betray" as the translation of παραδώσει in v. 12.

15. A classic theological explication of this theme of cross-shaped discipleship, though with reference to Matthew's Sermon on the Mount rather than with specific reference to Mark, is Dietrich Bonhoeffer, *Discipleship*, Dietrich Bonhoeffer Works, vol. 4, trans. Barbara Green and Reinhard Krauss (Minneapolis: Fortress, 2003).

The Crucified One

it would certainly be appropriate to describe the life of discipleship as a life of "cruciformity," a way of life inspired by and modeled after the example of Jesus's self-giving and suffering.

It is necessary, however, to distinguish Mark's portrayal of obediently following after Jesus's example from the Pauline interpretation of cruciformity, as Michael Gorman has explicated it. The difference lies in *the absence, within Mark's story, of any notion of participatory union with Christ*. Here is how Gorman describes Paul's understanding of cruciformity: "Cruciformity is an ongoing pattern of *living in Christ* and of dying *with* him that produces a Christlike (cruciform) person. Cruciform existence is what being Christ's servant, *indwelling him and being indwelt by him*, living with and for and 'according to' him is all about, for both individuals and communities."[16]

The italicized phrases in this quotation (with the italics supplied for emphasis) highlight distinctive features of Paul's theology that find no direct analogue in Mark. Mark offers no indication that the risen Jesus is to be a continuing living presence in the community of his followers; instead, Mark leaves his readers with this tantalizing proclamation of Jesus's absence: "He has been raised; he is not here" (Mark 16:6). Still less does Mark envision Jesus's followers as *indwelling* their Lord or experiencing a mysterious union with him in which they are indwelt by him. By contrast, Mark's Jesus has simply given his disciples, both by precept and by example, a paradigmatic portrayal of the cross-shaped servanthood that should define their own life in the world, their own costly, responsive obedience to the good news of the inbreaking kingdom of God.

That is not to say that Mark would dispute Paul's theological proclamation or disapprove of it. But the gospel that Mark has written bears no trace of the *participatory* soteriology that Gorman has rightly discerned in Paul's letters. Instead, Mark offers an austere call to follow after Jesus's example in trust that such faithful following will finally somehow serve God's redemptive purposes in the world.

The strange open ending of Mark's Gospel is also the beginning of the strange life of discipleship that is to characterize the vocation of all who seek to follow him. Even after Jesus has been raised from the dead, to know him rightly is to know him as the Crucified One. Mark drives this home one final time in his mysterious resurrection narrative, a resurrection narrative without an appearance of the risen Jesus. The women who discover the empty tomb find only an unnamed "young man, dressed in a white robe," who addresses

---

16. Gorman, *Cruciformity*, 48–49, emphasis mine.

them with astonishing, but enigmatic, news: "Jesus you are seeking, the Nazarene, the Crucified One (τὸν ἐσταυρωμένον). He is risen; he is not here" (Mark 16:5-6, my translation). The perfect tense of the participle ἐσταυρωμένον implies much; it implies that the action of the verb continues in effect into the present. Although Jesus is risen and the tomb is empty, his identity remains marked by the crucifixion. Even as he goes before his followers again to Galilee, he is still to be known as "the Crucified One." And they, precisely insofar as they follow him, are also to be marked by the sign of the cross.

.... *Chapter 3*

Luke and the Cross:
A Vision of Crucicentric Discipleship

Frank E. Dicken

Dietrich Bonhoeffer writes in his now classic *The Cost of Discipleship*:

> The cross is laid on every Christian. The first Christ-suffering which every man must experience is the call to abandon the attachments of this world. It is that dying of the old man which is the result of his encounter with Christ. As we embark upon discipleship we surrender ourselves to Christ in union with his death—we give over our lives to death. Thus it begins; the cross is not the terrible end to an otherwise godfearing and happy life, but it meets us at the beginning of our communion with Christ. When Christ calls a man, he bids him come and die.[1]

Bonhoeffer's statement is an apt summary for the task at hand—an exploration of Luke's teaching about the cross. Scholarly work on Luke's view of the cross has tended to focus on soteriological aspects of Jesus's death.[2] While it is easy to understand this tendency, soteriology is not the primary focus of

---

1. Dietrich Bonhoeffer, *The Cost of Discipleship* (New York: Simon & Schuster, 1959), 89.
2. E.g., Peter Doble, *The Paradox of Salvation: Luke's Theology of the Cross* (Cambridge:

As one of my former professors, Michael Gorman, through his teaching, guidance, and expertise, helped shape me as an interpreter of the New Testament and as a follower of Jesus. I am grateful for the numerous ways he helped and supported me as a hopeful PhD applicant and in the early years of my work as an academic. It is truly one of the highlights of my career to be able to write this essay in his honor.

the third evangelist's discussion of the cross.³ Certainly, Jesus's death is "for" others (Luke 22:19–20), but Lukan soteriology involves healing, exorcisms, restoration, forgiveness of sins, and more.⁴ For Luke, Christ's death on the cross is part and parcel of Luke's primary point of emphasis: Jesus's resurrection and exaltation.⁵

When Luke discusses the cross, his primary concern is discipleship—the cross that followers of Jesus must faithfully carry daily is in view. To be sure, Jesus is crucified, but it is on a cross he does not carry. In fact, Luke only uses the verb σταυρόω four times in narrating Jesus's death.⁶ Luke exclusively uses

---

Cambridge University Press, 2005) and the more recent monograph, Benjamin R. Wilson, *The Saving Cross of the Suffering Christ*, BZNW 223 (Berlin: Walter de Gruyter, 2016).

3. Charles H. Talbert rightly points out that Jesus offers salvation both before and after his death in Luke and Acts ("The Place of the Resurrection in the Theology of Luke," *Int* 46 [1992]: 22–23).

4. See e.g., Joel B. Green, *The Theology of the Gospel of Luke*, New Testament Theology (Cambridge: Cambridge University Press, 1995), 76–101. On the lack of salvific significance of Jesus's cross in Luke, see Isak J. du Plessis, "The Saving Significance of Jesus and His Death on the Cross in Luke's Gospel—Focussing on Luke 22:19b–20," *Neot* 28 (1994): 523–40; Joel B. Green, *The Gospel of Luke*, NICNT (Grand Rapids: Eerdmans, 1997), 764. For the effects of Jesus's death in Luke, see Joseph A. Fitzmyer, *The Gospel According to Luke I–IX*, AB 28 (Garden City, NY: Doubleday, 1981), 219–27.

5. Werner Georg Kümmel rightly argues that the soteriological significance of Jesus's death on the cross is not entirely absent in Luke, but the third evangelist does not stress it ("Current Theological Accusations Against Luke," *ANQ* 16 [1975]: 131–45). Similarly, Fitzmyer notes that this is a matter of emphasis and does not diminish Jesus's work on the cross (*Luke I–IX*, 22–23). See also Darrell L. Bock, *A Theology of Luke and Acts* (Grand Rapids: Zondervan, 2012), 203–4. Even the language used in the pivotal transition of the narrative from Galilee to Jerusalem (9:51) reflects this emphasis. There Luke states that Jesus sets out for Jerusalem as the time approached for him to be "taken up" (ἀνάλημψις), which refers not to Jesus's death but his ascension (Luke uses the cognate verb ἀναλαμβάνω at Acts 1:2, 11, 22 to refer to the ascension). See BDAG, 67; Green, *Gospel of Luke*, 403; Charles H. Talbert, "The Way of the Lukan Jesus: Dimensions of Lukan Spirituality," *PRSt* 9 (1982): 237–49.

6. Luke uses the verb σταυρόω a total of six times. The verb occurs three times prior to the Lukan crucifixion on the lips of those who wish to see Jesus dead (Luke 23:21 [twice], 23), once in describing the actual crucifixion (23:33), and twice in the resurrection narratives (24:7, 20). By way of comparison, the verb occurs seven times in Mark's and six times in Matthew's respective crucifixion narratives. Matthew's Jesus even names crucifixion as the means of his death (Matt 20:19; 26:2), which neither the Lukan nor the Markan Jesus does. On Simon carrying the cross, while the assumption of I. Howard Marshall that Jesus initially carried the cross (*Commentary on Luke*, NIGTC [Grand Rapids: Eerdmans, 1978], 863) was likely true historically (see especially the contrasting account of John 19:17), the third evangelist clearly states that Simon carried the cross.

the noun σταυρός to refer to the cross carried by those who follow Jesus.[7] Luke's view of the cross is more ecclesiological than christological or soteriological. Therefore, this essay will argue that Luke's teaching concerning the cross presents a vision of crucicentric discipleship, i.e., the central metaphor for following Jesus is bearing one's cross.[8] In order to demonstrate this, the essay will proceed in three parts, with each section corresponding to the tripartite geographical division of the gospel: the Galilean ministry narrative (Luke 4:14–9:50), the journey/travel narrative (9:51–19:27), and the Jerusalem/passion narrative (19:28–24:53).[9] Each of these three sections includes Luke's depiction of Jesus as suffering-and-rising Messiah and a portrayal of Jesus's disciples as cross-carriers.[10] As will be discussed below, the Galilean ministry narrative establishes Jesus's identity as the suffering-and-rising Messiah. Likewise, in this first section, Luke establishes the identity of Jesus's disciples as those who take up a cross and follow Jesus. Then, the travel narrative shows Jesus faithfully progressing toward his death and exaltation in Jerusalem. Similarly, the journey narrative portrays the disciples as those who faithfully carry a cross in order to follow Jesus. Finally, the Jerusalem narrative actualizes the identities and faithfulness of both Jesus and the disciples. Jesus, of course, is crucified and raised from the dead. Discipleship is actualized in the Jerusalem narrative when Simon of Cyrene quite literally bears a cross and follows Jesus, thus becoming a model of discipleship. The following is an overview of the structure of the argument of the essay:

---

7. The noun only occurs in Luke at 9:23; 14:27; 23:26. Again, by comparison, Mark uses the noun to refer to the disciple's cross (8:34), Simon carrying the cross (15:21), and Jesus's cross twice (15:30, 32). Matthew uses σταυρός for the disciple's cross twice (10:38; 16:24), Simon carrying the cross (27:32), and Jesus's cross twice (27:40, 42).

8. The term "crucicentric" is a nod to one of the leading emphases of Prof. Gorman's scholarly career, cruciformity. For Luke, discipleship is not cross-shaped (cruciform) but rather is envisioned by the central metaphor of cross-bearing (crucicentric). The methodology employed in the essay falls within standard exegetical and narrative-critical parameters.

9. Scholars disagree on where the Jerusalem narrative begins (19:28 or 19:45). There are other minor differences, but there is widespread agreement on a tripartite division of the Third Gospel. See e.g., Hans Conzelmann, *The Theology of St. Luke*, trans. Goeffrey Buswell (London: Faber and Faber, 1960), 27; Charles H. Talbert, *Reading Luke: A Literary and Theological Commentary on the Third Gospel* (New York: Crossroad, 1988), v–vi. Luke 1:1–4:13 is sometimes included with the Galilean ministry section. I have chosen to exclude it here since Jesus's public ministry begins in the Nazareth synagogue scene.

10. Dennis M. Sweetland, *Our Journey with Jesus: Discipleship According to Luke–Acts*, Good News Studies 23 (Collegeville, MN: Liturgical Press, 1990), 107.

	Function vis-à-vis the cross	Jesus	Disciples
Galilean Ministry (4:14–9:50)	Establishes identity	Jesus is suffering-and-rising Messiah (9:21–22, 44)	Disciples take up the cross and follow Jesus (9:23–27)
Travel Narrative (9:51–19:27)	Demonstrates faithfulness to identity	Jesus journeys to Jerusalem knowing his fate (11:45–54; 13:33–35; 17:25; 18:31–34)	Disciples carry the cross and follow Jesus (14:27)
Jerusalem/ Passion (19:28–24:53)	Actualizes identity	Jesus is crucified and raised from the dead (23:32–24:53)	Simon of Cyrene bears the cross and follows Jesus (23:26)

Crucicentric Discipleship: Identity and Faithfulness

The Cross as Identity Marker (Luke 9:18–50)

Jesus's Identity: Suffering-and-Rising Messiah

In the chapters preceding Luke 9, the third evangelist utilizes titular Christology to form a matrix of mutually informing identifiers for Jesus that appear throughout the gospel. Beginning in the birth narratives (Luke 1–2), the author portrays Jesus in distinct but overlapping ways. Luke's initial descriptors of Jesus are Son of the Most High and King of Israel (1:32–33). Once Jesus is born, Luke's angels refer to Jesus as the Savior, a designation equated with the title "Messiah," which is defined appositively as "the Lord" (σωτὴρ ὅς ἐστιν χριστὸς κύριος; 2:11). It has been established that these five epithets—Son of God, King of Israel, Savior, Messiah, and Lord—are various ways of referring to the Davidic Messiah/King of Israel.[11] That Luke uses all five titles in introducing Jesus shows that they mutually inform each other.[12]

---

11. See, e.g., Raymond E. Brown, *The Birth of the Messiah*, 2nd ed. (New York: Doubleday, 1993), 310–11, 424–25.

12. Green, *Gospel of Luke*, 89; Sweetland, *Our Journey*, 86–87.

For Luke, these mutually informing descriptors form the initial impression of Jesus in the Third Gospel. The Galilean portion of the narrative (Luke 4:14–9:50) confirms that impression. The temptation narratives show Jesus to be the Son of God (4:1–13). Jesus is the anointed one (Messiah/King) in the Nazareth synagogue scene (4:14–30). In the accounts of Jesus's miracles and teaching, he is Lord (5:12; 6:5; 7:6, 13, 19). In portraying Jesus as Savior, Luke recounts several miracles in which Jesus heals physical infirmities (6:9; 7:50; cf. 4:18). Moving beyond the titles revealed in the birth narratives, Luke adds one more christological title when depicting Jesus as Israel's teacher: Son of Man (5:24; 7:34; 9:22). This final title is equated with "Lord" in the Sabbath controversies between Jesus and the Jewish religious leaders (6:1–11, esp. 6:5). There are certainly distinctions between these titles to maintain. However, Luke's regular shifting between them helps the reader remember the others when one is employed.

In this way, the birth and Galilean ministry portions of Luke lay the groundwork for the overall depiction of Jesus as the suffering-and-rising Messiah by the third evangelist. The theme of Jesus's identity culminates in Luke 9 with Peter's response that reveals his belief that Jesus is the Messiah (9:20).[13] The preceding discussion of the interrelatedness of the designations that form Luke's titular Christology is important at this juncture. The Lukan Jesus's tacit agreement with Peter leads directly to the first Lukan passion prediction. Here Jesus refers to himself with his favored self-designation, Son of Man, in order to define his messiahship for the disciples (9:21–22).[14] As Messiah/Son of Man, Jesus will suffer, be rejected and killed, and raised on the third day.[15]

This first prediction is soon followed by a second abbreviated prediction to form an *inclusio* (Luke 9:44). This enclosed section includes two short narratives that further confirm Jesus's identity as it has been revealed up to this point in the narrative. The first is the transfiguration account which confirms Jesus's status as Son of God (9:28–36, esp. 9:35).[16] The second is a healing miracle that

---

13. Sverre Bøe (*Cross-Bearing in Luke*, WUNT 2/278 [Mohr Siebeck, 2010], 80), Holly Beers (*The Followers of Jesus as the Servant: Luke's Model from Isaiah for the Disciples in Luke–Acts*, LNTS 535 [London: Bloomsbury/T & T Clark, 2015], 109), and Donald E. Miller ("Luke 9:18–24," *Int* 37 [1983]: 65) all agree that this section is crucial for Luke's formation of Jesus's identity. Fitzmyer also points out that the identification of Jesus as Messiah recalls the birth narratives (*Luke I–IX*, 771).

14. Wilson, *Saving Cross*, 43.

15. Again, notice that for Jesus the emphasis is on the resurrection, not the cross, though the latter obviously plays a crucial role in Jesus's identity as Messiah/Son of Man. Fitzmyer, *Luke I–IX*, 781.

16. Wilson, *Saving Cross*, 45.

serves to further highlight Jesus's status as Savior (9:37–43). Thus, the climax of the Galilean ministry of Jesus serves as an early narrative summary of Jesus's identity, an identity that is inextricably bound to his divinely ordained destiny to die and be raised.[17] The Lukan Jesus is the suffering-and-rising Messiah.

The Disciples' Identity: Self-Denial and Taking up a Cross

There is another short section of text in the *inclusio* noted above. Following Jesus's first passion prediction, he immediately shifts his attention to his disciples' identity.[18] The first mention of a cross in Luke's Gospel refers to the disciples' crosses (Luke 9:23–27).[19] Up to this point in the narrative, Luke has shown that disciples are followers of Jesus who often make significant personal sacrifices to follow Jesus. For example, Simon Peter, James and John, and Levi the tax collector left *everything* (πᾶς) to follow Jesus (5:11, 28).[20] In another instance, Luke tells of a larger group of disciples who follow Jesus, some of whom are women of relatively high social standing who support Jesus and other disciples out of their own financial resources (8:1–3).

However, Luke's Jesus does not specify the nature of discipleship until 9:23–27. In this passage "Jesus applies the function of suffering, rejection, and death in his own life to the life of anyone who" wishes to follow him.[21] The condition of following Jesus (lit. "if anyone wishes to come after me")[22] is met as disciples obey three commands: denial of self (ἀρνησάσθω), taking up (ἀράτω) their own cross daily, and following (ἀκολουθείτω) Jesus. The first two commands are aorist indicating conceptually complete actions (despite the call to carry

---

17. Wilson, *Saving Cross*, 45. On Luke's use of δεῖ (9:22; cf. 2:49; 4:43; 17:25; 21:9; 22:37; 24:7, 26, 44) to denote God's action at work in the life and ministry of Jesus, see Green, *Gospel of Luke*, 22.

18. Bøe, *Cross-Bearing in Luke*, 80–81; Miller, "Luke 9:18–24," 64; Sharyn Dowd, "Luke 9:18–27: 'Daily' Cross-Bearing for Jesus' Sake," *RevExp* 112 (2015): 620. On the close connection between Luke 9:21–22 and 9:23–27 in contrast to Mark, see John Nolland, *Luke 9:21–18:34*, WBC 35b (Waco, TX: Word, 1993), 475–76.

19. Luke appears to follow Mark by never having Jesus refer to his death *on the cross* (cf. Mark 8:31; 9:31; 10:33–34). Matthew is distinct as Jesus twice speaks of his crucifixion (Matt 20:19; 26:2).

20. This is reiterated later in the gospel as Peter, once again speaking on behalf of the group, states that they have left their homes to follow Jesus (18:28).

21. Dowd, "Luke 9:18–27," 619. See also Nolland, *Luke 9:21–18:34*, 482.

22. A phrase that anticipates the journey narrative as Bøe indicates (*Cross-Bearing in Luke*, 95).

one's cross daily)[23] and are epexegetical—denying self and taking up the cross are two closely related ways of conveying a pattern of life for Jesus's followers.[24] The final command switches to the present tense indicating the continuous sense is already found in the protasis.[25]

The call to take up the cross daily (καθ' ἡμέραν), a clear Lukan redaction, emphasizes the ongoing nature of discipleship.[26] This also means that this cross is not a literal one but rather the self-denying actions that would bring social stigma and shame similar to that experienced by one being led away to crucifixion. This makes sense of Jesus's statement that some of his disciples will not taste death before they see the kingdom of God (Luke 9:27); they will live despite carrying a cross. The daily lives of Jesus's followers will consist of denying themselves and carrying a cross. Luke further explains (γάρ) this manner of discipleship as the voluntary loss of one's entire physical life[27] in order to save it (9:24)[28] and sharing in Jesus's shame (9:26), ostensibly by engaging in the everyday acts that taking up a metaphorical cross entails.[29] This explanation magnifies the motif of metaphorical death set by the command to carry a cross. In this way, just as Jesus's own identity is bound up with suffering, so too his disciples' identities are bound up with self-denial and the metaphorical suffering of daily cross-bearing. For Luke, to follow the suffering-and-rising Messiah is to lead a crucicentric life.

The Cross as Costly Faithfulness (Luke 14:25-33)

The previous section shows how Luke utilizes Jesus's initial passion predictions as the culmination of Jesus's Galilean ministry. Much of the first third of Luke's Gospel is taken up with the question of Jesus's identity as the Davidic Messiah

---

23. Bøe, *Cross-Bearing in Luke*, 91–92; Green, *Gospel of Luke*, 373.

24. Bøe, *Cross-Bearing in Luke*, 91, 98–99; Dowd, "Luke 9:18–27," 620; J. Duncan M. Derrett, "Taking Up the Cross and Turning the Cheek," in *Alternative Approaches to New Testament Study*, ed. A. E. Harvey (Plymouth: SPCK, 1985), 62. Contra Michael P. Green who sees the actions as chronological ("The Meaning of Cross-Bearing," *BSac* 140 [1983]: 121).

25. Green, *Gospel of Luke*, 373; Miller, "Luke 9:18–24," 66.

26. Anton Fridrichsen, *Exegetical Writings: A Selection*, trans. Chrys C. Caragounis and Tord Fornberg, WUNT 1/76 (Tübingen: J. C. B. Mohr [Paul Siebeck], 1994), 42; Nolland, *Luke 9:21–18:34*, 482.

27. Fitzmyer defines ἀρνέομαι aptly: "adopt an attitude in life that is not self-centered, but that authentically allows one to identify one's conduct with Jesus and his mission" (*Luke I–IX*, 787). See BDAG, 132–33 on ἀρνέομαι and 1098–1100 on ψυχή.

28. 9:25 explains (γάρ) 9:24. Bøe, *Cross-Bearing in Luke*, 142; Nolland, *Luke 9:21–18:34*, 483.

29. Marshall, *Luke*, 373; Fridrichsen, *Exegetical Writings*, 42; Dowd, "Luke 9:18–27," 621.

who will suffer and be raised. The *inclusio* formed by the initial passion predictions also reveals the true identity of Jesus's disciples as those who voluntarily lose their lives in self-denial and by taking up a cross. In the next section of Luke's Gospel, commonly referred to as the "travel" or "journey" narrative (Luke 9:51–19:27), Luke will both reiterate Jesus's identity as the suffering-and-rising Messiah and elaborate upon the disciples' identities by showing the costly faithfulness required to carry one's cross.

Jesus's Impending Death and Exaltation in Jerusalem

The Lukan journey narrative begins with Jesus "setting his face" toward Jerusalem (Luke 9:51). When the journey toward Jerusalem begins, Luke indicates that Jesus resolutely adopts his identity as suffering-and-rising Messiah.[30] To emphasize this, Luke makes no fewer than four references to Jesus's impending death in Jerusalem: two are implicit (11:37–54; 13:33–35) and two are explicit passion predictions by Jesus (17:25; 18:31–34). In this way Luke's travel narrative demonstrates that Jesus faithfully embraces his identity as the suffering-and-rising Messiah.[31]

There is increasing specificity in the four references to Christ's passion in the travel narrative, from implicit statements by Jesus that prophets are killed in Jerusalem to the explicit enumeration of the ordeals he will undergo. In the journey narrative these four statements serve both a proleptic and analeptic function. Proleptically they anticipate the passion narrative proper and thus carry the narrative forward. As analepses, they recall the initial passion predictions (Luke 9:21–22, 44) which established Jesus's identity as suffering-and-rising Messiah. The Lukan travel narrative shows that Jesus understands his divinely directed end and so he faithfully journeys from Galilee to Jerusalem. Jesus's identity was established in the Galilean ministry portion of Luke. The journey narrative confirms it.

The first passage that implicitly speaks of Jesus's passion is Luke 11:37–54. Here Jesus is dining at the home of a Pharisee and the host is amazed that Jesus does not participate in ceremonial washing before eating. This provides Jesus an opportunity to launch into a lengthy polemic against the gathered Pharisees and Jewish legal experts. As part of this polemic Jesus accuses the religious

---

30. The verb στηρίζω connotes firmness of purpose. Nolland, *Luke 9:21–18:34*, 535; BDAG, 945.

31. Talbert writes that Luke depicts Jesus's suffering as an "ultimate act of obedience or faithfulness to God" ("Way of the Lukan Jesus," 244–45).

leaders of approving of their ancestors having killed the prophets by building tombs for those ancestors (11:47–48). Jesus demonstrates (διὰ τοῦτο) their guilt in the matter by referring to the Wisdom of God which states that the current generation will be guilty of killing and persecuting all of the apostles and prophets sent to it by God (11:49–52).[32] This subtle hint anticipates both Jesus's eventual death and the opposition his apostles will face.

In a later conversation with a group of Pharisees, Jesus more clearly anticipates his death as a prophet in the city of Jerusalem (Luke 13:33–35).[33] Several Pharisees initiate this brief interaction by warning Jesus that Herod (Antipas) wants to kill him (13:31–32). Jesus states that the Pharisees are to tell Herod about the ongoing miraculous activities that prompted Herod to want to see and now kill Jesus (cf. 9:7–9).[34] Jesus's double statement about continuing his work for two days and finishing it on the third (13:32–33) collapses the crucifixion and resurrection into a single event. The slightly different language of these two verses allows this twofold referent. The occurrence of τρίτος in 13:32 is surely a veiled reference to his resurrection.[35] However, 13:33 indicates that on the day after today and tomorrow, Jesus will continue on his way to Jerusalem where prophets are killed (13:34).[36] The passage ends by anticipating the triumphal entry into Jerusalem (13:35; cf. 19:38). Alongside 11:37–54, Jesus's reference here to the third day, the day after tomorrow, and the anticipation of his entry into Jerusalem once again reiterate his identity as the suffering-and-rising Messiah and his faithfulness in that role.[37]

Luke's journey narrative also contains two explicit passion predictions. The first is a brief aside in a passage that is otherwise concerned with God's judgment (Luke 17:22–37). According to Luke, Jesus affirms that the kingdom of

32. Marshall, *Luke*, 502; Nolland, *Luke 9:21–18:34*, 668.
33. Raymond E. Brown, *The Death of the Messiah*, vol. 2 (New York: Doubleday, 1994), 1430. David P. Moessner also relates 13:33–35 to 11:47–52 (*Lord of the Banquet: The Literary and Theological Significance of the Lukan Travel Narrative* [Harrisburg, PA: Trinity Press International, 1989], 155).
34. See Frank Dicken, *Herod as a Composite Character in Luke-Acts*, WUNT 2/375 (Tübingen: Mohr Siebeck, 2014), 100–105.
35. Fitzmyer, *Luke I–IX*, 781. Τρίτος regularly refers to the day of resurrection and exaltation in Luke's Gospel (9:22; 18:33; 24:7, 21, 46).
36. On Luke's portrayal of Jesus as a prophet, see Moessner, *Lord of the Banquet*, 46–50.
37. Green, *Gospel of Luke*, 538. A third text, Luke 12:50, complements these two passion inferences. That verse appears in a pericope dealing primarily with Jesus's exaltation and accompanying judgment on the earth, but his figurative baptism (i.e., his suffering and death) is a precursor to those events. Like the implicit prediction of 13:33–35, 12:49–56 closely relates Jesus's suffering and exaltation. See Moessner, *Lord of the Banquet*, 153.

FRANK E. DICKEN

God is already present, not future, in response to a question posed by a group of Pharisees concerning the arrival of the kingdom (17:20–21). Jesus then turns to his disciples about a related matter: the revelation of the Son of Man.[38] In the midst of this discussion, Jesus states that the Son of Man must (δεῖ) suffer and be rejected by the current generation (17:25). This deliberately recalls the first passion prediction which also mentions Jesus's suffering and rejection (9:22), showing once again that Jesus willingly accepts his role in God's plan.[39] This passage also hearkens back to 11:47–52 with Jesus's accusation against "this generation" which will cause the suffering of the Son of Man.[40]

The final passion prediction of the journey narrative is also Jesus's penultimate instructions to his followers before he enters Jerusalem (Luke 18:31–33).[41] As in the other explicit passion predictions Jesus speaks of himself as the Son of Man. However, three new pieces of information emerge in this passage: (1) the prophets of Israel have in some sense foretold the suffering of the Son of Man, (2) Jesus will be handed over to gentiles, and (3) mockery, insults, spitting, and flogging will precede Jesus's death. The first of these newly revealed aspects of Jesus's passion anticipates the resurrection since the risen Jesus emphasizes the fulfillment of the prophets in his appearances to his disciples (24:26–27, 46).[42] The second aspect anticipates Pilate's and the Roman soldiers' roles in Jesus's death (23:1–49). The third outlines what happens to Jesus after his arrest and before his execution (22:63–23:31). The journey motif also resumes more clearly after this final prediction as Jesus only makes one more stop, Jericho, on his way to Jerusalem (18:35), thereby recalling the resolution with which he began the journey from Galilee and the divine necessity compelling the Son of Man toward Jerusalem.[43] This text serves to round out the depiction of Jesus in the Third Gospel leaving no doubt in the reader's mind concerning how Luke wishes to portray him: Jesus is faithful to his task as suffering-and-rising Messiah.

These four passages demonstrate that Jesus's passion is a key motif of the Lukan journey narrative. Jesus's identity was established in the birth narratives

---

38. John T. Carroll, *Luke: A Commentary*, NTL (Louisville: Westminster John Knox, 2012), 347–48.

39. Wilson, *Saving Cross*, 49; Green, *Gospel of Luke*, 633–34; Nolland, *Luke 9:21–18:34*, 859.

40. Moessner, *Lord of the Banquet*, 97–98. Additionally, as Marshall states, the passage confirms Jesus's identity as the Son of Man (*Luke*, 661).

41. Jesus's final teaching to his disciples in the journey narrative may also be an allusion to his impending rejection in Jerusalem (19:11–27).

42. Green, *Gospel of Luke*, 660.

43. Moessner, *Lord of the Banquet*, 168; Wilson, *Saving Cross*, 47.

and the Galilean ministry. The travel narrative reinforces that identity and shows Jesus to be faithful to it as he moves steadily toward his destiny. However, the only reference to a cross in the middle section of Luke is to the one that disciples must carry. Just as in the Galilean ministry, self-denial and carrying a cross are central to the disciple's identity. And just as Jesus's identity as the faithful suffering-and-rising Messiah was confirmed and elaborated upon by Luke in the journey narrative, so this second instruction for the disciples elaborates upon what it means for disciples to carry their crosses faithfully.

The Disciples' Cross-Bearing Explained

As in the Galilean ministry narrative, despite repeated references to Jesus's death, the only mention of a cross in the journey narrative is the one carried by disciples as a mark of their discipleship (Luke 14:27).[44] This cross logion is one of three parallel statements found in a larger pericope that deals with the costly faithfulness required of those who want to become disciples (14:25–33). With these three statements the Lukan Jesus elaborates on the self-denial and cross-bearing required of his followers.

The three parallel definitions of discipleship are found at Luke 14:26, 27, 33, each of which states negatively a condition for discipleship:[45]

14:26—if someone comes to me and does not hate family and life
14:27—whoever does not carry a cross and follow me
14:33—anyone who does not surrender all possessions

Each ends with the same phrase: that one cannot be my disciple (οὐ δύναται εἶναί μου μαθητής). The effect of this parallelism is to place hatred of family, hatred of life, and the renunciation of possessions on the same plane as what is already known about discipleship (9:24), namely that one must deny self and take up a cross. A few comments on 14:26 and 14:33 are in order before turning to the second cross logion.

The first condition, hatred of family and life, is the necessary corequisite for coming *to* Jesus.[46] As the disciple comes to Jesus to enter into such a rela-

---

44. Nolland, *Luke 9:21–18:34*, 741. The above analysis of the passion predictions in the journey narrative demonstrates that Green is incorrect in stating that the passion context is absent from this cross logion ("The Meaning of Cross-Bearing," 121).

45. Green, *Gospel of Luke*, 567.

46. Τίς is the subject of both indicatives (ἔρχεται, μισεῖ), which are joined with a simple καί. The preposition πρός denotes entering into a friendly relationship with another party (BDAG, 874 [3.d.β]).

tionship, the immediate family (father, mother, wife, children, brothers, and sisters) is the object of the disciple's hatred.⁴⁷ Textual proximity links hating one's life with cross-bearing in the present context. This link is strengthened as Jesus's call for disciples to hate their own lives (ψυχή) here recalls his earlier explanation of taking up the cross as losing one's life (Luke 9:24). In short, this first condition for being a disciple of Jesus is about trading a person's primary identity marker and support network in the Greco-Roman world—the immediate family—for being identified as part of Jesus's personal network, i.e., being identified with and by the one who is bound to suffer and die.⁴⁸

The condition of surrendering one's possessions (Luke 14:33) should be understood more broadly than "stuff someone owns" in light of the connotations of ὑπάρχω, which include both material and monetary goods.⁴⁹ According to Luke, all of this (πᾶσιν τοῖς ὑπάρχουσιν) must be renounced (ἀποτάσσεται) by the one wishing to be a disciple of Jesus. Such renunciation is a repeated discipleship motif in Luke. During the Galilean ministry, a group of wealthy women serve as concrete examples of the call to discipleship by both following Jesus and supporting him and the other disciples with their resources (ἐκ τῶν ὑπαρχόντων αὐταῖς, 8:3). Jesus later calls his followers to sell their possessions (πωλήσατε τὰ ὑπάρχοντα ὑμῶν) and give alms (12:33). Near the end of the journey narrative, Zacchaeus becomes an exemplar of this instruction by giving half of his possessions to the poor (τὰ ἡμίσιά μου τῶν ὑπαρχόντων τοῖς πτωχοῖς δίδωμι, 19:8).⁵⁰ Two short parables (14:28–32) illustrate the immense investment of capital (both literal and figurative) required to be a follower of Jesus and become the points of comparison (οὕτως οὖν) for the divestment of all of one's worldly goods.⁵¹ "This verse demands 'possessions-denial' in addition to self-denial and family denial."⁵² The disciple of Jesus is thus marked

---

47. As Bøe states, hatred toward family is strong language meant to convey the prioritization of faithfulness to Jesus over one's family (*Cross-Bearing in Luke*, 168–69). Note that Jesus had earlier called potential followers to this priority (9:57–62) and later commends his disciples for leaving their families to follow him (18:28–30). See also Dowd, "Luke 9:18–27," 620.

48. On the tremendous social costs associated with breaking family ties in the first century CE, see Bøe, *Cross-Bearing in Luke*, 40–41. I disagree with Bøe that this saying does not illuminate the call to carry one's cross.

49. Dowd, "Luke 9:18–27," 620; Nolland, *Luke 9:21–18:34*, 764; BDAG, 1029.

50. For more examples, see chapter four of Christopher M. Hays, *Renouncing Everything: Money and Discipleship in Luke* (Mahwah, NJ: Paulist, 2016).

51. The word οὖν shows that what follows is a deduction from these parables. See Bøe, *Cross-Bearing in Luke*, 193.

52. Bøe, *Cross-Bearing in Luke*, 195.

out in the world by downward social mobility through voluntary poverty and/or financial support of others.

Carrying a cross is the requisite third condition for discipleship in this pericope. The language of Luke 14:27 is strikingly similar to 9:23: εἴ τις θέλει ὀπίσω μου ἔρχεσθαι (9:23) and ὅστις . . . ἔρχεται ὀπίσω μου (14:27). The word ὀπίσω is a standard way to denote following someone.[53] The language of discipleship is quite literally to go "behind" Jesus. Reflective of the advancement of the narrative, the shift in language shows progression from 9:23 to 14:27 with the former calling disciples to "take up" (αἴρω) their crosses and the latter calling them to "carry" (βαστάζω) their crosses.[54] The disciples' cross-bearing also intensifies in the journey narrative. At 9:23 the self-denial and taking up the cross were metaphorical as disciples are instructed to undertake the latter task daily. While a metaphorical death similar to that envisioned at 9:23–27 is almost certainly in view at 14:27, the context of the Lukan travel narrative adds the possibility of Jesus's disciples facing a literal death.[55] In the first implicit passion prediction of the journey narrative (11:37–54), Jesus has already stated that some of the prophets and apostles sent to Israel will be killed and persecuted. The "apostles" in view here are surely the group of twelve disciples chosen by Jesus out of the larger group of his followers (6:13; 9:10; 17:5; 22:14). Here the cost associated with discipleship rises even beyond hatred of family and renunciation of possessions to facing the possibility of physical persecution and/or death. This is the ultimate expression of self-denial and hatred of one's life.

The threads of cross-carrying discipleship that are woven throughout the first two sections of Luke's Gospel come together in this passage as self-denial and cross-carrying are put in stark terms. Luke portrays faithfulness as disciples prioritizing following Jesus over their families in order to identify with and be identified by Jesus.[56] They must renounce their possessions and give up any social status that may have come with them. They must carry the cross,

---

53. LN 36.35; BDAG, 716 (2.a).
54. Bøe notes that βαστάζω has a durative connotation (*Cross-Bearing in Luke*, 183–84).
55. See 9:24. Pace Bøe, 188.
56. For an elaboration of the ecclesial dimensions of discipleship (e.g., faith, repentance, mission, prayer, praise, critique of empire, etc.) that Luke includes in the journey narrative, see chapter 5 of Green, *Theology*. Due to space, I am focusing on the pericope in which the cross logion appears and attempting to capture those ecclesial dimensions with the term "faithfulness." See also Green who argues that cross-bearing is a metaphor for obedience and submission to Jesus ("The Meaning of Cross-Bearing," 127).

enduring the shame associated with that act. Discipleship costs everything, up to and including one's very life.[57]

Simon of Cyrene: Model of Discipleship (Luke 23:26)

The Cross of the Suffering-and-Rising Messiah

There are no explicit passion predictions in the Jerusalem narrative, but there continue to be proleptic references to Jesus's death. The first is the parable of the vineyard and the tenant farmers (Luke 20:9–18), the point of which is clear: the son who is sent by the vineyard owner and killed by the tenant workers represents Jesus. The parable is polemic against the religious leaders who have expressed increased hostility toward Jesus and even a desire to kill him (20:19; cf. 19:47–48; 20:1–2, 20).[58] This parable and the surrounding statements of the intentions of the religious leaders confirm what is already known from the preceding narrative—that Jesus will meet his fate in Jerusalem. The second prolepsis is Jesus's statement that the bread eaten during his final Passover meal is his body given for his disciples and the accompanying wine is his blood poured out for them (22:19–20).[59] These are clear allusions to his impending death.[60]

When Jesus speaks of his body as bread and blood as wine, he also evokes the earlier repeated references to his suffering and death in Jerusalem. Along with this, at Luke 22:22 Jesus once again refers to himself as the Son of Man and his imminent betrayal, thus pulling the narrative threads of Jesus's identity together. This recalls the initial passion predictions in which he used the same self-referent, spoke of rejection by the religious leaders (who are already working with Judas, 22:3–6), and mentioned betrayal (9:21–22, 44). The Lukan passion narrative actualizes Jesus's identity as suffering-and-rising Messiah.

To further reinforce Jesus's identity as he is facing death, Luke once again combines the various titles that he has already used for Jesus in creating the christological matrix of the birth and Galilean ministry narratives. After Jesus is arrested and mocked (Luke 22:54, 63–65; cf. 18:32–33), he is brought before an assembly of the religious leaders for questioning. Here three of the christolog-

---

57. As Beers puts it, disciples of Jesus must endure "suffering and sacrifice" (*Followers of Jesus*, 109).

58. Green, *Gospel of Luke*, 709.

59. Jesus is aware that this is the last meal before his suffering (πάσχω) and rejection (ἀποδοκιμάζω, 22:15, 17; cf. 9:22).

60. John Nolland, *Luke 18:35–24:53*, WBC 35c (Waco, TX: Word, 1993), 1053.

Luke and the Cross

ical titles—Messiah, Son of Man, and Son of God—appear together with little distinction and a fourth, "king," is used by Pilate in the ensuing episode. In this way, the passion narrative brings Luke's emphasis on Jesus's identity full circle so that throughout the gospel Jesus is the suffering-and-rising Messiah.[61]

The crucifixion narrative is the first time Luke mentions a cross in connection with Jesus's death (Luke 23:32–46).[62] In line with his depiction of Jesus's faithfulness to his identity, Luke presents Jesus as a righteous sufferer on the cross. Both Pilate and Herod have already declared Jesus innocent (23:14, 15, 22) and the centurion at the cross deems him "righteous" (δίκαιος, 23:47).[63] Despite his innocence and righteousness, but in line with his identity and faithfulness, the crucifixion and the accompanying events are the suffering of the suffering-and-rising Messiah.

Luke holds these two aspects of Jesus's identity together, even in the resurrection accounts. Twice Luke includes a reference to the crucifixion in statements that focalize the passion predictions. The first is the announcement of the two men in dazzling clothes to the women who come to the tomb with spices for Jesus's body. These men tell the women to remember that Jesus had told them that he would be handed over, crucified, and rise again (Luke 24:7). The second post-resurrection reference to the crucifixion is when the two travelers on the road to Emmaus recount to an incognito Jesus that Jesus had been handed over by the religious leaders to be condemned and crucified (24:20). Both of these statements contain elements of the various passion predictions examined above—the title "Son of Man," Jesus being handed over, the resurrection, the involvement of the religious leaders, and the condemnation of

---

61. Wilson, *Saving Cross*, 103–6.

62. Luke utilizes consistent language throughout the gospel to speak of Jesus's death, especially in the passages discussed in this essay: πάσχω (9:22; 17:25; 22:15; 24:26, 46); ἀποδοκιμάζω (9:22; 17:25; 20:17); ἀποκτείνω (9:22; 11:49; 13:34; 18:33; 20:14–15); παραδίδωμι (9:44; 18:32; 22:4, 6, 21–22, 48); ἀπόλυμμι (13:33; 20:16). While it is almost certain that Luke's readers knew that Jesus died on a cross, the point here is that Luke reserves specific reference to crosses prior to the crucifixion to the one taken up and carried by Jesus's disciples. In this way, Luke is similar to Mark but expands the instructions concerning discipleship by including a second cross logion, as does Matthew. Contrary to the Matthean Jesus, however, Luke's Jesus never mentions a cross as the means of his execution. Throughout Luke, the cross belongs to disciples, a point driven home in the passion narrative as Simon carries Jesus's cross.

63. I am following Brown in viewing Jesus as both righteous and innocent in his death on the cross (*Death*, 2:1163–67). On Jesus's innocence, see Heather M. Gorman, *Interweaving Innocence: A Rhetorical Analysis of Luke's Passion Narrative (Luke 22:66–23:49)* (Eugene, OR: Pickwick, 2015).

Jesus to death—and focalize them in light of Jesus's actual suffering and rising. However, in the Third Gospel, Jesus never told his disciples that he would be crucified; that information is only known to the characters in retrospect.[64]

Finally, Luke's Jesus makes two statements that are reminiscent of the passion predictions and encapsulate his identity as suffering-and-rising Messiah. The first is a question to the two Emmaus road travelers, and the second is part of a larger set of instructions to the disciples (Luke 24:26, 46). In both, Jesus refers to himself as Messiah. The question on the road to Emmaus indicates that the Messiah's suffering and rising was a divinely directed series of events (ἔδει) that could be deduced from Moses and the prophets (24:26–27). Similarly, the instructions to the disciples cast his suffering and resurrection as the fulfillment of Scripture (οὕτως γέγραπται). The narrative of the gospel ends with Jesus being carried up to heaven, the very thing he set out resolutely for Jerusalem to accomplish.

Luke's crucifixion and resurrection narratives thus serve as a proper climax and resolution to the narrative portrayal of Jesus as the suffering-and-rising Messiah. While the cross of Christ never appears in the narrative before the crucifixion, Jesus regularly relates the prospect of his death and resurrection in Jerusalem both to his disciples and to wider audiences. When Luke brings the cross into the story, he actualizes the predicted sufferings of the Messiah. The resurrection and exaltation confirm Jesus's identity. Further, as Luke has done all along, he parallels Jesus's sufferings with the anticipated cross-bearing expected of disciples. In the crucifixion narrative, then, it is no mistake that a person follows Jesus and bears the cross to the place of crucifixion.

Discipleship Actualized: Simon of Cyrene

The minor character Simon of Cyrene is, for Luke, a model of Christian discipleship. Joseph Fitzmyer writes concerning Simon carrying the cross, "Without saying that Simon was a disciple, Luke thus depicts him in the attitude of a Christian disciple."[65] Or as Brian Blount remarks, "Simon evokes a positive image because he follows. . . . The Christian community is urged to be like

---

64. Green, *Gospel of Luke*, 838; Fitzmyer, *Luke I–IX*, 785.
65. Joseph A. Fitzmyer, *The Gospel According to Luke X–XXIV*, AB 28a (Garden City, NY: Doubleday, 1985), 1497. See also Marion L. Soards, "Tradition, Composition, and Theology in Jesus' Speech to the 'Daughters of Jerusalem' (Luke 23.26–32)," *Bib* 68 (1987): 227. Simon's actual discipleship is immaterial in the Lukan narrative. To my mind, it seems highly unlikely that his name (and those of two of his children in Mark's Gospel) would be preserved in the gospel traditions if he did not become a disciple.

Luke and the Cross

Simon."[66] In the character of Simon, Luke actualizes the point that a follower of Jesus is marked out in the world as a cross-bearer.

The single verse in which Simon appears (Luke 23:26) contains two indications that Christian discipleship is in view.[67] First, Luke states that the purpose of the cross being placed on Simon is for him to bear it (ἐπέθηκαν αὐτῷ τὸν σταυρὸν φέρειν).[68] The use of φέρω here shows progression from the initial call for disciples to "take up" (αἴρω, 9:23) the cross, then to "carry" (βαστάζω, 14:27), and now to "bear" (φέρω). After one takes up the cross, βαστάζω connotes carrying a burdensome object, and φέρω connotes bearing a burden from one place to another.[69] Though Simon is not mentioned again, presumably he carries the cross from where Jesus was condemned to the place called The Skull where Jesus is executed. The second indication that discipleship is in view is Simon bearing the cross behind Jesus (ὄπισθεν τοῦ Ἰησοῦ).[70] This recalls Jesus's first description of discipleship in which those who wish to follow him (ὀπίσω μου ἔρχεσθαι) are those who deny self and take up the cross (9:23).[71] The two terms, ὄπισθεν and ὀπίσω, are synonymous in these contexts.[72] Simon is quite literally a cross-bearing follower of Jesus.[73]

Up to this point, the disciples are portrayed as unable to understand Jesus's passion predictions (Luke 9:37-43, 45-50; 18:34). Unlike the other Synoptic Gospels, however, the disciples do not defect from Jesus in Luke's arrest scene.[74] Instead, they remain faithful to the call to follow Jesus (as the jour-

---

66. Brian K. Blount, "A Socio-Rhetorical Analysis of Simon of Cyrene: Mark 15:21 and Its Parallels," *Semeia* 64 (1993): 194.

67. Peter Dschulnigg, "Kreuzigung und Tod Jesu nach Lk 23,26-49," SNTSU 33 (2008): 119; Green, *Gospel of Luke*, 813-14. Contra Bøe, *Cross-Bearing in Luke*, 216.

68. The "they" who place the cross on Simon are almost certainly Roman soldiers under Pilate's command. See Stephanie B. Crowder, *Simon of Cyrene: A Case of Roman Conscription*, Studies in Biblical Literature 46 (New York: Peter Lang, 2002), 48.

69. See LN 15.187, 188 and Bøe, *Cross-Bearing in Luke*, 183-84, 210-11.

70. Blount, "Socio-Rhetorical Analysis," 189.

71. Franz Georg Untergassmair states that neither of the other two Synoptists recalls as clearly as Luke does here the demands to carry the cross (*Kreuzweg und Kreuzigung Jesu*, Paderborner Theologische Studien 10 [Paderborn: Ferdinand Schöningh, 1980], 173). Cf. Dschulnigg, "Kreuzigung und Tod Jesu," 119.

72. BDAG, 715-16, lists both as improper prepositions with the genitive that denote a place "behind" someone. See Bøe, *Cross-Bearing in Luke*, 95-96, 213.

73. I agree with Crowder who is careful to point out that Simon is not actually a disciple because he has been conscripted to carry Jesus's cross (*Simon of Cyrene*, 31-37). Thus, I choose to refer to Simon as a model of discipleship and not a model disciple. See Untergassmair who refers to Simon as an ideal figure for subsequent disciples (*Kreuzweg*, 173).

74. Cf. Mark 14:50; Matt 26:56. See Fitzmyer, *Luke I-IX*, 785.

ney narrative call has illustrated) and only need enlightenment concerning the meaning of Jesus's sufferings.[75] Jesus himself provides this enlightenment when he appears to them after the resurrection and opens their minds to understand the Scriptures (24:44–46).[76] Therefore, while the example of Simon does not correct the disciples' nonunderstanding, it does actualize the call to discipleship in Luke. Fitzmyer captures this succinctly, "Luke has Christianized Simon."[77] Once Jesus's disciples receive retrospective understanding of his death (understanding shared by readers of Luke at the conclusion of the gospel), Simon of Cyrene's participation in Jesus's execution becomes a model of the cross-bearing discipleship to which Jesus has called those who wish to follow him.[78]

Conclusion

This essay has explored Luke's teaching on the cross and shown that the third evangelist focuses primarily on the metaphorical cross taken up by followers of Jesus. The above discussions raise three questions that cannot be explored here because of space. The first concerns the nature of discipleship in the book of Acts: Does Luke's second volume depict the disciples as cross-bearers? The similarities between the portrayals of Jesus in Luke's Gospel and his disciples in Acts are well-documented.[79] A glance at the various sufferings endured by the apostles in Acts seems to point toward a positive response to the question, but the issue needs to be examined. The second question is, does the exaltation of Jesus imply that those who follow him will experience a similar exaltation after enduring the suffering of cross-bearing? Jesus's resurrection is one of the core teachings of the apostles' speeches in Acts, but what about the resurrections of his disciples? Arthur Just sees cross-bearing as preserving "a Lukan theme that suffering must always precede glory."[80] A starting point for such

75. Wilson, *Saving Cross*, 56.
76. See Joshua L. Mann, "What Is Opened in Luke 24:45, the Mind or the Scriptures?," *JBL* 135 (2016): 799–806.
77. Fitzmyer, *Luke I–IX*, 785.
78. See Helen K. Bond, "Paragon of Discipleship?: Simon of Cyrene in the Markan Passion Narrative," in *Matthew and Mark across Perspectives: Essays in Honour of Stephen C. Barton and William R. Telford*, ed. Kristian A. Bendoraitis and Nijay K. Gupta, LNTS 538 (London: Bloomsbury/T & T Clark, 2016), 19; Dschulnigg, "Kreuzigung und Tod Jesu," 119–20.
79. See, e.g., Sean A. Adams, *The Genre of Acts and Collected Biography*, SNTSMS 156 (Cambridge: Cambridge University Press, 2013), chapters 5–6.
80. Arthur A. Just, *The Ongoing Feast: Table Fellowship and Eschatology at Emmaus* (Collegeville, MN: Liturgical Press, 1993), 20.

a study might be Stephen's vision of the exalted Lord during his execution by the religious leaders in Jerusalem (Acts 7:55–60). Further exploration of the teaching of Acts on the resurrection of the dead is beyond the scope of the present essay but certainly worthy of future study. The third question concerns practical theology—what does it look like in a contemporary setting to bear a cross? There are surely broad implications for the church, but this is ultimately within the purview of the preacher, pastor, or priest leading local Christian communities.[81]

This essay has been limited to the Third Gospel where Luke presents both Jesus and Jesus's disciples as those whose identities are shaped by a call to suffering. Luke's Jesus is the suffering-and-rising Messiah and his disciples are those who take up their respective crosses and follow him. Jesus faithfully sets out for Jerusalem knowing the fate that awaits him there. Similarly, disciples must not only take up their crosses but faithfully carry them as they journey with their Lord. Luke's passion narrative actualizes Jesus's identity as the suffering-and-rising Messiah. The crucifixion narrative of the Third Gospel provides an actualization of the cross-centered identity of Jesus's disciples when Simon of Cyrene follows Jesus after taking up, carrying, and bearing the cross of the suffering-and-rising Messiah. For Luke, Bonhoeffer is correct—the cross is indeed laid on every Christian. Discipleship is crucicentric.

---

81. See note 56 above.

Chapter 4

The Johannine Cross as Revelation of the Father: Finding a Cruciform God in the Fourth Gospel

Christopher W. Skinner

It is an inescapable truth that the Johannine prologue (John 1:1–18) lays the foundation for our ability to understand the remainder of the Fourth Gospel. In a comprehensive revelation that looks back to "the beginning" (vv. 1a, 2) and progresses to the incarnation of the Word (v. 14), all while proleptically announcing the Word's rejection by the world (vv. 10–11) and triumph over darkness (v. 5), we are given a lens through which to interpret the words and works of the Johannine Jesus. The prologue's climactic statement announces that Jesus is the one who reveals the Father to the world (μονογενὴς θεὸς ὁ ὢν εἰς τὸν κόλπον τοῦ πατρὸς ἐκεῖνος ἐξηγήσατο, 1:18). In the narrative that follows, one can hardly comprehend Jesus's words or deeds apart from this critically important insight—a reality that stands in contrast to the various presentations of Jesus in the Synoptics.

John's conception of Jesus as revealer is foundational to our understanding of the gospel's christological program and much has been made of this theme in Johannine scholarship. In his epoch-making commentary on the Gospel of John, Rudolf Bultmann devotes nearly fifty pages to an examination of John's emphasis on Jesus as revealer. He notes:

> The cosmic and saving event is grounded in the eternity and unity of the divine will: the Logos is not an act of revelation by God, limited to the temporal order but is pre-existent.... [John's] *idea of God* is therefore determined from the outset by the *idea of revelation*. To speak of God, means: to speak of his revelation; and to speak of his revelation, means: to speak of

The Johannine Cross as Revelation of the Father

God. And revelation is not here intended in any general sense; it is rather the saving will of God that can be experienced in the incarnate Revealer.[1]

Bultmann's treatment of Jesus as revealer in many ways sets the agenda for his brilliant, if tendentious, reading of the gospel. But it is important to note that for Bultmann, the crucifixion of Jesus was merely the culmination of the work begun in his incarnation; for him the Johannine cross has no special salvific significance. Rather, the *incarnation* is what really matters for understanding the gospel's position on salvation.[2] Bultmann is not alone in this assertion.[3] Teasing out the role of the cross in Johannine theology has proven to be a task fraught with difficulties. Some have argued that the death of Jesus should be understood in vicarious terms.[4] Others have argued that the cross is the primary means by which Jesus returns to the Father and thus gives life. Still others assert that the cross represents Jesus as victorious.[5]

The present study is concerned with investigating the cross event in the Fourth Gospel, especially as it relates to the Johannine conception of God. As our starting point, we assume that, as J. T. Forestell has persuasively argued, although in a way very different than Bultmann, revelation is the central theme of Johannine theology.[6] With that in mind, we aim to explore the cross (1) in

---

1. Rudolf Bultmann, *The Gospel of John*, trans. G. R. Beasley-Murray, R. W. N. Hoare, J. K. Riches (Philadelphia: Westminster, 1971), 35 (italics original); cf. also the discussion of Jesus-as-revealer in Bultmann's *Theology of the New Testament*, 2 vols., trans. Kendrick Grobel (New York: Charles Scribner's Sons, 1955), 2:40–49.

2. "In John, Jesus' death has no preeminent importance for salvation, but is the accomplishment of the 'work' which began with the incarnation: the last demonstration of the obedience (14:31) which governs the whole life of Jesus" (Bultmann, *Theology of the New Testament*, 2:52).

3. Among others, see Alfred Wikenhauser, *Das Evangelium nach Johannes*, RNT 4 (Regensburg: F. Putset, 1961); Siegried Schulz, *Das Evangelium nach Johannes*, NTD 4 (Göttingen: Vandenhoeck & Ruprecht, 1975).

4. On this assertion, see the insightful discussion in the chapter entitled "The Death of Jesus in John," in William Loader, *Jesus in John's Gospel: Structure and Issues in Johannine Christology* (Grand Rapids: Eerdmans, 2017), 147–281.

5. See the helpful survey of scholarly opinion in John Morgan-Wynne, *The Cross in the Johannine Writings* (Eugene, OR: Pickwick, 2011); cf. also, John Dennis, "Jesus' Death in John's Gospel: A Survey of Research from Bultmann to the Present with Special Reference to the Johannine Hyper-Texts," *CurBR* 4 (2006): 331–63.

6. Cf. J. Terence Forestell, who writes that "the evangelist presents the work of Jesus as a work of revelation. This revelation concerns the mystery of his own person in relation to the Father and to men. It is neither conceptual knowledge about God nor esoteric knowledge about the true nature of the self; it is a communication to men of that life which the Father

light of Jesus's role as revealer of the Father and (2) in conversation with Michael J. Gorman's articulation of cruciformity in some of our earliest Christian writings.[7] We will explore two questions: First, insofar as John's Jesus is the revealer, *what does his crucifixion reveal about the Father*? Or to ask it differently, how does the cross event demonstrate what the Father is like within the Johannine thought world? Second, how does that understanding of cross-as-revelation intersect with Gorman's presentation of a "narrative spirituality of the cross"?

We will begin by examining how proleptic statements in the gospel anticipate Jesus's crucifixion, after which we will examine John 13:1–17—a text that both anticipates and helps explain the revelatory significance of the Johannine cross event. After these texts help us come to terms with the revelatory "how and what" of Jesus's death in John, we will explore the potential value Gorman's notion of cruciformity has for our understanding of God in the Fourth Gospel.

Anticipating the Cross: Johannine Prolepsis

Prolepsis is a feature within narrative literature "that consists of narrating or evoking in advance an event that will take place later."[8] Even a cursory reading of the gospel reveals this as a common feature of Johannine discourse. Gilbert van Belle has helpfully noted that the term "prolepsis" is used to describe both a Greek grammatical construction and a literary device.[9] We are concerned

---

has in himself and which he has given to the Son" (*The Word of the Cross*, AnBib 57 [Rome: Biblical Institute Press, 1974], 17–57, here 57).

7. E.g., Michael J. Gorman, *Cruciformity: Paul's Narrative Spirituality of the Cross* (Grand Rapids: Eerdmans, 2001); *Inhabiting the Cruciform God: Kenosis, Justification, and Theosis in Paul's Narrative Soteriology* (Grand Rapids: Eerdmans, 2009); "Cruciformity according to Jesus and Paul," in *Unity and Diversity in the Gospels and Paul: Essays in Honor of Frank J. Matera*, ECL 7, ed. Christopher W. Skinner and Kelly R. Iverson (Atlanta: SBL Press, 2012), 173–201; "Paul and the Cruciform Way of God in Christ," *JMTh* 2 (2013): 64–83; "Cruciform or Resurrectiform? Paul's Paradoxical Practice of Participation in Christ," *ExAud* 33 (2017): 60–83.

8. Gerard Genette, *Narrative Discourse: An Essay in Method* (Ithaca, NY: Cornell University Press, 1983), 40. Shlomith Rimmon-Kenan notes similarly that prolepsis is "a narration of a story-event at a point before earlier events have been mentioned. The narration, as it were, takes an excursion into the future of the story" (*Narrative Fiction: Contemporary Poetics* [London: Routledge, 1983], 46).

9. Gilbert van Belle, "Prolepsis in the Gospel of John," *NovT* 43 (2001): 334–47, here 335. For a discussion of the former category in the traditional grammars, see A. T. Robertson, *A Grammar of the Greek New Testament in the Light of Historical Research*, 3rd ed. (Nashville:

here with the latter category. Additionally, Adele Reinhartz, relying upon categories provided by Gerard Genette, has divided the Johannine rhetorical device into two sub-categories: (1) external predictive prolepses, or statements which refer to events that will take place outside the temporal framework of the narrative, and (2) internal predictive prolepses, or events which are eventually narrated within the gospel.[10] Again, we are concerned here with the latter category, and even more restrictively concerned with those prolepses that anticipate Jesus's death.[11] Reinhartz has also argued that John's use of prolepsis sets Jesus apart, at least in part, as a prophet in the mold of Moses and other great prophets in the Hebrew Bible. Recognizing the revelatory value of these predictive statements, she notes:

> The main purpose of this device is not, however, to indicate Jesus' place among the prophets but to point to his unique identity as the Son of God, who has been given the authority to speak God's words and to do God's works in the world. . . . Hence the crucifixion-resurrection event . . . is not to be viewed as a rupture or a crisis in the relationship between God and the believer, *but as a bridge, or perhaps a ladder*, which, by means of the paraclete, *allows revelation to continue*.[12]

It is thus important to realize that prolepsis is one of the primary ways in which the evangelist prepares the audience for Jesus's death. As such, our appreciation of how these texts function will help us further apprehend the

---

Broadman Press, 1934), 423; F. Blass, A. Debrunner, and R. Funk, eds. *A Greek Grammar of the New Testament and Other Early Christian Literature* (Chicago: University of Chicago Press, 1961), 252; Maximillian Zerwick, SJ, *Biblical Greek: Illustrated by Examples*, 4th ed. (Rome: Editrice Pontificio Istituto Biblico, 1994), 84–85. In his "Liste des caracteristiques stylistiques," Marie-Émile Boismard is the first commentator to identify the grammatical construction as a *uniquely Johannine feature*. He identifies eight passages in the Fourth Gospel under the title, "Prolepse" (4:35; 5:42; 7:27; 9:8, 29; 11:31; 14:17; 16:4), contrasting these with only eight other occurrences across the Synoptics and Acts (M.-É. Boismard, A. Lamouille, and G. Rochais, *L'évangile de Jean Commentaire, Synopse des quatre évangiles en français*, 3 [Paris: Cerf, 1977], 514b). For a fuller perspective, compare Turner's discussion of the grammatical construction in each of the canonical gospels (James H. Moulton and Nigel Turner, *A Grammar of New Testament Greek, Volume IV: Style* [Edinburgh: T & T Clark, 1976], 12, 16, 33, 36, 47, 69, 70, 93, 151).

10. Adele Reinhartz, "Jesus as Prophet: Predictive Prolepses in the Fourth Gospel," *JSNT* 36 (1989): 3–16, here 4.

11. Examples that fall into Reinhartz's second category but do not concern the death of Jesus include 4:21; 14:16, 26; 15:26.

12. Reinhartz, "Jesus as Prophet," 12 (emphasis added).

revelatory value of the crucifixion. Leading up to the revelatory ὑπόδειγμα in John 13, there are five specific instances in which Jesus or the narrator proleptically announces his death: 2:19–22; 3:14–15; 8:21–30; 10:11–18; 12:12–30. We will briefly examine each here.

John 2:19–22: Temple Logion as Paradigmatic

Taking into account the development of John's narrative rhetoric, we are still coming to terms with what has been revealed in 1:1–18 when we reach 2:19–22. There we read:

> Jesus said to them, "Destroy this temple and in three days I will raise it." Then "the Jews" said to him, "It has taken forty-six years to build this temple, and you will raise it in three days?" But he had been speaking of the temple of his body. Therefore, when he was raised from the dead, his disciples remembered that he said this. And they believed the scripture and the word which Jesus had spoken.[13]

This narratorial clarification is the first reference to the death of Jesus and as such, is a paradigmatic moment for the audience. Everything that has been revealed about the Johannine Jesus to this point must be interpreted in anticipation of his impending death and resurrection. We now know that there is *revelatory value* not just in Jesus's signs and speeches but also in his forthcoming death, but we are yet to discover what his death is actually meant to reveal.

John 3:14–15: What Does It Mean to Be "Lifted Up"?

At the end of his initial encounter with Nicodemus, Jesus chides "the teacher of Israel" for his ignorance about earthly and heavenly matters (John 3:10–12). After commenting that only one individual has both ascended into heaven and descended to earth—the Son of Man—Jesus tells Nicodemus, "And just as Moses lifted up (ὕψωσεν) the serpent in the wilderness, so must the Son of Man be lifted up (ὑψωθῆναι), in order that everyone who believes in him might have eternal life" (vv. 14–15). This is an obvious reference to the story

---

13. All translations in this chapter are those of the author unless otherwise specified. There is not space here to rehearse the linguistic and theological difficulties associated with translating οἱ Ἰουδαῖοι in John. I have chosen to translate the phrase—placed in quotes—as "the Jews," in recognition of these concerns.

in Num 21:6-9 where, in response to the grumbling of the people, the Lord allows venomous serpents to enter the camp and bite the Israelites, after which many die. In turn, the Israelites petition Moses for relief from the poisonous serpents and the Lord provides a solution: Moses is to fashion a bronze serpent and lift it up on a pole. Whoever has been bitten and looks on the bronze serpent will live.

At least one element of this parallel is clear: whoever looks upon (viz., acknowledges) Jesus will find life. But what is the significance of the verb ὑψόω? While it is important to note that the verb refers to the literal raising of an object into the sky, it can also be used figuratively of exaltation.[14] Jesus is "lifted up" both literally and metaphorically during his crucifixion, so both meanings are likely operative here.[15] While it might seem odd in some instances to think of the crucifixion as a moment of exaltation, this is actually a key emphasis in the Johannine presentation of Jesus's "glorification."[16] Thus, we have here the second reference to the death of Jesus, *and the first reference to what it will accomplish*: it brings eternal life.

John 8:21-30: Where Is Jesus Going?

By the time the audience reaches this pericope, there has been a steadily advancing antagonism between Jesus and various groups: his brothers (John 7:1-9), various attendees at the Feast of Tabernacles (7:10-24), the crowds (7:25-31, 40-44), and the Jewish leaders (7:45-52; 8:12-20). Announcing his

---

14. E.g., Ps 117:28, LXX: θεός μου εἶ σύ, καὶ ὑψώσω σε ("You are my God, and I will lift you up" [viz., "glorify you"]).

15. A number of Johannine interpreters see the Son of Man as a descending and ascending figure whose real home is in heaven, with the implication that ὑψόω also means "to ascend" in this particular context. I regard this as problematic first on the basis of its use in 3:14. There is no sense in Num 21 in which the serpent ascends into heaven. A second problem for this thesis is the use of the verb in John 12:32-33, where ὑψόω is used "to indicate the kind of death he was going to die." On the assertion that ὑψόω refers to Jesus's ascension, see Loader, *Jesus in John's Gospel*. Cf. also, John Ashton who argues that ὑψόω means "raise" or "exalt" and represents Jesus's ascent to heaven rather than the crucifixion (*Understanding the Fourth Gospel* [Oxford: Oxford University Press, 2007], 468).

16. Cf. John 7:39; 12:23, 28; 13:31-32; 16:14; 17:1, 4, 5. BDAG notes that the Aramaic equivalent of ὑψωθῆναι is אזדקיף, which can mean both "to be exalted," and "to be crucified or hanged" (s.v. ὑψόω, 1046). Additionally, Keener observes that the combination of ὑψόω (lifting up) and δοξάζω (exaltation/glorification) is found in the tradition of the Suffering Servant in Isa 52 (Craig S. Keener, *The Gospel of John: A Commentary, Volume 1* [Grand Rapids: Baker Academic, 2003], 566).

departure once again, Jesus tells the religious leaders that he is going away and that they are incapable of following him (8:21). Like others in the narrative, the leaders become obsessed with the literal meaning of Jesus's words and fail to understand their deeper significance. They wonder aloud if he plans to kill himself (8:22). This confusion leads to an even more antagonistic exchange where Jesus points out their inability to understand because they are "from below," while he has come "from above." After a few back-and-forth interactions (8:22–26), the narrator clarifies that the religious authorities failed to understand that Jesus had been talking to them about the Father (8:27). At this moment Jesus announces: "When you have lifted up (ὑψώσητε) the Son of Man, then you will know that 'I am' and that I do nothing on my own. Rather, I say those things which the Father has instructed me to say" (8:28). This culminates in many people believing in Jesus (8:30).

In this third proleptic announcement of Jesus's death, we again see (1) ὑψόω used in reference to the crucifixion and (2) Jesus's reference to himself as the Son of Man. Also present is the assertion that the actions of Jesus correspond fully to the will of the Father and as a result, the Father is pleased with him. We thus continue to see a steadily unfolding picture of how the death of Jesus is proleptically announced and what that death reveals about the Father.

John 10:11–18: The Good Shepherd Will Lay Down His Life

On four different occasions in the so-called Good Shepherd discourse (John 10:1–18), Jesus again discusses his impending death, this time in terms of "laying down his life" for the sheep (vv. 11, 15, 17, 18). Jesus is the faithful shepherd who, in deference to the will of the Father, lays down his life on behalf of his people (viz., "the sheep"). Bultmann has argued that the phrase lay down one's life (τιθέναι τὴν ψυχήν) "means to stake one's life, to risk it, to be prepared to lay it down as in LXX Judg. 12.3; I Sam 19.5; 28.21."[17] Similarly, Susan Hylen has recently argued that the language of laying down one's life need not explicitly refer to death here but denotes the *risking* of one's life, especially as this relates

---

17. Bultmann, *The Gospel of John*, 370n5. Other commentators opt for a soft rendering here. For example, J. Ramsey Michaels notes, "What makes a shepherd 'good' is that he 'lays down his life for the sheep,' that is, *he puts his very life on the line* to protect his flock" (*The Gospel of John*, NICNT [Grand Rapids: Eerdmans, 2010], 585). Similarly, Marianne Meye Thompson comments, "Precisely because the shepherd faithfully guards his sheep, he puts himself in their place, willingly *facing death* so that they may live. The shepherd does so because the sheep belong to him (10:12, 14) and he cares for them (v. 13): a hired hand has no vested interest in the sheep" (*John*, NTL [Louisville: Westminster John Knox, 2015], 226).

to discipleship.[18] This suggestion is compelling on grammatical grounds, and I do not wish to dispute that such an idea could be present. However, this suggestion fails to take into account that this passage is *principally about Christology*. The immediate context of this παροιμία is a dispute between Jesus and the Pharisees over who is fit to lead God's flock, and both predicated ἐγώ εἰμι statements (10:7, 11, 14) and proleptic announcements are expressly related to the Fourth Gospel's presentation of Christology, which I have further argued is intimately connected to the evangelist's emphasis on revelation. Therefore, even if "to risk one's life" is an acceptable translation of the phrase τιθέναι τὴν ψυχήν elsewhere within Greek literature, it does not capture the *primary* sense of the phrase used here or throughout the rest of the Fourth Gospel (cf. e.g., 13:37; 15:13). These four references (10:11, 15, 17, 18) are explicitly about Jesus laying down his life and should be understood as pointing to his impending death, which the audience has, by now, begun to anticipate.

John 12:12–30: A Triumphal Entry Lost on the Disciples

As the crowds gather in Jerusalem in preparation for the gospel's third Passover, Jesus is acclaimed as king (John 12:12–13a). During his triumphal entry into Jerusalem they shout, "Hosanna! Blessed is the one who comes in the name of the Lord! Blessed is the king of Israel!" (v. 13b). The evangelist connects this event—specifically the act of Jesus riding on a young donkey—to the prophecy in Zech 9:9 (John 12:14–15). This is obviously a moment dripping with both christological and soteriological significance, but as we have come to expect, it is completely lost on the disciples. Similar to the comment in 2:19–22, the narrator notes that the disciples did not initially understand this event. Only after Jesus is glorified (viz., crucified and resurrected) are they able to remember these events and realize both *what was written about* and *what was done to* Jesus (ἀλλ' ὅτε ἐδοξάσθη Ἰησοῦς τότε ἐμνήσθησαν ὅτι ταῦτα ἦν ἐπ' αὐτῷ γεγραμμένα καὶ ταῦτα ἐποίησαν αὐτῷ, 12:16). Here again we have the tension between John's narration of present-time events alongside the anticipation of a future, post-resurrection viewpoint. The crucifixion is in view as the audience grapples with the revelation that Jesus is the long-awaited messianic king.

Taken together, the cumulative force of these five scenes (2:19–22; 3:14–15; 8:21–30; 10:11–18; 12:12–30) points the audience ever forward as it both wres-

---

18. Susan E. Hylen, "The Shepherd's Risk: Thinking Metaphorically with John's Gospel," *BibInt* 24 (2016): 382–99.

tles with the reality of Jesus's death and unpacks the revelatory significance of the Johannine cross event. What the audience has learned so far is that Jesus pleases the Father by doing his will and by voluntarily laying down his life for humanity, which will result in eternal life for those who acknowledge him. This still leaves us with the question: What exactly does the death of Jesus reveal about the Father?

Prefiguring the Cross: Jesus's ὑπόδειγμα (John 13:1–17)[19]

At the outset of the Farewell Discourse,[20] Jesus provides for his disciples an example (ὑπόδειγμα, John 13:15) that finally begins fleshing out how the cross will reveal the nature and will of the Father. We soon learn that this ὑπόδειγμα functions more like an implicit command to the disciples, and by implication is meant to extend beyond the particular behaviors associated with washing another person's feet. It is, quite literally, an "example" that prefigures the cross.

The scene is set just before the Passover (John 13:1a), when Jesus knows his "hour" is approaching.[21] Jesus loves his own who are in the world "to the end" (εἰς τέλος, v. 1d). This phrase, like many throughout the gospel, likely carries several different shades of meaning. It can be used to suggest that Jesus's love endures to the very end (viz., his crucifixion). However, εἰς τέλος can also indicate the ultimate "goal" or "aim" of an activity and can thus be understood to describe Jesus loving his own "fully" or "completely." Taken in this way, the phrase indicates that the activity this statement anticipates—Jesus's washing of his disciples' feet as an exemplar of this service to humanity on the cross—is an embodiment of the fullest or most complete expression of his love for them. This is an important point insofar as it lays the groundwork for our appreciation of the christological and revelatory significance of the footwashing.

Knowing that his departure is near, Jesus demonstrates the extent of his

---

19. Some of the material in this section is adapted from my chapter "Love One Another: The Johannine Love Command in the Farewell Discourse," in *Johannine Ethics: The Moral World of the Gospel and Epistles of John*, ed. Sherri Brown and Christopher W. Skinner (Minneapolis: Fortress, 2017), 23–42. It is used here with the permission of the publisher.

20. There remains significant debate among scholars over what material belongs to the Farewell Discourse. My discussion here assumes that all of 13:1–17:26 falls into the category of what the evangelist intends as a farewell address.

21. Jesus's hour (ὥρα) is a particularly important theme in John. It appears in passages meant to evoke the impending crucifixion and resurrection events. Jesus has previously spoken about his hour in 2:4; 4:21, 23; 5:25, 28; 7:30; 8:20; 12:23, 27.

The Johannine Cross as Revelation of the Father

love toward the disciples while providing them with a model on which to base their future service to others in his name. First, the narrator reports that the devil had already put it in mind that Judas Iscariot should betray Jesus. This statement is meant to recall Jesus's earlier comment to his disciples: "Have I not chosen you, the Twelve? But one of you is a devil" (καὶ ἐξ ὑμῶν εἷς διάβολός ἐστιν, John 6:70). Commentators recognize a Semitic idiom in verse 2 ("to put in mind"),[22] which is best expressed in Barrett's translation: "the devil had already *made up his mind* that Judas should betray him."[23] R. Alan Culpepper points out that the heart of the devil rather than the heart of Judas is the object of "put it into" (βάλλω εἰς).[24] At the same time, the audience learns that Jesus knows "everything has been handed over to him by the Father," and that just as he has come from the Father, he will soon return to him. This sets up a critical contrast between the heart/mind of the devil (John 13:2) and the heart/mind of Jesus (vv. 1, 3). Later, in v. 20, Satan will enter into Judas and the two worlds will clash. God's design is being enacted in Jesus while Satan's design is worked out in the actions of Judas.

In John 13:4 Jesus rises from the meal, removes his outer garments (τίθησιν τὰ ἱμάτια), and takes a towel (λαβὼν λέντιον) to wrap around his waist. It is important to highlight the use of τίθημι and λαμβάνω (here and in v. 12) as they call attention back to the image of the Good Shepherd in 10:11-18. There, Jesus announced that the Good Shepherd lays down his life (τὴν ψυχὴν αὐτοῦ τίθησιν, 10:11, 15, 17, 18) in order to take it back up again (ἵνα πάλιν λάβω αὐτήν, 10:17, 18). The use of τίθημι also recalls the words of Jesus in 11:34, when he inquires about the burial place of Lazarus: "Where have they put him?" (ποῦ τεθείκατε αὐτόν;). These linguistic cues here in verse 4 link to the Good Shepherd discourse and the encounter with Lazarus and look forward to the crucifixion and resurrection of Jesus, thus signaling his actions here as both *symbolic and prophetic*. They also serve to highlight the extent of Jesus's

---

22. We see this construction in Job 22:22 (LXX): καὶ ἀνάλαβε τὰ ῥήματα αὐτοῦ ἐν καρδίᾳ σου (and lay up these words in your heart); the corresponding Hebrew phrase in the MT is וְשִׂים אֲמָרָיו בִּלְבָבֶךָ. Another example from the LXX that does not have a counterpart in the MT is 1 Sam 29:10: καὶ λόγον λοιμὸν μὴ θῇς ἐν καρδίᾳ σου ("and do not put an evil word in your heart").

23. C. K. Barrett, *The Gospel according to St. John: An Introduction with Commentary and Notes on the Greek Text*, 2nd ed. (Philadelphia: Westminster, 1978), 439. Brown translates the idiom as "*The devil had already induced Judas*, son of Simon, the Iscariot, to betray Jesus" (Raymond E. Brown, *The Gospel according to John XIII-XXI*, AB 29a [Garden City, NY: Doubleday, 1970], 548, emphasis added).

24. R. Alan Culpepper, "The Johannine *hypodeigma*: A Reading of John 13:1-38," *Semeia* 53 (1981): 133-52, here 136.

service to his disciples. On this point, Barrett comments, "When Jesus lays aside his garments in preparation for his act of humility and cleansing he foreshadows the laying down of his life."[25] This point cannot be emphasized strongly enough. The footwashing is *symbolic* in that it provides a depiction of sacrificial self-giving, and *prophetic* in that it anticipates *Jesus's ultimate act of sacrificial self-giving*—his death on behalf of the world.

Jesus begins in earnest to wash and dry the disciples' feet (John 13:5), which leads to a brief exchange with an incredulous and uncomprehending Peter (vv. 6–9). In the course of their conversation, Jesus comments that though Peter fails to understand now, he will understand in the future. This present-future schema appears in numerous passages throughout the gospel, where the audience is invited to reflect on the narrated events from two perspectives: one related to the real-time narration of events and one from a distinctly post-resurrection perspective. When Jesus tells Peter that he will understand *in the future*, he is pointing forward to a time when all that has happened will be explained by and interpreted through the lens of crucifixion and resurrection. Peter's misplaced literalism, and in fact initial rejection of the footwashing (see vv. 6, 8a), misses the larger point that this symbolic and prophetic action has consequences beyond both a *particular time period* and a *particular type of service*. Emphasis should not be placed on the "here and now" but on the future; likewise, emphasis should not be placed on a particular type of service (viz., the literal practice of footwashing) but rather on various forms of sacrificial self-giving—the highest of which is embodied in the crucifixion of Jesus on behalf of his followers. This will become clearer only in a future, post-resurrection perspective.

Jesus's explanation at the close of the footwashing reinforces our understanding of this event as both symbolic and prophetic (John 13:12–17). It is somewhat ironic that Jesus asks his disciples—who are often represented by the voice of Peter—if they understand what he has just done for them. It seems unlikely that they have, given Peter's protestations and requests during his dialogue with Jesus in vv. 6–9. Their Lord and Teacher seemingly instructs them to continue washing one another's feet (v. 14b),[26] but if our interpretation of Jesus's actions ends there, we will be guilty of the same type of misplaced literalism displayed by characters throughout the gospel. An agenda of outward

---

25. Barrett, *Gospel according to St. John*, 439. Brown also sees potential parallels between the present text and 10:11, 15, 17, 18 (*Gospel according to John XIII–XXI*, 551).

26. On the suggestion that this ὑπόδειγμα is to be regarded as a literal command to continue the footwashing, see the discussion in Michaels, *The Gospel of John*, 735–36.

behavior that is characterized by sacrificial self-giving—beyond the simple behavioral parameters associated with footwashing—is at the heart of this command. "Jesus' instruction is a call to his disciples to repeat in their lives what he has done for them. He has given them the example of a loving gift of self in love, symbolized by the foot washing, which they must now repeat."[27] This point becomes clearer in verse 15: "I have given you an example [ὑπόδειγμα], in order that, just as I have done for you, you should also do." This example clearly anticipates his sacrificial self-giving in the form of his death on the cross, but it also prescribes a certain normative ethic.[28]

The term ὑπόδειγμα, translated variously as "example" and "model," appears in several contexts associated with noble death and righteous behavior, and provides for the disciples and the audience a link between the sacrificial self-giving of the footwashing and that of the death of Jesus.[29] That Jesus's death should be connected to the example of footwashing as the premier display of sacrificial self-giving is not a new suggestion, and it fits neatly within the cumulative narrative rhetoric of the gospel to this point. Having learned of Jesus's "arrival" through incarnation (John 1:14), the audience is now being systematically prepared for his departure in a return to the Father. This departure is the *telos* of Jesus's ministry, which will result in the sending of the παράκλητος, who will further prepare the disciples to live as Jesus instructed and as the Father commands. The footwashing is not to be regarded as an end unto itself but as an event that invites the disciples into the mode of sacrificial self-giving soon to be realized in the crucifixion. Barrett's comment here is instructive: "There stands first a symbolic narrative, the washing of the disciples' feet, which prefigures the crucifixion itself, and in doing so points the way to the interpretation of the crucifixion. The public acts of Jesus on Calvary, and his private act in the presence of his disciples, are alike in that each is an act of humility and service, and that each proceeds from the love of Jesus for

---

27. Francis J. Moloney, *Glory Not Dishonor: Reading John 13–21* (Minneapolis: Fortress, 1998), 16.

28. On the question of whether normative ethics can be derived from the Fourth Gospel, see the various essays in Brown and Skinner, eds., *Johannine Ethics*.

29. E.g., 2 Macc 6:28 (NABRE): "I will leave to the young a noble example (ὑπόδειγμα) of how to die willingly and nobly for the revered and holy laws"; 4 Macc 17:22–23 (NRSV): "And through the blood of those devout ones and their death as an atoning sacrifice, divine Providence preserved Israel that previously had been mistreated. For the tyrant Antiochus, when he saw the courage of their virtue and their endurance under the tortures, proclaimed them to his soldiers as an example (ὑπόδειγμα)"; Sir 44:16 (NABRE): "Enoch walked with the Lord, and was taken that succeeding generations might learn by his example (ὑπόδειγμα)." For more on these parallels, see Culpepper, "Johannine *hypodeigma*," 142–43.

his own."³⁰ Having both provided an example for his disciples (vv. 1–17) and celebrated a final meal (vv. 18–30), Jesus will begin to speak in detail about his departure. In verses 34–35 he announces, "I give you a new commandment: love one another. As I have loved you, so you must love one another. By this everyone will know you are my disciples, if you love one another." Three times in the span of these two verses Jesus instructs his disciples to love one another, and in that same context he notes, "as I have loved you." There can be little doubt that this hearkens back to the image of 13:1, where Jesus loves his disciples εἰς τέλος. By imitating the manner in which he has demonstrated his own love toward them—what I have termed sacrificial self-giving—the disciples will be a light to all humanity. While it must be admitted that the audience still has much to learn about the meaning of the crucifixion in John, this passage, more than any other in the gospel, has elucidated the significance of Jesus's forthcoming death.

We are thus now in a position to begin deliberating on the question: What does the Johannine cross event reveal about the Father?

1. First, the God of the Fourth Gospel is concerned to initiate and maintain a relationship with humanity. If the incarnation is the means of inaugurating this relationship, the cross is the means of securing it once and for all.
2. Second, insofar as the cross-anticipating-ὑπόδειγμα is characterized by sacrificial self-giving, it is possible to affirm that the God of the Fourth Gospel is characterized by an attitude of sacrificial self-giving. The crucifixion of Jesus is quite literally an act of service to humanity.
3. God's act of entering into relationship with and serving humanity is ultimately rooted in and driven by his love. ³¹

The God of the Fourth Gospel loves, seeks out, draws near to, serves, and secures a relationship with humanity by means of the cross. This ignominious and torturous death is actually, for John, an unveiling of the heart of the Father toward the world. How does this description of the Father in John intersect, if at all, with ideas about cruciformity that have been advanced by Gorman?

---

30. Barrett, *Gospel according to St. John*, 346.
31. We see this as early as 3:16–17. On the importance of this text for our understanding of the gospel, see Francis J. Moloney, *Love in the Gospel of John: An Exegetical, Theological, and Literary Study* (Grand Rapids: Baker Academic, 2013), esp. 56–61.

The Johannine Cross as Revelation of the Father

Cruciformity in John?

Michael Gorman has written extensively about cruciformity in Paul and has similarly applied the term to the teaching of Jesus in Mark's Gospel.[32] However, his work on John has focused more on ideas of mission and theosis, though cruciformity plays a role in those deliberations.[33] Based upon the above discussion, what can we say of John's relationship to notions of cruciformity? Is it possible to affirm that the Fourth Gospel also provides its audience with some vision of a cruciform God?

At its core, cruciformity—as articulated by Gorman—is about conforming to the death of Christ and all that implies. He writes:

> Cruciformity is the spiritual-moral dimension of the theology of the death of Jesus by crucifixion found in Paul, in the rest of the New Testament, and throughout much of the Christian tradition. With respect to Paul, at least, this conformity to the crucified Messiah is not an abstract moral principle but a spiritual, or even mystical, reality. This mystical reality is rooted, paradoxically, in a profoundly this-worldly reality (Jesus' crucifixion) and produces, no less paradoxically, a variety of very this-worldly results.[34]

Frank Matera helpfully reminds us that it is ever important to respect the diverse unity of New Testament theologies, and thus avoid conflating the various voices at work in the New Testament.[35] In this case we can and probably should draw important parallels between major foci in Pauline and Johannine texts without attempting to equate the two. With that in mind, however, we can affirm that John's presentation of the cross event and its significance aligns with this initial description provided by Gorman. For John, Jesus's crucifixion is a return to the Father that results in the sending of the παράκλητος (John 14:16). This sending will produce a mystical or spiritual reality (to use Gorman's

---

32. Cf. bibliographic details in n. 7 above. While the term "cruciform" existed in the Christian theological lexicon prior to Gorman's work on the subject, it is safe to say that his articulation of "cruciformity" is the primary one to which theologians refer when they use the term in contemporary theological discourse.

33. Cf. Michael J. Gorman, *Abide and Go: Missional Theosis in the Gospel of John* (Eugene, OR: Cascade, 2018).

34. Gorman, "Paul and the Cruciform Way of God in Christ," 66.

35. This is a major emphasis in Matera's published work; nowhere is it more prominently on display than in his study, *New Testament Theology: Exploring Diversity and Unity* (Louisville: Westminster John Knox, 2007).

words) that will, among other things, lay bare the truth to those who believe (16:8–11), guide believers into truth (16:13), speak words of truth (16:14–15), and instruct future disciples (16:26–27). All of these are—again, to use Gorman's words—"very this-worldly results." Without drawing a straight line from Paul to the Fourth Gospel, we can easily recognize these points of "cruciform overlap" between the two.

Gorman continues:

> Cruciformity, then, is cross-shaped existence in Jesus the Messiah. It is letting the cross of the crucified Messiah be the shape, as well as the source, of life in him. It is participating in and embodying the cross.... In fact, we might even refer to the ethical results of this indwelling as non-identical repetition, as long as the qualifier "by the power of the Spirit" is included. As we will now see, the events that are repeated are constituted by the narrative of Christ's self-giving faith and love that were quintessentially expressed in his (incarnation and) death on the cross.[36]

Again, we see notable points of contact between this description and the picture presented in the Fourth Gospel. In Johannine terms, the ὑπόδειγμα of chapter 13—which serves as an exemplar for the cross—is an invitation to Jesus's followers to, in Gorman's words, "let the cross of the crucified Messiah be the shape, as well as the source, of life in him." While the practice of washing one another's feet may in fact be a repeatable phenomenon and mode of worship-in-remembrance, it is not the immediate focal point of Jesus's teaching here. Rather, he is calling for other forms of sacrificial service, which Gorman, borrowing the language of John Milbank, has labeled, "non-identical repetition." And when the παράκλητος comes, they will live and move and breathe in and through its power. On this very passage Gorman comments, "since Jesus is the 'unique self-exegesis of God' ... then *Jesus* in motion is *God* in motion; the act of foot washing tells us something profound, not only about the self-giving love of Jesus, but also about the gratuitous, hospitable, kenotic love of God."[37]

There is not space in this brief chapter to explore all the nuances arising from the breadth of Gorman's exposition of cruciformity. Such an ambitious endeavor could easily occupy an entire monograph. The more modest pursuit in this essay has been to explore the possibility of locating a cruciform vision of

---

36. Gorman, "Paul and the Cruciform Way of God in Christ," 67.
37. Gorman, *Abide and Go*, 87.

God in the Fourth Gospel. We can recognize that John—with his own autonomous voice—provides a unique spin on the cruciform God in ways that are both similar to and different from that which has been articulated by Gorman in his treatments of Paul and Mark. John demonstrates the critical importance of the cross and its implications for (1) God's divine condescension in pursuing and entering into relationship with humanity, (2) ongoing discipleship by means of the Spirit-Paraclete, and (3) the impartation of eternal life. In these we see the Johannine version of a cruciform God, and in this way, Gorman's work remains both instructive and suggestive for our ongoing attempts to speak meaningfully about the theological outlook of the Fourth Gospel and other early Christian texts.[38]

---

38. Since 2005, Mike Gorman has been a mentor to me both personally and professionally, and more importantly, he has been a friend. It is not an overstatement to say that I would not be where I am in this field without Mike's influence, help, and friendship. I have the highest regard for Mike as a teacher, scholar, husband, father, grandfather, and man of faith. It is one of the great privileges of my vocational life to count Mike among my friends. I offer this essay as a very small token of both my great esteem for him and my appreciation for his impact upon my life and career.

Chapter 5

Cruciformity and the Believer's Governing Faculties: Rethinking Ἡγέομαι in Philippians

Nijay K. Gupta

Perhaps more than any other book, Michael Gorman's *Cruciformity* inspired me to dig deeper into Pauline theology and eventually go on for doctoral studies and a career in Pauline studies.[1] *Cruciformity* helped me to discover the cross at the heart of Paul's theology, and a pattern and way of life—what Gorman calls a "narrative spirituality" based on the story of Christ—that made history and theology come alive. And I have been passing on his teaching on cruciformity for fifteen years. While my students easily and immediately resonate with this approach to Paul's spirituality, I sometimes receive questions like these: If cruciformity is about service and sacrifice, how does it function as a form of leadership? If it is deferential and self-giving, will it not inevitably lead to a loss of control, lack of self-care and self-value, or inherent powerlessness? A few years ago, I taught the concept of Pauline cruciformity to a group of students in a counseling program, and their response was: that sounds exhausting!

These conversations have led me to revisit the concept of cruciformity, especially as it appears so centrally in Philippians, from the perspective of leadership. If cruciformity is about serving, giving, and conforming to the death of Christ, what place is there for having a ministry of influence and self-determination? And, if we try to contextualize this within the situation behind Philippians, one might imagine the Philippians wondering: *How do*

---

1. Michael J. Gorman, *Cruciformity: Paul's Narrative Spirituality of the Cross* (Grand Rapids: Eerdmans, 2001).

you, Paul, conceive of cruciform leadership as you sit in chains in prison facing an unknown future? And how ought we, Philippians, to conceive of cruciform leadership, as a small group of followers of Jesus who are facing persecution and opprobrium? These are important questions, and a comprehensive answer goes far beyond the scope of this brief essay. Limiting our purview to Philippians, we will argue that an intriguing clue toward Paul's perspective on this can be found in his use of the verb ἡγέομαι.

The simple verbal meaning of ἡγέομαι, especially as Paul tends to use it in Philippians, is "I consider, regard." But it should also be recognized that this is a polysemous word and can mean "I rule, govern." The argument I wish to make is this: in Philippians, Paul has reason to play off of these two different meanings of the word, and he represents cruciform thought as a form of self-determination and Christian leadership in any and all circumstances. We will spend the majority of our time determining how Paul uses ἡγέομαι rhetorically and theologically in Philippians, and then we will draw out some implications at the end for refining the concept of Pauline cruciformity.

Philippians and a Cruciform Epistemology

To begin with, it is helpful to survey why and how Paul communicates a cruciform mindset in Philippians. We can be fairly certain that, though this church was not suffering from dire communal problems, Paul *was* concerned with their adoption of a right way of thinking about suffering, community, and Christian life. In chapter 1, Paul reorients the Philippians toward his own imprisonment, encouraging them to see it not as a mark of doom or failure but as an unexpected opportunity to see the gospel spread in an important place. In the second chapter, Paul turns to the Philippian community and their interrelationships. The love and grace of God in Jesus Christ and the Spirit serve as a model and inspiration for oneness of community and the importance of generous love and other-regard (Phil 2:1-2). They must fight temptations to compete with or criticize one another for the sake of gaining personal honor; instead, they ought to prize humility and deference borne out of a spirit of unity (2:3-4). The Christ hymn (2:6-11) clearly establishes Jesus Christ as the perfect example of this theoretical humility. But it is important how Paul frames this encomium.[2] The introductory statement in 2:5 focuses

---

2. In terms of the nature and genre of the Christ hymn, see Adela Yarbro Collins, "Psalms, Philippians 2:6-11, and the Origins of Christology," *BibInt* 11 (2003): 361-72; John Reumann, *Philippians*, AB 33B (New Haven: Yale University Press, 2008), 333-77; Mat-

on the *mindset* of Christ: "Let the same mind be in you that was in Christ Jesus."[3] Here Paul uses the verb φρονέω (which he employs ten times total in this letter) in reference to the shaping of a proper way of thinking. This is borne out in the Christ hymn, as the focus lies not on the activity of Christ per se but on his humble mindset (2:6-8), which led to benevolent action and obedience to the Father.

In chapter 3, Paul presents how he has come to reflect differently on his own past and his former pursuit of righteousness before God. He had formerly assumed certain indicators demonstrated his righteousness and status but eventually came to consider all those things null in view of the supreme value of knowing Christ and being found in him (Phil 3:8-9).[4] He calls the Philippians to adopt the same mindset (3:15). Paul warns them of certain misguided believers who are "enemies of the cross," who do not comprehend the true gospel, and whose "minds are set on earthly things" (3:18-19). In the final chapter, Paul offers numerous pieces of advice, including a call to unity and peace and an exhortation to set their minds, not on worries, fears, and problems, but on all such things that are true, virtuous, and excellent (4:4-8). One can see, just from this brief summary of Philippians, that *right thinking* is a key theme in this letter.[5] Part of this Paul communicates through the repeated

---

thew E. Gordley, *New Testament Christological Hymns* (Downers Grove, IL: InterVarsity Press, 2018), 79-110.

3. There is a long-standing debate about whether or not this verse is designed to focus on emulation ("that was in Christ Jesus") or result ("which is yours in Christ Jesus"); I find convincing the majority view that emulation is the most natural reading (see Gordon Fee, *Paul's Letter to the Philippians*, NICNT [Grand Rapids: Eerdmans, 1995], 200-201).

4. Joseph Hellerman, *Embracing Shared Ministry: Power and Status in the Early Church and Why It Matters Today* (Grand Rapids: Kregel, 2013), 127-33.

5. In the last thirty years or so, we have seen a surge of interest in Pauline epistemology; see J. Louis Martyn, "Epistemology and the Turn of the Ages: 2 Corinthians 5:16," in *Christian History and Interpretation*, ed. W. R. Farmer, C. F. D. Moule, and R. Niebuhr (Cambridge: Cambridge University Press, 1967), 269-87; Alexandra Brown, *The Cross and Human Transformation: Paul's Apocalyptic Word in 1 Corinthians* (Minneapolis: Fortress, 1995); Richard B. Hays, *The Moral Vision of the New Testament* (San Francisco: HarperSanFrancisco, 1996), 193-206; Ian W. Scott, *Paul's Way of Knowing: Story, Experience, and the Spirit* (Grand Rapids: Baker Academic, 2009); Mary Healy, "Knowledge and Mystery: A Study of Pauline Epistemology," in *The Bible and Epistemology*, ed. Mary Healy and Robin Parry (Milton Keynes, UK: Paternoster, 2007), 134-58; Craig S. Keener, *The Mind of the Spirit* (Grand Rapids: Baker Academic, 2016); specifically on Philippians see Wayne A. Meeks, "The Man from Heaven in Paul's Letter to the Philippians," in *The Future of Early Christianity: Essays in Honor of Helmut Koester*, ed. Birger Pearson (Minneapolis: Fortress, 1991), 329-36.

Cruciformity and the Believer's Governing Faculties

use of φρονέω, but he deploys a wide variety of epistemological and noetic terms to address this (e.g., βλέπω, γνῶσις, νόημα, λογίζομαι).[6] Aside from φρονέω, the most important epistemological term in Philippians is ἡγέομαι (again, meaning "I consider, regard, think"). This verb is only used by Paul eight times in the undisputed letters, six of which appear in Philippians (2:3, 6, 25; 3:7, 8 [x2]). It refers to the way that a person treats something as true, right, or valuable.

> 2:3: "in humility *regard* others as better than yourselves."
> 2:6: "[he] did not *regard* equality with God as something to be exploited."
> 2:25: "I have *considered* it necessary to send Epaphroditus to you." (NET)
> 3:7–8: "Yet whatever gains I had, these I have come to *regard* as loss because of Christ. More than that, I *regard* everything as loss because of the surpassing value of knowing Christ Jesus my Lord. For his sake I have suffered the loss of all things, and I *regard* them as rubbish, in order that I may gain Christ."

The tendency here is for Paul to employ this verb in reference to a conscious, often countercultural, mindset that establishes and reinforces a specific set of values; as if to say, the world tries to squeeze you into its thinking mold, but believers must resist this and reshape their minds to conform to Christ's way of knowing and thinking (cf. Rom 8:6–7; 12:1–2; Phil 3:18–19). I do not pretend to be the only one who has noticed the focus on right-thinking in Philippians.[7] But what I believe has been unrecognized or underestimated is the fact that the verb ἡγέομαι has two different meanings ("I consider" and "I lead/govern"). Now, conventional interpretive wisdom reminds us that a word only means one thing at one time in a given discourse, and therefore the reader ought to select the correct meaning according to the context (and set aside any other meaning).[8] And all major English translations (RSV, NRSV, NIV, NET, ESV) *rightly* opt for the noetic/epistemological category for the uses of ἡγέομαι in Philippians. But I wish to open up the possibility that Paul may have intended a double meaning in this text that brought the second meaning (e.g., governance) into view for rhetorical purposes. Just to lay all my cards out on the table, I wonder if Paul may have purposely used ἡγέομαι repeatedly in

---

6. See Keener, *The Mind of the Spirit*, 217–36.
7. See Meeks, "Man from Heaven;" Craig S. Wansink, *Chained in Christ* (Sheffield: Sheffield Academic, 1996), 143–45; Stephen Fowl, *Philippians*, THNTC (Grand Rapids: Eerdmans, 2005), 28–29.
8. See James Barr's classic critique of what he calls "illegitimate totality transfer" (*The Semantics of Biblical Language* [London: Oxford University Press, 1961], 218).

Philippians (as he put pen to paper while sitting in prison) to communicate to the Philippian believers that rightly thinking about God, and choosing to imitate the thought-patterns and mindset of Christ, is a key form of leadership and self-determination, the competent and even valiant employment of one's "governing faculties" in a way that runs against the grain of social and cultural acceptability. In order to make this case, first we will engage with how hellenophones used ἡγέομαι in reference to governance. Then we will demonstrate how this leadership meaning is encouraged (even if subtly) by Paul in Philippians. Finally, we will draw out the implications this might have for the question of cruciformity, empowerment, and leadership.

Ἡγέομαι and Leadership

Despite the frequent usage of ἡγέομαι in Philippians, Moulton and Milligan observe that the noetic meaning of ἡγέομαι is not commonly found in Hellenistic literature. Much more often one sees the use of this verb in relation to leadership and governance.[9] And on scale this also appears to be the case when the Greek Bible is in view. For example, in LXX Gen 49, Jacob prophesies to his sons that "A ruler (ἄρχων) shall not be wanting from Ioudas [Judah] and a leader (ἡγούμενος) from his thighs until the things stored up for him come, and he is the expectation of nations" (49:10 NETS). In LXX Exodus, we read that the Lord guided (ἡγέομαι) his people in the wilderness in cloud by day and fire by night. In LXX Micah, the rulers of the house of Jacob are called οἱ ἡγούμενοι (3:9, 11; cf. Jer 4:22). This leadership meaning of ἡγέομαι was apparently not technical language for a specific office or role but a basic term like the English word "leader"—it could be used for general matters (like a teacher or counselor giving "guidance") but also for executive activity such as serving as the ruler or governor of a people (cf. Sir 10:2; 41:17). In more political-oriented statements, there is a tendency for authors to use the participial form of ἡγέομαι (ἡγούμενος) in parallel to ἄρχων ("ruler"; cf. e.g., LXX Ps 67:28; LXX Dan 2:48; Jdt 7:8; 1 Macc 9:30; Sir 46:18).

In the New Testament, we find ἡγέομαι almost thirty times, again often in reference to leadership. Matthew quotes Mic 5:2 (LXX 5:1): "And you, Bethlehem, in the land of Judah, are by no means least among the rulers of Judah; for from you shall come a ruler who is to shepherd my people Israel" (2:6). It is interesting to note that LXX Mic 5:1 does not have the word "rulers" here but

---

9. J. H. Moulton and G. Milligan, *The Vocabulary of the Greek Testament* (London: Hodder & Stoughton, 1914–1929), 277.

"thousands" (χιλιάσιν); yet we do see a match with the second clause about the coming of a "ruler" to shepherd the people. Matthew here employs the word ἡγέομαι, while LXX Micah has ἄρχων. Perhaps even more interesting than that is the fact that Matthew uses here both the nominalized form ἡγεμών ("rulers" of Judah) *and* the participial form ἡγούμενος (a "ruler" shall come)—this variation was normal for Greek literature in this time period. Matthew used the noun form repeatedly in his gospel, particularly in reference to an official government leader (cf. Matt 23:24–33). Luke used the noun ἡγεμών to designate the "governor" Felix (Acts 23–24 passim).

The epistle to the Hebrews shows a mix of meaning-uses of ἡγέομαι. Several times, the author uses it with the idea of "think/consider" (Heb 10:29; 11:11, 26). And on a handful of other occasions he employs the leadership meaning (13:7, 17, 24). As for Paul, he did not use ἡγέομαι explicitly in reference to the activity of leadership in his extant letters; instead, he preferred terms like προΐστημι to communicate activities like management ("to give oversight"; cf. Rom 12:8; 1 Thess 5:12).

So, looking at the material presented so far, we can conclude the following.

1. The verb ἡγέομαι has two completely different possible meanings: "to consider" and "to lead."
2. The second meaning is far more commonly found in Hellenistic literature, though the usage entirely depends on the writer's discourse purposes and needs.
3. The Greek Bible demonstrates usage of both types of meanings.
4. Paul uses ἡγέομαι only explicitly in reference to the noetic meaning ("to consider").

Is it possible that in Philippians Paul may have had a reason for teasing out the leadership nuance of this word as well?[10] Why? And how would you be able to prove this? I do think Paul was playing with a bit of double meaning in his use of this word in Philippians. In order to make as strong of a case as possible, we will need to examine the Christ hymn (Phil 2:6–11) more closely.

---

10. Again, I am sensitive to Barr's concern for overloading meaning into a single word. And I agree that writers intend one meaning of a word in any given discursive situation. But I think we would all say that discourses that carry poetic qualities can break out of the boundaries of normal semantic-rhetorical habits. Hence, we can identify numerous occasions where Paul engaged in wordplay. I would argue that what I am positing in this essay breaks conventional rules of word usage, but the context (especially the Christ hymn) lends itself to just this sort of wordplay.

Ἡγέομαι, the Christ Hymn, and the Stratified Roman Authority System

In this section, we will make the case that Paul's appeal to a Roman-style authority system and hierarchy in Philippians encourages the reader to rethink Paul's use of ἡγέομαι from a sociopolitical standpoint. Before we directly address the key terms relevant to this discussion, I wish to make appeal to Joseph Hellerman's cogent analysis of the Christ hymn with a view toward the Roman *cursus honorum*.[11] Hellerman has argued that the Christ hymn intentionally parodies the Roman *cursus honorum*, or race for honors, which involved a set of political offices within the Roman senatorial class. Elites sought to climb this ladder of glorification, so to speak, in order to advance politically. What the Christ hymn presents is a powerful subversion of the *cursus* which shows someone at the top (the glorious pre-incarnate Christ) purposefully move *down* the ladder, as it were, on a *cursus pudorum* (a route of "ignominies") out of humble obedience to God to fulfill the divine plan of redemption. Hellerman has presented a remarkable framework for understanding the nature and structure of the Christ hymn. And I find the way he plays off of Roman political ideology to be convincing. This has inspired for me *another* way of looking at the political dynamics of the Christ hymn, not in fundamental contradistinction to Hellerman's proposal but as a complement.

Let us begin in the middle of the Christ hymn with Phil 2:8: Christ lowered himself, becoming ὑπήκοος to the point of death, even death on a cross. Traditionally, ὑπήκοος is translated as "obedient" in English. This is a fair translation, but one might wonder why Paul used γινομαι + ὑπήκοος rather than simply a form of ὑπακούω (cf. Phil 2:12).[12] The word ὑπήκοος is an adjective, and certainly implies obedience, but often functions in reference to someone who is in a position of being under the authority of someone else; i.e., a "subject" (LXX Deut 20:11; Josh 17:13; Prov 4:3). The reason why it is helpful to make this distinction between the verb (ὑπακούω, "I obey") and the adjective (ὑπήκοος, "subject") is because the latter is often found in a stratified list of members of society in Hellenistic literature.[13]

There is ample evidence that writers within the Greco-Roman world

---

11. Joseph Hellerman, *Reconstructing Honor in Roman Philippi*, SNTSMS 132 (Cambridge: Cambridge University Press, 2007).

12. Or he could have used a variety of other verbs: ὑποτάσσω, πειθαρχέω, πείθω, etc.

13. The technical difference between using ὑπήκοος and ὑπακούω is that the former (as an adjective) refers to a state-of-being or status, while the latter (as a verb) refers to an action.

Cruciformity and the Believer's Governing Faculties

thought broadly in terms of "rulers" and "those who are ruled." We can imagine an invisible dividing line; above that line are those persons who are associated with governance, rulership, and executive authority. We see the following terms connected to those roles.

ἡγεμών/ἡγούμενος (leader)[14]
ἄρχων (ruler)[15]
κύριος (lord, ruler)[16]
βασιλεύς (king)[17]
δεσπότης (master)[18]
τύραννος (tyrant)[19]

The top two in this list are by far the most commonly used in reference to political leaders in general. The bottom two are far less common. When it comes to the ruled, there are fewer terms used, but they are found regularly.

ὑπήκοος (subject)[20]
δοῦλος (slave)[21]

If you have been glancing at the footnote references, it is clear that Philo often referred to these roles as general classifications. And he frequently did so to make a statement about God, overcoming passions, the power of the mind, or the nature of social reality. We will examine a few key texts from his many

---

14. Josephus, *Ant.* 14.84; Philo, *Opif.* 142; *Conf.* 54; *Migr.* 8; *Somn.* 1.162; *Gig.* 46; *Decal.* 166; *Prob.* 154; Appian, *Foreign Wars* 10.56.
15. Philo, *Leg.* 3.88; *Jos. Asen.* 24:15.
16. Josephus, *J. W.* 5.248; 1 Esd 6:27.
17. Josephus, *Ant.* 20.47; Sibyl. 8:111; Plutarch, *Ant.* 61.1; Athenaeus, *Deipn.* 1.9b.
18. Philo, *Gig.* 46.
19. Philo, *Ebr.* 198.
20. See *Aristeas* 253; Josephus, *Ant.* 2.212; *J. W.* 2.97; Appian, *Civil War* 1.35 (τούτου γὰρ δὴ μάλιστα ἐπεθύμουν ὡς ἑνὶ τῷδε αὐτίκα ἡγεμόνες ἀντὶ ὑπηκόων ἐσόμενοι; "They desired this especially because by that one step they would become rulers instead of subjects"). Plutarch mentions that the Carthaginians are subservient to their rulers, harsh to their subjects (ὑπήκοον τοῖς ἄρχουσι, βαρὺ τοῖς ὑπηκόοις; *Marriage Advice* 3). We ought also to add the verbal form ὑπακούω (see *Aristeas* 44).
21. Dio, *Orations* 64.6; Philo, *Opif.* 165, *Alleg.* 3.88; *Cher.* 83; *Sacr.* 9; for rulers (ἡγεμών), slaves (δοῦλος), subjects (ὑπήκοος), see Arr. *Anabasis* 7.9.3; Philo, *Spec.* 2.48. Philo is quite insistent and transparent about the natural ruling order: "For among all those nations who have any regard for virtue, the older men are esteemed above the younger, and teachers above their pupils, and benefactors above those who have received kindnesses from them, and rulers above their subjects, and masters above their slaves (ἄρχοντες ὑπηκόων καὶ δεσπόται δούλων)" (*Spec.* 2:226).

tractates to illustrate how Philo viewed the political spectrum. Eventually it will become clear how resonant this is with Paul's Christ hymn.

We begin with Philo's *De cherubim*. Philo points out that no human has absolute power in the world. In the bigger scheme of things, mortals are like subjects (ὑπήκοος) and slaves (δοῦλος), so there must be a great ruler (ἡγεμών) and lord (κύριος), one great and all-powerful ruler (ἄρχων) and leader (ἡγεμών), one God to whom all say, "all things belong to him (πάντα αὐτοῦ κτήματα)" (*Cher.* 83). So, here, Philo uses what he presumes to be a common understanding of political stratification to explain the supremacy of God. Elsewhere, he takes this same schema for granted and applies it to the relationship between the (corruptible) senses and the mind. According to Philo, the mind ought to rule the person, not the senses, which are easily swayed by pleasures. But, Philo warns, the mind can be tricked and corrupted by the senses, leading to the person's degradation or demise. The mind can be wooed by the senses and manipulated, and when that happens, in the internal anthropological ecosystem, the mind becomes a subject (ὑπήκοος) instead of a ruler (ἡγεμών), a slave (δοῦλος) instead of a master (δεσπότης), an exile (φυγάς) instead of a citizen (πολίτης), mortal (θνητός) rather than immortal (ἀθάνατος) (*Opif.* 165).[22]

We will revisit Philo later, but let us turn now to Paul's Christ hymn in Philippians where it should become obvious just how resonant that Pauline text is with the framework of these political metaphors used by Philo and others. The Christ hymn (Phil 2:6–11) is probably best understood as exalted encomium, offering a kind of parabolic tale of the story of Jesus's initial high position, his humble self-lowering in obedience to God the Father, and his subsequent super-exaltation to the highest place with the highest name. Scholars have long hunted for and debated the most substantial conceptual background for the Christ hymn, with many options finding some favor including Adam typology, Wisdom typology, the Roman *cursus honorum*, and Isaianic themes.[23] Without taking the time to confirm or refute any of these, I simply wish to include in this conversation what I think by now should be a self-evident observation—a number of terms used by Paul in the Christ hymn correlate with Greco-Roman sociopolitical stratification as we have described above. In fact, it seems to me

---

22. Notice how similar Philo's thinking is to Plutarch when the latter explains that "there is not any law or ordinance more worthy and powerful than knowledge; nor is it fitting that the mind, provided it be truly and really free by nature, should be a subject (ὑπήκοος) or slave (δοῦλος) to anyone, but it ought to govern all (ἀλλὰ πάντων ἄρχοντα εἶναι)" (*Mor.* 9).

23. For a helpful summary of scholarship, see Gregory P. Fewster, "The Philippians 'Christ Hymn': Trends in Critical Scholarship," *CurBR* 13 (2015): 191–206.

that Paul goes *out of his way* to use several of the common class terms that represent rulers and the ruled, namely κύριος, ὑπήκοος, and δοῦλος (and ἡγέομαι, though we will need to spend more time looking at its semantic function).

In the scene-setting statement of Phil 2:6, Paul asserts that Jesus Christ was initially "in the form of God" and had "equality with God"—whatever precisely this means is unclear but the gist is intuitive; what Paul is getting at is that Jesus was easily on the ruler side of the political equation, on par with terms like ἡγεμών or ἄρχων, perhaps even κύριος. He fit the glory and status of ruler. In the ancient world, kingship was viewed as a divine right, a position that is in keeping with the proper nature of society. There are those who are born to rule, and others who are born to be ruled. But what is remarkable about this figure, Jesus Christ, is that he did not dwell on clinging to this status or role. What is implicitly asserted in 2:6 is that God the Father called upon Jesus Christ to take off the crown, lay down the scepter, and step down into a lower station—more than that, to relinquish all the privileges of his status. It is not surprising to see the use of the verb κενόω in political contexts; after all, kings and kingdoms rise and fall, cities are destroyed, fortunes are lost, treasuries are emptied. But the tendency is to see κενόω in the passive: filled things are often emptied *against one's will* (Josephus, *Ant.* 10.3; 14.484; *J. W.* 1.355; 2.457). But what is remarkable about the Christ hymn is how Paul shows Jesus emptying *himself*—what sort of ruler would do this? What would motivate such self-inflicted loss?

Paul explicates this self-emptying by saying that Jesus took the form of a δοῦλος (Phil 2:7). Again, if Paul was intentionally drawing on this spectrum of Roman social stratification, there is nothing lower on the scale than δοῦλος. It is important to be clear, though, that the earthly Christ did not become an actual δοῦλος. But this fits the story Paul tells in the hymn insofar as the downward movement from high glory was so drastic, it is *as if* a ruler chose to become a slave. In 2:7 Paul refers twice to Jesus becoming the form of a mortal (ἄνθρωπος), implying that previously he had the form of something greater (divine?). A special mission caused, for Jesus, a great humbling, such that this ruler must now become a subject (ὑπήκοος; Phil 2:8). Here is where it is crucial to understand why Paul uses ὑπήκοος (a word used only three times in the NT, once elsewhere in Paul, 2 Cor 2:9). Most lexicons gloss this as "obedient," but two clarifications or provisos need to be made here. First, the adjective more properly refers to subjection, so "subject" is likely a better English translation. Secondly, given the overall context of the Christ hymn (and its intentional sociopolitical orientation), the use of ὑπήκοος seems to have more to do with where Jesus Christ places himself as one who is ruled, rather than the focus being on the activity of obedience per se.

Paul carries this story forward by explaining that Jesus became a subject, one who is governed or ruled by another, and stuck with that role, even to the point of death on a cross. But if Jesus becomes the subject, if he sinks down voluntarily to the category of ruled, *who is the ruler?* Paul leaves this unstated in Phil 2:8. In fact, in 2:6–8, God is not specifically mentioned as one who sends Jesus to earth in human form (even though Paul is willing to say as much in Gal 4:4). There are probably two reasons for this. First, it is important for Paul to point out that Jesus *willingly and voluntarily* abdicated his position, rather than being forced by someone else. But that does not mean Jesus becomes a subject to himself per se in 2:8. That would be going too far. We may catch a sense of the divine passive here in 2:8—God the Father is the implied leader or master, hence God's exaltation of Jesus in 2:9. And we might say that Jesus's self-emptying and self-lowering also puts him into the hands of his enemies, the rulers of the earth (which, of course, is how the gospels play out this scenario). One might think, then, of the Christ hymn positioning Jesus as subject to *two* masters, evil ones that end up killing him and God the Father, who wills that redemption come from this loving self-sacrifice. Jesus, then, serves as a kind "double-agent," subject both to the powers that crucify him and also to the Father who calls him to obedience.[24] While this notion of "double agency" may seem far-fetched, Paul appears to use this same concept in Phil 1 when he argues that Rome put him in chains (potentially for his demise), but God has purposed these chains in actuality to magnify and propel the gospel (see Phil 1:12–17).

Because of Jesus's willingness to subject himself to the Father's will, and in the process become a subject to worldly powers, God promotes Christ with ultimate and supreme status and authority (Phil 2:9–11), paradoxically attaining that most glorious position of preeminence that belongs to God alone (again see Philo, *Cher.* 83). Identifying the sociopolitical language in the Christ hymn no doubt adds even more richness to a dense and deep passage, but I wish to go one step further and argue that this context invokes a rethinking of how Paul uses ἡγέομαι in the Christ hymn (2:6), and furthermore in Philippians as a whole (cf. 2:3, 25; 3:7–8). According to 2:6, though Jesus had already possessed "ruler" status, he did not *regard* this form something to cling to. Of course it makes good sense to translate ἡγέομαι here as "regard" or "consider," following the verb's noetic/cognitive semantic value. But I wonder whether it may be appropriate to read

---

24. See my article which gives a detailed argumentation of this interpretation, "To Whom Was Christ a Slave (Phil 2:7)? Double Agency and the Specters of Sin and Death in Philippians," *HBT* 32 (2010): 1–16.

into ἡγέομαι a layer of the "leadership" meaning that it can bear. Why? Because if we think of the Christ hymn as a whole signaling attentiveness to the Roman rulership social system (slave, lord, subject), ἡγέομαι fits so exquisitely well as another piece of that puzzle that it might make the reader do a double take, at the very least sensing intentional wordplay. But to what end?

I would not translate ἡγέομαι in Philippians any differently than English translations already do, but what I might detect is an expression that no matter what one's position or status in life, there is great power and "ownership," as it were, in choosing how one thinks. The will to see the world a certain way, to control one's own epistemology, to focus the mind and commit oneself to a certain value system—that is a self-determined form of leadership, the employment of what we might call the "governing faculties."

Can we read this into Paul, Philippians, and the Christ hymn? Is this wishful thinking—a semantic and exegetical stretch? Ultimately, one cannot make an open-and-shut case for what I am arguing here, but I wish to point out that more than once Philo seems to be doing a similar sort of thing. Allow me to offer these possible analogies. In his work *De agricultura*, Philo breaks down the allegorical meaning of Gen 46:31–34 (where Joseph coaches his family about their integration into Egyptian society). If the king of Egypt should ask them what they do (for work), they are to say they keep livestock. Under these circumstances, they cannot divulge their true identity as holy and royal beings such as they are in association with their God (*Agr.* 57–59). They have to play the part, so to speak, of being mere "shepherds" in order to move their family forward.

Later in this same section, Philo explains that, though Jacob and his sons had to wander and sojourn, they clung inwardly to the divine promise of having their own land. So also, Philo posits, "every soul of a wise man has heaven for its country," though the "house of the body" is a temporary lodge (*Agr.* 65 [Yonge]). Regardless of the exact external situation, under subjugation or left wandering, Philo encourages his readers to believe that the mind is the "ruler of the flock (ἀγελάρχης)," and the mind governs (ἀφηγέομαι) the flock of the soul. But, Philo warns, names and titles can be deceiving. One might be called a "keeper of sheep" (κτηνοτρόφος) and actually do nothing more than tend animals. But one might appear to do the same thing and be called a "shepherd" (ποιμήν)—and this person actually is a king and a leader (*Agr.* 66). Here and elsewhere Philo is quick to associate true leadership with a state of mind—that makes all the difference.

Let us now look at the overall flow of the Christ hymn, taking into account how Paul might have been playing with status roles that were well-recognized in Greco-Roman society. Christ, initially in the position of a sovereign, equal to God, lowers himself intentionally even to the point of losing his grand status entirely—one might even say he was no better off than a δοῦλος (slave). He moves from being on the ruler side of the equation to being a ὑπήκοος and δοῦλος, to the point of crucifixion. But because he chose to be obedient to the commands of the great Father, he was super-appointed to an even higher position, now sharing in the unique title κύριος (2:11). If we look at the overall flow of Phil 1–3, Paul was trying to convince these Philippian believers that they could find hope and joy in imitating the humble and cruciform mindset of Jesus Christ. And the Christ hymn serves as a crucial word picture or "master story" to model this perspective.[25] And we can easily see the role that epistemological language plays in all of this. Paul repeatedly uses words like ἡγέομαι in reference to how one makes up their mind or chooses to attribute value to something. And ἡγέομαι is important for the Christ hymn. In the context of this hymn, so much of the action appears to be out of the hands of the hero of the story, Jesus Christ. He is (tacitly) called by God to lower himself. He succumbs to punishment as a worst-of-society criminal. In what sense, then, does Jesus Christ serve as a model *leader* for the Philippians? Surely, the answer is found in how Jesus Christ *chose to see reality*, how he focused his mind's eye to see beyond present circumstances alone and the superficial judgment of the masses. And those with eyes to see and ears to hear this "master story" might also pick up on a clever double meaning of ἡγέομαι (2:6) in the context of a passage where political status markers are all over the place. Yes, Christ had to become a "slave" and "subject"—those who are governed and even subjugated by others in society. Their fate, so to speak, is not in their "control." The imprisoned Paul would add—*my own fate is unclear*. But even in such circumstances, leadership is called for, and there is great power in correct perception, leading by thinking rightly about the world and how God sees the world.

Implications for Cruciformity?

Before drawing out the implications the above argument has for the concept of cruciformity in Paul, allow me to briefly summarize. We have argued that theological epistemology is especially prominent in Philippians. That is, Paul appears to have invested in underscoring that suffering and shame, as well as glorification, honor, and hope, must be seen from the right perspective. In

---

25. See especially Michael J. Gorman, *Becoming the Gospel: Paul, Participation, and Mission* (Grand Rapids: Eerdmans, 2015), 105–41.

Cruciformity and the Believer's Governing Faculties

reference to these matters, Paul employs several terms of cognition including ἡγέομαι. But we introduced the idea that Paul may have also intentionally played upon the (unrelated) meaning of ἡγέομαι, "to lead." With the Christ hymn especially in view, we made the case that Paul was appealing to a familiar sociopolitical typology whereby the world can be divided into the ruling and the ruled. In fact, the Christ hymn employs several of the terms that fit that cultural framework. What is incredible about the hero (Jesus) of this poetic encomium is that he voluntarily moves down from the level of ruler to subject and even to slave. One could easily see this as pure folly, an irresponsible abdication of power that has left the hero with nothing, right? But we must recall *how* Paul introduces the Christ hymn. He exhorts the Philippians to emulate the *mindset* of Jesus Christ (2:5), the one who disregarded his privileged status (2:6) in order to be fully obedient to the redemptive plan of God. For Paul, the humble lowliness of Jesus Christ was not a complete relinquishment of his leadership, but rather a *demonstration* of it, because of the power of his *choice* and the dynamic potential of his *mindset*.

We can revisit now the concerns and questions that my students have presented about the concept of cruciformity. Does it inevitably lead to powerlessness? Does it obviate self-determination? Paul would answer, μὴ γένοιτο! With a view toward Philippians, I conclude with these claims.

1. *Power can come from the strangest of places.* While it is true that empowered leaders have the potential to effect great change, Paul would have been the first to recognize that God can use anyone in any position to show his glory. Paul communicates this to the Philippians when he talks about how his "chains" have served to magnify and display the gospel of Jesus Christ to people he could never have reached otherwise (Phil 1:12–13).
2. *You often have more resources than you think.* Despite Paul's restrictive imprisonment, he obviously had many different resources at his disposal. For example, he received an encouraging gift from the Philippians themselves, and he had the aid of Epaphroditus and Timothy. Cruciformity is ultimately about *obedience to God*, not about having nothing per se. I liken it to the Parable of the Pearl—this man was so entranced by this valuable item that he considered everything else loss (Matt 13:45–46). While Paul was forced to accept his current situation as a prisoner, he was certainly not resourceless.
3. *You may not be able to control everything in life, but you can always control your perspective and values.* Again, this is why Paul returns again

and again to the matter of right-thinking in this letter. Cruciformity is an orientation and act of faith, a way of thinking and living that is against the grain. It is transformation by the renewal of the mind; it is being willingly crucified to the world and having the world crucified to oneself. Paul's letter to the Philippians *itself* is a powerful testimony to his ability to demonstrate leadership while also being in chains. Sharing his story and his wisdom, his attitude and his mindset—even if death was near—testifies to how he saw his role as an apostolic leader.

Conclusion

In this essay, our goal has been to revisit the nature of Pauline cruciformity and address the question of how one can serve as a *leader* while also demonstrating cruciform spirituality. To some interpreters and readers, it can seem like a contradiction: *cruciformity is about weakness, "leadership" is about power.* But for Paul cruciformity is not ultimately about weakness, suffering, or death; it is about obedience to God whatever the cost. In the end, this kind of obedience leads to loss, undoubtedly. Perhaps loss of status or resources. But we have attempted to make the case that Paul saw an indispensable form of "leadership" and power in the way one chooses to think, to see the world, and to affirm godly values. All these things can happen even from a prison cell—or worse. And the epistle to the Philippians itself is a testimony to the change-making potential of that kind of leadership.

PART TWO

Participation in Christ, One with God

Chapter 6

Grasping and Being Grasped: Gift and Agency in Paul

Stephen E. Fowl

It is itself an honor to contribute to a volume honoring Mike Gorman. For many years now, our offices have been only a couple of miles apart. The demands of our jobs, however, mean that we often see each other more at the annual meeting of the Society of Bibilical Literature than we do in Baltimore. In addition to being spatially close to each other, Mike and I share common approaches to Paul and his letters and to the importance of training students to read those letters theologically. We also share a love of Philippians. Given these common delights, I want to offer Mike this essay. It will engage what I take to be one of the most significant books on Paul of the past twenty years:

My title is a reference to a section of Phil 3:12: καὶ καταλάβω, ἐφ᾽ ᾧ καὶ κατελήμφθην ὑπὸ Χριστοῦ. The NRSV translates this clause, "I press on to make it my own, because Christ Jesus has made me his own." This recognizes that the Greek uses the same verb for what Paul does and what Christ has done for Paul. Nevertheless, I see two problems with the translation. First, the Greek καταλάμβανω, really is about grabbing, seizing, taking hold of something. Second, I am following Joseph Fitzmyer in reading the elliptical Greek phrase, ἐφ᾽ ᾧ, consecutively as the object of the verb (see "The Consecutive Meaning of ἐφ᾽ ᾧ in Romans 5:12," *NTS* 39 [1993]: 321–39). The NRSV translates the phrase as describing a cause (i.e., I press on to make it my own, *because* Christ Jesus made me his own). I would translate this part of the verse "I reach out to grab that for which Christ first grabbed me." The difference here is that Paul is not describing the reason he is grabbing or reaching out. Rather, he is talking about the object of his grabbing, which is the object Christ has always wanted for him.

89

John Barclay's *Paul and the Gift*.¹ I will point out some possible tensions within Barclay's account of Paul's reception of the Christ-gift in Romans and suggest that a close reading and a theological account of Phil 3 can help to resolve some of those tensions in ways that are closely aligned with Paul's thought, conform to Mike's interest in cruciformity and participation, and also are true to what I take to be the great insights Barclay offers in *Paul and the Gift*.

Gift and Agency in Paul

I begin with a brief disclaimer: many Enlightenment debates about human agency, with their typical concerns about human freedom and autonomy, with their attempts to separate agents and acts, either do not apply to Paul very well or will mislead us when we apply them to Paul. Indeed, one need not be a biblical scholar or theologian to find such notions of agency particularly problematic. For some time now any number of masters of suspicion, ranging from Freud and Marx to contemporary feminist and postcolonial theorists, has attacked notions of autonomy and freedom that underwrite strong concerns with agency. In addition, those interested in character ethics, which depends on seeing agents and actions as deeply embedded within narratives, have long muddied any clear and distinct separations between agents and their actions. All that is to say that Enlightenment notions of human agency are not likely to help one to read Paul better. In addition, as a corollary to this point, I want to note that because Paul sees his life as a gift from God many post-Enlightenment critics of modern notions of agency will not find Paul's account any more congenial.²

No discussion of gift and agency in Paul can begin without first engaging with John Barclay's monumental volume, *Paul and the Gift*. Barclay's study injects needed clarity into the ways in which scholars think of notions of gift and grace. In particular, he examines how reflections on gift and grace tend to elevate specific aspects of gift and grace above all other possible ways of understanding these terms. Barclay describes this as "perfecting" an aspect of grace, "The drawing out of a concept to the end-of-the-line extreme."³ Having noted the various ways gift and grace might be perfected, Barclay is then able to organize usefully a wide array of discussions of gift and grace in Paul ranging from Marcion and

---

1. John M. G. Barclay, *Paul and the Gift* (Grand Rapids: Eerdmans, 2015).
2. Barclay makes some similar points in his introduction to *Divine and Human Agency in Paul and his Cultural Environment*, ed. John M. G. Barclay and Simon Gathercole (Edinburgh: T & T Clark, 2006), 3–5.
3. Barclay, *Paul and the Gift*, 4.

Grasping and Being Grasped

Augustine through the Reformers and down to contemporary theologians and biblical scholars. Then, prior to engaging in a detailed examination of grace in Romans and Galatians, Barclay explores and illustrates the diversity of views about grace in several Second Temple texts. Barclay agrees with Sanders and others that Second Temple Judaism was well acquainted with the idea of grace. He sharpens this point in ways that advance our understanding. He shows that just as modern scholars of Paul perfect specific aspects of grace, so Second Temple Judaism, too, tends to perfect grace in a number of distinct ways. "Grace is everywhere in Second Temple Judaism but not everywhere the same."[4]

All of this work allows Barclay to advance, and perhaps even resolve, what had become a rather stale debate in Pauline scholarship. In Pauline studies those adopting and those opposed to the "new perspective" on Paul have reached a sort of impasse. The more traditional approach to Paul, an approach often linked to Augustine and Luther, emphasized that for Paul, salvation was a gift from God offered despite human sinfulness. God's offer of this gift to Paul freed him from a life wracked by sin and guilt. This is a scenario that may more closely match Augustine and Luther than Paul. This emphasis also tended to treat Judaism as a religion devoid of grace by which one could only achieve a self-created righteousness through the works of Torah. This either created misplaced self-righteousness or guilt-driven despair in its adherents.

The so-called new perspective responded to this by noting that the traditional approach was driven by a false conception of Second Temple Judaism, which was in fact a grace-filled religion. To understand Paul rightly, one could only do so in the light of a realistic picture of the Judaism of his day, also recognizing the fact that Paul never stopped thinking of himself as a Jew. He held his convictions about Jesus the Messiah to be compatible with Judaism. The animating force for many of his writings was not how he found relief from his introspective conscience. Instead, these writings are rooted in Paul's mission to the gentiles and his (and his communities') concerns with how and in what ways God was joining Jews and Gentiles into one body in Christ.

One of the great achievements of *Paul and the Gift* is Barclay's great skill in recognizing that the traditional approach was correct in elevating the incongruity of God's gift in Christ, a gift given without any regard for the worth or virtue of the recipients. At the same time, Barclay recognizes that the new perspective's emphasis on understanding Paul within the context of the Judaism of his day is essential. Because Barclay had already shown that Second Temple Judaism did not have a single view about grace/gift, he could both

---

4. Barclay, *Paul and the Gift*, 6.

respect the emphasis on the incongruity of grace and fit it within the variety of ways the notion of grace is perfected in Second Temple Judaism. In the light of this variety, Barclay presents Paul's arguments in Romans and Galatians as inner-Jewish arguments about how the Christ-gift, manifesting the incongruity of God's grace, played out against other fully Jewish ways of understanding grace. In particular, he puts Paul's way of perfecting grace in conversation with another way of perfecting grace common in Second Temple Judaism. This view argued that if God's gift giving did not take some account of human worth and righteousness, the moral coherence of the cosmos would be threatened, if not undermined. "Thus, the foil to Paul's theology is not a human self-righteousness that attempts to earn salvation, but the natural assumption that when God acts in saving benevolence, he distributes his gifts to those we consider fitting or worthy."[5]

As Barclay masterfully demonstrates, gift giving in Paul's world (and our own) is a practice soaked in social, material, political, and relational conventions. Understanding these conventions provides a crucial framework for understanding any particular act of gift giving. At the same time, we only understand specific acts of gift giving when they are set within a narrative context. These contexts show that gift giving is never just the handing of a gift from one party to another. Gift giving is a complex practice marked and shaped by present and past particularities as well as future hopes. This is why I would argue that the heart of *Paul and the Gift* is Barclay's discussion of Galatians and Romans. In these epistles Paul unpacks a narrative of God's gift of Christ to the world, a gift that is both cosmic in its scope and effects and also soaked in the particulars of God's dealings with Israel and with the redemption of all peoples. To support his argument Barclay offers rich and textured readings of both Romans and Galatians. These readings help sustain his argument that Paul tends to "perfect" grace in a way that elevates the incongruity of God's gift in Christ.

Gift, Agency, and Processes of Participation

Without question, *Paul and the Gift* is a master work of Pauline scholarship. I have no desire to diminish the scope and power of its achievements. At the

---

5. Barclay, *Paul and the Gift*, 541. (Hereafter, page references are given in parentheses in the text.) In calling this view a "foil" to Paul's theology, Barclay is not engaging in the type of "mirror-reading" he so famously criticized in "Mirror Reading a Polemical Letter: Galatians as a Test Case," *JSNT* 31 (1987): 73–93. He is primarily noting that Paul's approach to God's gift in Christ is both consistent with some views of his Jewish contemporaries and at odds with other views.

Grasping and Being Grasped

same time, there are some unresolved tensions in Barclay's account that I believe can be addressed by bringing in other Pauline texts and reading those texts in the light of the perspectives of cruciformity and participation that have animated Mike Gorman's work. To do this, I will raise some questions about Barclay's account in Romans, pointing out some of its rough edges. Then I will suggest that an account of Phil 3 that focuses more on the ongoing process of participation in Christ can help round out some of these rough edges.

As with Galatians, Barclay argues that Paul perfects his notion of grace in terms of incongruity, that the Christ-gift is given without regard for the worth of the recipients. The issue that comes into focus in Rom 5–8 is whether and how a gift that is unconditioned by the worth of the recipients relates to the continuing common life of those recipients. "What begins as an *unfitting* gift founds the *fit* between the lives of believers and the final outcome of salvation. Does this mean that grace is operative as incongruous gift only at the *start* of a believer's life? Does it disappear thereafter or turn into something else?" (493).

At this point in the book, Barclay is clear in his answer. "The length at which Paul here describes this double sided phenomenon, and the event of baptism that stands at its core ([Rom] 6:1–14), enables us to see how the incongruous grace of life in Christ in an important sense *remains incongruous* with the condition of believers even while they 'bear fruit for God' (7:14) and please God through the Spirit (8:1–13)" (494). A lot seems to depend on what Barclay means by "the condition" of believers. Romans 5–6 seems crucial here. The "Adamic condition" is slavery to sin and death. This condition is countered by the gift of God in Christ. This gift establishes an alternative and superior political space into which believers enter through baptism. Baptism both accomplishes and signifies a change of citizenship and allegiance that renders any desire to remain in the realm of sin incoherent.

Entering the realm established and sustained by the Christ-gift entails a set of obligations. Barclay notes that nobody in Paul's world would have thought that this diminishes the gratuity of the Christ-gift. Moreover, the realm of Christ is not just created by the Christ-gift, it is sustained by the continuing presence of Christ through the Spirit. In this sense it could be seen as remaining incongruous. The gift of the Spirit is no more dependent on the worth of the recipients than the Christ-gift is. As I understand Barclay's notion of incongruity, this makes sense. The sustenance of the community of Christ does not depend upon the moral worth of the community members. Paul clearly seems to recognize that although they have left the realm of sin and death and are no longer subject to Sin as a power, they will, nonetheless, commit various transgressions.

Barclay, however, wants to say more. The lives of believers are in a state of incongruity to the extent that they are still subject to death. "This puts their lives in a state of permanent incongruity: in one respect they are bound to death ('on account of sin,' that is, as a residue of their Adamic heritage, [Rom] 8:10); in another they are alive, in an eternal 'life from the dead' that in its source and character is the life of Christ" (501). Although they are citizens of the ultimately victorious realm of Christ, believers continue also to live in a world marked by sin and death. Although the character of the death of our bodies is transformed by the gift of Christ, this side of the eschaton we will still die.

Although this is true, it simply reflects the sort of incongruity between believers' present state and their ultimate end, not the sort of incongruity Barclay has used to interpret Galatians and Romans. Even recognizing that mortal bodies have yet to put on immortality, one must also say that even if it is not possible to specify in advance how resurrected bodies are continuous with mortal bodies, there must be some continuities. How else would one know oneself or others in the resurrection? Christ's own resurrected body maintained sufficient continuities with his earthly body that his disciples could recognize him, even if not always immediately. At this point Barclay seems to be speaking of two different types of incongruity. The incongruity between mortal and resurrected bodies is of a very different sort than the incongruity between the giver of an unconditioned gift and its recipients that drives this notion in the rest of the book.

Moreover, in his account of Rom 12–15 Barclay recognizes that there is a moral efficacy in God's gift (see chapter 16).[6] The newness of life arising from believers' participation in the Christ-gift calls forth, invites, and entails a range of practices; it requires the transformation and reorientation of other practices. Barclay is also correct to note that sustaining such newness of life does not require subsequent series of graces. Rather, it seems much more like the Christ-gift, which is given to the Romans without any consideration of their worth, is meant to effect the transformations that the particular shape of this gift implies and entails. "In that sense, what began as a morally incongruous gift will be completed as a morally congruous gift" (518).

I take it that the point Barclay wants to make when he says, "The incon-

---

6. Barclay treats this as a separate perfection of grace. As we will see, one of the things that I believe is true of Romans but even clearer in Philippians is that what Barclay treats as a separate perfection of grace is inextricably bound up in Paul's understanding of the incongruity of the Christ-gift.

gruous grace of life in Christ in an important sense *remains incongruous* with the condition of believers even while they 'bear fruit for God' (7:14) and please God through the Spirit (8:1–13)," becomes clearer in the following sentences. "Right up to the moment of resurrection a believer remains *simil mortuus et vivens*. What is given to them is not a new set of competencies added to their previous capacities, nor an enhancement of their previous selves: what is given is a death and the emergence from that death of a new self, essentially 'eccentric' in its dependence on the resurrection life of Christ" (518).

Barclay goes on to note that this does not diminish the agency of believers. Rather, it transforms it from an agency that is antagonistic to or competitive with God to an agency that is derived from Christ and cooperates with Christ.

The element of this picture that troubles me somewhat is how Barclay or anyone else knows that the new life given to believers "is not a new set of competencies added to their previous capacities, nor an enhancement of their previous selves." It seems possible, and perhaps even likely, that Paul could agree that participation in the death and resurrection of Christ does produce a new self, dependent on Christ, and also recognize that this need not obliterate previous capacities and might entail the perfection of their previous selves. Moreover, for believers, death is not something that establishes an enduring incongruency in their lives. Rather, its power to obliterate life is undermined and destroyed so that on both sides of death there are significant congruities in the lives of believers. If that is the case, then the moral, spiritual, and communal transformations Paul sees as essential to participation in Christ are inextricably bound up in Paul's understanding of the incongruity of the Christ-gift.[7] It is thus not another perfection but a further way in which Paul rounds out and specifies the precise nature of the incongruity between the Christ-gift and the lives of believers.

Processes of Participation: Philippians 3

In what follows I want to sketch out these possibilities by examining Phil 3.[8] Part of the challenge for any of us in speaking about Paul's approach to the Christ-gift is that the offering of a gift is both an event in itself, and an event that invites and evokes a longer stream of events, relationships, and practices.

7. Treating this issue as a specification of what Paul imagines participation in Christ to entail is in line with Mike Gorman's overall approach to soteriology. See *The Death of the Messiah and the Birth of the New Covenant* (Eugene, OR: Cascade, 2014).

8. Barclay's magnificent volume only deals with Romans and Galatians and concludes with some promissory notes about future work on other epistles.

Moreover, the offering of the Christ-gift not only invites a new and ongoing set of relationships with God and others, but it also transforms one's past relationships, or one's perceptions of those relationships, with God and others. Barclay is certainly correct to note that with regard to the various ways grace can be perfected, emphasizing one perfection does not imply all of the other perfections. Nevertheless, it would seem to be the case that Paul would argue that emphasizing the incongruity of the Christ-gift might also entail some of the other perfections of grace. At this point, Mike Gorman might suggest that the notion of participation in Christ helps us comprehend both the incongruity of the Christ-gift and the new and ongoing relationships with God and others into which Paul invites and indeed expects his congregations to participate. Moreover, it provides his congregations with new ways of perceiving their past relationships with God and others. Indeed, one might begin by noting that Paul's deep commitments to rightly understanding his past and the pasts of all believers reflect an ongoing commitment to recognizing both the radical transformations inherent in the Christ-gift and that gift's capacity to enable Paul to reconceive lines of continuity in his own life.

To see this, we can do no better than engage Phil 3. In a relatively compact set of verses Paul speaks about himself in ways that make his notions of moral formation and transformation and reformation discernable. In addition, this passage concludes with Paul's admonition to the Philippians to imitate him and those who think, act, and feel in a manner similar to him. Thus, there is some sense in which Paul thinks of his own experience as exemplary if not normative. At the same time, we can see some of the complexities involved in trying sharply to distinguish the interactions between God's incongruously gracious work in Paul's life and Paul's own actions in the light of his apprehension of Christ's apprehension of him.

In this passage Paul presents the connections between divine gift and the new life this gift invites and evokes as so deeply intertwined that it is not easy to separate them. Indeed, Paul hopes that participation in Christ means that one's life in Christ should be formed in such a way that it becomes difficult and largely unimportant to make such a separation.

Paul's account of himself in Phil 3 is a story of formation, transformation, and reformation as he speaks about his life prior to and after his encounter with the resurrected Christ. Paul offers this account as a way of contrasting his views with those he characterizes as dogs, evil workers, and mutilators (3:2).[9] Ultimately, Paul will note that the manner of life these people follow

---

9. Within both Greco-Roman and Jewish writings, calling someone a dog is a fairly

renders them "enemies of the cross" (3:18). Scholars have devoted a good deal of attention to identify these people more precisely. For my purposes, it is not important to do that.[10] It is sufficient to say that in contrast to those who walk as enemies of the cross, Paul offers his account of himself as a way of exemplifying the patterns of thinking, acting, and feeling appropriate to those who are "friends" rather than enemies of the cross. In doing this, Paul is carrying on an argument that begins at the end of Phil 1 and is highlighted by the admonition to display the same pattern of thinking, acting, and feeling Christ displayed in 2:5–11. Paul's account recognizes that his understanding of the Christ-gift emphasized that gift's sharp incongruity with his own sense of what was worthwhile and meritorious in him. It also builds upon that understanding to advocate new patterns of thinking, feeling, and acting that he—with the Spirit's aid—seeks to embody with the goal of diminishing that incongruity. At the same time, this account also relies on continuities between Paul's past and his present and future. For example, both before and after encountering Christ Paul considers himself a Jew. There is both elimination and destruction but also enhancement and renewal of that same self.

After reading through Paul's rather impressive account of his achievements in Judaism in Phil 3:4–6 it is tempting to characterize Paul's life prior to Christ as one of unrelenting self-advancement. On this view, one gets a picture in which Paul relied on himself prior to Christ and relied on God's grace after that point. Paul speaks of his past as a prime example of having confidence in the flesh, even to the extent of being blameless with regard to the righteousness found in the law. Thus, Paul must be speaking here about a transformation

---

common form of insult. It provides contemporary readers with little if any purchase on identifying these people. In 2 Cor 11:13, 15 and in Matt 9:37–38 the term "evil workers" is used to speak of various Christian missionaries. The Psalter has numerous references to "workers of iniquity" but none of these texts provide clear insight into the characters Paul is concerned with here in Philippians. The term "mutilators" (κατατομή) seems to be a derisory play on the Greek word for circumcision (περιτομή). This term is also related to the verb used in the LXX for pagan self-mutilation (Lev 21:5; 1 Kgs 18:28; Isa 15:2; Hos 7:14). Paul's description, thus, would seem to mark out these people as Jewish. Moreover, this group's unworthy focus on the Philippian Christians would indicate that they are Jewish Christians rather than non-Christian Jews. Given this limited information, however, it is difficult to make a more precise identification. See Stephen Fowl, *Philippians*, THNTC (Grand Rapids: Eerdmans, 2005), 145–47.

10. If pressed, I would speculate that the characters Paul wants the Philippians to beware of are those Jewish Christians who would advocate that gentile Christians take on the forms and practices of Judaism to avoid Roman persecution (Fowl, *Philippians*, 147–49). Nothing I advocate here, however, depends on whether this speculation is correct.

from confidence in his own achievements in the flesh to a dependence on God's gracious activity in Christ, a transformation from dependence on works to dependence on grace. Although one can read 3:1–11 this way, I think it is a mistake to do so.

Instead, it is important to recognize that although Paul uses language that rightly identifies his transformation as unanticipated and so radical that it leads him to count all of his previous assets as losses, there are also some underlying continuities between Paul's views before and after he is grabbed by Christ that I would like to note here. In Phil 3:4–6, Paul points to a life that he once considered virtuous.[11] Indeed, he would expect that anyone familiar with Judaism would have easily recognized his virtue. This recognition would have rested on a set of assumptions that Paul and his Jewish peers would have shared to varying degrees. They would all have assumed that: God had graciously chosen the people of Israel to be blessed and to be a blessing; participation in this people presumed a loving response to God's gracious initiative; one way of enacting such love between God and humans was in the giving of the law by God and human devotion to that law. Although Jews disagreed with each other over the specific shape and pattern of such devotion, they all agreed that the law held the key to righteous living and faithful participation in the life of the people of God. In fact, it was only because they shared these perceptions and assumptions that Jews could then argue with each other over the proper shape and pattern of a life devoted to God. Thus, the fact that those things which Paul counts as "assets" (3:4–6) his peers would have also counted as "assets," also reflects a prior set of assumptions. One could even say Paul and his Jewish peers share a prior commitment to a story about God's gracious creation of and intervention into the world, a story in which God's covenantal faithfulness will ultimately result in God's redemption of the people of God. Thus, when Paul speaks of being blameless according to the righteousness

---

11. Being circumcised on the eighth day is Paul's reference to the fact that he was circumcised when he was eight days old. Being a member of the people of Israel and the tribe of Benjamin reflects the notion that he was not a proselyte. Indeed, Benjamin is the only one of Jacob's twelve sons born in the Promised Land (Gen 35:16–17). Paul's namesake, Saul, Israel's initial king, was a Benjaminite. Only Benjamin and Judah remained loyal to the Davidic house. When Paul calls himself a "Hebrew born of Hebrews" in 3:5 it may mean that Paul spoke/read Hebrew as Markus Bockmuehl argues (*The Epistle to the Philippians*, BNTC [London: A & C Black, 1998], 196). Although this may be true, it would have to be squared with the fact that when Paul quotes Scripture, he seems always to rely on the Greek translation. It is, of course, possible that Paul read and spoke Hebrew and for missionary purposes relied on versions of the LXX in his letters.

found in the law, he says this to reflect the depth of his love for God and his devotion to God's prior and gracious initiative in calling Abraham and in sending the law through Moses. Yes, he comes to see this devotion as misdirected. One does not get the impression, however, that, prior to Christ, Paul found this devotion to be anything other than a testimony to his love for the God who first loved him.

Indeed, Paul's account here in Phil 3:4–6 has much in common with the notions and perfections of grace Barclay finds in Philo (and to a lesser degree in Wisdom of Solomon). I will quote his concluding comments on Philo at length:

> If the world is ordered by a system of values instituted by God himself, and if the superior values represent God's own nature and the virtues closest to himself, it is natural that God should reward what is most like himself with the gifts of his grace. To do otherwise as a matter of principle would render God's generosity contradictory to his goodness, a random or self-defeating beneficence that would cut against the values of the cosmos. But God is no arbitrary giver. He rewards the values he has instituted himself, and thus ensures that rightly ordered humans can reach the perfection that he has graciously designed for them to attain. (238)

Without mitigating the incongruous nature of the Christ-gift, Paul in Philippians also seems to agree with the basic structure of Barclay's account of this perfection of grace. In the light of Christ, Paul has come to recognize a set of virtues that are closest to God's own nature. Indeed, they are directly displayed in the life, death, and exaltation of Christ as narrated in 2:6–11. Conforming oneself to the virtues closest to God's own nature would result in divine favor and further gracious gifts. This seems to presume continuities between Paul's pre- and post-Christ self. A central aspect of the dramatic change Paul narrates in Phil 3 is a change in his understanding of the "system of values initiated by God himself." These values are summarized in the pattern of thinking, feeling, and acting displayed by Christ in 2:5–11. When one reads this passage along with several others, such as 1:27–30, where Paul claims that God has granted the Philippians not only the grace of believing in Christ but also of suffering for his sake, it also indicates that the gracious gifts God bestows on those who adopt the patterns of thinking, feeling, and acting displayed by Christ are not precisely what those outside of Christ would consider gracious gifts. Nevertheless, there is a basic structural continuity between the position Barclay attributes to Philo and others and Paul's argument in Philippians.

One might extrapolate from these verses to summarize Paul's pre-Christ views about God's gift and his subsequent response in this way: The story of God's creation of the world and of God's continued gracious interaction with the world is a story in which God is working to draw all creation to Godself through the people of Israel. As a Jew, Paul's life was given a particular purpose and end as a character within this drama of God's redemption of the world. The initiation and unfolding of this drama all hinge on God's prior gracious activity. As one who rightly perceived the *telos* of this drama, the challenge confronting Paul or any other person was the challenge to form and order their thoughts, actions, and feelings in such ways as to fit their lives appropriately into this drama. Such formation depended upon God's help, both directly and indirectly; it required prayer and study, conversation and action; it involved coming to perceive the specific situations in which one found oneself as episodes that one needed to fit within the drama of God's redemption of the world. It also required Paul to employ his God-given skills, gifts, and capacities in a life together with others engaged in the same tasks. Aligning Paul's self with this divine drama also required the formation of a sort of practical reasoning. Within this movement of divinely ordered practical reasoning, when one failed or strayed or sinned, the gracious God of Israel had made ample provision for repenting, reforming, and becoming reconciled to God and others without necessarily requiring one to reconfigure or reconstitute the entire drama of God's salvation and one's place in that drama.

In Phil 3:6 Paul offers a thumbnail sketch of such practical reasoning at work. When faced with what the pre-Christian Paul (or Saul) and others took to be a grave internal threat to Judaism, he violently sought to root out those Jews proclaiming a false and dangerous message about Jesus being the Messiah. No doubt few could match the claim that their love of God led them to persecute heretics. Although from the perspective of being in Christ, Paul will in 1 Cor 15:9 note that his actions as a persecutor render him the "least of the apostles," from his pre-Christian perspective he does not flinch in mentioning these activities as a mark of virtue. Within such a perspective Paul was doing God a great service and his willingness to act so decisively on God's behalf was a mark of virtue in a manner similar to Phinehas (Num 25; Ps 106).

When Paul is "grabbed" by Christ, however, he both has to reconstitute and reconfigure the entire drama of God's salvation and he must, with the Spirit's help, have his practical reasoning reformed so that it is properly focused on and enlivened by the resurrected Christ who reflects the true values of the cosmos. Christ rips Paul out of the drama in which he formerly participated, but he does not leave him floating free, nor does Christ obliterate Paul's prior self.

Instead Paul finds himself in a radically revised drama of God's redemption of the world. It is a drama that has been unfolding from before the foundation of the world but has only now been revealed to him, and he must, as he did before, continue to seek to fit himself appropriately into that drama. Now, however, he rightly understands that this drama reaches both its climax and its proper end in Christ. From this perspective, being grabbed by Christ does and does not transform Paul as an agent. Both before and after Christ Paul is still more like an actor following someone else's script and direction than he is like an autonomous agent creating his own path through worlds freely chosen and constructed.

God certainly provides a new direction and end for Paul's life. As with his life in Judaism, however, this new end and direction is God's gift to Paul. It is not something that Paul would have chosen for himself apart from God's gracious intervention into his life and his world. At the same time, Paul does not seem to have any difficulty in thinking that humans are responsible for their actions and dispositions as Romans, Galatians, and the Corinthian letters all make abundantly clear. This is because the primary focus of human responsibility is to God and not to oneself.

Moreover, although his pattern of thinking, feeling, and acting has been profoundly disrupted, Paul does not abandon practical reasoning altogether. Instead, to use the language of Phil 3:19, Paul would admit that he once had a φρόνησις directed by earthly considerations which is being transformed into a φρόνησις revealed and enabled by Christ (cf. 2:5).

These represent some of the most significant structural or conceptual continuities between Paul's life before and after being grabbed by Christ. The thing that has changed and has changed decisively is Paul's understanding of God's drama of salvation. As Paul argues more fully in Romans and Galatians, God only ever had one plan to redeem the world. Apart from and until the mystery of Christ was revealed to the world, however, Paul could not have grasped this. It is only once he has been grabbed by Christ that Paul can begin, with the Spirit's help, to reorder his patterns of thinking, feeling, and acting in ways that conform to patterns of thinking, feeling, and acting displayed in Christ. If one is to keep thinking in the terms that Barclay uses for thinking about the perfections of grace, Phil 3 indicates both that there is an incongruity to God's gift of Christ and that the gift is effective. Barclay speaks of efficacy as a perfection of grace in the following way, "a perfect gift may also be figured as that which fully achieves that which it was designed to do" (73). Paul clearly reflects this view in 1:6 when he expresses his confidence that the God "who began a good work in you will carry it through to completion at the day of

Christ." That, however, is not all that Paul wants to say. In a sense, the efficacy of the gift depends upon the incongruity between the giver and the receiver and works to eliminate it.

Paul no longer strives for nor even values the habits, dispositions, and activities that marked his former life. They are so much garbage to him now. As a result, as Phil 3:10–11 describes, Paul's life is now directed toward a newly perceived *telos*. Paul is learning how to become a friend of the cross, one who wants to know Christ and the power of his resurrection, to share in his sufferings, and even to be conformed to Christ's death so that he may attain the resurrection of the dead.[12] Paul's desires here in 3:10–11 reflect the standard of fidelity and a goal toward which he now orients his life.

Philippians 3:10–14 indicates that God's work in Paul happens by re-ordering Paul's desires and affections rather than obliterating them. He now seeks to grab that for which Christ first grabbed him. Paul is coming to love that which Christ loves for him. He desires different things, in different ways, and toward a different end. Nevertheless, they are still his desires. The "death" Paul and all believers undergo in baptism begins a participation in Christ's resurrected life. This resurrected life is moving toward the perfection of his prior self, not its obliteration. Yes, Paul's body died at some point. Nevertheless, from the perspective of being in Christ, there is much less incongruity between the mortal Paul and the resurrected Paul than Barclay suggests. As Paul will note in 3:21, Christ will transform (μετασχηματίσει) our bodies, not destroy them. Indeed, as Paul has already asserted in 1:20 he plans to continue to "magnify" Christ in his body whether he lives or dies. Death, no doubt, remains an enemy awaiting subjection to Christ. Here in Philippians, at least, Paul does not seem to take the continued presence of death in the world as a significant marker of incongruity (at least in the sense Barclay speaks of it) in the lives of believers.

Without question, God's grace is the effective cause of this transformation in Paul. Nevertheless, Paul describes this transformation in terms of changed or reordered desires. In the context of Phil 3:8–12, the verb ἡγοῦμαι used with nouns regarding profit and loss and the use of διώκω with a specific goal in 3:12 are ways of describing aspects of desiring. These are not simply God's desires for Paul, as the first-person singular indicates, they are Paul's desires, too. Whatever one wants to say about the effective nature of God's gift to Paul, Paul also has to come to desire on his own for himself the things God desires for him.

---

12. See Gorman's discussion in *Cruciformity: Paul's Narrative Spirituality of the Cross* (Grand Rapids: Eerdmans, 2001), 330–32.

Grasping and Being Grasped

To better understand this, one will have to move beyond thinking simply in terms of perfecting God's grace. As the next several verses make clear, Paul's transformation is hardly complete. He still has some way to go. Paul's point here is not to draw a contrast between those who have already reached this goal and himself. Rather, he wants to contrast his current situation with where he wants to end up, and to show how his vision of this end shapes his present behavior.[13]

He continues to reach out, strain forward, press on toward this end (Phil 3:13–14). Most modern commentators assume that Paul is indicating that at some eschatological point in the future Paul would take possession of the "prize of the upward call of God in Christ Jesus." This, of course, is implied by Paul's language here and reflects the efficacy of God's gift. At the same time, this claim raises a number of theological issues which most modern commentators ignore but were important elements in patristic discussions of these verses. For example, would Paul's possession of his prize mean that his desire for God would be satisfied? Would he stop reaching out toward what lies ahead because he had finally reached it? If the answer to these questions were yes, it might, among other things, seriously compromise one's doctrine of God and God's economy of salvation.[14] It would indicate that somehow God could be comprehended in such a way that one could become sated with God. In this light, Gregory of Nyssa, developing themes initially found in Origen, offered a very particular account of the importance of continually stretching out toward God, even after the eschaton.[15] As Nyssa describes it, the proper end of the Christian life is not represented by the attainment of a particular state. Rather, it is the believer's eternal end to grow continually in virtue and love of God. In reflecting on Moses's insatiable capacity to desire God and to grow in virtue, even though he had already achieved great intimacy with God, Nyssa notes that a soul once set on its upward course "will always make its flight yet higher—by its desire of the heavenly things *straining ahead for what is still to come*, as the Apostle says."[16] Growth in virtue is an activity which,

---

13. Paul also says that he forgets what lies behind him. Given that Phil 3:2–8 make it abundantly clear that Paul's memory has not failed him, it would seem that his point here is that he does not allow his past to encumber him.

14. I do not mean to imply here that Nyssa's way of approaching these matters is the only theologically responsible way to do this. Nevertheless, even those theologians who do not follow Nyssa must come up with alternative answers to these issues. My point is that modern commentators largely ignore these matters altogether.

15. See Nyssa's *Life of Moses* 225–26.

16. *Life of Moses* 225.

"causes its capacity to grow through exertion; this kind of activity alone does not slacken its intensity by the effort, but increases it."[17] Nyssa reads Paul to say that the life of a believer is one of ever deepening communion with God in a way that can never be sated. The more one attains, the more one desires. Paradoxically, then, the perfection of this gift is to never be completed. In some sense this requires that the agency of Paul and other believers is dynamic, always intact and active.

Throughout this passage the effective working of God's gift presumes the continued presence of other discrete actors like Paul. These believers work in concert to exemplify, in a manner capable of imitation, the formation and transformation of one another's loves and desires. Indeed, God's incongruous Christ-gift founds a community or communities of believers. God works effectively in their common life to bring the community to its proper end at the day of Christ (Phil 1:6). This is not to say that all believers in Philippi moved in lock step toward this goal. They each have their own identity, capacities, and selves. These are transformed and perfected by the Spirit in ways appropriate to each. Nevertheless, they are united in a common life that shares common patterns of thinking, feeling, and acting as well as habits and practices they all aim to avoid and the disposition to seek the benefit of others rather than themselves (2:1–4).

Conclusion

Whether and how this means that Paul thinks of himself or that we ought to think of Paul as an agent in the modern senses of this term is at best uncertain. Instead we can note that Christ grabs Paul with the aim of getting Paul to grab back. Paul could not have and would not have apprehended Christ on his own. He depends upon Christ's prior gracious activity. Christ's apprehension of Paul begins a transformation that will ultimately fit Paul to grasp better that heavenly prize for which God has called him. Paul understands that his transformation is not yet complete (perhaps there is also a sense in which it will never be completed). As Paul reminds the Philippians, God is ultimately the one who both started a good work in them and will bring it to completion on the day of Christ (Phil 1:6). Nevertheless, Paul also urges the Philippians to act, think, and feel in particular ways, fully assuming that they have the capacities to do this. The transformations that Paul seeks for himself and for the Philippians will have the effect of better fitting them both to love what Christ

17. *Life of Moses* 226.

loves for them, and also to participate better or more fully in that end for which Christ grabbed them. Even here, however, the Spirit's help is essential.

Thus, what we see here is a complex intertwining of God's gracious work in the lives of believers with their loving response in thought, word, and deed, which, with God's help, forms and transforms believers so that they are ever more receptive to God's grace, and so on. Christ's grabbing of Paul and Paul's reaching out to grab Christ is designed to draw them ever closer so that it is not only increasingly difficult to disentangle these strands of grace and response, it becomes less and less important to do so.

Barclay's *Paul and the Gift* cracks open new vistas for thinking about Paul and grace. That he did not engage Philippians is hardly a criticism of his work. In extending that work into other Pauline letters, such as Philippians, however, I hope to have made the case that many of the sharp disjunctions that Barclay notes in Romans and Galatians between the Christ-gift and the communities of believers founded and sustained by that gift are refined in Philippians and perhaps better accounted for in terms of Mike Gorman's work on cruciformity and participation, showing that these disjunctions may not be so sharp after all.

Chapter 7

Baptized into Christ: Romans 6:3–4—*the* Text on Baptism and Participation

Klyne Snodgrass

No one has done more to emphasize participation with Christ than Michael Gorman,[1] and no text focuses more on participation ideas than Rom 6, a text that is not about baptism but uses baptism as proof that Christians have died to sin (v. 2). I am honored to offer these thoughts to one who has contributed so much, both with his scholarship and with his life.

I have argued earlier that participation is the language both scholars and the church should recover and emphasize,[2] for the gospel is a gospel of participation, and participation does not allow for the passivity we find in many who claim to believe. Faith is indeed obedience, as Michael has argued.[3] Some people are so fearful of salvation by works that obedience never happens. The misunderstanding of salvation by works may always be an issue, but it is not the problem of most people in the modern era who are more likely not to care about works at all. The problem Rom 6 confronts is somewhat similar—the

---

1. See e.g., his *Cruciformity: Paul's Narrative Spirituality of the Cross* (Grand Rapids: Eerdmans, 2001), 32: "Paul conceives of identification with and participation in the death of Jesus as the believer's fundamental experience of Christ" and 131: "Faith, then, for Paul is first of all cruciform participation with Christ that liberates participants from the hostile powers that rule human existence and brings them into the powerful sphere of Christ's benevolent lordship and community."

2. "The Gospel of Participation," in *Earliest Christianity within the Boundaries of Judaism: Essays in Honor of Bruce Chilton*, ed. Alan J. Avery-Peck, Craig A. Evans, and Jacob Neusner (Leiden: Brill, 2016), 413–30.

3. Gorman, *Cruciformity*, 133.

thought that grace enables sin instead of requiring a radically ethical transformation to life with Christ.

No one can say any part of Romans has been neglected, but Rom 6 still has not been given its due.[4] With justice N. T. Wright accuses interpreters of tiptoeing around Rom 6,[5] but Rom 6 is *the* chapter on participation and on dying and rising with Christ. Surely dying and rising with Christ, being in Christ, and participation with Christ are central features of Paul's thought, whatever else is said. Dying and rising with Christ and the conviction of being in Christ summarize well what Paul understands by "faith," but participation, dying and rising with Christ, and the conviction of being in Christ are all rooted in Paul's understanding of being *baptized into* Christ. To understand being baptized into Christ involves one in a *fascinating* discussion of important issues, not least the following: the origin of baptism and its significance, the prepositions used with baptismal language and their intent, the significance of the resulting variety of baptismal expressions, the question to what degree the language is metaphorical, and the theological result of taking Paul's words seriously.

If there is any doubt that Rom 6:1–11 is about participation with Christ, note the following:

> Three references to "baptized into" (v. 3: ἐβαπτίσθημεν εἰς Χριστὸν Ἰησοῦν, εἰς τὸν θάνατον αὐτοῦ ἐβαπτίσθημεν, v. 4: διὰ τοῦ βαπτίσματος εἰς τὸν θάνατον)
> Four occurrences of "with" compounds (v. 4: συνετάφημεν, v. 5: σύμφυτοι, v. 6: συνεσταυρώθη, v.8: συζήσομεν)
> One occurrence of "with Christ" (v. 8: σὺν Χριστῷ)
> One occurrence of "in Christ Jesus" (v. 11: ἐν Χριστῷ Ἰησοῦ)
> One occurrence of "just as Christ... thus also we" (v. 4: ὥσπερ... Χριστὸς ... οὕτως καὶ ἡμεῖς)

This text is not about participation; it is about death to sin, but participation with Christ mirrored in baptism is the center of Paul's theology and the means by which he makes his theological-ethical argument.

---

4. There are relatively few monographs on Rom 6, and Mark Reasoner in his history of the interpretation of Romans omits chapter 6 entirely, as well as chapter 2 and everything after 13:7. See his *Romans in Full Circle: A History of Interpretation* (Louisville: Westminster John Knox, 2005).

5. "Response to Kevin Vanhoozer," in *Jesus, Paul and the People of God: A Theological Dialogue with N. T. Wright*, ed. Nicholas Perrin and Richard B. Hays (Downers Grove, IL: IVP Academic, 2011), 261.

Baptism

The short of it is that we have not done justice to baptism and its significance for Paul, even if in Corinth, at least, he did not baptize many people (1 Cor 1:13-17). In crucial contexts where Paul addressed issues concerning how people should live because of the gospel, he frequently turned to baptism. Thirty-five years prior to the writing of Romans, from all we know, *baptism* did not exist. What happened to make baptism foundational for Paul's thinking?

The Origins of Baptism

How little we know about the origin of baptism is striking. Certainly, ritual washings in the OT and Judaism, especially with the use of *miqwa'ot*, provide an important background for the origin of baptism, but they do not explain *why* baptism began, and some real oddities exist. *Miqwa'ot* emerged in the second century BCE during the Hasmonean rule as a means to ritual purity but are infrequent in Palestine after 70 CE.[6] Full immersion was required so that water touched all parts of the body.[7] People often speak of Jewish proselyte baptism as a possible background for Christian baptism, but increasingly an early date for proselyte baptism is rejected.[8] Proselyte baptism is not mentioned in places where one would expect it, such as with the conversion of Aseneth in Joseph and Aseneth, of Achior in Jdt 14:10, of Izates in Josephus, *Ant.* 20.34-46, anywhere else in Josephus or Philo, or in the Mishnah tractate on *Miqwa'ot*. Texts supposedly about proselyte baptism are later than the NT, and some texts, such as *m. Pes.* 8:8 and Epictetus, *Diatr.* 2.9.19-21, presumed to be about proselyte baptism, are not.[9] Further, "proselyte baptism" is a mis-

---

6. Jonathan D. Lawrence, *Washing in Water: Trajectories of Ritual Bathing in the Hebrew Bible and Second Temple Literature*, AcBib 23 (Atlanta: SBL Press, 2006), 190. See also E. P. Sanders, *Jewish Law from Jesus to the Mishnah: Five Studies* (London: SCM, 1990), 214-27.

7. See, e.g., 11Q19 XLV, 15-16, and note the depth of surviving *miqwa'ot*. See also *m. Miqw.* 1:7-2:2; 8:5-9:3. A *miqweh* was required to hold at least forty *seahs* of water, enough to cover a body.

8. Shaye J. D. Cohen, "Is 'Proselyte Baptism' Mentioned in the Mishnah? The Interpretation of *m. Pesahim* 8.8 (= *m. Eduyot* 5.2)," in *Pursuing the Text: Studies in Honor of Ben Zion Wacholder on the Occasion of His Seventieth Birthday*, ed. John C. Reeves and John Kampen, JSOTSup 184 (Sheffield: Sheffield Academic Press, 1994), 278-92; Lars Hartman, *'Into the Name of the Lord Jesus': Baptism in the Early Church* (Edinburgh: T & T Clark, 1997), 5-8, 31; Everett Ferguson, *Baptism in the Early Church: History, Theology, and Liturgy in the First Five Centuries* (Grand Rapids: Eerdmans, 2009), 76-82, 86. See also G. R. Beasley-Murray, *Baptism in the New Testament* (Grand Rapids: Eerdmans, 1962), 18-31.

9. See Cohen, "Is 'Proselyte Baptism' Mentioned in the Mishnah?," 291-92; Ferguson,

nomer. The first lustration of many lustrations is *not* a baptism. If the first sure reference to proselyte baptism is *b. Yeb* 46a,[10] even those arguing for the origin of proselyte baptism at the end of the first century are on shaky ground, given the uncertainty of rabbinic attributions.

Certainly, Christian baptism develops from the practice of John the Baptist, but why did *he* start baptizing? Although some suggest his baptisms were repeatable like Jewish lustrations,[11] that is unlikely. It fits neither the aorist verb tenses in the description of what was said at Jesus's baptism and the exchange in Acts 19:1-5 nor the use of the singular βάπτισμα. If John were merely asking people to do in the Jordan River what they were doing in a *miqweh*, he would have had no impact. His baptism was not a lustration. Whereas lustration was self-administered, John baptized people. That he did so in the Jordan in relation to his message about the kingdom made baptism an eschatological act. His baptism points to the expectation that God would purify his people in the last days.[12] But why was this act called βάπτισμα resulting in John being known as ὁ βαπτιστής, and what Hebrew/Aramaic term lay behind this language? People presume it would be טבל,[13] but here is a real oddity. The verb for ablutions in the OT is רחץ, not טבל, which in the OT is used of dipping a finger or foot,

---

Baptism in the Early Church, 76-80; and W. A. Oldfather's footnote in the Loeb translation of Epictetus's *Discourses*, 272-73.

10. Adela Collins, "The Origin of Baptism," *Studia Liturgica* 19 (1989): 28-46, 34. This tradition is connected to Rabbis Eliezer ben Hyrcanus and Joshua ben Hananiah active from 90 to 130 CE. The reliability of the tradition is another story. See also Ferguson, *Baptism in the Early Church*, 78. Shaye Cohen, with hesitation, dates this rather bare, legal ceremony to the second or early third century ("The Rabbinic Conversion Ceremony," in his *The Beginnings of Jewishness: Boundaries, Varieties, Uncertainties* [Berkeley: University of California Press, 1999], 198-238). Dieter Sänger says there is no explicit reference to proselyte baptism prior to 135 CE and points to *Sifre on Numbers* 108 (on Num 15:14) and to *b. Ker.* 9a for the explicit connection of circumcision, baptism, and sacrifice for entrance into the covenant ("'Ist er heraufgestiegen, gilt er in jeder Hinsicht als ein Israelit' (bYev 47b): Das Proselytentauchbad im frühen Judentum," in *Ablution, Initiation, and Baptism/Waschungen, Initiation, und Taufe*, 3 vols., ed. David Hellholm, Tor Vegge, Øyvind Norderval, and Chiste Hellholm, BZNW 176 [Berlin: De Gruyter, 2011], 1:291-334).

11. Among others, see Bruce Chilton, "John the Baptist: His Immersion and His Death," in *Dimensions of Baptism: Biblical and Theological Studies*, ed. Stanley E. Porter and Anthony R. Cross, JSNTSup 234 (Sheffield: Sheffield Academic Press, 2002), 25-44, 37.

12. See e.g., Isa 4:2-4; Ezek 26:35-36; Zech 13:1. See also Hartman, *'Into the Name of the Lord Jesus,'* 9-22; and Robert L. Webb, *John the Baptizer and Prophet: A Socio-Historical Study*, JSNTSup 62 (Sheffield: Sheffield Academic, 1991), 196-202.

13. See James D. G. Dunn, *Jesus Remembered*, vol. 1 of *Christianity in the Making* (Grand Rapids: Eerdmans, 2003), 356.

etc. and is not used of immersion except in reference to Namaan in 2 Kgs 5.[14] Was John suggesting Jews needed cleansing as much as a gentile? Probably there is no allusion to Namaan, for there is no suggestion of dipping seven times. Further, טבל is *not* used of the frequent ritual washings mentioned in the Qumran scrolls, except for three occurrences all in the same document.[15] Yet, טבל is *the* language used in the Mishnah and later rabbinic writings for ritual immersions.[16] What caused the change in language? Is it because rabbis wanted to emphasize full immersion, which רחץ did not necessarily do?[17] That is not convincing, given that טבל in the OT does not usually mean full immersion either.

The concern among Jews for ritual purity was not devoid of concern for moral living, at least among some groups. The people at Qumran connected the two and viewed ritual washing without moral change as ineffective.[18] (See 1QS II, 25–III, 8;[19] V, 13–15; 4Q 255, f.2, 1–5; 4Q 257, f.3, 6–14; 4Q 414 f.2, ii, 3–4; 4Q 512 f.2 ii, 3–4). Like John's baptism to some degree, they viewed their washings as preparation for the end. The same connection with moral living is evident too in *Sib. Or.* 4:162–165. John's baptism seems to have had less concern for ritual purity and much more focus on cleansing from sin and promotion of righteous living. He sought to prepare a righteous group of people for the coming kingdom. Surely though there is an implicit anti-temple critique in his calling people to baptism in the Jordan rather than ritual cleansing in a *miqweh* for entrance into the temple complex.[20] What was true of John's baptism apparently is mirrored in Jesus's baptism and in any baptizing he or his disciples did (as in John 3:22 and 4:1–2). Surely the early church's continuation of baptism

---

14. And metaphorically of Job in Job 9:31.

15. 4Q 274 (4Q Tohorot A) 2i, 4–5. There is one occurrence of הטבילה referring to an immersion pool in 3Q 15 (3Q Copper Scroll) I, 11–12.

16. Note too tractate *m. Tebul Yom*.

17. Lawrence, *Washing in Water*, 110n70.

18. See the treatment of the connection between ritual and moral purity by Samuli Siikavirta, *Baptism and Cognition in Romans 6-8: Paul's Ethics beyond 'Indicative' and 'Imperative,'* WUNT 2/407 (Tübingen: Mohr-Siebeck, 2015), 55–67.

19. The translation of ll.4b–5a in the Dead Sea Scrolls Electronic Library as "He cannot be sanctified by baptism in oceans and rivers, nor purified by mere ritual bathing" is misleading. The word "baptism" translates no Hebrew word. Assumedly it is used in the translation because of יתקדש meaning "to consecrate," but notice l.9 where the same form is translated "purged." Whether this washing was for initiation is uncertain.

20. See Ferguson, *Baptism in the Early Church*, 90. Of course, *miqwa'ot* were in many places not connected to the temple.

Baptized into Christ

is rooted in the baptism of Jesus and in his command to baptize.[21] Both John's eschatological and moral emphases continue with Christian baptism, but any anti-temple emphasis seems to have been lost.

Baptism and Death

Another area where justice has not been done to βαπτίζειν language is its association with death. People know Paul associated baptism with death, but they do not think much about such a connection before Paul. They usually think instead of washing/cleansing, and three of the four occurrences of the word in the LXX have this meaning (2 Kgs 5:14; Jdt 12:7; and Sir 34:25; the fourth occurrence, Isa 21:4, is metaphorical of being overwhelmed by transgression). James Dunn even argues baptism was *not* an obvious symbol of death, notes Jesus's association of the two (Mark 10:38/Luke 12:50), and says the connection is probably Christian.[22] Perhaps it is not an obvious symbol of death to us, but it was in the ancient world. Philo does not use βαπτίζειν of washing at all, Josephus has this meaning only in relation to John the Baptist, and few other Greek writers use the word of washing. Except for one literal occurrence for sinking in water, Philo only uses the word metaphorically of the soul or mind being overwhelmed by passions. Apart from reference to John the Baptist, Josephus uses the word of ships sinking, of people drowning, of people drowning someone else, of a city being destroyed, and metaphorically of drunkenness.[23] The most graphic text is *J. W.* 2.476, which describes a man "baptizing" his sword into his own entrails. When Josephus discusses the lustrations of the Essenes or of Bannus (*Life* 11–12), he does not use βαπτίζειν.

When one looks at ancient Greek literature more broadly, the uses evident in Philo and Josephus are frequent: references to ships sinking, people drowning or being drowned, a knife "baptized" into a fetus, and metaphorical uses of being overwhelmed by passions or drunkenness.[24] Lucian, *Timon* 44 is graphic: "If another be swept past me by a winter torrent, and stretch out his hands for

---

21. However one deals with Matt 28:19–20. See the discussion in Beasley-Murray, *Baptism in the New Testament*, 70–88.

22. James D. G. Dunn, *Romans 1–8*, WBC 38A (Dallas: Word, 1988), 312; similarly, Ferguson surprisingly says destruction does not inhere in the word (*Baptism in the Early Church*, 49, 52).

23. See respectively as examples *Ant.* 9.212; *J. W.* 3.423; *Ant.* 15.55; *J. W.* 3.196; *Ant.* 10.169.

24. E.g., Chariton, *Chaer.* 3.4.6.3; Diodorus Siculus, *Library* 16.80; Soranus, *Gynecology* 2.63; Plato, *Symposium* 176b.

aid, then let mine press him down head under (κεφαλὴν βαπτίζοντα), that he never rise again." Occurrences with the meaning "washing" are rare.[25]

Nor does Paul explicitly connect washing and baptism. The language of 1 Cor 6:11 (ἀπελούσασθε ... ἐν τῷ ὀνόματι τοῦ κυρίου Ἰησοῦ Χριστοῦ καὶ ἐν τῷ πνεύματι τοῦ θεοῦ ἡμῶν) *probably* alludes to baptism. Ephesians 5:26 and Titus 3:5 are less convincing but may also be texts about washing that allude to baptism. Still, washing is just not a Pauline emphasis with baptism.

If the connection to washing is infrequent in Paul's world, the connection to death is not. Baptism frequently pointed to death, and Jesus's association of baptism and death should not be ignored. Mark 10:38/Luke 12:50 cannot refer to washing. Paul's contemporaries would find his statements connecting baptism and death unsurprising. Some scholars have seen the connection. Karl Barth said baptism implied a threat of death, and Sanday and Headlam described baptism as a sort of funeral.[26] Martin Luther more poignantly said, "Your baptism is nothing less than grace clutching you by the throat: a gracefull throttling by which your sin is submerged in order that you may remain under grace. Come thus to thy baptism. Give thyself up to be drowned in baptism and killed by the mercy of thy dear God, saying: 'Drown me and throttle me, dear Lord, for henceforth I will gladly die to sin with Thy Son.'"[27] We will not do justice to Paul and Rom 6 without seeing the connection of baptism

---

25. For one example see Plutarch, *Superst.* section 3: "then call in the old crone who performs magic purifications, dip yourself in the ocean, and sit down on the ground and spend the whole day there."

26. See respectively Karl Barth, *The Teaching of the Church Regarding Baptism*, trans. Ernest A. Payne (London: SCM, 1948), 11; and William Sanday and Arthur C. Headlam, *A Critical and Exegetical Commentary on the Epistle to the Romans*, 2nd ed., ICC (Edinburgh: T & T Clark, 1896), 157. Whether death was implied with the baptism of John and with baptism in Acts cannot be shown. Some think death is implied with John's baptism, e.g., Hartmut Stegemann, *The Library of Qumran: On the Essenes, Qumran, John the Baptist, and Jesus* (Grand Rapids: Eerdmans, 1993), 219; Morna Hooker, "John's Baptism: A Prophetic Sign," in *The Holy Spirit and Christian Origins: Essays in Honor of James D. G. Dunn*, ed. Graham N. Stanton, Bruce W. Longenecker, and Stephen C. Barton (Grand Rapids: Eerdmans, 2004), 22-40, 24; and J. Ysebaert, *Greek Baptismal Terminology: Its Origins and Early Development, Græcitas Christianorum Primæva* (Nijmegen: Dekker & Van de Vegt, 1962), 39. If John's baptism implied death, then early Christian baptism did as well. The focus on repentance and the Spirit could point in this direction.

27. This statement is from a sermon on Rom 6:3-11 preached on the sixth Sunday after Trinity. The translation is from Karl Barth's *The Epistle to the Romans* (London: Oxford University Press, 1933), 194. A more sedate translation is in *Sermons by Martin Luther*, ed. and trans. John Nicholas Lenker (Grand Rapids: Baker, 1988), VIII:122.

and death, a connection evident as well in 1 Cor 1:13 ("Paul was not crucified for you, was he, or were you baptized into the name of Paul?").

Tradition

People often suggest Rom 6:3-4 reflects early Christian tradition, and there are good grounds for the suggestion.[28] Several other texts have the same or similar language—Rom 13:14; Gal 3:26-29; 4:7; 1 Cor 12:12-13; Col 2:12-13, 20; 3:1-5, 9-11; Eph 4:22-24. Note the following common themes:

- Baptized into (ἐβαπτίσθημεν εἰς)—Rom 6:3 into Christ/his death; Gal 3:27 into Christ; 1 Cor 12:13 into his body
- Buried with him through/in baptism—Rom 6:4; Col 2:12
- The old being crucified with Christ—Rom 6:6 and putting off the old being and putting on the new—Col 3:9-11; Eph 4:22-24; cf. Rom 6:4 for "newness"
- Putting on Christ/the Lord—Gal 3:27; Rom 13:14
- Unity established through the removal of divisions between Jews and Gentiles, slaves and free, and male and female—Gal 3:28; 1 Cor 12:13; Col 3:11[29]—which is based on Joel 2:28-32 (Hebrew 3:1-5)
- Crucifixion with/dying with Christ—Rom 6:5, 6, 8; Col 2:20; 3:1-5[30]
- Focus on resurrection—Rom 6:4-5, 8-9; Col 2:12-13; 3:1
- End of slavery—Rom 6:6-7; Gal 4:7

The parallels are striking, and while one cannot *prove* Paul used early baptismal tradition in these texts, it is likely, especially because of ἀγνοεῖτε in Rom 6:3 ("Are you unaware?"). Paul does not refer to baptism much, and we should be careful not to assume allusions without strong evidence. The mention of water is not proof of reference to baptism, but the texts listed above

---

28. E.g., Ulrich Wilckens, *Der Brief an die Römer*, 3 vols., EKKNT (Zürich: Benziger, 1980), 2:11; Dunn, *Romans 1-8*, 308. There is no basis for Hans Dieter Betz's view that Paul was correcting an inadequate understanding ("Transferring a Ritual: Paul's Interpretation of Baptism in Romans 6," in *Paul in His Hellenistic Context*, ed. Troels Engberg-Pedersen [Minneapolis: Fortress, 1995], 84-118).

29. Only Gal 3:28 mentions male and female. Although 1 Cor 7:7-24 is not explicitly about baptism, it does reflect the social divisions of Gal 3:28, treating male/female relations while also mentioning the categories of circumcised/uncircumcised and slave/free. Does this text, too, mirror baptismal thinking?

30. Dying and rising with Christ appears elsewhere, of course. See Rom 8:11-13; 2 Cor 4:10-12; Gal 2:19-20; Phil 3:9-11.

either mention baptism explicitly, are in a context where baptism is explicit, or have language paralleling such texts (such as Rom 13:14). At the very least we must say that baptismal language permeated Paul's thought and provided the theological foundation at crucial times in his discourse with churches about the significance of life in Christ.

Prepositions

Prepositions are notoriously ambiguous, sometimes interchangeable, and frustratingly unclear, nowhere more so than with βαπτίζειν. Compare:

Matt 3:6 (καὶ ἐβαπτίζοντο ἐν τῷ Ἰορδάνῃ ποταμῷ) and 3:11 (βαπτίζω ἐν ὕδατι ... βαπτίσει ἐν πνεύματι ἁγίῳ καὶ πυρί[31]) with Mark 1:9 (ἐβαπτίσθη εἰς τὸν Ἰορδάνην) and John 3:23 (βαπτίζων ἐν Αἰνὼν)
Matt 28:19 (βαπτίζοντες αὐτοὺς εἰς τὸ ὄνομα τοῦ πατρὸς καὶ τοῦ υἱοῦ καὶ τοῦ ἁγίου πνεύματος) with Acts 2:38 (βαπτισθήτω ἕκαστος ὑμῶν ἐπὶ τῷ ὀνόματι Ἰησοῦ Χριστοῦ), 10:48 (ἐν τῷ ὀνόματι Ἰησοῦ Χριστοῦ βαπτισθῆναι), 19:5 (ἐβαπτίσθησαν εἰς τὸ ὄνομα τοῦ κυρίου Ἰησοῦ), and 1 Cor 1:13 (εἰς τὸ ὄνομα Παύλου ἐβαπτίσθητε)

The element for baptism can be expressed with either ἐν or εἰς,[32] but ἐν in Matt 3:11/John 1:26 could be instrumental, and in John 3:23 designates the area, not the element. Baptism can be on the name (ἐπί, presumably "on the basis of the name"), in the name (ἐν), or into the name (εἰς), but what is intended with the last two?

The preposition εἰς has quite varied possible nuances: in, on, into, unto, to, at, toward, about, for, for the purpose of, and against. The central idea seems to be direction toward, but for us to designate a nuance means we determine the nuance *we need in English* or some other language to understand the relations in Greek. The nuance is controlled more by the surrounding words than by the preposition. Like all words, by itself a preposition has only possible meaning until set in relation to other words. With a directional preposition like εἰς the verbal ideas are especially important, but because of aporia in all language, much has to be filled in from the broader context.

---

31. Several texts in Mark, Luke, and Acts have the bare dative with ὕδωρ but use ἐν with πνεῦμα (Mark 1:8; Luke 3:16; Acts 1:5; 11:16).
32. Εἰς and ἐν can be used interchangeably, apparently evidenced by Matt 5:34-35 which has "... μὴ ὀμόσαι ... μήτε ἐν τῇ γῇ ... μήτε εἰς Ἱεροσόλυμα." Paul does not use them interchangeably. See Murray J. Harris, *Prepositions and Theology in the Greek New Testament: An Essential Reference Resource for Exegesis* (Grand Rapids: Zondervan, 2012), 85-86.

The difficulty with εἰς is especially evident with some texts. What do the following mean?

Matt 10:41: ὁ δεχόμενος προφήτην εἰς ὄνομα προφήτου—in keeping with what the prophet stands for? with respect for who he is?

Matt 18:20: οὗ γάρ εἰσιν δύο ἢ τρεῖς συνηγμένοι εἰς τὸ ἐμὸν ὄνομα—unto the honoring of my name/me? (Cf. 1 Cor 5:4)

2 Cor 1:21: ὁ δὲ βεβαιῶν ἡμᾶς σὺν ὑμῖν εἰς Χριστὸν καὶ χρίσας ἡμᾶς θεός—established into Christ, similar to baptized into Christ's body (1 Cor 12:13)? The following verse (ὁ καὶ σφραγισάμενος ἡμᾶς καὶ δοὺς τὸν ἀρραβῶνα τοῦ πνεύματος ἐν ταῖς καρδίαις ἡμῶν) suggests this text is also about baptism.[33]

With βαπτίζειν εἰς, one of the important questions is whether there is a difference between ἐν τῷ ὀνόματι Ἰησοῦ Χριστοῦ, εἰς τὸ ὄνομα τοῦ κυρίου, and εἰς Χριστόν. Some, like C. E. B. Cranfield, assume all such expressions are equivalent,[34] but that is not the case. Baptism ἐν τῷ ὀνόματι Ἰησοῦ Χριστοῦ occurs only in Acts 10:48,[35] but what the expression means is not obvious. The verb is passive. It is one thing to do something in the name of Jesus, but it is quite another thing to have something done to you in the name of Jesus. This text could mean baptized with reference to Jesus, on the basis of who Jesus is, or it could be an allusion to the name of Jesus being called upon by the baptized person or by the one baptizing (see Acts 2:38; 22:16). It is possible there is an allusion to Joel 2:28-32, obviously a crucial text for NT thought about salvation and baptism for three reasons: (1) the gift of the Spirit associated with baptism and faith;[36] (2) the removal of the distinctions between Jew and gentile, slave and free, and male and female;[37] (3) the emphasis on calling on the name of the Lord.[38]

The phrase βαπτίζειν εἰς does not occur frequently, only at Matt 28:19; Acts 8:16; 19:3, 4, 5; Rom 6:3, 4; 1 Cor 1:13, 15; 10:2; 12:13; and Gal 3:27. The meaning of the texts in Matthew and Acts is difficult to determine, for there is little

---

33. See Hartman, 'Into the Name of the Lord Jesus,' 68.

34. C. E. B. Cranfield, *A Critical and Exegetical Commentary on the Epistle to the Romans*, 2 vols., ICC (Edinburgh: T & T Clark, 1975 and 1979), 1:301.

35. If 1 Cor 6:11 alludes to baptism, it could be a second occurrence, but ἐν here could be instrumental: "But you were washed, set apart, and acquitted by the name of the Lord Jesus Christ and by the Spirit of our God."

36. E.g., Acts 2:38; Gal 3:14.

37. Gal 3:28.

38. Acts 2:17-21, 38; 9:14, 21; 15:17; 22:16; Rom 10:13; 1 Cor 1:2; Jas 2:7.

help in the context.³⁹ With Paul it is different. Paul shows awareness of the expression βαπτίζειν εἰς τὸ ὄνομα in treating divisions at Corinth (1 Cor 1:13, 15), but *he only uses βαπτίζειν εἰς when treating baptism*. Whether his use of the shorter form should be understood as equivalent to βαπτίζειν εἰς τὸ ὄνομα is debated⁴⁰ and depends on the meaning attached to the latter. Ὄνομα could be merely a cipher for Christ, and the two would be the same. W. Heitmüller thought the phrase was adapted from accounting, that something was posted in someone's name, and thought it conveyed ownership.⁴¹ This is hardly convincing for βαπτίζειν and the NT uses, even if "ownership" is a factor on other grounds. Some take the phrase to mean baptized "with reference to Christ," often seeing it as parallel to לשׁם in the OT.⁴² This does not do justice to Paul's texts. The expression does not merely say "This is a Christian baptism," as if opposed to John's baptism or as if there were another kind. Some think Paul meant something like baptized "into the fellowship of people who belong to Christ"—that is, into the church,⁴³ but this does no justice to the depth of Paul's thought. With βαπτίζειν εἰς Paul means baptized *into* Christ. Baptism moves one into Christ. It is directional, incorporative, eschatological, and a life-changing event.

Romans 6:3-4

Just when one wants to take Paul's words seriously, however, the discussion becomes difficult, partly because people understand terms differently, partly because of the influence of confessional traditions, partly because of wanting to avoid crass misunderstanding and the devaluing of, or overemphasis on, baptism, and partly because people have difficulty understanding how we can be in another person—e.g., E. P. Sanders's saying we lack a category of reality

---

39. BDAG, "βαπτίζω," 164, says Acts 19:3 "means, as the answer shows, *in reference to what (baptism) were you baptized?* i.e. what kind of baptism did you receive?" I do not think the examples are convincing. Should it be "to what did you commit yourself in baptizing?"

40. E.g., Rudolf Schnackenburg says there is no difference (*Baptism in the Thought of St. Paul: A Study in Pauline Theology*, trans. G. R. Beasley-Murray [Oxford: Basil Blackwell, 1964], 23) while Ferguson says there is (*Baptism in the Early Church*, 155–56).

41. Wilheim Heitmüller, *"Im Namen Jesu": Eine sprach- und religionsgeschichtliche Untersuchung zum Neuen Testament, speziell zur altchristlichen Taufe* (Göttingen: Vandenhoeck & Ruprecht, 1903), 100–109, 127.

42. E.g., Beasley-Murray, *Baptism in the New Testament*, 129–30, 147; Dunn, *Romans 1–8*, 311. Often people suggest this and then proceed to a much deeper meaning.

43. Craig Blomberg, *It Is Fulfilled: A New Testament Theology* (Waco: Baylor University Press, 2018), 319.

to appropriate Paul's thought.[44] Most want to argue that baptism is not merely a symbol but also that it is not magic. Some understand βαπτίζειν εἰς in a local/spatial sense, but others, like R. Schnackenburg, downplay a local sense. Yet he speaks of a profound ontological relation, but what does that mean?[45] He like several others is guilty of using double talk, seemingly diminishing Paul's language and then making sweeping statements that emphasize participation at some deep level. Some are happy to speak of mysticism, especially Albert Schweitzer and Alfred Wikenhauser,[46] while others would not get near the word. Schweitzer and Wikenhauser shun the idea that union with Christ is merely subjective, with the latter insisting it is objective,[47] but what does "objective" mean in such a context? The relation of faith and baptism is a major issue. Is baptism the event that establishes union with Christ,[48] or is it an affirmation of a union already established on other grounds?[49] Does Paul speak metaphorically in Rom 6 of baptism as spiritual baptism while physical baptism is a secondary issue?[50] I doubt Paul would agree. Being baptized into Christ—into union with Christ—is a wonderful and absolutely essential feature of Christian thinking, but what does it really mean?

Perhaps the place to start is with the question whether Paul's use of baptism is metaphorical. James Dunn pointed to Jesus's use of baptism as a metaphor for death and suggested Paul mirrored that use to explain the beginning of salvation as baptism into death. In doing so Dunn states that the metaphor of baptism "had been quite far removed in conception from the actual performance of baptism in water."[51] He admits the rite may still be connected to the metaphor, but his argument has not found much acceptance or treatment

---

44. E. P. Sanders, *Paul and Palestinian Judaism: A Comparison of Patterns of Religion* (Philadelphia: Fortress, 1977), 522–23.

45. Schnackenburg, *Baptism in the Thought of St. Paul*, 21–23.

46. Albert Schweitzer, *The Mysticism of Paul the Apostle*, trans. William Montgomery (London: Black, 1931) and Alfred Wikenhauser, *Pauline Mysticism: Christ in the Mystical Teaching of St. Paul*, trans. Joseph Cunningham (New York: Herder and Herder, 1960).

47. Wikenhauser, *Pauline Mysticism*, 42, 94, 103–5, 124.

48. Schweitzer, *The Mysticism of Paul the Apostle*, 19, 116–17, 206, 261; Wikenhauser, *Pauline Mysticism*, 63, 100, 104–5, 109–18, 123–32, 144–48, 153.

49. Cranfield, *A Critical and Exegetical Commentary on the Epistle to the Romans*, 303.

50. Constantine R. Campbell, *Paul and Union with Christ: An Exegetical and Theological Study* (Grand Rapids: Zondervan, 2012), 336.

51. Dunn, *The Theology of Paul the Apostle* (Grand Rapids: Eerdmans, 1998), 452; and see his "Baptized as Metaphor," in *Baptism, the New Testament and the Church: Historical and Contemporary Studies*, ed. Stanley F. Porter and Anthony R. Cross, JSNTSup 171 (Sheffield: Sheffield Academic Press, 1999), 294–310.

and understandably so. If Rom 6:3–4, Gal 3:26–29, and related texts reflect an early Christian tradition, then baptism has to be front and center. Even if Paul did not think of the act of baptism, his readers certainly would, but the issue is more complicated. The word "baptized" is not metaphorical, but "into Christ" and "into his death" are. One is not "literally" plunged into another person, and death is not an entity into which one can be plunged while still living. These expressions are not literal, but that does not make them any less real. What do the words "literal" and "metaphorical" even mean? Metaphor joins two seemingly unrelated ideas to create a new and forceful framework for understanding, and nearly all language is metaphorical to some degree—and we hardly even notice. For example, 1 Cor 3:10–15 is almost entirely metaphor, and its meaning is obvious and enlightening. Of course, it is not sufficient to say something is metaphorical without saying what the metaphor intends.

A key ingredient in understanding Rom 6 is Paul's Adam-Christ contrast with the resulting focus on two realms or lordships, one into which sin, death, and law entered and ruled and one into which grace came, brought life, and rules (5:12–21).[52] If through Adam sin came, through Christ grace came, and people live either in sin and in the flesh or in grace and in Christ. Paul has a spheres of influence theology,[53] and baptism plays a key role in such thinking.

Baptism marks the movement into a new sphere of existence. In Gal 3:27 baptism into Christ means that one is clothed with Christ. One is taken into and determined by his existence. One lives in his sphere of existence and is determined by his character, life, and dominion. In 1 Cor 12:13 one is taken into the body of Christ along with others of faith. They are all part of his body and are to live reflecting that unity. In Rom 6:3–4 one is moved into the sphere of Christ's existence, his death, and his life with the result that one lives under grace (6:14). Paul understood that baptism expresses so close an involvement and *solidarity* with Christ that one owns and participates in the narrative of his death and his life. What happened to Christ happens to believers.[54] This is Paul's understanding of the meaning of faith, as the use of σύμφυτοι in 6:5 shows, regardless of whether one understands the term as "grafted onto" or

---

52. Among many see Robert C. Tannehill, *Dying and Rising with Christ* (Berlin: Alfred Töpelmann, 1967), esp. 7–43.

53. Which is the assumption of his "in Christ" theology and his description of life "under sin." See the description of Paul's transfer terms in E. P. Sanders, *Paul, the Law, and the Jewish People* (Philadelphia: Fortress, 1983), 7–10.

54. Arland J. Hultgren, *Paul's Letter to the Romans: A Commentary* (Grand Rapids: Eerdmans, 2011), 246.

merely as "united with."⁵⁵ One is joined to Christ so that Christ becomes the environment in which the baptized lives.

Romans 7:1–6, especially v. 4, provides commentary on Paul's thought. Romans 6:3 says you were baptized into Christ and into his death; Rom 7:4 says you died to the law through the body of Christ so you might be joined to another. A death has occurred, breaking all previous commitments, and one is *joined to Christ to live in newness of life*. The two texts are affirming the same reality.

At issue are questions of identity. Is identity dominated and determined by sin, death, and the old age or by Christ, grace, and newness of life? Paul does not mean baptized into Christ literally, but he does point to a reality. The thinking with βαπτίζειν εἰς in Rom 6:3–4 and related texts is the basis of and origin of Paul's whole "in Christ" theology.

One cannot be baptized into Christ or the body of Christ without being baptized into the death of Christ, as Rom 6:3–6 insists. Faith means one identifies with the death of Christ and with—or because of—the life of Christ. The focus of the text is on death, a participation and identification with the death of Christ and thereby having died to the old realm.⁵⁶ Christian faith for Paul means being crucified with Christ and a resultant death of one's old being (Rom 6:6–7; cf. Gal 2:19 and Col 2:12). The concern is transformation of life. If you died to sin, why would you still live in it (6:2; cf. Col 2:20)?

Romans 6:4 speaks of being buried (συνετάφημεν) with Christ in baptism, probably alluding to the tradition in 1 Cor 15:3–4. The only other occurrence of this verb is in Col 2:12, again in connection with baptism. The idea in Rom 6:6 of being crucified with Christ (συνεσταυρώθη) is closely related, and this verb elsewhere in Pauline material occurs only in Gal 2:19. It is important to emphasize that these verses do not mean "crucified and buried like Christ" but "with him"—that there is a participation, a solidarity with Christ in his death and with Christ in being buried.

Does the language of burial reflect the rite of immersion? It is here that some odd things are said and that people are guilty of double talk. Can we convince ourselves that, seen from the outside, the ritual has little resemblance to the meaning or that the focus in Rom 6 is not on the ritual but on the event of baptism?⁵⁷ As we have seen, baptism is often a metaphor for death and often

---

55. Or "assimilated to." See the discussion in Cranfield, *A Critical and Exegetical Commentary on the Epistle to the Romans*, 306–8.

56. See Sorin Sabou, *Between Horror and Hope: Paul's Metaphorical Language of Death in Romans 6:1–11*, Paternoster Biblical Monographs (Eugene, OR: Wipf & Stock, 2006).

57. For the first see Hans Dieter Betz, "Transferring a Ritual," 114; for the second see

associated with going under water. People display ingenuity trying to diminish the idea of immersion. Howard Marshall even suggests βαπτίζειν also could mean "sprinkle" because the Spirit comes down from above, even though he admits immersion was the rule in the early church.[58] Similarly Schnackenburg downplays the idea that βαπτίζειν necessarily includes immersion, but then grants that Paul will have thought of the rite of immersion in which the person disappeared under the water as into a grave.[59] Whatever one decides about the mode and timing of baptism, as nearly all admit, immersion was the practice of the early church. If that is the case, it is difficult to think that "buried with" would not bring to mind going under the water. Even if Paul did not intend the image, his readers would have assumed it.

Another issue requiring attention is the "eschatological reserve" of Rom 6:1-10. In focusing on participation with Christ's death, did Paul, as some suggest, intentionally refrain from saying that believers also participate in his resurrection? James Dunn, for example, grants that a sharing in Christ's risen life is implied, but the believer is not yet able to share in the resurrection in the same way he or she can share in Christ's death. He argues Paul refused to extend the association to resurrection with the result that the whole life of the believer "is suspended between Christ's death and Christ's resurrection." Believers do not yet share in Christ's resurrection.[60] Biblical faith resides, indeed, in the tension of the now and the not-yet, and because of triumphalism eschatological reserve is necessary, but Dunn's "suspension" creates an odd picture and results from a literalistic reading that does no justice to the context. Sharing in the resurrection is not a focus in 6:1-10 because the focus is on the implications of *dying* to sin. The thirteen references to death and its implications dominate. Sharing in the resurrection is assumed or 6:4b makes no sense (ἵνα ὥσπερ ἠγέρθη Χριστὸς ἐκ νεκρῶν διὰ τῆς δόξης τοῦ πατρός, οὕτως καὶ ἡμεῖς ἐν καινότητι ζωῆς περιπατήσωμεν), and neither would 6:11 and 13 (οὕτως καὶ ὑμεῖς λογίζεσθε ἑαυτοὺς ... ζῶντας δὲ τῷ θεῷ ἐν Χριστῷ Ἰησοῦ ... ἀλλὰ παραστήσατε ἑαυτοὺς τῷ θεῷ ὡσεὶ ἐκ νεκρῶν ζῶντας). What besides participation with the resurrection can account for the transition from 6:4a to

---

Douglas Moo, *Romans 1-8*, Wycliffe Exegetical Commentary (Chicago: Moody, 1991), 379. He grants that a secondary allusion to the rite is possible.

58. I. Howard Marshall, "The Meaning of the Verb 'Baptize,'" in *Dimensions of Baptism: Biblical and Theological Studies*, ed. Stanley E. Porter and Anthony R. Cross, JSNTSup 234 (Sheffield: Sheffield Academic Press, 2002), 8-24, esp. 23. βαπτίζειν is not used in relation to the pouring out of the Spirit.

59. Schnackenburg, *Baptism in the Thought of St. Paul*, 22-34.

60. Dunn, *Romans 1-8*, 314, 316, 330-33, at 331.

6:4b? Further, Rom 7:4, which expresses the same theology as 6:2–6, is proof that Paul had no hesitation in speaking of participation in Christ's resurrection (ὑμεῖς ἐθανατώθητε τῷ νόμῳ διὰ τοῦ σώματος τοῦ Χριστοῦ, εἰς τὸ γενέσθαι ὑμᾶς ἑτέρῳ, τῷ ἐκ νεκρῶν ἐγερθέντι, ἵνα καρποφορήσωμεν τῷ θεῷ).[61]

But can βαπτίζειν εἰς Χριστόν be taken so strongly of solidarity with Christ when 1 Cor 10:2 has πάντες εἰς τὸν Μωϋσῆν ἐβαπτίσθησαν ἐν τῇ νεφέλῃ καὶ ἐν τῇ θαλάσσῃ? This text leads some to retreat to understanding βαπτίζειν εἰς as "with reference to," but again this does not do justice to the way context determines meaning. Baptized into Moses is an analogy and not a very precise one at that. The purpose of this section of 1 Corinthians is to prevent people from thinking baptism and the Lord's Supper had some magical effect that did not require corresponding reality in life. With the exodus, people did not even get wet, and their relation to Moses was nowhere close to the relation with Christ. The point of the language is only to say, "These people had a similar experience in relation to Moses and to water and food, but it did not save them," as 10:6 shows. One cannot use this passage to diminish Rom 6:3.

But what is the relation of faith and baptism? Does baptism create the union with faith being essential, or does baptism only mirror a preexisting union?[62] Our problems result often from the fact that we separate the two, but I doubt that early Christians did. Every indication is that they thought of faith and baptism as one comprehensive act. They knew that baptism by itself did nothing, as 1 Cor 10:2–6 shows; the ritual was not magic. The ritual was valid and effective when it expressed what it portrayed, an identification with the narrative of Christ's life, death, and resurrection. That identification is the act of faith, and if there were hours or days between identification and baptism, that would not matter. The early Christians would not have understood faith without baptism,[63] and baptism without faith would have been nonsensical. In this connection we should also think of the relation of πιστεύειν εἰς Χριστόν and βαπτίζειν εἰς Χριστόν. The phrase πιστεύειν εἰς Χριστόν and related expressions are not frequent outside Johannine material, but they do occur, and they occur in important texts like Gal 2:16.[64] In my estimation both expressions express the solidarity with Christ that is faith.

Alfred Wikenhauser said, "Paul considers it a self-evident fact that as soon

---

61. Rom 8:11 and 13 are relevant as well, unless one interprets them as referring to future eschatology.

62. See p. 117, above.

63. Note 1 Pet 3:21: baptism, "as an appeal to God for a good conscience," saves "through the resurrection of Jesus Christ."

64. See also Acts 10:43; 14:23; 20:21; 24:24; Rom 4:18; Phil 1:29; Col 2:5; 1 Pet 1:21.

as a man becomes a Christian he enters upon this vital union with Christ."[65] His language may be patriarchal, but the theology is right on target. Christians who built cross-shaped or hexagonal baptistries, the hexagonal depicting the sixth day, knew that baptism was an identification with the death of Christ. Others built octagonal ones to depict the resurrection.[66] Cyril of Jerusalem says about baptism, "In that same moment you were dying and being born, and that saving water was at once your grave and your mother."[67] As with Paul, from death comes life. Cyril also says that as people are led to the pool, they enact Christ's being laid in the sepulcher. Similarly, Ambrose describes neophytes as fastened to Christ just as Christ was fastened to the cross and says the baptismal font has the shape and appearance of a tomb.[68] These people understood solidarity with Christ, his death, and his life.

Two other issues deserve attention. If dying and rising are a pattern for Christian living, why is baptism a one-off experience? Repeated baptisms would make sense, but baptism was viewed as an initiatory and unique rite. That can only be because it was viewed as marking union with Christ, a permanent union that did not need to be reestablished.

Finally, the Christology undergirding baptism is striking. Why did these early Christians very quickly view Jesus of Nazareth as more than an individual and someone in whom others could reside, be joined to, enveloped by, and determined by? That has no real parallel and has to be a result of their convictions about Christ's death on their behalf and the significance of his resurrection.[69]

---

65. *The Mysticism of Paul the Apostle*, 93.

66. See Robin M. Jensen, *Baptismal Imagery in Early Christianity: Ritual, Visual, and Theological Dimensions* (Grand Rapids: Baker, 2012), 140–213.

67. Cyril of Jerusalem, *On the Mysteries* 2.4 (*NPNF2* 7.148). The quotation is from Jensen, *Baptismal Imagery in Early Christianity*, 140.

68. Ambrose, *The Sacraments* 2.23.

69. M. David Litwa points to analogies to deification in the ancient world, but this is quite different from incorporation into a recent historical figure (see his book *We Are Being Transformed: Deification in Paul's Soteriology*, BZNW 187 [Berlin: De Gruyter, 2012]).

Chapter 8

The Holy Spirit, Justification, and Participation in the Divine Life in Galatians

Ben C. Blackwell

In a recent essay on Gal 2:15–21, Michael Gorman identifies the key themes that permeate his wider treatments of justification in Paul.[1] In contrast to readings that see the discussion of 2:19–20 as distinct from Paul's argument about justification, Gorman reads participation in Christ's death and life as essential to understanding the content of justification, as well as its means and mode. He writes: "According to Gal 2:15–21, justification is participation not only in Messiah's death, but also his resurrection, which means that justification entails resurrection to new life, that is, the emergence of a new self indwelt by the (Spirit of the) Messiah and living in proper relation to God."[2] In identifying the connection between justification and resurrection, Gorman

---

1. Michael J. Gorman, "Reading Gal 2:15–21 Theologically: Beyond Old and New, Beyond West and East," in *Participation, Justification, and Conversion: Eastern Orthodox Interpretation of Paul and the Debate between "Old and New Perspectives on Paul*," ed. Athanasios Despotis, WUNT 2/442 (Tübingen: Mohr Siebeck, 2017), 315–47. Gorman has recently revised and republished this essay in *Participating in Christ: Explorations in Paul's Theology and Spirituality* (Grand Rapids: Baker Academic, 2019), 11–149. I will, however, be referring to the original form of the essay in what follows. For his related discussions about justification, see *Inhabiting the Cruciform God: Kenosis, Justification, and Theosis in Paul's Narrative Soteriology* (Grand Rapids: Eerdmans, 2009), 40–104; *Becoming the Gospel: Paul, Participation, and Mission* (Grand Rapids: Eerdmans, 2015), 212–96.
2. Gorman, "Reading Gal 2:15–21 Theologically," 332, emphasis removed. Gorman's reading is also supported in this recent monograph: Andrew K. Boakye, *Death and Life: Resurrection, Restoration, and Rectification in Paul's Letter to the Galatians* (Eugene, OR: Pickwick, 2017).

highlights the agency of the Spirit. Since the Spirit is not explicitly named in Gal 2:15–21, he draws in the implications of the passage immediately following (3:1–6) and other associations between the Spirit and life in the letter (e.g., 5:25; 6:8).

This reading stands at odds with much of contemporary scholarship (as I demonstrate below), so the question of its validity arises. Accordingly, in this essay I will test his reading by focusing on the Galatians material following 2:15–21, exploring the relationship of the Spirit and justification in Gal 3 more closely. In vindication of Gorman's position, I will argue that justification entails acquittal before God and participation in the divine life through Christ and the Holy Spirit as fulfillment of a new covenant hope. Before establishing this thesis with a view toward Galatians, I will first briefly narrate some of the historical issues that influence why most scholarship misses this relationship of the Spirit and justification.

Justification and the Spirit in the History of Interpretation

Contemporary discussions of justification, whether in support of or in distinction to the "Lutheran" reading, are highly shaped by dynamics that arose in the Reformation.[3] While the Spirit continues to play a strong role in Roman Catholic theologies of justification,[4] the Spirit does not play a central role in most Protestant discussions since the focus is on Christ's righteousness and forgiveness.[5] Early Lutheran traditions associated justification with regeneration, but Protestant perspectives that later came to dominance rule out some of these earlier positions, and the later positions most influence contemporary discussions.[6]

A focus on forgiveness is evident in the Lutheran tradition, but with regard to one's union with Christ, Luther often maintained a continuity between justification and regeneration as the joint result of faith.[7] Luther emphasized

---

3. Cf. James B. Prothro, "An Unhelpful Label: Reading the 'Lutheran' Reading of Paul," *JSNT* 39 (2016): 119–40.

4. Note how the Holy Spirit is the subject of the first three affirmations regarding justification in the *Catechism of the Catholic Church* §§1987–1989.

5. See, for example, Stephen Westerholm, *Perspectives Old and New on Paul: The "Lutheran" Paul and His Critics* (Grand Rapids: Eerdmans, 2004), 274–78.

6. Stephen J. Chester details this transition in *Reading Paul with the Reformers: Reconciling Old and New Perspectives* (Grand Rapids: Eerdmans, 2017), 175–318.

7. See, for example, Luther's comments on Gal 2:16, 19–20 and 3:13 in his *Lectures on Galatians 1535* (LW 26.129–30, 166, 281–83).

the imputation of Christ's righteousness, but he also framed this in terms of union with Christ, which thus takes the doctrine beyond a status declaration.[8] This identification between justification and regeneration is also reflected in Melanchthon's *Apology for the Augsburg Confession* (1530), as we see in *Apology* 4:72, 78, 117.[9] By the time of the Formula of Concord (1577) a distinction between justification and regeneration is made using an *ordo salutis* (*Epitome* 3:8; *Strong Declaration* 3:10–23).[10] While the Formula repeatedly makes clear that the Spirit enacts justification and regeneration/vivification, the tendency in the tradition is to focus upon the Spirit's specific role in the latter. This model of the Formula is also evident in Calvin's *Institutes* where he describes participation in Christ as a *duplex gratia*, which includes both justification as blamelessness before God by Christ's righteousness and regeneration as sanctification by Christ's Spirit for a blameless and pure life (3.11.1).[11] These are simultaneous and yet distinct, both deriving from union with Christ through the Spirit (3.11.5, 10), yet Christ's righteousness is the focus of justification and the Spirit's agency with regeneration. Calvin emphasizes forgiveness as the primary focus of justification and critiques those who, in his view, confuse justification and regeneration: Osiander (3.11.5–12) and Augustine, who "subsumes grace under sanctification, by which we are reborn in newness of life through the Spirit" (3.11.15).[12] These Reformation theologians set the whole divine-human relationship in a participatory framework of union with Christ, but the strong distinction between justification and regeneration/vivification becomes calcified, with the result that justification is treated as distinct from the Holy Spirit's work in most contemporary biblical scholarship.

We see this explicitly in two of the three major approaches to justification which reflect this later Protestant reading. Mapping contemporary approaches is always an artificial exercise, but we can discern three major approaches to justification in scholarship. Each has multiple proponents sharing common

---

8. Stephen Chester, "It Is No Longer I Who Live: Justification by Faith and Participation in Christ in Martin Luther's Exegesis of Galatians," *NTS* 55 (2009): 315–37.

9. Alistair McGrath argues that Melanchthon shifts after this, moving more towards the vision of the Formula (*Iustitia Dei: A History of the Doctrine of Justification*, 3rd ed. [Cambridge: Cambridge University Press, 2005], 238).

10. John Reumann, "Justification by Faith in Pauline Thought: A Lutheran View," in *Rereading Paul Together: Protestant and Catholic Perspectives on Justification*, ed. David E. Aune (Grand Rapids: Baker Academic, 2006), 111–12.

11. It is important to note that Calvin treats regeneration and vivification in his discussion of repentance and sanctification (3.3.1–9).

12. John Calvin, *The Institutes of the Christian Religion*, ed. John T. McNeill, trans. Ford Lewis Battles, 2 vols., LCC (Philadelphia: Westminster, 1960), 753.

perspectives. My purpose here is to give a brief taxonomy rather than to defend or explain the various nuances to each position.[13] All three positions make use of terms like "forensic," "juridical," etc., so to prevent confusion I will avoid using commonly appropriated (and disputed) terms for labeling. Rather, this taxonomy focuses on their major proposition within a problem-solution framework. The three positions are "justification as acquittal," "justification as rectification," and "justification as covenant membership." The justification as acquittal position, reflected by Stephen Westerholm, highlights believers' freedom from God's wrath as they are acquitted, with reconciliation and forgiveness being the primary focus of justification.[14] The justification as rectification position, reflected by Martinus de Boer, highlights believers' freedom from evil powers such as Sin and Death, such that liberation and even transformation are the primary focus.[15] The justification as covenant membership position, reflected by N. T. Wright, highlights believers' freedom from communal divisions as they are declared members of the covenant family of God.[16]

With this taxonomy in mind, we can return to our interest in the Spirit (and regeneration/vivification) in relation to justification. Mapping the place of these topics in terms of justification would take the whole essay, but it is safe to say that these are not central issues within the current discussion, with the exception of the rectification approach which does relate vivification to justification. Brief consideration of the subject indexes of contemporary treatments of justification reveal that the Spirit and life are muted in the discussion or only briefly mentioned. To be sure, it is common among all traditions to note that the Spirit leads believers to faith, making the Spirit essential to the wider process.[17] However, for the acquittal and covenant membership positions, the Spirit's role in justification is not immediately clear because justifi-

---

13. For further explorations of this taxonomy, see my *Participating in the Righteousness of God: Justification in Pauline Theology* (Grand Rapids: Eerdmans, forthcoming). For an alternate taxonomy, see James B. Prothro, *Both Judge and Justifier: Biblical Legal Language and the Act of Justifying in Paul*, WUNT 2/461 (Tübingen: Mohr Siebeck, 2018), 6–26.

14. Cf. Westerholm, *Perspectives Old and New*, 275–77. See also Thomas R. Schreiner, *Faith Alone: The Doctrine of Justification* (Grand Rapids: Zondervan, 2015).

15. Martinus C. de Boer, "Paul's Use and Interpretation of a Justification Tradition in Galatians 2.15–21," *JSNT* 28 (2005): 210. See also other members of the "apocalyptic" school, such as Douglas A. Campbell, *The Deliverance of God: An Apocalyptic Rereading of Justification in Paul* (Grand Rapids: Eerdmans, 2009).

16. N. T. Wright, *Paul and the Faithfulness of God* (Minneapolis: Fortress, 2013), 991. See also James D. G. Dunn, "The New Perspective: Whence, What, and Whither?," in *The New Perspective on Paul*, rev. ed. (Grand Rapids: Eerdmans, 2008), 1–97.

17. Support is drawn from 1 Cor 2 and 12 (as well as John 14 and 16).

The Holy Spirit, Justification, and Participation in the Divine Life

cation primarily entails (only) a status declaration. Westerholm makes little mention of the Spirit in his *Perspectives Old and New on Paul*,[18] and he only mentions the life/justification connection in a footnote in order to support an *ordo salutis* position, thus distinguishing them.[19] Wright does frame his whole treatment of justification under the heading "Election Reworked around the Spirit."[20] He argues for a coordination between one's present justification as a status and the righteousness in the final acquittal of one's life lived by the Spirit.[21] However, Wright also expressly rejects identifying justification with the Spirit's work of regeneration or transformation.[22] In contrast, de Boer holds these conceptions more closely together. When commenting on Gal 3:14, he notes that the "Spirit provides the basis for justification."[23] In his discussion, however, he does not triangulate justification, the Spirit, and life/regeneration. For example, in his discussion of Gal 3:21, he maintains a distinction between justification and life.[24] Accordingly, we see how Westerholm and Wright repeat the distinction between justification and regeneration representative of the late Reformation position, though without explicit attribution. They appear to hold a distinction-without-separation model, though in their protestations the tone is more a distinction-through-separation.

Michael Gorman's inclusion of the Spirit is thus unique among these readings and warrants further evaluation. According to Gorman's reading, Paul gives distinct emphasis to "life" (or vivification) in his discussion of justification, and this is the explicit basis for his coordination between justification and the Spirit.

---

18. Westerholm explicitly excludes "the gift of the Spirit" from justification here: "Righteousness, Cosmic and Microcosmic," in *Apocalyptic Paul: Cosmos and Anthropos in Romans 5–8*, ed. Beverly Roberts Gaventa (Waco: Baylor University Press, 2013), 26–27.

19. Westerholm, *Perspectives Old and New on Paul*, 294n94. See also his firm distinction between justification and transformation in 277–78n39.

20. Wright, *Paul and the Faithfulness of God*, 912–1042.

21. In his *Justification: God's Plan and Paul's Vision* (Downers Grove, IL: IVP Academic, 2009), Wright makes the relationship clear: "The present verdict gives the *assurance that* the future verdict will match it; the Spirit gives the *power through which* that future verdict, when given, will be seen to be in accordance with the life that the believer has then lived" (251, emphasis original).

22. Wright, *Paul and the Faithfulness of God*, 952–60. An exegetical quandary arises when considering the connection between the Spirit and adoption in Wright's work. Since he considers justification as adoption into God's family (959), then how is the Spirit's presence not constitutive of justification? Becoming "children of God" through the Spirit seems to create not only a new status but a new state of being.

23. Martinus C. de Boer, *Galatians: A Commentary*, NTL (Louisville: Westminster John Knox, 2011), 215n312.

24. De Boer, *Galatians*, 233, see esp. n. 346.

Exploring Galatians

With his focus on faith and works of the law, Paul's discussion of justification usually comes in contexts related to Jew-gentile relationships. Given the influence of these related issues, scholars sometimes miss how the Holy Spirit and life also appear regularly in Paul's discussion. Justification and the Spirit occur together briefly at times, such as in 1 Cor 6:11 or Rom 14:17, but also in more extended discussions like 2 Cor 3 or Rom 8. Thus, our conclusions here regarding Gal 2:15–3:14 appear in the wider Pauline tradition. We will proceed progressively through Paul's argument.

Galatians 2:11–21

Extending his discussion of the Antioch incident (Gal 2:11–14), Paul gives his first treatment of justification in this letter with 2:15–21. He employs justification language without giving explicit semantic context or definitional phrases to clarify the meaning of God's act of justifying (δικαιόω).[25] Rather, the argument focuses on the *means to* justification, through Christ-faith or works of the law, rather than the *content of* justification: "a person is justified not by the works of the law but through Christ-faith" (Gal 2:16).[26] Paul presumes his audience already understands his language, and the implication is that Paul is using the language in a manner familiar with a shared lexical context, in particular in accord with Septuagint traditions.[27] While we have to attend to the specifically forensic shape of that lexical register from these wider theological contexts to understand how Paul is using it here, David deSilva notes that Paul points us directly to the forensic nature of the Septuagint tradition within his initial use of the term δικαιόω: "Paul's reconfiguration of Psalm 143:2 ('do not enter into judgment with your slave, for no living being will be acquitted before

---

25. In contrast to 2 Corinthians and Romans, Galatians is virtually devoid of other co-textual forensic language, most specifically the frequent antonym κατακρίνω (and its cognates).

26. There does not seem to be any distinction between Paul's use of the prepositions ἐκ, διά, and ἐν when used with regard to πίστις or ἔργα. While I have inclinations in the πίστις Χριστοῦ debate, I will use the ambiguous "Christ-faith" so as not to distract from either position, both of which have their own merits. For the sake of space, I also will bypass the debates about "works of the law."

27. See, e.g., John M. G. Barclay, *Paul and the Gift* (Grand Rapids: Eerdmans, 2015), 375–77; Prothro, *Both Judge and Justifier*, 127–39.

you') at the end of 2:16 suggests God's judgment" informs his use.[28] Later, Paul speaks of being justified "before God" (παρὰ τῷ θεῷ, 3:11), which also points to God's role as divine judge. James Prothro provides a helpful account of the Hellenistic Jewish context for justification, and he describes what we find in Galatians as a bilateral legal contention, where we have two parties—humans standing before God as judge in a covenant lawsuit.[29]

While not emphasizing the content of justification, Paul's argument provides the basis for discerning its meaning. The nature of the Christ-gift provides the best evidence for what Paul thinks justification entails, namely, forgiveness of sins. While Paul does not directly contrast being righteous and being a sinner here as he does elsewhere (e.g., Rom 3:23–24), there is an implicit contrast between the concepts since terminology related to both are in Gal 2:15–17. Likewise, in Gal 1:4 Paul describes how Christ "gave himself for our sins to set us free from the present evil age." While the gift "for our sins" is oblique, God's act of justification of sinners on account of the Christ-gift in 2:16–17 would seem to entail acquittal in a bilateral judgment and thus forgiveness of those sins.

One's standing before God (with regard to sin) is not, however, the only issue Paul raises. He also notes how the Christ-gift redeems believers from this evil age (Gal 1:4). Among the evil powers that interpreters focus on are the στοιχεῖα τοῦ κόσμου (4:3, 9), but in the justification discourse (2:15–21) the topic of *death* is at issue, particularly in relation to the law, and death remains part of his discourse on justification in 3:10–14.[30] After reiterating that no one can be justified by works of the law (2:16–17), Paul turns to a first-person account to express how he died to the law, being crucified with Christ, but he also lives with Christ (2:19–20). Against the charge that justification by faith led to sin and transgression, Paul argues that justification entails life (and therefore obedience). Explaining how death and life with Christ in 2:19–20 extends and explains what justification entails, Scott Shauf argues:

> Structurally, v. 20 is an expansion of v. 19 and thus along with vv. 18–19 a part of the answer to the objection of v. 17. . . . Verse 17 presents a *specific* charge against Paul's doctrine of justification, and vv. 18–20 are all presented

---

28. David A. deSilva, *Galatians*, NICNT (Grand Rapids: Eerdmans, 2018), 217.

29. Against counter-readings by Wright and de Boer/Martyn, Prothro (*Both Judge and Justifier*, 127–55) gives a compelling interpretation that supports a bilateral reading of justification in Galatians.

30. Cf. the parallel issue of "corruption" related to the flesh in Gal 6:7–8, which is contrasted with life.

as a response to the charge. Yet in v. 21 Paul concludes with a very *general* denial that righteousness comes through the law.³¹

In particular, Shauf contends that 2:20 allows Paul to shift the issues from *the law*, which relates specifically to Jewish Christians, to *life in Christ*, which relates to all Christians, and thus this opens his argument to the primarily gentile audience at Galatia.

Paul uses Christ's love-inspired gift of death (and life) in Gal 2:20 to substantiate God's gift of righteousness in 2:21. Since there are no discourse markers signaling that the direction of the argument has moved away from justification in 2:19-20,³² the coordination between the gift in 2:20 and 2:21 leads one to affirm that the gift of dying and rising with Christ through faith in 2:19-20 depicts the gift of righteousness through the death of Christ in 2:21.³³ Gorman helpfully describes participation in Christ's death as the mode of justification, whereas participating in his life is what justification entails.³⁴ This identification with the experience of Christ's life is supported by the parallels between justification and life in the passage:

[a] *being justified* by faith [ἐκ/διὰ πίστεως] (2:16) and *living* by faith [ἐν πίστει] (2:20)

[b] *being justified* in Christ [ἐν Χριστῷ] (2:17) and *being co-crucified* with Christ [Χριστῷ] (2:19)

[c] *being justified* in Christ [ἐν Χριστῷ] (2:17) and *living* to God [θεῷ] (2:19)

[d] *being justified* in Christ [ἐν Χριστῷ] (2:17) and Χριστός *living* in me [ἐν ἐμοί] (2:20)

While each parallel is not equally informative, Paul does not go out of his way to distinguish between them, which supports the reading that he sees δικαιόω and ζάω as coordinate. Rather than seeing Gal 2:19-20 as an excursus from Paul's justification argument in 2:15-18, 21,³⁵ several items reinforce the inter-

---

31. Scott Shauf, "Galatians 2:20 in Context," *NTS* 52 (2006): 97, emphasis original.

32. Calvin makes a distinction here between justification as acceptance and regeneration as empowered activity: John Calvin, *Galatians, Ephesians, Philippians and Colossians* (Grand Rapids: Eerdmans, 1965 [1548]), 43.

33. For his argument on the implicit role of the Spirit in 2:19-20, see Gordon D. Fee, *God's Empowering Presence: The Holy Spirit in the Letters of Paul* (Peabody, MA: Hendrickson, 1994), 373-77.

34. Gorman, "Reading Gal 2:15-21," 325-34.

35. Note, for example, two interpreters from differing perspectives that see 2:19-20

connection of dying and rising with Christ and justification: the Christ-gift as the basis for both, the parallel use of terms, and the continuous flow of the argument. The experience of (death and) life in Christ is the most direct exposition of what justification entails in the letter so far, and the later connection between the concepts in 3:10–14 and 3:21 confirms this reading.

Applying Prothro's taxonomy, this serves as an example of a trilateral judgment where God's justifying act rectifies the human problem with regard to an external agent. The third party in this trial scene is death (via the law). Justification in this model is not merely a status declaration because the problem is not merely a status problem. As Prothro and Downing spell out, ancient trials did not distinguish between the verbal declaration and the execution of the judgment.[36] Drawing from the shared Hellenistic Jewish framework in play here (and reflected in Paul's other letters), the problem of condemnation before God in a bilateral framework is met with God's gracious justification.[37] Moving beyond the bilateral, Paul distinctly emphasizes death and life in this divine-human encounter, by which he is drawing together the execution of the verdict of death and life with its declaration. An important aspect of Prothro's work is that the bilateral and trilateral perspectives need not be played off against one another since the two are often merged in LXX traditions.[38] In that case, being set right before God (bilateral) is not at odds with being rectified before one's

---

as somehow distinct from his argument about justification: Beverly Roberts Gaventa ("The Singularity of the Gospel Revisited" in *Galatians and Christian Theology: Justification, the Gospel, and Ethics in Paul's Letter,* ed. Mark W. Elliott et al. [Grand Rapids: Baker, 2014], 187–99) and N. T. Wright ("Messiahship in Galatians?" in *Galatians and Christian Theology,* 3–23). Though seeing justification in terms of life fits closely to Gaventa's understanding of rectification, she still distinguishes the two when she writes: "By moving to the language of 'death' and 'life,' Paul has again shifted his discourse; the register of the argument changes. The canvas on which Paul depicts the gospel has enlarged from legal language to existential language. The question is no longer about making things right (rectifying or justifying) and how that is done; instead, it concerns death and life" (194–95). While approaching justification from a different direction, Wright identifies an antithesis between being "in Messiah" and "Messiah in me": "To be 'in the Messiah' is a matter of *status,* of who one is in God's eyes. To have the Messiah living within one is a matter of actual, personal, inner transformation" (21, emphasis original).

36. F. Gerald Downing, "Justification as Acquittal? A Critical Examination of Judicial Verdicts in Paul's Literary and Actual Contexts," *CBQ* 74 (2012): 298–318; Prothro, *Both Judge and Justifier,* 57–61.

37. Paul regularly treats "condemnation" as an antonym to justification, and condemnation is identified with "death" (2 Cor 3:9; Rom 5:15–21; 8:1–2).

38. Prothro, *Both Judge and Justifier,* 89–94.

enemies (trilateral). In other words, as believers are acquitted before God by God in Christ, they are also rectified with regard to the problem of death.[39]

To speak of justification in terms of vivification might sound like treating grace or righteousness as objects which are transferred from God to the believer. In contrast, the presence of Christ himself is the grace which creates this new life: "Christ lives in me" (Gal 2:20). Thus, this experience of vivification is not the basis on which believers have hope; rather, Christ is their hope just as he is their life.[40] In that way, there is no source for concern here that a door has been opened for moral action as the basis for justification. Indeed, the thrust is far and away on divine agency rather than human agency—"it is no longer I who live, but it is Christ who lives in me" (2:20). And yet, this divine act of giving life in the event of justification is what creates the ground for moral action as "[living] to God" (2:19). While vivification in these verses includes both the divine act of restoring one to life from the dead and the cooperative accomplishment of moral action, justification appears to focus on the former aspect of vivification as a completed event, already present. Capturing this element, Luther aptly argues that the moral act cannot precede initial life, because God must first make the tree alive (as justification) before it can produce fruit.[41]

Paul concludes his first section on justification (Gal 2:11–21) with an emphasis on the gift of the crucified Christ as the basis for the gift of righteousness. This emphasis on the crucified Christ is important because it grounds the next section of his argument, which coordinates justification with the Spirit as the blessing of the Abrahamic covenant (3:1–14).

Galatians 3:1–14

In Gal 3:1–5 Paul focuses directly on the Galatians' experience of the Holy Spirit but does not mention justification, so it could be seen as merely an argument from experience distinct from his justification discourse. His use of καθώς in 3:6 (linking the wider argument of Abraham, justification, and

---

39. Cowan rightly notes the intersection of life and God's legal act in justification, but he tries unsuccessfully to distinguish the objective status of life from its subjective experience, thus echoing Calvin's distinction: J. Andrew Cowan, "The Legal Significance of Christ's Risen Life: Union with Christ and Justification in Galatians 2.17–20," *JSNT* 40 (2018): 453–72.

40. In this regard, see deSilva's response to the separation of justification and transformation: *Galatians*, 250n371.

41. Luther, *Commentary on Galatians*, LW 26.169. It is in this context that Luther speaks about an "alien life." This "alien life" must be a subjective experience and it parallels his use of "alien righteousness" elsewhere.

faith to the experience of the Spirit) points to a more substantial progression in the argument. Paul's return to the Spirit in relation to Abraham in 3:14 as the climax of the argument further confirms this connection.[42]

As with his discussion of justification in the previous section, Paul argues from a shared knowledge with the Galatians and so does not fully explain this experience of the Spirit. As before, his primary purpose is to accentuate the distinction between the different (possible) means to this experience: the contrast is between faith and works of the law (Gal 3:2, 5). In light of 3:1–5 alone we cannot determine a distinct relationship between the experience of the Spirit and justification, though both the experience of the Spirit (3:2, 5) and justification (2:16[x2]) happen "from (the message of) faith" (ἐξ [ἀκοῆς] πίστεως). More clarity comes with the conclusion of this paragraph about the Spirit. Paul introduces his quotation of Gen 15:5 with "just as" (καθώς). Read in conjunction with 3:5, Paul argues that God supplies them with the Spirit by faith, *just as* Abraham was justified by faith (3:6).[43] Fung thus argues that Paul "seems to take it for granted that Abraham's being justified by faith *proves* that the Galatians must have received the Spirit by faith also; and this argument falls to the ground *unless* the reception of the Spirit is in some sense equated with justification."[44]

How does the Spirit relate to Abraham's justification by faith? Is there something more than just the common term "faith" that enables Paul to leapfrog to this other discussion? Abraham is a primary focus for the rest this chapter (Gal 3:6–29) and much of the next (4:21–5:1), and Paul will link not only faith but also the Spirit to Abraham in 3:14. Lee describes the interconnection as coordinate types of evidence for justification by faith—evidence from experience of the Spirit (3:1–5) and then evidence from Scripture (3:6–14)—such that the Spirit is *not* the blessing of Abraham (justification).[45] However, in line with my following argument, Stanley maintains that 3:1–14 is "a single,

---

42. For a summary of how interpreters associate the Spirit and Abraham's blessing, see Chee-Chiew Lee, *The Blessing of Abraham, the Spirit, and Justification: Their Relationship and Significance for Understanding Paul's Theology* (Eugene, OR: Pickwick, 2013), 4–11.

43. Translations and commentators are divided about whether 3:6 ends the paragraph with 3:1–5 or starts a new paragraph. In either case, the καθώς establishes a firm connection with the previous Spirit argument.

44. Ronald Y. K. Fung, "Justification, Sonship, and the Gift of the Spirit: Their Mutual Relationships as Seen in Galatians 3–4," *China Graduate School of Theology Journal* 3 (1987): 75–76.

45. Lee, *The Blessing of Abraham*, 24–34. She does extend the role of the Spirit in final justification and helpfully incorporates a covenantal setting (205).

interconnected argument concerning... the Spirit" and Abraham's blessing.[46] Paul's argument in the next two paragraphs (3:7-9 and 3:10-13) proceeds in two coordinate steps, setting the groundwork for 3:14 by establishing the basis for and the nature of Abraham's blessing.

In step one, Paul argues that those of faith (especially the gentiles) are children of Abraham and that they receive God's blessing with him (Gal 3:7-9). Within this argument, Paul gives the most direct evidence that justification is identified with "blessing": God's act of justifying gentiles is foretold as a promise that the gentiles will be blessed in Abraham (3:8). The association between having faith like Abraham and becoming his children becomes the center of focus in a following section (3:15-4:30).[47] In that later discussion, several items are worth noting with regard to being a child of Abraham through faith in Christ: this is equivalent to being a child of God (3:26-29), and this makes one an heir of the promise (3:18) and therefore a recipient of the Spirit (4:4-6). There appears to be an order of experience in 4:5-6, namely becoming sons and then receiving the Spirit into their hearts.[48] The order, however, is reversed in 4:29, where the free children are those "born according to the Spirit" (τὸν [γεννήσαντα] κατὰ πνεῦμα). Reading 4:6 and 4:29 together, we see that becoming children and experiencing the Spirit are reciprocal and do not form an *ordo*.[49] The only discernable *ordo* is that faith precedes both. Thus, Paul coordinates the presence of the Spirit with becoming a child (which in theological language is "regeneration"), and this happens together with justification. After establishing that people from all nations who have faith like Abraham receive his blessing as his children in 3:6-9 as the first step of this argument, Paul can then explore the nature of that blessing.

In step two, Paul argues that the nature of that blessing is (the experience of) life rather than cursing, which is death (Gal 3:10-13). He uses a series of intertextual references to bring his law/faith contrast in connection with his death/life contrast: law brings cursing as death in contrast to faith, which

---

46. Christopher D. Stanley, "'Under a Curse': A Fresh Reading of Galatians 3:10-14," *NTS* 36 (1990): 493.

47. As we noted, Paul assumes a common knowledge about the Spirit (and justification) with the Galatians, so we must draw in his wider statements in the letter to understand his argument.

48. Gorman notes the intertextual connection to Ezek 36:26 through the "heart" reference ("Reading Gal 2:15-21," 334).

49. So, Sam K. Williams, "Justification and the Spirit in Galatians," *JSNT* 29 (1987): 97n12; *pace* Fung, "Justification," 91.

The Holy Spirit, Justification, and Participation in the Divine Life

brings blessing as life.⁵⁰ This language of blessing (εὐλογία) and cursing (κατάρα) has strong resonance with Jewish covenantal passages in the LXX, namely, Gen 12 and 22 (with Abraham) and Deut 27–30 (with Moses). By pointing out a chiasm in the argument, Lee identifies how life is at the center of Paul's argument: faith (3:6; 3:14b), blessing (3:7–9; 3:14a), curse (3:10; 3:13), and life (3:11, 12).⁵¹ Employing Hab 2:4, Paul draws this life argument into his justification discourse. He writes: "no one is justified before God by the law; for 'The one who is righteous by faith will live (ζήσεται)'" (3:11).⁵² This is then contrasted with the inability to experience life through the law as he quotes Lev 18:5 (Gal 3:12). Noting the relation between justification and life, Preston Sprinkle brings out the connection: "the phrase 'justified by the law' (3:11a) corresponds positively to 'life by doing these things' (3:12b) and negatively to 'life by faith' (3:11b)."⁵³ Just as "to 'live by them' (3:12b) is to be 'justified by law' (3:11a)," so also to (really) live is to be justified by faith (3:11).⁵⁴ In contrast to the curse of death from which Christ redeemed believers, they have the blessing of life through faith, which is none other than justification.

As the climax of the section, Paul draws Abraham back into this argument and concludes: Christ redeemed believers "in order that in Christ Jesus the blessing of Abraham might come to the Gentiles, so that we might receive the promise of the Spirit through faith" (Gal 3:14).⁵⁵ This draws together the two premises from the two previous paragraphs but with a variation. The first idea

---

50. Many take the curse to be the problem of exile. I do not rule out the possibility of exile as a covenant curse here, but we should attend more closely to Paul's explicit language related to death, not least because it more closely coheres with his wider use of life language in the letter. Cf. Rodrigo J. Morales, *The Spirit and the Restoration of Israel: New Exodus and New Creation Motifs in Galatians*, WUNT 2/282 (Tübingen: Mohr Siebeck, 2010), 91–93. Pace John Anthony Dunne, *Persecution and Participation in Galatians*, WUNT 2/454 (Tübingen: Mohr Siebeck, 2017), 83, esp. n. 162.

51. Lee, *The Blessing of Abraham*, 32.

52. I have maintained the word order of the Greek so as to maintain the emphasis on life.

53. Preston M. Sprinkle, *Law and Life: The Interpretation of Leviticus 18:5 in Early Judaism and in Paul*, WUNT 2/241 (Tübingen: Mohr Siebeck, 2008), 139.

54. Sprinkle, *Law and Life*, 139. In this way, Sprinkle argues that justification and life are to be identified together rather than viewing justification as merely leading to life.

55. Matthew Thiessen argues that the "promise of the Spirit" is directly related to Abraham's faith represented in Gen 15:5 and 22:16–18 in the promise that his descendants would be like stars, not merely quantitatively but also qualitatively. That is, they would experience astral qualities, among which is a pneumatic existence (*Paul and the Gentile Problem* [Oxford: Oxford University Press, 2016], 129–48). While I am not convinced by his material *pneuma* argument, Thiessen's wider connections between Abraham's faith and the promise of his descendants' transformation is suggestive.

is that the gentiles who share his faith share his blessing reflects 3:6-9 directly. The second is parallel to 3:10-13, but he describes the covenant blessing in 3:14 as *the Spirit* rather than *life* as from 3:10-13. He thus uses metonymy, substituting the Spirit for life, as cause for effect. We see this relationship articulated when Paul later argues that the Spirit is the agent of life in the present (5:25) and the future (6:8). Indeed, his affirmation of "[since] we live by the Spirit" (5:25) serves as a programmatic summary of his wider discussion of the liberating experience of the Spirit in 5:2-24. Thus, with the metonymy in 3:14, we have firm grounds for interpreting the "promise of the Spirit" as the blessing of the life through the agency of the Spirit.[56]

This clarifies the relationship of the Spirit and life, but how does this Spirit-given life relate to justification? Drawing from Gal 2:15-21, we already saw that justification was primarily articulated as Christ *living* in the believer. Paul's whole purpose in 2:15-3:14 is to establish faith as the means to the justifying experience, in contrast to the law, which leads to death and cursing. Galatians 3:1-5, with its focus on the Spirit, might have merely seemed like an argument from experience, but Paul's overall argument shows that the experience of the Spirit is central to his justification argument. By faith believers experience justification and life like Abraham (3:6) just as (καθώς) they will receive the blessing of the Spirit who gives life by faith in the manner of Abraham (3:14). Accordingly, 3:1-5 is not just a side excursus as an argument from experience about the Spirit; rather, 3:1-5 is a pivotal aspect of the argument that establishes the reality of life through Christ *and the Spirit* as described in 3:6-14. The coordination of justification with redemption and life sets justification in a trilateral framework here, where believers are not only set right before God (3:11) but also with regard to death (via the law) as an opposing party.

As a result of Paul's extended discussion, we see that justification entails forgiveness and also embodying the life of Christ, and this justification-as-life is actualized by the vivifying presence of the Spirit. Does this cohere with his later discussions of justification in the letter? While justification is the primary focus of Gal 2-3, Paul moves on to other topics such as adoption, inheritance, and freedom from the flesh after 3:14. Exploring the interconnection of these

---

56. Fee agrees: "The 'blessing of Abraham' is not simply 'justification by faith.' Rather, it points towards the eschatological life now available to Jews and Gentiles alike, effected through Christ's death, but realized through the dynamic ministry of the Spirit—and all of this by faith" (*God's Empowering Presence*, 395). However, he also makes a distinction between "positional" righteousness and the "experiential" presence of the Spirit, so he does not see the argument as an identification between the two (368-69, 378n33).

Galatians 3:21 and 5:4-5

Throughout the letter, Paul's argument is that the Galatians have already experienced the life of Christ and the Spirit, so the law is shown to be unnecessary. Reiterating this, Paul writes in Gal 3:21: "If a law had been given which could make alive, then righteousness would indeed come through the law." Since this "righteousness" is not by law, the direct implication is that true righteousness is by faith, which in the context of the letter is none other than justification by faith. Given the structure of the sentence, the parallel is not easy to catch. Rephrasing to put it in more direct terms, he says: "If a law had been given which could make alive, then the law would justify." Notice how being "made alive" (ζωοποιέω) and "righteousness" (δικαιοσύνη) are the two hypothetical outcomes from the law, which Paul uses interchangeably. Using life identically with justification could seem to be a rhetorical flourish, but in light of this association in 2:15-21 and 3:10-14, we should view righteousness and life as metonyms, with the cause (righteousness) standing for the effect (life).[57] This expectation of justification and life is cast as freedom for those under sin (representing a trilateral framework) and as a *promise* realized in those who believe (3:22). By uniting justification and life as the fulfillment of the promise, this draws the Spirit's agency as the promised blessing into the frame, such that justification, life, and the Spirit are triangulated again as in 3:14.[58]

Paul returns to the topic of justification in chapter 5, when he again contrasts justification by the law and the hope of righteousness by faith in the Spirit (Gal 5:4-5). In contrast to those who are cut off from Christ by seeking to be justified by the law (5:4), those who participate in Christ by the Spirit have the hope of righteousness (5:5). The immediately consecutive prepositional phrases—"by faith" (ἐκ πίστεως) and "in the Spirit" (πνεύματι)—makes determining the role of the Spirit here ambiguous: is faith by the Spirit or is the hope of righteousness by the Spirit? Given the earlier context, the latter is most likely since Paul has already stated that the Spirit comes by faith (3:2, 5) and thus brings righteousness and life (3:6-14, 21). While Paul's focus has been on the present reality of the life through Christ and the Spirit to this point,

---

57. See especially, E. P. Sanders, "Patterns of Religion in Paul and Rabbinic Judaism: A Holistic Method of Comparison," *HTR* 66 (1973): 470.

58. Cf. Fung, "Justification," 84.

this verse points toward a yet future experience with the language of the hope of righteousness. This reflects the assurance of believers before God at the final judgment and their expectation of resurrection life as the instantiation of their justification and vindication. Thus, present justification through the Spirit assures final justification through the Spirit.

Conclusion

In Galatians Paul argues strongly that the blessings of God are received through faith and not through works of the law, and he grounds that argument in a soteriological vision explained largely in terms of justification and established by the presence of God through Christ and the Spirit. What we have seen then is a vindication of Michael Gorman's reading in terms of life and the Spirit in response to wider debates regarding justification in light of Reformation history.

Justification in Galatians

Though Paul assumes the Galatians share a basic conception of justification from Jewish theological contexts, he still provides adequate information from the letter in which we were able to draw out a nuanced understanding of his justification teaching. The language is fundamentally forensic, in that God's justifying action is set in terms of the covenant lawsuit framework from the Septuagint which includes bilateral and trilateral perspectives. As such, my reading draws from key aspects from each of the three main approaches in scholarship.

In terms of justification as acquittal, we can see that Paul sets justification in the context of the problem of human sin before God. In a bilateral manner, God has a covenant lawsuit against humanity for their sin and disobedience. As they are justified before God because of his grace expressed in the death and resurrection of Christ, believers are acquitted for their sins and forgiven. While this acquittal implies forgiveness, we should note that Paul never explicitly characterizes justification as forgiveness in the letter. This coheres with other letters where God is cast as the judge, and humans bear his wrath and condemnation for their sin (e.g., Rom 5:12–21). In response, his acquittal entails forgiveness (Rom 4:3–8).

While Paul assumes and works from the justification as acquittal model in Galatians, he also extends the language specifically in the direction of justification as rectification. While forgiveness is never explicitly mentioned, he does relate justification multiple times to the issues of life and death, in terms of participation in Christ and the Spirit. This places justification in a trilateral contention: sin and other evil powers also stand in a contention against humanity. As God justifies those of faith, he rectifies the problem of death by giving them life through the presence of Christ and the Spirit.

Accordingly, the language of justification entails being set right with regard to God and to their opponents, as we see the bilateral and trilateral come together.[59] This is made evident in other letters with the language of condemnation (again, e.g., Rom 5:12–21). Humans stand condemned before God (and his law) because of sin, but this condemnation is not just a divine declaration or status. Rather, Paul's letters consistently speak of the execution of the judgment of death as constitutive of condemnation. That is, the two stand in a metonymical relationship which has collapsed upon itself. To speak of condemnation is to speak of condemnation-as-death. BDAG, accordingly, writes about κατάκριμα: "In this and the cognates that follow the use of the term 'condemnation' does not denote merely a pronouncement of guilt [s. κρίνω 5], but the adjudication of punishment."[60] As the direct antithesis to condemnation, Paul presents the hope of justification. Like condemnation-as-death, justification and life stand in a metonymical relationship that has collapsed in on itself. To speak of justification is to speak of justification-as-life. Indeed, BDAG again captures this clearly when describing δικαιόω: "Since Paul views God's justifying action in close connection with the power of Christ's resurrection, there is sometimes no clear distinction between the justifying action of acquittal and the gift of new life through the Holy Spirit as God's activity in promoting uprightness in believers."[61] In other words, God rectifies the problem of sin, not just forgiving but correcting and restoring what was broken. In the words of Habakkuk: "The one righteous by faith will live."[62] Thus, Gorman's reading

---

59. Gaventa rightly focuses on the "singularity of the gospel" but misses the unified vision bringing together justification and life ("The Singularity of the Gospel Revisited," 194–95).

60. BDAG, 519.

61. BDAG, 249.

62. Aguilar argues similarly: "The relationship between justification and vivification ... is an unbreakable relationship in which one could not exist without the other." José E. Aguilar, "Justification and the Spirit in Paul: Is there a relationship?," in *Il Verbo di Dio è vivo. Studi sul Nuovo Testamento in onore del Card. Vanhoye*, ed. J. E. Aguilar, F. Manzi, F. Urso, C. Zesatti; AnBib 165 (Rome: Pontifical Biblical Institute, 2007), 377. Others have associated justification with believers' experience of *future* life at the judgment (as well as present reconciliation). E.g., Charles H. Cosgrove, "Justification in Paul: A Linguistic

stands apart from acquittal and covenant membership readings that minimize this interconnection.[63]

In terms of the justification as covenant membership reading, we noted how justification as forgiveness and life is a covenantal reality. The theological framework for understanding justification is the septuagintal framework of a *covenant* lawsuit.[64] The covenant framework is evident from Paul's explicitly covenantal language of blessing and cursing, as well as life and death, and Paul explicitly frames his wider argument in covenantal terms in the letter (Gal 3:15, 17; 4:24). By drawing together the hope of forgiveness in terms of life through the Spirit, we see explicitly new covenant language in Galatians.[65] As such, we can speak of justification as a distinctly covenantal experience, though it would be limiting to describe justification as covenant membership (i.e., as merely a status). Rather, the focus of this new covenant restoration is holistic, including individual and communal aspects. Paul captures the individual aspect as justification—a new covenant acquittal bringing new life through Christ and the Spirit—but does not separate this from his new covenant communal unity of Jews and gentiles.

When viewed holistically, we see justification in Galatians as entailing for-

---

and Theological Reflection," *JBL* 106 (1987): 653–70; Karl Donfried, "Justification and Last Judgment in Paul," *ZNW* 67 (1976): 90–110.

63. Stephen Westerholm notes dying and rising to new life in Christ as a related concept to justification, but he argues that these (and other metaphors like redemption, reconciliation, etc.) are "neither synonymous nor interchangeable" with justification (*Justification Reconsidered: Rethinking A Pauline Theme* [Grand Rapids: Eerdmans, 2013], 11). James D. G. Dunn, for his otherwise informed and comprehensive contributions to justification, makes almost no mention of life (or the Spirit). He only raises the topic in relation to Lev 18:5, which he interprets as a manner of living (*The Theology of Paul the Apostle* [Grand Rapids: Eerdmans, 1998], 373). Responding to critiques about a lack of emphasis on eschatological judgment, Dunn focuses on the way of living and eternal life ("The New Perspective: Whence, What and Whither," 71–77). Exceptions outside of the rectification tradition that explicitly discuss the interaction of justification and vivification are noteworthy: Mark Seifrid, *Christ, our Righteousness: Paul's Theology of Justification*, NSBT 9 (Leicester: Apollos, 2000); Richard B. Gaffin, Jr., *By Faith, Not By Sight: Paul and the Order of Salvation*, 2nd ed. (Phillipsburg: P & R Publishing, 2013); G. K. Beale, "The Role of Resurrection in the Already-and-Not-Yet Phases of Justification," in *For the Fame of God's Name: Essays in Honor of John Piper*, ed. Sam Storms and Justin Taylor (Wheaton, IL: Crossway, 2010), 190–212; Chester, *Reading Paul with the Reformers*, 415–16.

64. See Prothro's *Both Judge and Justifier* for exposition of the OT framework (62–104) as well as his qualified support of covenant in Galatians (144–45).

65. Boakye argues this strongly (*Death and Life*). Paul also employs a new covenant framework with regard to justification in 2 Cor 3 and Rom 8.

giveness and new life as a new covenant reality. As such, this reading captures aspects of acquittal, rectification, and covenant expectations.

Justification, the Spirit, and Ecumenical Discussion

With justification seen in this wider framework, we can more easily see a place for the Spirit in Paul's justification theology. Rather than approaching the intersection of justification and the experience of the Spirit as distinct-but-not-separate or as justification leading to the Spirit's presence in an *ordo salutis*, Paul unites the work of the Spirit and justification, particularly in the act of vivification as the Spirit mediates the life of Christ to believers. A variety of NT texts associate the Spirit and forgiveness, particularly when triangulated with baptism (Acts 2:38; Titus 3:5–7). This is likely an implication of Paul's argumentation here (given the inclusion of baptismal language in Gal 3:26–29), but the greater focus in Galatians is participation in God's life as a new covenant reality.

Paul frames this eschatological, new covenant expectation in terms of the Messiah's death and resurrection. In God's act of giving life to the dead through the Spirit, believers embody the life of Christ. This life is an eschatological reality and unites the beginning, middle, and end of Christian experience. Aguilar, who argues strongly for the identification of justification and vivification in terms of the Spirit, uses this eschatological framework to distinguish them: "The association of justification and the reception of the Spirit cannot be understood as an identity between both. A confirmation of this is the fact that justification does not appear expressed in terms of a partial realization, as in the case of the reception [of aspects of the Spirit], but as fully realized."[66]

While I affirm the full realization of the justification in faith and baptism with Aguilar, he misses the already/not yet aspect of the experience of the Spirit which equally matches the already/not yet experience of justification and vivification. These are all truly actuated in the present, but their revelation is not fully evident until final judgment. Meyer captures this when he recounts the Spirit as the "first-fruits" (Rom 8:23) and "promissory down-payment" (2 Cor 1:22; 5:5; cf. Eph 1:14): "These metaphors do not mean that the Spirit is given partially now in anticipation or in place of a full endowment later on. The Spirit *is* itself and as such the 'first-fruits,' anticipatory of redemption."[67]

---

66. Aguilar, "Justification and the Spirit in Paul," 376.
67. Paul W. Meyer, "The Holy Spirit in the Pauline Letters: A Contextual Exploration," *Int* 33 (1979): 12, emphasis original.

This parallels exactly Paul's theology of justification, and Turner helpfully captures the eschatological nature of the Spirit's presence: "Receiving the Spirit introduces the Christian experimentally [sic] to the whole tension of salvation history: the 'already' and the 'not yet' of Christian life. In receiving the gift of the Spirit we become aware of God's pronouncement of 'not guilty' over us and yet this assurance is only the first instalment of the reality which we hope to receive by the same Spirit."[68] Believers are not partially justified, awaiting a later fullness. Rather, through the Spirit they are justified by Christ-faith fully and this assures their final justification at the last judgment. In the same way, they truly live now in Christ and through the Spirit, even as their present justification. They await the full revelation of that justification-as-life until their resurrection at the parousia and final judgment.

This already/not yet experience of justification, life, and the Spirit allows this reading to fit within historical Protestant understandings but without some of the artificial limitations of the later Protestant divisions. By using "life" to speak to the initial experience, the ongoing walk of obedience, and bodily resurrection, Paul links each step of the process. Justification focuses most directly on the initial and ultimate experience of "life," each with an emphasis on divine agency. God's act of justification entails his act of vivification and regeneration, though the latter two include more than justification. The distinct-but-not-separate model represented by Calvin and the Formula of Concord makes a distinction that does not hold up exegetically, and so Luther and the voice of Melanchthon in his *Apology for the Augsburg Confession* fits Paul better. This does not minimize the need for divine agency in vivification because the model of new life is that of Christ's own resurrection. No one raises themselves, not even Christ. Accordingly, this does not present a back door for human agency to merit salvation. Vivification is not the basis for acceptance but is a new creation event which therefore stands as the basis for a restored moral agency. This model unites the beginning and purpose of the Christian life with its telos—participating in the life of God. As a result, Christian moral action is not a disjunctive step but a natural outgrowth of justification. As Luther remarks, fruit is a natural outgrowth of a tree newly formed. The new life of God begets "living to God," both of which are in Christ and through the Spirit.

This is not to return to or build up a model of grace or righteousness as an object to be transferred, but grace is a divine self-gift, a gift of the divine presence. Believers participate in Christ and the Spirit, and therefore participate

---

68. M. M. B. Turner, "The Significance of Spirit Endowment for Paul," *VE* 9 (1975): 60.

in the divine life as Christ and the Spirit live in and through them, something that is both relational and ontological.[69] In this way, Michael Gorman is right to describe justification as theosis,[70] since theosis is just that, participating in the life of God. In this way, justification, from a Pauline perspective which accounts for acquittal and rectification in a new covenant context, presents the ground for renewed opportunities in ecumenical theology rather than the basis for ecclesial division. We already see this in recent ecumenical scholarship, with "The Joint Declaration on the Doctrine of Justification,"[71] as well as with charismatic and Pentecostal theologies.[72] Thus, Michael Gorman's work in Paul not only serves to reunite concepts that have been separated but can stand as the basis for reuniting ecclesiastical communities as well, not unlike Paul's own intention when using justification to reunite Jewish and gentile Christians.[73]

---

69. Cf. Volker Rabens, "The Holy Spirit and Deification in Paul: A 'Western' Perspective," in *The Holy Spirit and the Church according to the New Testament. Sixth International East-West Symposium of New Testament Scholars, Belgrade, August 25 to 31, 2013*, ed. Predrag Dragutinovic, Karl-Wilhelm Niebuhr, and James Buchanan Wallace, WUNT 1/354 (Tübingen: Mohr Siebeck, 2016), 203.

70. E.g., Gorman, *Inhabiting*, 90–93, but it rightly runs through most of his works.

71. Though not directly part of the Joint Declaration discussions, Peter J. Leithart's argument for justification as God's "deliverdict" reflects ecumenical discussions that transcend polarization (*Delivered from the Elements of the World: Atonement, Justification, Mission* [Downers Grove, IL: IVP Academic, 2016]).

72. E.g., Frank D. Macchia, *Justified in the Spirit: Creation, Redemption, and the Triune God* (Grand Rapids: Eerdmans, 2010).

73. I am grateful to Jason Maston, Jim Prothro, and John Kincaid for their feedback on this essay.

.... *Chapter 9*

Participation in Christ in 1 Peter

Dennis R. Edwards

Thanks in large part to Michael J. Gorman, scholars are using "participation" to describe the apostle Paul's soteriology. In the opening pages of *Becoming the Gospel: Paul, Participation, and Mission*, Gorman explains that participation is a kind of "umbrella term" that covers other metaphors for what Christ accomplished for humanity, such as liberation, transformation, and justification.[1] Gorman also employs other terms that may be less familiar for Western Christians like theosis, deification, Christification, and Christosis, which "adequately summarize this transformative reality of Spirit-enabled, Christlike participation in the life and mission of God."[2] These terms, however, are problematic for some scholars and other readers of the Bible who are not part of the Eastern Orthodox Church.[3] In this essay I do not consider whether

---

1. Michael J. Gorman, *Becoming the Gospel: Paul, Participation, and Mission*, The Gospel and Our Culture Series (Grand Rapids: Eerdmans, 2015), 25.
2. Gorman, *Becoming the Gospel*, 7.
3. Cf. Ben C. Blackwell, *Christosis: Engaging Paul's Soteriology with His Patristic Interpreters* (Grand Rapids: Eerdmans, 2016), xxx.

On a personal note, I offer my thanks to Michael Gorman for his scholarship and friendship. Not only has Michael's work been a blessing and help to me, so has his role as dean for my years of teaching at the Ecumenical Institute of Theology. Mike's pastoral nature had a profound impact on me—as well as on many others. I offer these words from the Hebrew Scriptures, echoed in 1 Pet 2:6 as a blessing for him: "See, I am laying in Zion a stone, a cornerstone chosen and precious; and whoever believes in him will not be put to shame."

theosis and the related terms are helpful, but I do explore the notion of participation in 1 Peter. Initially, I suggest that 1 Peter makes its own contribution to our understanding of participation in Christ and does not simply copy Paul's teachings, as some scholars allege. However, I do borrow from Pauline studies of participation to explore 1 Peter's presentation of: (1) Jesus's participation in the human condition; (2) participation in Christ through suffering and subsequent glorification; (3) holiness as evidence of divine kinship.

The classic text for exploring participation in Christ in the NT is 2 Pet 1:4: "Thus he has given us, through these things, his precious and very great promises, so that through them you may escape from the corruption that is in the world because of lust, and may become participants of the divine nature." This verse raises questions concerning in what sense human beings become sharers (κοινωνοὶ) in God's nature.[4] Interest in participation, or what it means to share in divine nature, expanded to include Pauline studies, especially given the apostle Paul's proclivity for using "in Christ" and similar phrases, along with κοινωνία (and its cognates).[5] However, not much has been written concerning 1 Peter's teachings on participation given that 1 Peter has historically been associated with 2 Peter, and has also been thought to echo Paul's teachings.[6] Authorship of 2 Peter has long been debated as many scholars deny that the apostle Peter wrote the letter and take the writing to be a clear example of NT pseudepigrapha.[7] James M. Starr points out, "While assessments vary of how much 2 Peter made use of 1 Peter, it is safe to conclude at least that 2 Peter was familiar enough with 1 Peter to see fit to link his epistle to 1 Peter's."[8] Questions of authorship aside, it seems reasonable to investigate whether or not there is a Petrine teaching of sharing in Christ. This essay attempts to describe participation, or sharing, in Christ within 1 Peter. Although I argue that 1 Peter does not depend directly upon Paul, we may use the fruit of Pauline studies when examining 1 Peter.

---

4. See James M. Starr, *Sharers in Divine Nature: 2 Peter 1:4 in Its Hellenistic Context*, ConBNT 33 (Stockholm: Almqvist & Wiksell International, 2000); Richard Bauckham, *Jude, 2 Peter*, WBC 50 (Waco: Word Books, 1983), 179–82; Paul M. Collins, *Partaking in Divine Nature: Deification and Communion*, TTCT (London: T & T Clark, 2010), 42; Jörg Frey, *The Letter of Jude and the Second Letter of Peter: A Theological Commentary* (Waco: Baylor University Press, 2018), 261–69.

5. Blackwell, *Christosis*, 3.

6. Starr has a brief discussion of 1 Peter (*Sharers in Divine Nature*, 221–23).

7. For recent synopses of the issues concerning Petrine authorship, see David A. deSilva, *An Introduction to the New Testament: Contexts, Methods and Ministry Formation* (Downers Grove, IL: IVP Academic, 2018), 777–81; Frey, *The Letter of Jude and the Second Letter of Peter*, 213–20.

8. Starr, *Sharers in Divine Nature*, 221.

First Peter uses some of the formal language of sharing (i.e., κοινωνία) and also describes believers as members of a new family through new birth. Such ideas are similar to those found in Paul's writings as well as the Gospel of John. However, 1 Peter does not generally use the same vocabulary as Paul. Even the new birth language in 1 Pet 1:3, 23 is different from the discussion of new birth in John 3. Yet, with different vocabulary and different emphases, 1 Peter does teach that believers participate in Christ by becoming like him, especially as those who endure suffering without retaliation. I argue that Peter's use of Isa 53:4–6 functions similarly to Phil 2:6–11 in that it shows how participation in Christ follows from Christ's participation in the human condition. As Gorman shows with respect to Paul, believers' participation in Christ relates not only to future salvation but also to present mission in the world. While this missional notion is not the focus of this paper, I hope to show how that topic might be explored in the future.

First Peter's Alleged Dependence upon Paul[9]

First Peter demonstrates a view of salvation as participation similar to that of Paul. For example, Paul's frequent "in Christ" formulation occurs three times in 1 Peter (3:16; 5:10, 14) but not in other NT writings. Gorman notes that the language of being "in Christ" is one of Paul's linguistic features that points to the centrality of participation in Paul's theology.[10] Although 1 Peter does not focus on the language of justification (but note the use of δίκαιος in 3:12, 18; 4:18), the letter encourages believers to become the gospel through participation in Christ, specifically in the context of suffering. Daniel G. Powers, within his discussion of Paul's understanding of the vicarious death of Jesus, examines the formula "Christ died for us" and notes, "the same basic formula with minor variations can be found in other New Testament writings that show no influence of Paul; namely, Hebrews and the Gospel of John."[11] Powers also mentions 1 Pet 2:21 and 3:18 but adds, "1 Peter is generally thought to be influenced by Paul."[12] For a time, scholars considered 1 Peter to be heavily influenced by Paul. Francis W. Beare, in the mid-twentieth century, asserted that 1 Peter

---

9. I discuss the issues surrounding the authorship of 1 Peter in *1 Peter*, Story of God Bible Commentary (Grand Rapids: Zondervan, 2017), 18–20. For simplicity, in this essay I refer to the author of 1 Peter as "Peter."

10. Gorman, *Becoming the Gospel*, 26, 29.

11. Daniel G. Powers, *Salvation through Participation: An Examination of the Notion of the Believers' Corporate Unity with Christ in Early Christian Soteriology*, CBET 29 (Leuven; Sterling, VA: Peeters, 2001), 38.

12. Powers, *Salvation through Participation*, 38n10 (see also 49n50).

is strongly marked by the impress of Pauline theological ideas, and in language the dependence upon St. Paul is undeniably great. All through the Epistle, we have the impression that we are reading the work of a man who is steeped in the Pauline letters, who is so imbued with them that he uses St. Paul's words and phrases without conscious search, as his own thoroughly-assimilated vocabulary of religion. Entire passages are little more than an expansion or restatement of Pauline texts, and whole verses are a kind of mosaic of Pauline words and forms of expression. As a theologian, the writer has a mind of his own and is no mere echo of Paul, but it is abundantly evident that he has formed himself on Paul's writings.[13]

Regardless of the commonalities, 1 Peter should not be viewed as merely a reworking of Pauline thought. Peter contextualizes similar pre-Pauline ideas and offers his own perspective on participation in Christ. Rather than dismiss 1 Peter's theology of salvation as merely parroting Paul, we do well to explore how 1 Peter contributes to our understanding of the union between Christ and his followers. It may be that 1 Peter's notion of participation is not entirely dependent upon Paul. First Peter's theology of salvation certainly resonates with Pauline thought, but there are noteworthy differences. Paul J. Achtemeier juxtaposes references from 1 Peter and various passages from the Pauline corpus (especially Romans and Ephesians) and concludes, "While the relationship of 1 Peter to the Pauline way of theological reflection cannot be denied, how much of the 'Pauline' flavor of 1 Peter is the result of a common use of early liturgical or confessional material is difficult to say with precision. Similarly, whether the author of 1 Peter was aware of the Pauline letters, or had read them, or whether the 'Pauline' material in 1 Peter had already passed into common tradition by the time 1 Peter was written is equally difficult to demonstrate."[14] John H. Elliott's conclusion is that, "The notion of a supposed 'Paulinism' of 1 Peter has no solid basis in the textual evidence and ought finally be abandoned. It is high time for 1 Peter to be liberated from its 'Pauline captivity' and read as a distinctive voice of the early Church."[15] Other scholars

---

13. Francis Wright Beare, *The First Epistle of Peter: The Greek Text with Introduction and Notes* (Oxford: Blackwell, 1947), 25.

14. Paul J. Achtemeier, *1 Peter*, Hermeneia (Minneapolis: Fortress, 1996), 15-19. Cf. Powers, who observes, with regard to Christ's vicarious death, that "there is a general consensus among scholars that this phrase ['Christ died for us'] does indeed represent a very early, traditional, pre-Pauline formula" (*Salvation through Participation*, 30). Hence, the author of 1 Peter need not have been dependent on Paul for such notions in his soteriology.

15. John H. Elliott, *1 Peter: A New Translation with Introduction and Commentary*, AB 37B (New York: Doubleday, 2001), 40.

share similar views.[16] David G. Horrell after surveying the evidence, offers a nuanced assessment:

> What these various examples show is that there are indeed close points of contact between 1 Peter and the Pauline tradition. The parallels do not suggest that there is a *literary* relationship between the texts, such as we see between the three Synoptic Gospels since the overlaps in wording are generally few and imprecise. But they do suggest that the author of 1 Peter knows and uses in his letter some forms and turns of phrase that reflect some knowledge of Paul's letters. However, this does not mean that we should regard 1 Peter as essentially 'Pauline' in character. . . . 1 Peter has its own distinctive character, its own particular use of tradition.[17]

It is not a foregone conclusion that 1 Peter is dependent upon Paul. However, studies of Pauline soteriology provide helpful tools for examining other NT writings. Our understanding of participation in Christ is deepened with increasing appreciation of how Christian tradition is communicated in 1 Peter.

Jesus's Participation in the Human Condition

In the NT, participation in Christ is predicated upon Christ's participation in human existence, especially the experience of suffering. Robert C. Tannehill, while exploring Rom 8:3, asserts that, "Atonement for sin presupposes the prior divine action of sending God's Son to participate in the human situation, an act in which the Son identifies with humanity in its need . . . through the Son, God participates in the situation of human need."[18] Tannehill goes on

---

16. There are many commentators who conclude that Peter uses common Christian tradition and does not copy Paul. For example, Joel B. Green argues that "Peter is doing more than mimicking early tradition. He appears to have his own access to those elements of the tradition also picked up by Matthew and Luke, Paul and James, and others, and like them he embeds those materials within his own constructive thought by way of addressing the needs of his audience" (*1 Peter*, THNTC [Grand Rapids: Eerdmans, 2007], 232). J. Ramsey Michaels claims, "Even where 1 Peter appears to be reflecting the thought or language of Paul, it always develops the Pauline ideas, images, or proof texts in such an independent fashion that a direct literary relationship is difficult to establish" (*1 Peter*, WBC 49 [Waco: Word Books, 1988], xliv).

17. David G. Horrell, *1 Peter*, NTG (New York: T & T Clark, 2008), 38 (italics original).

18. Robert C. Tannehill, *The Shape of the Gospel: New Testament Essays* (Eugene, OR: Cascade, 2007), 227.

to review other Pauline texts, particularly Gal 4:4-5, Phil 2:7-8, and 2 Cor 8:9, concluding that, "the self-renouncing identification of God's Son with humanity in its need is based on divine initiative. The participation is first of all divine participation in the human plight, which makes possible human participation in God's Son."[19] Gorman also recognizes how Christ's participation in humanity is the basis for the believer's participation in Christ. In *Becoming the Gospel: Paul, Participation, and Mission*, Gorman begins his argument for theosis in Romans by quoting Morna D. Hooker, Dietrich Bonhoeffer, and Wilhelm Wrede, respectively:

- "Christ became what we are—*adam*—in order that we might share in what he is—namely the true image of God" (Hooker).
- Christ "became like human beings, so that we would be like him" (Bonhoeffer).
- "Christ becomes what we are, that we through his death may become what he is" (Wrede).[20]

A few pages later, Gorman offers a summarizing dictum of Irenaeus's regarding theosis: "He [Jesus] became what we are, so that we might become what he is."[21]

First Peter likewise affirms that Christ's solidarity with humanity is for the purpose of human beings becoming like God. As part of his opening greeting, Peter offers a trinitarian description of his readers: "chosen and destined by God the Father and sanctified by the Spirit to be obedient to Jesus Christ and to be sprinkled with his blood" (1:2). While this is not a direct assertion of the divinity of Christ, Peter offers a picture of the Father, Son, and Spirit working together in the lives of the believers. Furthermore, it is likely that Peter at least affirmed Christ's preexistence. A few verses later, Peter refers to prophets "who prophesied of the grace that was to be yours" (1:10). Peter likely has OT prophets in view.[22] And if OT prophets are indeed the agents of the message,

---

19. Tannehill, *The Shape of the Gospel*, 229.
20. Gorman, *Becoming the Gospel*, 262. See also Michael J. Gorman, *Inhabiting the Cruciform God: Kenosis, Justification, and Theosis in Paul's Narrative Soteriology* (Grand Rapids: Eerdmans, 2009), 1–8.
21. Gorman, *Becoming the Gospel*, 268. In *Christosis*, Ben Blackwell explains, "In the process of restoring divine likeness, Irenaeus regularly employs his exchange formula: Christ became human so humans could become like him" (42).
22. Most commentators share this perspective. E.g., see Achtemeier, *1 Peter*, 108 and Elliott, *1 Peter*, 345.

then the assertion that the "Spirit of Christ" (1:11) was at work in those prophets is Peter's way of acknowledging Christ's preexistence, even if not a clear assertion of Christ's divinity. It is this Messiah (Christ) who, in the person of Jesus, shares in the human condition, especially with regard to suffering.

Because Jesus participated in human suffering, he provides an example for Peter's readers in much the same way that the *carmen Christi* of Phil 2:6–11 does for the Philippian Christians. Gorman has written much on Philippians, even referring to 2:6–11 as "Paul's master story."[23] Gorman argues that this master story is also Paul's story as well as that of the Philippians. The story serves to affirm the believers' participation in Christ and in God's mission to the world, especially in light of the pressures the Christians faced to conform to Roman ways. "Perhaps Paul worries that the Philippians will stop confessing that Jesus, rather than Caesar, is Lord and therefore return to public behaviors that demonstrate their loyalty to Rome and their acceptance of Roman values and ideologies—the Roman 'gospel,' the Roman master narrative."[24]

The pressure of 1 Peter's readers to conform to the Roman way of life is present throughout the letter, and 1 Pet 2:21–25 functions similarly in the letter as Phil 2:6–11 does in its context. Jesus, who suffered but did not retaliate, serves as the ultimate example for Peter's readers. There are several references in 1 Peter to the suffering of Jesus (e.g., 1:11; 3:18; 4:1, 13; 5:1), but 2:21–25 is one that clearly has Isaiah's Suffering Servant in view, even citing Isa 53:5:

> For to this you have been called, because Christ also suffered for you, leaving you an example, so that you should follow in his steps. "He committed no sin, and no deceit was found in his mouth." When he was abused, he did not return abuse; when he suffered, he did not threaten; but he entrusted himself to the one who judges justly. He himself bore our sins in his body on the cross, so that, free from sins, we might live for righteousness; by his wounds you have been healed.

Richard Bauckham asserts that Phil 2:6–11 reflects a Christian understanding of salvation and the mission of God found in Isaiah's Suffering Servant.[25] Early Christians, Bauckham argues, interpreted the person and mission of Jesus through the lens of Isaiah 40–66, equating the Servant of the Lord with

---

23. Gorman, *Inhabiting the Cruciform God*, 12; Gorman, *Becoming the Gospel*, 115.
24. Gorman, *Becoming the Gospel*, 114–15.
25. *Jesus and the God of Israel: God Crucified and Other Studies on the New Testament's Christology of Divine Identity* (Grand Rapids: Eerdmans, 2008), 197–210.

Participation in Christ in 1 Peter

Jesus Christ. Consequently, Phil 2:6–11 is Paul's way of describing how "the career of the Servant of the Lord, his suffering, humiliation, death and exaltation, is the way in which the sovereignty of the one true God comes to be acknowledged by all."[26] The suffering of Jesus is testimony of God's sovereignty, and the suffering of the followers of Jesus is testimony of their allegiance to Christ. The phrase at the start of 1 Pet 2:21, "for to this you have been called" points back to the abuse described in v. 20 and indicates that suffering is not meaningless; it serves a purpose. That purpose is found when considering the suffering of Christ. Indeed, in 1 Pet 2:21–25 we read how suffering characterized the ministry of the Messiah. What Christ went through on earth was for others—even slaves—and provides an example for encouragement and motivation. First Peter 2:21–25 focuses upon the catalytic impact that suffering can have; that is, in the same way that Christ serves as an example for Christian slaves because he endured unjust treatment, the attitude of these slaves during the heat of oppression can also be a witness to onlookers (2:15). Slaves are called to follow in the footsteps of Christ as 1 Pet 2:21–25 does not emphasize the resurrection of Christ but rather his death. Peter encourages his readers, in 2:21–25 and elsewhere, that in their suffering they are participating in Jesus by following in the footsteps of their Lord.

Κοινωνία—in Suffering and in Glory

Twice in 1 Peter the language of sharing, specifically κοινωνία or its cognates, occurs (4:13 and 5:1), and points to participation in suffering as well as in glory. Gorman concludes that, "the Pauline language of κοινωνία indicates a deep participation in Christ, especially in his death, that is shared with other believers and that comes to fruition in concrete practices of sacrificial, generous self-giving love and even suffering."[27] Peter's language of κοινωνία functions similarly in that believers, together, share in Christ's suffering and also demonstrate self-giving love (1:22; 2:17; 3:8; 4:8; 5:14).[28] For Peter, participation in the sufferings of Christ is a cause for great rejoicing.[29] Suffering itself is not

---

26. Bauckham, *Jesus and the God of Israel*, 206.
27. Gorman, *Becoming the Gospel*, 31.
28. In addition to Peter's explicit love language (i.e., φιλαδελφία and ἀγάπη), he employs other language of self-giving and mutuality (e.g., ὁμόφρων, συμπαθής, εὔσπλαγχνος, and ταπεινόφρων in 3:8; ταπεινοφροσύνην in 5:5; ταπεινώθητε in 5:6).
29. Joyful celebration is clearly emphasized in 4:13, as Peter twice uses the verb χαίρω ("rejoice") and also the verb ἀγαλλιάω ("be exceedingly joyful"). Cf. Jas 1:2 and Phil 4:4 (Gorman's evaluation of κοινωνία emerges chiefly from his study of Philippians).

enjoyable; Peter is not a masochist. Rejoicing is possible, however, because through suffering, the faithful follower of Jesus is assured eternal reward—an inheritance (1:4)—when Christ returns. Peter's readers suffer because of their identification with Jesus and are encouraged to endure their suffering with hope.

In 1 Pet 4:16, Peter admonishes the audience not to be ashamed if they suffer for bearing the name "Christian." The word Χριστιανός is rare in the NT (elsewhere only at Acts 11:26; 26:28), and most likely was initially an epithet, coined by outsiders.[30] But Peter attempts to turn an insult into a title of honor. David Horrell observes that, "The label Χριστιανός is a stigmatizing label associated not with a facet of personal identity—such as disability or disfigurement—but with a feature of social identity deriving from group membership. In relation to the term Χριστιανός, one thing that is interesting is that it is outsiders who heighten the salience of this label not only by coining it in the first place but also by making it, in judicial settings, *the* crucial identifier that determines whether a person is or is not a social deviant, whether they can be permitted to remain in society or not."[31] Horrell considers the work of social science and suggests that the use of Χριστιανός in 1 Pet 4:16 is an example of "the strategy of changing the values assigned to the attributes of the group, so that comparisons which were previously negative are now perceived as positive.... In other words terms and designators with a negative social-identity value are retained, but reclaimed and reinterpreted, with what we may perhaps call polemical pride, as positive ones." [32] A derogatory term is converted into a badge of honor. Shively T. J. Smith applies similar reasoning suggesting, "The cosmology of 1 Peter functions as a narrative of knowledge in which diaspora is transformed from a punitive and embarrassing situation to a condition of being the legitimate people of God. Instead of titles such as 'foreigner' and 'Christian' being pejorative and limiting, the letter tells them to embrace these as markers of the diaspora-Christian situation."[33]

Rather than enduring the shame heaped upon them by outsiders, Peter's

---

30. Michaels, *1 Peter*, 268–69. Michaels points out that the formation "Christian" is analogous to "Herodian," indicating "partisans of Christ" (268). But see Elias J. Bickerman who argues that the Antiochene Christians coined the term themselves ("The Name of Christians," *HTR* 42 [1949]: 109–124).

31. David G. Horrell, "The Label Χριστιανός: 1 Peter 4:16 and the Formation of Christian Identity," *JBL* 126 (2007): 377 (emphasis original).

32. Horrell, "The Label Χριστιανός," 379.

33. Shively T. J. Smith, *Strangers to Family: Diaspora and 1 Peter's Invention of God's Household* (Waco: Baylor University Press, 2016), 42.

readers were to find honor in their identification with Christ, even as they endured suffering. After their suffering, which Peter refers to as "a little while" (1 Pet 5:10), there will be glory. "To participate with Christ in suffering is to place oneself in the pattern of Christ's career as Peter portrays it. Drinking deeply from the scriptural wells of the Righteous Sufferer, Peter has plotted a path from suffering to glory for Jesus."[34] That path is emphasized in 1 Pet 3:18–22, even though vv. 19–21 are the subject of much confusion and discussion.[35] What is clear, in what may be part of a hymn or creedal statement, is that Christ's path starts with suffering (v. 18) and ends with exaltation (v. 22), as is the case with Phil 2:6–11.

Peter's readers are to follow the same path, from suffering to glory. Peter's other use of κοινωνία is in 1 Pet 5:1 where Peter, after acknowledging his role as a witness of the sufferings of Christ, asserts that he will share in the glory yet to be unveiled. In the meantime, the Christian family witnesses for Jesus through its humility (5:2–6). I say "family" because Peter's final section is full of familial language: "older" (5:1); "younger" (5:5); ἀδελφότης "fellowship of sisters and brothers" (5:9); "brother" (5:12); "she" or "sister" (5:13). The Christians to whom Peter writes are, as Gorman might put it, an *apologia* for the gospel.[36] It is also through the language of family—especially new birth (1:3)—that Peter gets at another aspect of participation: holiness.

Members of a New Family, Characterized by Holiness

While the term "Christian" reflects an allegiance to Christ, with believers sharing in the Lord's suffering and shame, the language of family amplifies the relationship. First Peter opens with what might appear to be contrasting descriptors of the recipients of the letter.[37] On the one hand, the first readers of the letter are described as "elect" (ἐκλεκτός), a designation intended to recall the unique relationship of God to God's OT people. This election, based upon God's foreknowledge (1 Pet 1:2), foreshadows descriptions that appear later in the letter, such as the echo of Exod 19:5–6 and reference to Hos 2:23 found in 1 Pet 2:9–10. Election indicates divine initiative. God calls people to live in a

---

34. Green, *1 Peter*, 154–55.
35. See Edwards, *1 Peter*, 158–67.
36. Gorman, *Becoming the Gospel*, 139–40. Gorman refers to the Philippians as an *apologia* for the gospel, particularly through suffering—Paul's and theirs.
37. The commentaries, including my own (Edwards, *1 Peter*) discuss the terms ἐκλεκτός, παρεπίδημος, διασπορά, and πάροικος (1 Pet 2:11) in more detail. My goal here is to emphasize kinship with God.

way that is distinct from the broader society, and that way of life is characterized by holiness (1:15–16). On the other hand, Peter refers to his audience as "exiles of the dispersion" (παρεπιδήμοις διασπορᾶς, 1:1).³⁸ Such language suggests distance, perhaps even from God.

Diaspora implies expulsion from a people's homeland. Shively Smith, after tracing the meaning of "diaspora" from its earliest usage with regard to Israel, points out that "social and cultural intellectual circles broadened the meaning of diaspora to encompass the migration and dispersal patterns of contemporary migrating populations (e.g., Africans, Armenians, Hispanics, Turks), not just Jews."³⁹ Given the history of Israel's relationship to land, diaspora might be viewed as punishment. If diaspora is a form of exile or forced migration, it might be reasonable to conclude that God was responsible for the removal of God's people from a particular geographic location. Smith, however, does not view dispersion as divine punishment. She explores terms from the Hebrew Bible related to exile and captivity (i.e., גולה, גלה, and גלות) and concludes that "diaspora" "is not used to translate those Hebrew words denoting exile and captivity. It also does not describe the tangible political and militaristic circumstances that gave rise to it like foreign conquests and mass deportations."⁴⁰ Although "diaspora" does mean "dispersion," the emphasis, particularly in 1 Peter, is distance from the dominant culture, not distance from God. Therefore, "elect exiles of the dispersion" is not a contradiction; rather, it describes the dynamic tension these early Christians faced. These people are not called into a relationship with God while simultaneously being pushed away by God. On the contrary, because of their calling (i.e., election), they are being alienated by the world (i.e., diaspora). As those rejected by society yet chosen by God, 1 Peter's readers are shown to be like their Lord, who was the stone rejected by humans but chosen and honored by God (2:4). One of the contributions of 1 Peter is to describe how Christians participate with God while experiencing rejection and the heat of oppression (1:6–7; 4:12).

Familial language is used throughout 1 Peter to explain God's affirmation of these elect exiles of the dispersion and to highlight their participation with God. In addition to family language found in chapter 5 (mentioned at the end of the section above), Peter refers to believers as those who experience new

---

38. Smith offers the hyphenated "elect-foreigners" as a "conjoined substantive." She designates the recipients as "elect-foreigners of the Diaspora" (*Strangers to Family*, 20). Whether or not the terms are taken as a compound noun, they still suggest a contradiction, or at least some ambiguity.

39. Smith, *Strangers to Family*, 7.

40. Smith, *Strangers to Family*, 7.

Participation in Christ in 1 Peter

birth (1:3, 23) and share in the family inheritance (1:4). Furthermore, Peter refers to God as Father (e.g., 1:2, 17) and to the believers as "obedient children" (1:14). Additionally, the church is called "household" (4:17). Participation in 1 Peter includes becoming part of a new family and adopting the values and behaviors of Jesus Christ, the model member of the family. In the opening chapter, when Peter refers to "new birth" (1:3, 23), he uses the only NT occurrences of the word, ἀναγεννάω ("beget again"). However, the concept of spiritual new birth is common in the NT, most notably in the Gospel of John (e.g., John 3:3–7).[41]

In *Abide and Go: Missional Theosis in the Gospel of John*, Gorman continues his exploration of theosis and mission.[42] He seems to have discovered what Collins has observed: "The Johannine corpus in the New Testament has many parallels with the Pauline corpus in terms of the themes of adoption and Christification, even if the vocabulary and phraseology are different."[43] Regarding the image of new birth, Gorman writes that, "those who are brought into relationship with Jesus receive the Spirit and become children of God, both of which imply participation in the divine life and sharing in the divine 'DNA.' Such sharing in God's life and such family resemblance imply participation in God's activity, or mission."[44] Indeed, new birth means a new family identity. In 1 Peter, this new identity entails deliverance "from the futile ways inherited from your ancestors" (1:18) and a commitment to holiness (1:16). "Filiation" is the technical term indicating the status of believers as children of God and is related to the concept of theosis, or deification. In the Pauline literature, adoption (υἱοθεσία) is the metaphor indicating filiation (Rom 8:15, 23; 9:4; Gal 4:5; Eph 1:5). In 1 Peter filiation is described as new birth. Those who become children of God take on attributes of God, including holiness.[45]

First Peter 1:16 echoes the OT Levitical command, "Be holy, for I am holy" (Lev 11:44, 45; 19:2; 20:7, 26). This command is linked to the notion of new birth, which is prominent in the first chapter of 1 Peter (noted above). The Christian community is described as children whose character is that of obe-

---

41. See Craig S. Keener, *The Gospel of John: A Commentary* (Peabody, MA: Hendrickson, 2010), 539–44; Matthew Vellanickal, *The Divine Sonship of Christians in the Johannine Writings*, AnBib 72 (Rome: Biblical Institute, 1977), esp. 163–213 (where Vellanickal details the Gospel of John's language of new birth).
42. Michael J. Gorman, *Abide and Go: Missional Theosis in the Gospel of John* (Eugene, OR: Cascade, 2018).
43. Collins, *Partaking in Divine Nature*, 46.
44. Gorman, *Abide and Go*, 56.
45. See Collins, *Partaking in Divine Nature*, 27–28.

dience to God (1 Pet 1:14).[46] God, the One who calls, is holy, and it is God's holiness that provides the foundation for the behavior of Peter's readers (1:15). First Peter employs the vocabulary of holiness and purity throughout the letter, using ἅγιος (and its cognates), as well as related words: ἄμωμος ("unblemished") and ἄσπιλος ("spotless") in 1:19 and καθαρός ("pure") in 1:22. Elliott catalogs 1 Peter's vocabulary of holiness and observes, "In 1 Peter, holiness is stressed as a paramount quality uniting believers with God and Jesus Christ and distinguishing them from nonbelievers."[47] Indeed, holiness indicates obedience to God but is not simply conformity to a code; holiness is the result of the relationship people have with God. Believers who are called into a relationship with God (1:1–2, 15; 2:9; 5:10), through new birth (i.e., filiation), are commanded to be holy. Holiness is evidence of union with Christ and leads to noticeable distinction from the broader culture. Holiness is devotion to God that results in separation from what is common or profane. That separation is based on the people of God becoming like God. Scot McKnight asserts that, "Holiness cannot be reduced to separation or difference. At a deeper level, holiness means 'devoted.'"[48] Regarding holiness in the OT, Morna Hooker observes, "in summoning Israel to be his people, God demanded that they should share his 'otherness.' They must 'consecrate' themselves to him—make themselves holy."[49] Both Hooker and McKnight suggest holiness is first of all devotion to God, or consecration. Hooker defines holiness as "living according to the revealed character of God" (5). She further explains that holiness for Israel did not mean being aloof and cutting off outsiders, but instead living in such a way as to reveal God's character to the other nations (5–6). With the revelation of Jesus Christ we find out what God is like, so "for the Christian, the command to 'be holy as I am holy,' is a command to be like Christ" (12). Gorman's observations surrounding holiness in Paul resonate with those of Hooker: "As a Jew Paul knows that to be holy is to be *Godlike*; as a Jew in Christ, he knows that to be holy is to be *Christlike*."[50]

The holiness of Christian communities should be a witness to unbelievers.

---

46. The phrase τέκνα ὑπακοῆς ("children of obedience") is a Semitic construction where "obedience" is an essential quality of "children."

47. Elliott, *1 Peter*, 361.

48. Scot McKnight, *A Fellowship of Differents: Showing the World God's Design for Life Together* (Grand Rapids: Zondervan, 2014), 117.

49. Morna D. Hooker, *Holiness and Mission: Learning from the Early Church about Mission in the City* (London: SCM, 2010), 4. Hereafter, page references are given in parentheses in the text.

50. Gorman, *Inhabiting the Cruciform God*, 113 (emphasis Gorman's).

Those who observe Christian believers ought to get some sense of what God values and what Jesus is like. This is to say that holiness has a missional component.[51] The community that 1 Peter addresses has the noble but challenging task of modeling Christlike behavior in hostile territory. The suffering of the believers, largely in the form of marginalization and verbal assault from unbelievers, is a direct result of the community's allegiance to Christ. As followers of Christ, the community withdraws from social activities that dishonor God (1 Pet 4:2–4) yet lives as model citizens who respect the government (2:13–17), even though the slaves and Christian wives within the community were prevented from enjoying the benefits of actual citizenship.

Betsy Bauman-Martin points out the vulnerability of the Christian community addressed in 1 Peter under the Roman Empire:

> 1 Peter was written in a time of, and for an audience that experienced, imperialism (an ideology that upholds the legitimacy of the economic and military control of one country by another), and colonialism (a practice which results from imperialism, specifically the settlement of groups from the more dominant country in the country of the conquered, often for means of control). Asia Minor, the site of the audience for 1 Peter, had experienced imperialism since the time of Alexander the Great and colonialism in the form of taxation and new religious demands, extraction of resources, including human ones, less autonomy for governors, and overall imperial supervision.[52]

Peter's audience, whose status was that of alien members of diaspora, were in a vulnerable position because their allegiance was to Jesus and not to the empire. It is from their vulnerable position that the early Christians to whom Peter writes witness to what Jesus is like. Gorman observes, with respect to Paul's Letter to the Romans, that the church challenged, albeit implicitly, the values of the Roman Empire.[53] The same could be said of 1 Peter's community. People without power or prestige rebuffed the allure of Roman society because life in Christ was more attractive, valuable, and rewarding. There is, of course, much more that could be said about how 1 Peter's community lived as witnesses of the *missio Dei*, but that is beyond the scope of this essay. In any case, 1 Peter

---

51. See Andy Johnson, *Holiness and the* Missio Dei (Eugene, OR: Cascade, 2016).
52. Betsy Bauman-Martin, "Speaking Jewish: Postcolonial Aliens and Strangers in First Peter," in *Reading First Peter with New Eyes: Methodological Reassessments of the Letter of First Peter*, ed. Robert L. Webb, LNTS 364 (London: T & T Clark, 2007), 157.
53. Gorman, *Becoming the Gospel*, 293–95.

affirms what Gorman says about Romans: "Theosis is political. It is counter- and alter-cultural. It is missional."[54]

Conclusions

I set out in this essay to demonstrate that 1 Peter's message resonates with Paul's, particularly with regard to participation in Christ. One can see the similarities without having to conclude that Peter merely copied Paul. It may be that 1 Peter and Paul are working from a common Christian tradition. But even though Peter does not necessarily borrow directly from Paul, we can employ Pauline studies as a helpful framework to gain insight into 1 Peter. Michael Gorman's work on theosis in Paul helps to provide a lens and language to explore salvation as participation in 1 Peter, as well as the nature of Christian mission under the Roman Empire.

Believers' participation in Christ follows from Christ's participation in the human condition. Whereas Phil 2:6-11 describes Christ's participation in humanity from Paul's perspective, 1 Pet 2:21-24 fills a similar role in 1 Peter. Christ, who suffered unjustly and did not retaliate, serves as a model for the entire Christian community but especially slaves, who faced the likelihood of physical abuse along with the verbal abuse other Christians experienced (1 Pet 2:20). Sharing in Christ includes conforming to Christ's behavior in the world. The believers in 1 Peter are admonished throughout the letter to participate in Christ. The formal language of sharing, κοινωνία, which appears much in Paul, also appears in 1 Peter and points to both participation in suffering as well as in glory. As the believers take on the shame of public scorn, bearing the epithet "Christian," they transform an insult into a badge of honor. The Christians participate in Christ's suffering (4:13) but look forward with joy (4:13; cf. 1:5-6, 8).

The language of family, which permeates 1 Peter, also describes what participation in Christ means. The family, with God as Father, produces obedient children who are holy like their Father. These children are holy not simply because of what they do or what they avoid but because they have a new nature; they have been born anew (1:3, 23). And children will receive an inheritance (1:4).

There is more to be said about 1 Peter and participation that is too much for one essay. For example, 1 Peter has been called a "baptism homily."[55] A brief

---

54. Gorman, *Becoming the Gospel*, 294.
55. See Horrell, *1 Peter*, 7-8.

Participation in Christ in 1 Peter

discussion of baptism occurs at 1 Pet 3:21. Baptism, as Gorman points out, is by its nature a participatory rite, identifying the believer with Christ and the Christian community.[56] There may be more to be explored concerning 1 Peter's depiction of baptism as participation in Christ. Furthermore, the fact that the Christian community in 1 Peter is called upon to be witnesses for Christ among hostile unbelievers, requires more missional readings of the letter.[57]

---

56. Gorman, *Becoming the Gospel*, 26–27.
57. See, e.g., Michael W. Goheen, *A Light to the Nations: The Missional Church and the Biblical Story* (Grand Rapids: Baker Academic, 2011) and Ross Hastings, *Missional God, Missional Church: Hope for Re-Evangelizing the West* (Downers Grove, IL: IVP Academic, 2012).

PART THREE

Becoming the Gospel in Mission

Chapter 10

"Follow Me": The Mandate for Mission in the Gospel of John

Sherri Brown

In recent years, scholars of the Johannine literature have begun exploring the ethical implications of these texts with renewed interest, often challenging long-standing stereotypes of the absence of such mandates in favor of christological and/or sectarian concerns.[1] Some have further challenged the traditional presuppositions of what it means to be "ethical" and what constitutes "ethical mandates."[2] Such scholars look instead to genre, characterization, as well as the action implied in Jesus's teaching through invitation, imperative, and mimetic exhortation.[3] Harold Attridge further explores the evangelist's

---

1. See esp. the diverse essays in Sherri Brown and Christopher W. Skinner, eds., *Johannine Ethics: The Moral World of the Gospel and Letters of John* (Minneapolis: Fortress, 2017) and Jan G. van der Watt and Ruben Zimmerman, eds., *Rethinking the Ethics of John: "Implicit Ethics" in the Johannine Writings, Kontexte und Normen neutestamentlicher Ethik/Contexts and Norms of New Testament Ethics*, vol. 3, WUNT 1/291 (Tübingen: Mohr Siebeck, 2012).

2. See the discussions in Michael Labahn, "'It's Only Love'—Is That All? Limits and Potentials of Johannine 'Ethic': A Critical Evaluation of Research," in *Rethinking the Ethics of John*, 3–43; Christopher W. Skinner, "Introduction: (How) Can We Talk about Johannine Ethics? Looking Back and Moving Forward," in *Johannine Ethics*, xvii–xxxvi. See also Sookgoo Shin, *Ethics in the Gospel of John: Discipleship as Moral Progress*, BibInt 168 (Leiden: Brill, 2019); D. Moody Smith, "Ethics and the Interpretation of the Fourth Gospel," in *Word, Theology, and Community in John*, ed. John Painter, R. Alan Culpepper, and Fernando F. Segovia (St. Louis: Chalice, 2002), 109–22; Lindsey M. Trozzo, *Exploring Johannine Ethics: A Rhetorical Approach to Moral Efficacy in the Fourth Gospel Narrative*, WUNT 2/449 (Tübingen: Mohr Siebeck, 2017).

3. See Cornelis Bennema, *Mimesis in the Johannine Literature: A Study in Johannine Eth-*

interest in dialoguing with other first-century ethical thinkers, especially the Stoics.[4] He claims, "the evangelist presents an alternative rationale for a foundational ethical principle, that right reason, not emotion, should guide life," and this reason "must be grounded in acceptance of the revealed truth that Jesus teaches and embodies."[5]

A corresponding extension of this developing interest lies in the study of Johannine spirituality. Scholars such as Dorothy Lee, Andrew Lincoln, Teresa Okure, and Sandra Schneiders have moved away from a focus on a spiritual interiority that is disconnected from concrete this-worldly existence to explore the Johannine approach to mission.[6] In his important contribution to the discussion, Michael Gorman identifies such an approach as reading John through a "missional hermeneutic."[7] He summarizes the claims of "missional theosis" in his recent study of the Fourth Gospel in the following thesis statement.

> Johannine spirituality fundamentally consists in the mutual indwelling of the Triune God (Father, Son, and Spirit) and Jesus' disciples such that disciples *participate* in the divine love and life, and therefore in the life-giving mission of God, thereby both *demonstrating their likeness to God as God's children* and *becoming more and more like God as they become like his Son*

---

ics, LNTS 498 (London: Bloomsbury/T & T Clark, 2017) and the essays in Christopher W. Skinner, ed., *Characters and Characterization in the Gospel of John*, LNTS 461 (London: Bloomsbury/T & T Clark, 2013).

4. Harrold W. Attridge, "An Emotional Jesus and Stoic Traditions," in *Stoicism in Early Christianity*, ed. Tuomas Rasimus, Troels Engberg-Pedersen, and Ismo Dunderburg (Peabody, MA: Hendrickson, 2010), 77–92; "Divine Sovereignty and Human Responsibility in the Fourth Gospel," in *Revealed Wisdom: Studies in Apocalyptic in Honour of Christopher Rowland*, ed. John Ashton, AJEC 88 (Leiden: Brill, 2014), 183–99; "Quaestiones Disputatae: Are John's Ethics Apolitical?," *NTS* 62 (2016): 484–97.

5. Harold W. Attridge, "Johannine Ethics and Ethical Discourse," in *Scripture and Social Justice: Catholic and Ecumenical Essays*, ed. Anathea E. Portier-Young and Gregory E. Sterling (Lanham, MD: Lexington Books/Fortress Academic, 2018), 179.

6. Dorothy Lee, *Hallowed in Truth and Love: Spirituality in the Johannine Literature* (Eugene, OR: Wipf & Stock, 2012); Andrew T. Lincoln, "The Johannine Vision of the Church," in *The Oxford Handbook of Ecclesiology*, ed. Paul Avis (Oxford: Oxford University Press, 2018), 99–118; Teresa Okure, *The Johannine Approach to Mission: A Contextual Study of John 4.1–42*, WUNT 2/31 (Tübingen: Mohr Siebeck, 1988); Sandra M. Schneiders, *Jesus Risen in Our Midst: Essays on the Resurrection of Jesus in the Fourth Gospel* (Collegeville, MN: Liturgical Press, 2013).

7. Michael Gorman, *Abide and Go: Missional Theosis in the Gospel of John* (Eugene, OR: Cascade, 2018), 2–8.

by the work of the Spirit. This spirituality can be summarized in the phrase "abide and go," based on John 15.[8]

That is to say, transformative participation in the life of God through the incarnation of the divine into the earthly (by way of believing that Jesus is the Christ and Son of God and entering into the resulting relationship [John 1:10–14]) bestows a union of divine indwelling that then creates an outward turning toward mission, inclusion, and active, justice-seeking discipleship. The current essay builds upon this scholarly interest and tracks the narrative unfolding of John's establishment of what it means to be children of God and the invitations and imperatives that ensue for all disciples, which culminate in a mandate for mission in the new covenant.

Through both narration and direct summons, characters in and audiences of the Gospel of John are beckoned to deeper relationship with God through Jesus as he challenges them to open themselves to what God is doing in their lives now. Indeed, Jesus's first words of the gospel, the query "what are you seeking?" (1:38, my translation) set the tone for the invitation-as-imperative (or, imperative-as-invitation): "come and see," made to both his first and all potential disciples (1:38–39). The primary commandments presented across the narrative are to receive and believe Jesus is Christ and Son of God, which is manifested in abiding and loving one another in community (1:12; 13:34–35). Further, Jesus tasks inquisitors to know the truth so that it will set them free (8:31–32; 18:37–38). Some respond positively; others do not, but the hope for those who do is to have life in Jesus's name (20:30–31). Jesus's final challenge of the gospel, then, is for those who believe and love to "follow me"—the underlying imperative of the entire gospel (21:22), punctuated in the lives of real disciples who must live by Jesus's command to believe without seeing. But this is not just a call to an interior spirituality; rather, it is a challenge to participate in the divine indwelling relationship by living the way Jesus lived: a life of concrete action through receiving, loving, and abiding with others in this world. This is the gospel's mandate for mission, and its purpose is to prepare audiences to do just that.

The Call to Receive and Believe

The Johannine narrative is often noted to be a gospel of encounters as Jesus interacts with people in the midst of their celebrations (John 2:1–12),

---

8. Gorman, *Abide and Go*, 8 (italics original).

their questioning (3:1–21), their daily lives (4:1–42), their ritual lives (5–10), and their suffering (11:1–44). A careful reading also reveals that "belief" as a noun (πίστις) does not occur in the Fourth Gospel, but forms of the verb "to believe" (πιστεύειν) occur regularly and often (ninety-eight times).[9] Thus, believing in John's Gospel is always dynamic and rightly described in terms of an action, or better, an active journey powered by encountering others along the way. Authentic believing is unreserved openness to God, readiness to accept the truth, and an unqualified loyalty to the reality one experiences.[10] The journey of believing could, therefore, be multifaceted, reflecting both the evangelist's christological claims of how relationship with God is achieved *and* how the children of God interact with the world around them. Believing, therefore, is also an ethical imperative of the evangelist and the foundation of the ethical life.

The invitation to receive and believe begins in the prologue (John 1:1–18) and extends, in detail, across the often-called Book of Signs (1:19–12:50).[11] Although continuing through the narrative's climax and resolution, the primary discourse of this imperative falls in Jesus's public ministry. Much like the prologues in ancient Greek dramas, John's prologue gives audiences a synthesis of events to come (1:1–18). It tells audiences the *who* and the *what* of the events at hand but leaves open the *how*. The subsequent drama *shows* what the prologue *tells* since the story itself is necessary to understand how the events play out.[12] The core proclamation of John's prologue is that the Word of God in human form is the gift of truth that empowers those who receive and believe in him to become children of God.[13] If the prologue is the gateway into the narrative, this

---

9. See also, Raymond E. Brown, *The Gospel according to John, I–XII*, AB 29 (Garden City, NY: Doubleday, 1966), 512–14; Lee, *Hallowed*, 135; Derek Tovey, *Jesus, Story of God: John's Story of Jesus* (Adelaide: ATF, 2007), 103–37.

10. Sandra M. Schneiders, *Written That You May Believe: Encountering Jesus in the Fourth Gospel* (New York: Crossroad, 1999), 87.

11. So Brown, *The Gospel according to John, I–XII*, cxxxviii–cxliv.

12. "Showing" and "telling" are the means by which narratives reveal character (Wayne C. Booth, *The Rhetoric of Fiction*, 2nd ed. [Chicago: University of Chicago Press, 1983], 3–9). See also Tom Thatcher, "Jesus, Judas, and Peter: Character by Contrast in the Fourth Gospel," *BSac* 153 (1996): 435–48; W. J. Harvey, *Character and the Novel* (Ithaca, NY: Cornell University Press, 1965), 32.

13. For a full treatment of my understanding of the structure and content of the prologue, see Sherri Brown, *Gift upon Gift: Covenant through Word in the Gospel of John*, Princeton Theological Monograph Series (Eugene, OR: Pickwick, 2010), 78–95; and Sherri Brown and Francis J. Moloney, *Interpreting the Gospel and Letters of John: An Interpretation* (Grand Rapids: Eerdmans, 2017), 163–77. This argument is drawn largely from the work of R. Alan

core proclamation is also the heart of the gospel message. The establishment of childhood in God through the Word of God incarnate in Jesus the Christ is the culmination of all God's dealings with the world, the goal of the Creator and creation. The claim is that those who receive the Word (v. 12a) will be given the power to become children of God (v. 12b), but how does one go about this receiving? By believing in his name (v. 12c).[14]

Alan Culpepper's work on the prologue alerts us to the way the evangelist begins with cosmic assertions of the eternal nature of God and God's Word and moves to more specific claims of the interaction of the Word of God in creation in terms of a familial relationship (John 1:1–11). The crux of the prologue is that Jesus gives those who receive and believe in him "power to become children of God" (v. 12). John can then proclaim the incarnation of the Word in Jesus Christ as God's promised gift of truth to humankind who, in turn, reveals God to all who receive him (vv. 13–18).[15] If v. 12 is indeed the central thesis, or, in Culpepper's words, "the pivot," of the prologue, this proclamation also indicates the aim of the entire mission of both Christ and the narrative that shares this good news.[16] The crux of the prologue, and, thus, the force of the narrative the prologue introduces, is the mission of the Word of God who gives "power to become children of God" as well as the necessary response-in-action of receiving and believing.

John 1:9–10 flow from the final words of vv. 6–8 and return focus to the light, further characterized by way of truth (τὸ φῶς τὸ ἀληθινὸν, v. 9). The true light whose enlightening reign reaches everyone was coming into the world. The incarnation foreshadowed here comes to pass in the counterpart to these verses, v. 14. The imminent conflict of the gospel story is also reaffirmed,

---

Culpepper, "The Pivot of John's Prologue," *NTS* 27 (1980): 1–31; and Francis J. Moloney, *Belief in the Word: Reading John 1–4* (Minneapolis: Fortress, 1993), 36–45.

14. Recognizing the complexity of these verses, Culpepper acknowledges that more than one structuring technique may well be in play. Thus, any diagram should be open to the fluidity of the evangelist's style. He defers to the work of Talbert: "Imperfections of form are the rule in antiquity.... It was, moreover, a stated rule that perfect symmetry was to be avoided (e.g., Horace, *On the Art of Poetry*, 347 ff.; Longinus, *On the Sublime*, 33, I; Demetrius, *On Style*, 5, 250)." See Charles H. Talbert, "Artistry and Theology: An Analysis of the Architecture of Jn 1,19–5,47," *CBQ* 32 (1970): 362. Culpepper thus claims the framework of the prologue is a chiasm that turns on the pivot of v. 12b ("The Pivot of John's Prologue," 8).

15. Culpepper, "The Pivot of John's Prologue," 7–31.

16. For discussion, see John Painter, "The Prologue as an Hermeneutical Key to Reading the Fourth Gospel," in *Studies in the Gospel of John and its Christology: Festschrift Gilbert van Belle*, ed. Joseph Verheyden, Geert van Oyen, Michael Labahn, and Reimund Bieringer, BETL 265 (Leuven: Peeters, 2014), 37–60.

this time in terms of knowledge (v. 10; see v. 8). Verse 11 provides powerful parallelism to this disconnect between the light and the world through the intimate language of "his own." The *logos*, instrumental giver of life and light in intimate relationship with God, comes into what is his own and is not received by them, his own people. Giving, receiving, and rejecting in relationship thus become the operative interactivity of the incarnation of the Word. At v. 12 the audience arrives at the pivot of the prologue (v. 12b) and the hinges upon which the pivot turns (vv. 12a and 12c).[17] This pivot, therefore, also profoundly affects the corresponding elements that balance the prologue.[18] The claim is that those who receive the Word are given the power to become children of God, and one goes about receiving him by *believing in his name* (v. 12c). The remainder of the prologue can thus be studied in terms of the revelation of God that makes this possible and how becoming "children of God" could be the *telos* of John's Gospel.

If John 1:12c describes the role of "receivers" in this relationship, then v. 13 describes the role of God and the "how" of becoming God's children. Spiritual

---

17. Culpepper, "Pivot," 15–17. In delineating the "laws of chiastic structures," Lund claims that the "very core of the message is found in the central line" (Nils Wilhelm Lund, *Chiasmus in the New Testament: A Study in Formgeschichte* [Chapel Hill: University of North Carolina Press, 1942], 46). The balance of the three phrases of v. 12 can be lost in English translations. The RSV, NRSV, and NIV, e.g., present v. 12c in apposition to v. 12a and thus directly following it, reading v. 12acb: "but to all who received him, who believed in his name, he gave power to become children of God." By contrast, the evangelist's syntax allows the central assertion of the Word's giving action to be framed by the introduction (v. 12a) and description (v. 12c) of potential recipients of the gift of the Word. These corresponding phrases thus hinge the core assertion (v. 12b) which is the crux of the prologue's message to audiences. Brown does not identify a chiasm, but he also correlates these phrases (*The Gospel according to John, I–XII*, 10). Although Ernst Käsemann's analysis of the prologue takes a different approach, he too identifies this verse as the climax: "Verse 12 specifies the gift which is his to bestow and the goal of his redeeming effectiveness" ("The Structure and Purpose of the Prologue to John's Gospel," in *New Testament Questions of Today* [London: SCM, 1969], 151–52).

18. The correspondence of receiving the Word to become children of God also suggests that "while Israel, which had been given the Torah, nevertheless rejected the Logos, some others, not necessarily Israel by virtue of flesh-and-blood parentage, became children of God via their receiving of the *Logos Asarkos*" (Daniel Boyarin, "The Gospel of the Memra: Jewish Binitarianism and the Prologue to John," *HTR* 94 [2001]: 278). See also C. H. Dodd, *The Interpretation of the Fourth Gospel* (Cambridge: Cambridge University Press, 1960), 271. Ernst Käsemann asserts that v. 12 "could be regarded as the culmination of the whole . . . [of] what was achieved by the manifestation of the Revealer" ("Structure and Purpose of the Prologue," 152). Although he wrongly assesses the prologue as an example of early Christian Gnosticism, Käsemann's insights on v. 12 extend beyond this perspective.

birth comes from above.[19] As a result of the Word's coming into the world and the rejection by his own, the "privilege of becoming the covenant people of God" changes forever.[20] Then, corresponding to the proclamation in vv. 9–10, v. 14 announces how the true light came into the world, who the *logos* becomes, and what is given in the process: "And the Word became flesh." The incarnation of the Word of God is made possible by the plan of God to reenvision the covenant people as children of spiritual, not human, birth. Just as God's action in giving and Israel's action in "receiving" the covenantal giving of Torah changed the nature of God's relationship with creation, the giving of the Word incarnate, while very much in accord with that history, once again decisively alters the manner by which creation can "receive" and relate to God (vv. 16–17). The mission of the Word that has become human in Jesus the Christ and Son of God is to make God the Father known and to give the gift of truth that empowers those who receive and believe in him to become children of God (vv. 12, 18).

John's Gospel will narrate the "how" of the covenantal claim that the prologue introduces. The initial summons is to receive the Word of God (John 1:12, 16). Later, John the Baptist, the true witness to Jesus as the Word of God (1:6–8, 15, 19–36), proclaims, "No one can receive anything except what has been given from heaven" (3:27). He goes on to explain his role as the one who prepares and rejoices for the one who is to come (3:28–36). Still later, while instructing his disciples about the inclusion of all who believe (regardless of ethnic identity, 4:36), Jesus teaches that, "The reaper is already receiving wages and is gathering fruit for eternal life, so that sower and reaper may rejoice together." Reaping those who have not been sowed, including Samaritans and other gentiles, is possible for the Word of God in human form: Jesus Christ. In the context of the Feast of Tabernacles, Jesus opposes receiving circumcision to the promise of receiving the Spirit of God (7:23, 39), while in 10:18, Jesus confirms to the crowds that he has "received" the command from his Father to lay down his life on his own accord: "I have power to lay it down, and I have power to

---

19. Verse 13 stands in apposition to v. 12 and corresponds antithetically to v. 11. Raymond Brown questions the use of αἱμάτων in the plural to mean natural descent. Lacking a better interpretation, however, he concludes this must have been the evangelist's intention (Brown, *The Gospel according to John, I–XII*, 11). Frank Kermode, in his study of the axioms of "being" and "becoming" in the prologue, notes: "we meet in v. 13 a paradoxical style of becoming (of birth) which is actually a form of being: being born not of the stuff of becoming, being born into being" ("St. John as Poet," *JSNT* 28 [1986]: 10).

20. John W. Pryor, "Covenant and Community in John's Gospel," *RTR* 47 (1988): 48. Heritage and ethnic identity have become irrelevant to birth from God.

take it up again." Later, in his last discourse to his disciples that prepares them for his coming departure and their new leadership roles, Jesus teaches, "Very truly, I tell you, whoever receives one whom I send receives me; and whoever receives me receives him who sent me" (13:20); and then reinforces the power of receiving, "Until now you have not asked for anything in my name. Ask and you will receive, so that your joy may be complete" (16:24).

The constitutive call to "believe in the word" of God in Jesus is revealed across the Book of Signs and climaxes in the so-called Last Discourse of Jesus to his disciples (John 13–17). Indeed, believing is the only legitimate response to the revelation of God in Jesus.[21] Although the initial summons to believe in Jesus as the Word of God incarnate comes in 1:12, it is introduced in 1:7 with John the Baptist, who becomes the paradigmatic witness to Jesus, the Lamb of God: "He came as a witness to testify to the light, so that all might believe through him" (1:7–8, 15, 19–28, 29–36; 3:22–36). So, how does one manifest this hospitality to the Word of God in their concrete lives? By actualizing this receiving and believing in relationship.

Jesus's summons, "come and see" (John 1:38–39) sets this tone for his entire mission. The prologue has claimed that Jesus, whose glory "we" have all "seen," has likewise "seen" God and reveals him to all (1:14, 18). This is confirmed by John the Baptist who sees the Spirit alighting upon Jesus and bears witness to such (1:33–34). Accordingly, Jesus calls all those he encounters to open themselves and see what God is doing in him, now, in their presence (1:46, 50–51; 3:1–21; 4:1–29; 5:11–47; 6:30–58; 8:50–59; 9:1–41; 12:45–50; 14:7–20; 20:25–29). Likewise, the evangelist calls audiences of the gospel to do the same. The first chapter of the gospel comes to a close as the gathering of these first disciples is completed. John has witnessed to Jesus as the Lamb of God and Son of God (1:29, 34, 36). The imperative-as-invitation to "come and see" will recur across this narrative of the good news: when Philip calls Nathanael (1:46), when the Samaritan woman calls her fellow villagers (4:29), and even when "the Jews" call Jesus to Lazarus's tomb (11:34). Discipleship in the Fourth Gospel was introduced as receiving and believing and now has the ongoing aspect of being and abiding with Jesus (1:38). Both the disciples and audiences are ripe for the revelation of God in Jesus, the Son of Man (1:51).

That said, his disciples are only able to begin to believe in him and his true glory when he turns the water to wine in Cana (John 2:1–11). Authentic believing only comes after his resurrection when hindsight becomes more acute: "After he was raised from the dead, his disciples remembered that he had said

---

21. Lee, *Hallowed*, 135.

this; and they believed the scripture and the word that Jesus had spoken" (2:22). Nonetheless, all but one seem committed to this journey (6:59–71; 11:1–17). The crowds of Jewish people, however, prove tougher nuts to crack (2:23–25; 5:10–47; 6:29–51; 7:31–52; 8:12–59; 10:24–41; 12:36–50). Individuals of all walks of life do rise to Jesus's challenge and struggle to believe in his true nature, including Nicodemus (3:1–21), the Samaritan woman (4:1–29), the Samaritan villagers (4:39–44), the royal official (a Roman? 4:45–54), Martha (11:20–30), Mary (11:28–40; 12:1–8), and even some of the masses (10:42). Indeed, it is in dialogue with Nicodemus, who is struggling to move beyond his traditional background, that Jesus gives his eponymous teaching:

> For God so loved the world that he gave his only Son, so that everyone who believes in him may not perish but may have eternal life. Indeed, God did not send the Son into the world to condemn the world, but in order that the world might be saved through him. Those who believe in him are not condemned; but those who do not believe are condemned already, because they have not believed in the name of the only Son of God. (3:16–18)

Once Jesus's hour has arrived (John 12:23), Jesus restricts his final teaching to his own—the believers that he has gathered across his public ministry (13:1) and begins to prepare them to become leaders in his absence following his coming earthly departure (13:19; see all of 13:1–17:26). His teaching on the fundamental aspect of believing comes to its apex in John 14 and 16. He begins what many understand as the discourse proper with, "Do not let your hearts be troubled. Believe in God, believe also in me" (14:1; also 14:29). He commands them to forego fear and invites them rather to believe. This is the essence of his public ministry. He expands it now in terms of his abiding relationship with God the Father (14:2–29; again in 16:23–33). Jesus culminates his call to the journey of believing in his final prayer, first for himself, then for those there with him, and finally for all those who will come to believe (17:1–26). The evangelist can then turn to his potential audiences and focus upon their believing, at the foot of the cross (19:35), through the witness of the Beloved Disciple (20:8), and finally through Thomas, the voice of every-person:

> But Thomas (who was called the Twin), one of the twelve, was not with them when Jesus came. So the other disciples told him, "We have seen the Lord." But he said to them, "Unless I see the mark of the nails in his hands, and put my finger in the mark of the nails and my hand in his side, I will not believe."

> A week later his disciples were again in the house, and Thomas was with them. Although the doors were shut, Jesus came and stood among them and said, "Peace be with you." Then he said to Thomas, "Put your finger here and see my hands. Reach out your hand and put it in my side. Do not doubt but believe."
>
> Thomas answered him, "My Lord and my God!"
>
> Jesus said to him, "Have you believed because you have seen me? Blessed are those who have not seen and yet have come to believe." (20:24–29)

Then we can circle back to the prologue, but now through the lens of the encounters of Jesus's own with the risen Christ. Jesus's final teaching on believing in the gospel is to bless those who can rise to the challenge of believing without seeing (John 20:29). The evangelist can then affirm his purpose in writing, that audiences of the first century and all time might believe that Jesus is the Christ and Son of God and thereby have life in his name (20:30–31). Dorothy Lee suggests that it is impossible to explore the depth and breadth of John's spirituality without reckoning with believing, "To believe, and go on believing, despite adversity and discouragement, is intrinsic to Johannine spirituality, and expresses something of the purpose of the Gospel (20:30–31)."[22] The community continues to receive Christ, the Word of God, through each other, activating their ongoing believing by cultivating their love for one another and responding both to each other's needs and to each other's teaching.[23] The Fourth Evangelist teaches that in the ongoing lives of the community, believing is practiced by receiving the Word of God, *by receiving one another*. This is the means to having life in Christ's name—the purpose of the good news—and therefore a foundational ethical imperative of the gospel.

The Command to Abide and Love One Another

Jesus's public ministry is marked by the call to receive God through him by way of believing, though he also speaks of the love of God for creation and all who dwell in it (e.g., John 3:16–17). In the section often called the Book of Glory (John 13–20), Jesus presents the new commandment to love one another and to abide in him as the Son of God the Father. As introduced in that first

---

22. Lee, *Hallowed*, 135; see also Johannes Beutler, S. J., "Faith and Confession: The Purpose of John," in *Word, Theology, and Community in John*, ed. J. Painter, R. A. Culpepper, and F. F. Segovia (St. Louis: Chalice, 2002), 19–31.

23. Lee, *Hallowed*, 133.

"Follow Me"

encounter with potential disciples in 1:38–39, believing is actualized in this life with Jesus as their model (ὑπόδειγμα, 13:15, 34–35).²⁴ The love of God and love of, and in, creation thus marks the second half of Jesus's mission in this world. On arrival at 13:1, audiences are products of their experience of 1:1–12:50, Jesus's public ministry. From the beginning, the evangelist has insinuated a theology of the cross that was marked by "the hour" which was "not yet," an inevitable movement toward a time to be determined by God (2:4; 7:6–8, 30; 8:20). Only when people from beyond the boundaries of Israel seek out Jesus does he announce that "the hour" has come (12:23). From that point, audiences are caught up in "the hour" as it moves toward consummation. Three times Jesus has referred to the cross as his necessary "lifting up" (3:14; 8:28; 12:32), and the narrator adds a comment after the final expression, so that there may be no doubts about what is meant by it: "He said this to indicate the kind of death he was to die" (12:33). The hour has come for Jesus to be "lifted up" in an ignominious death by way of crucifixion that will, paradoxically, also perfect his glorification. But, first, he must prepare his disciples for his coming death and their new roles after "the hour."

The form and content of the last discourse (John 13:1–17:26) has lent itself to considerable debate. Repetitions and discrepancies in sequence and content have resulted in various approaches to interpreting the scenes narrated within them.²⁵ The structure and content of this extended interaction begins with Jesus making God known through washing the feet of his disciples and sharing a final meal with them (13:1–38). The focus then turns to departure as Jesus promises God's abiding presence and guidance to the disciples (14:1–31). The heart of the discourse centers on a new covenant call for the disciples to abide, to love, and to be hated by the world (15:1–16:3). The remainder of the encounter revisits the theme of departure, now in terms of consequences of discipleship (16:4–33) before turning to Jesus's final prayer where he once again makes God known by consecrating the new community (17:1–26). The thematic symbolism across these chapters is complex and this segment of the gospel is often characterized generically as a "testament" or "farewell discourse." For the purposes of this study, Rekha Chennattu's study of John 13–17 as "discipleship discourses" and, more specifically, Theresa Okure's designation of the passage as "Jesus's Commentary on the Missionary Task," both in

---

24. Cornelis Benemma notes the importance of imitation (mimesis) across the last discourse (*Mimesis*, 58–62).

25. That said, the present discussion recognizes that, despite a potentially complex literary history, a final editor has woven John 13–17 into an intricate but fluid whole.

dialogue with Michael Gorman's summary statement of Jesus's teaching here as "abide and go," prove most insightful.[26]

John 13 introduces the themes of the discourse and serves as a foundational element of Jesus's elevation of his disciples to friends and leaders in their own rights. Beginning with the characterization of the disciples as Jesus's own, vv. 1–3 set the scene of a meal in which Jesus participates with "his own" whom he loves "to the end." Jesus's final meal with his disciples signifies the nature of their relationship: an intimate bond of friendship, shared knowledge, and acceptance that binds them as the new family of God. The foot washing symbolizes Jesus's self-sacrificing, perfecting love in relationship with them (13:4–20).[27] Through this ritual, Jesus invites them to participate in his mission and destiny in relationship with God: "Very truly, I tell you, whoever receives one whom I send receives me; and whoever receives me receives him who sent me" (13:20). Harold Attridge notes that John's fundamental ethical obligation emerges here in the command to love:[28]

> I give you a new commandment, that you love one another. Just as I have loved you, you also should love one another. By this everyone will know that you are my disciples, if you have love for one another. (13:34–35; see also 15:13)

Indeed, the "Beloved" Disciple emerges as the one who shares an intimate relationship with Jesus and the only disciple who travels in union with Jesus on his journey through the hour of his glorification. He becomes a model disciple and witness to Jesus's true destiny and meaning for the world, embodying Jesus's ensuing imperatives to love, to abide, and to go out to the world. As the final meal between Jesus and "his own" concludes and night falls, Judas, his betrayer (13:2), goes out to do what he must do (13:26–27), and Jesus begins to speak in earnest of the promises and obligation this missional relationship of mutual indwelling offers.[29]

---

26. Rekha M. Chennattu, *Johannine Discipleship as a Covenant Relationship* (Peabody, MA: Hendrickson, 2006), 196; Okure, *Johannine Mission*, 196–219; Gorman, *Abide and Go*, 71–132.

27. Jewish Scriptures narrate foot washing as a gesture of hospitality (Gen 18:4; 19:2; 24:32; 43:24; Judg 19:21; 1 Sam 25:41) and as preparation for meeting God (Exod 30:17–21).

28. "The Gospel thus presents a basic moral norm in generic forms of the cultural traditions that it cleverly interweaves. The Gospel is also structured as a kind of drama that drives home the significance of that moral norm by presenting an example of the 'greatest love' in the action of Jesus, who gave himself for his friends" (Attridge, "Johannine Ethics," 177).

29. Gorman, *Abide and Go*, 86–95.

The scene shifts at John 14:1 to a dialogue between Jesus and the disciples as a group, marked by his double use of the command to "believe" (14:1). Alongside believing, Jesus encourages the disciples through his imperative, "Do not let your hearts be troubled" (14:1, 27). Rather, they must focus on the promises he offers to those in relationship with him, including the indwelling presence of the divine (14:3, 12–21, 23, 28; see Exod 25:8), the knowledge of the divine (John 14:7, 17, 20–21, 26; see Exod 29:45–46; Lev 26:11–12), and the gift of peace (John 14:27; see Isa 9:6–7; 52:7; 57:19; Ezek 34:25; 37:26; Hag 2:9). Interspersed through these promises is the persisting call to believe and keep the commandments of his Word (John 14:1, 10–12), through the support and teaching of the Paraclete (the evangelist's designation for the Holy Spirit, 14:26; see also 15:26–27; 16:4–24), and in this way to love God (14:15, 21, 23–24). It all comes down to this.

Jesus turns to a more detailed exposition of this call. The heart of this missioning discourse begins with a metaphor of vine and branches that symbolically describes the relationship of mutuality between God, Jesus, and disciples, which culminates in the command to abide in Jesus and to love one another (15:1–17). This mutual indwelling language of abiding persists through the rest of the discourse.[30] The journey of believing for the disciples thus far has been one of pruning and cleansing as the branches of the vine. The challenge for the disciples from this point is to abide in the integral relationship of the vine and vintner. As he continues, Jesus identifies himself and his actions with the love of the Father, and therefore expands his call for the disciples to abide in his love. He further begins to integrate friendship with the love to which he is calling them. The love and fidelity the friends show to one another mirror God's own covenant faithfulness and sustain their mutual indwelling in a world that will challenge and even hate them (15:18–27).

Jesus then turns to the ramifications of the abiding relationship of love and friendship to which he calls his disciples (John 16:1–4). Shifting focus to the larger world, Jesus first warns them of the suffering and persecution they will encounter, then follows with both the reasons behind the trial and the rewards for their perseverance. Despite the hatred and alienation the members of the community may experience, they must not falter (see Exod 29:45–46; Jer 9:24; Isa 1:2). The consolation for standing fast in the midst of trial is the gift of the Paraclete (John 16:4–24). In the end, their hearts will rejoice, and their joy will be complete. Jesus frames his final teaching with reference to his hour (16:25–26a, 32–33) in which the disciples will face the consequences of their relationship with Jesus and yet also come into their own as children of God.

30. Gorman, *Abide and Go*, 96–106.

At its heart, Jesus reaffirms his origins and destiny with the Father, an intimacy that will also be shared with the disciples who love and believe in Jesus (16:26b–28). With these challenging words, Jesus then turns to his disciples for their response. Articulating their acceptance of the relationship including all its promises, obligations, and consequences, the disciples profess believing in Jesus and his word (16:29–30). Although they may not yet fully understand the mission of Jesus, his pending return to the Father, or his intended mission for them, this commitment is essential to sustain their ability to love and abide. Both the disciples in the story and subsequent audience of the story are challenged to decide for or against Jesus in terms of the believing and loving that have been the primary concerns of his teaching thus far.

Jesus's last discourse concludes with a prayer through which he consecrates the disciples as the first fruits of his community of believers, sealing their initiation process into the light of new life (John 17:1–26). After praying for strength for his coming ordeal (17:1–5), he turns his attention to his disciples (17:6–19). The prologue associated the "children of God" with those who receive Jesus, who is full of the gift of truth, and believe in his name (1:12). Here in this final prayer on behalf of his disciples, Jesus acknowledges that they have received his gift of truth and consecrates them in the name of the Father. Thus, he can say, "As you have sent me into the world, so I have sent them into the world" (17:18). The natural consequence of abiding in the truth of this relationship is going out into the world.[31] He then moves beyond them to *all* who will believe through *their* active word, thereby closing the prayer with his vision for the unity of the new covenant community (vv. 21–26). This oneness is based in mutual abiding in the relationship of God's love, which empowers all disciples to take on a leadership role in the new community Jesus has prepared for them. Jesus's time for teaching and physical dwelling with his own in this world must end so that the fullness of his hour of glorification may arrive.

Across John 13:1–17:26, Jesus reinterprets tradition in order to redefine and reestablish the identity of the community as the children of God who are to live active lives of mission and discipleship. Only then can he turn to the hour of his passion and glorification (18:1–19:42).

The Hope of Living in His Name

The conclusion to the body of John's Gospel is found at 20:30–31 and presents the purpose of this telling in the hope that all who believe will have "life in

---

31. Gorman, *Abide and Go*, 114–21.

his name."³² This hope is not introduced here; rather it is the culmination of the evangelist's teaching on ecclesiology: the gathering community of believers. John 20 begins to bring his story to a close with several accounts of appearances of the resurrected Jesus. Given the evangelist's understanding of the "lifting up" of Jesus through his crucifixion (John 3:14; 8:28; 12:32) as the ultimate glorification that "completes" his mission in the world (19:30), the evangelist is concerned to portray Jesus as continuing to fulfill the word that he spoke during his earthly ministry.³³ Through his interactions with the disciples in 20:1-29, Jesus fulfills his promises to return to them (14:18-19; 16:16); and they are able to begin to understand the word of Jesus about the raising of the temple of his body (2:19-22). The evangelist, as narrator, can then turn to audiences to bring them to their own cruces of faith decision, providing the purpose of what he has written (20:30-31):

> Of course, Jesus also did many other signs in the presence of his disciples that have not been written in this book; but these are written that you may go on believing that Jesus is the Christ, the Son of God, and that by believing you may have life in his name.³⁴

The telling of the activity that signifies who Jesus is was not exhausted by his story; rather, the evangelist has chosen from the wealth of traditions about Jesus in crafting his narrative. Here he uses his preferred term for Jesus's miraculous activity, σημεῖα ("signs") for the signifying role this activity carries throughout the gospel. The term also resonates with the "signs" of Moses on behalf of God during the Exodus narrative (Exod 4:8, 9, 17, 28, 30; 7:3; 10:1, 2), as well as God's own action to signify his glory in the Sinai

---

32. See, e.g., M.-J. Lagrange, *Évangile selon Saint Jean* (Paris: Gabalda, 1936), 520; Francis J. Moloney, *The Gospel of John*, SP 4 (Collegeville, MN: Liturgical Press, 1998), 542-44. A commentator who does not discuss 20:30-31 in terms of a conclusion is Edwyn C. Hoskyns, *The Fourth Gospel*, ed. F. N. Davey (London: Faber & Faber, 1947), 550. For the view that 20:30-31 forms the opening frame of a larger conclusion movement, see Fernando F. Segovia, "The Final Farewell of Jesus: A Reading of John 20:30-21:25," *Semeia* 53 (1991): 167-90.

33. Morna Hooker, *Endings: Invitations to Discipleship* (Peabody, MA: Hendrickson, 2003), 68.

34. Author's translation. For translating μὲν οὖν as "of course," see Raymond E. Brown, *The Gospel according to John XIII-XXI*, AB 29a (Garden City, NY: Doubleday, 1970), 1054. For translating Ἰησοῦς as the subject and ὁ Χριστὸς as the predicate nominative convertible proposition of v. 31, see Daniel B. Wallace, *Greek Grammar Beyond the Basics* (Grand Rapids: Zondervan, 1996), 46-47, against D. A. Carson, "The Purpose of the Fourth Gospel: John 20:31 Reconsidered," *JBL* 106 (1987): 639-51, esp. 642-44.

wilderness (Num 14:11, 22; Deut 4:34; 6:22; 7:19; 11:3; 16:38; 26:8; 29:3; 31:13, 17; 34:11).³⁵ At this crucial moment, the evangelist confirms his purpose in terms of what "is written" (γέγραπται). Incorporating a scriptural formula in this "unusual" way may indicate he understands that his writing has provided both binding commands and the articulation of fulfilled prophecy as part of, and quite possibly the completion of, the γραφή, the Scripture of God's action in the world.³⁶

By way of two final purpose clauses, the evangelist affirms his hope for his community of audiences.³⁷ A famous textual difficulty initiates the telling of this purpose as early manuscripts attest both the present subjunctive and the aorist subjunctive of the verb "to believe" (πιστεύειν).³⁸ The above translation opts for the present subjunctive, the exegetical force of which is that the evangelist is writing so that his community of believers who are making their own journeys of faith, which include facing doubt, opposition, and rejection, "may go on believing."³⁹ The second clause provides both the content ("that Jesus is the Christ, the Son of God") and the result ("life in his name") of that ongoing believing activity. Regardless of the mainstream social, cultural, and theological categories of the world that may put them out (see John 9:22; 12:42; 16:2), the Johannine community of audiences have chosen the path that fulfills Scripture and gives the true gift of life.

In terms of invitations to discipleship, this ending to the gospel's body opens the door for audiences to situate themselves as disciples of Jesus whose believing is affirmed and reaffirmed as they journey through living in his name. As Morna Hooker quips, "The book may have come to a tidy end, but John does not expect us to put the book back on our shelves with a sigh of

---

35. The "signs" refer to John's story as a whole rather than just the post-resurrection appearances (see Brown, *The Gospel according to John XIII–XXI*, 1055; Andrew T. Lincoln, *The Gospel According to Saint John*, BNTC 4 [London: Continuum, 2005], 506; Moloney, *John*, 544; Rudolf Schnackenburg, *The Gospel according to St. John*, 3 vols. [London/New York: Burns & Oates/Herder & Herder, 1968–82], 3:337).

36. Moloney, *John*, 544, building upon A. Obermann, *Die christologische Erfüllung der Schrift im Johannesevangelium: Eine Untersuchung zur johanneischen Hermeneutik anhand der Schriftzitate*, WUNT 283 (Tübingen: J. C. B. Mohr [Paul Siebeck], 1996), esp. 418–22.

37. For the syntax of the ἵνα clauses, see Wallace, *Greek Grammar*, 472. For the use of ἵνα clauses in Johannine literature for community instruction, see H. Riesenfeld, "Zu den johanneischen hina-Sätzen," *ST* 19 (1965): 213–20.

38. For detail, see Bruce Metzger, *A Textual Commentary on the Greek New Testament*, 2nd ed. (New York: United Bible Societies, 1994), 219–20.

39. So Brown, *The Gospel according to John XIII–XXI*, 1056; Lincoln, *Saint John*, 506–7; Moloney, *John*, 544; Schnackenburg, *St. John*, 3:337–38.

"Follow Me"

satisfaction and the thought that this was a good story: this is meant to be the kind of book that changes lives."[40] The epilogue, John 21, is a portrait of how that can happen.

The Challenge to Follow

The challenge to "follow me" is presented by Jesus to Peter in the epilogue to John's Gospel (21:19, 22), but it has been the underlying imperative of the entire gospel. The epilogue only punctuates this challenge in the lives of real disciples who live in Jesus's command to believe without seeing. As profound and provocative as the ending in 20:30–31 is, several threads of the narrative are still loose, including the fate and ongoing roles of Peter and the Beloved Disciple. The community the gospel engendered may have needed something more to understand and sustain this new life, and early audiences may have clamored for answers. If the evangelist has largely focused his narrative on the two "new commandments" *to believe* and *to love*, the resulting struggles can be summarized as an ecclesial problem (whom and how do we love?) and an authority problem (whom and what do we believe?).[41] After a brief introduction that presents the new setting (v. 1), the former is handled in the first scene of John 21 (vv. 2–14), and the latter in the second scene (vv. 15–23). This final act can then conclude, providing a second ending of the gospel now in the world of the audience (vv. 24–25). When the story of this chapter is told as an epilogue, after a pause or fade to black, then the corresponding shift of the spotlight is made from the life of the first generation to the life of those who have not seen and yet have the courage to believe (20:29), i.e., the ongoing community—audiences of all time.

The second part of John 21 properly situates authority in this inclusive church in an effort to answer questions of whom and how to believe. Peter is designated the leader, the head of the church; the Beloved Disciple is the witness, the paradigmatic disciple in the church. Jesus has brought Peter and the disciples around a new charcoal fire (ἀνθρακιά) and provided a meal of bread and fish (vv. 9–13). The charcoal fire is a narrative marker that calls to mind Peter's last scene of breach with Jesus (18:15–27). The meal calls to mind both their final meal together before Jesus's passion (13:11; which itself echoed the ritual covenant meals of the Jewish Scriptures; see Gen 26:26–30; 31:43–54;

---

40. Hooker, *Endings*, 74. The subtitle to Hooker's book is "*Invitations to Discipleship.*"
41. For this analysis of the issues at stake in John 21, see Moloney, *John*, 562–65.

Exod 24:5–11; Deut 27:6–7) and the sign and subsequent teaching of John 6.[42] Although all seven previously introduced disciples are involved in the meal and its aftermath, the narrator places a steady focus on Peter (vv. 3, 7, 11), and the reconciliation of Peter's relationship with Jesus takes center stage in the following verses (vv. 15–22). As Timothy Wiarda has noted, Jesus "confronts Peter at every stage in the narrative, upsetting his equilibrium and challenging him to make decisions and take new action."[43]

In the context of this meal, the central dialogue of the epilogue occurs. Jesus asks Peter three times if he loves him (ἀγαπᾷς με; John 21:15, 16; φιλεῖς με; v. 17), reconstituting Peter's three-time denial by that earlier charcoal fire into a binding relationship with the consequences of mission and leadership.[44] Jesus addresses Peter with the formal appellation, "Simon son of John" (v. 15), repeating his initial call of Peter to discipleship (1:42) and preparing the audience for Peter's restoration.[45] He initiates the dialogue with the comparative, "do you love me more than these?" (ἀγαπᾷς με πλέον τούτων;), a question that has generated much scholarly debate.[46] Ilaria Ramelli makes a convincing syntactical argument that the presence of the object pronoun "me" coupled with the absence of the subject pronoun "you" (which is unnecessary but commonly used by the evangelist for emphasis) leads the audience to focus not on the subject of Peter and how well he loves but on the object of Peter's love.[47] Understanding Jesus's question of Peter's love for him as a comparison to Peter's love for other things, including his former way of life symbolized by "these" freshly caught fish before them, calls to mind the absolute claim for love and commitment that God makes on those who enter into covenant in the Jewish Scriptures (see Deut 6:5; 7:9; 10:12; 11:1; 13:3; 30:36) which is set

---

42. Patrick E. Spencer, "Narrative Echoes in John 21: Intertextual Interpretation and Intratextual Connection," *JSNT* 75 (1999): 55, 59–60.

43. Timothy Wiarda, "John 21:1–23: Narrative Unity and its Implications," *JSNT* 46 (1992): 53–71.

44. This word choice is "gently significant" in the progression of the dialogue, see K. L. McKay, "Style and Significance in the Language of John 21:15–17," *NovT* 27 (1985): 319–33.

45. R. Alan Culpepper notes, "'Simon, son of John' . . . is repeated each time Jesus addresses Peter (21:15, 16, 17)" ("Peter as Exemplary Disciple in John 21:15–19," *PRSt* 37 [2010]: 171).

46. Chennattu (*Johannine Discipleship*, 174–75) and Wiarda ("John 21.1–23," 62–63), rightly argue that the comparison is between Peter's love for Jesus and his love for other things, including his former fishing life. Jesus is resolving Peter's mandate for mission.

47. Ilaria Ramelli, "'Simon Son of John, Do You Love Me?' Some Reflections on John 21:15," *NovT* 50 (2008): 332–50.

against everything else (Josh 22:5) and the claim that Jesus has made on his disciples (John 13–17).⁴⁸

The articulation of Jesus's threefold question and Peter's threefold response has also garnered much discussion regarding the meaning and exegetical intent of the two different words for love. Peter always responds to Jesus's question regarding his love by saying yes, but using a form of φιλέω, while Jesus uses ἀγαπάω the first two times he asks, then shifts to Peter's φιλέω the third time. The question is whether there is any difference in meaning between the two terms or if the usage is just part of the evangelist's internal thesaurus. In a recent appraisal of this issue, David Shepherd uses a narrative-critical approach to argue that regardless of whether there was a semantic distinction between the words in the larger milieu, the evangelist seems to make a distinction across the gospel, as Jesus tends to use ἀγαπάω in his calls to love, especially in the last discourse.⁴⁹ This would make Jesus's shift in wording a distinctive move toward Peter, something an early audience would hear and appreciate. This relationship is not just one-way human worship of the divine. Rather, the risen Christ is always actively participating, seeking out, and reconciling right relationship. Peter's "anguish" at this third query could then be the result of his realization that Jesus is both reconstituting his three-part denial as well as meeting Peter where he is, in all his imperfection and desire to chuck it all and go fishing.

This dialogue thus reconciles their breached relationship and renews Peter's role. Jesus's commands are integral to this reconstitution and articulate Peter's mission as action in service of the new community. Jesus's imperative for him is to "feed" and "tend" the flock (John 21:15, 16, 17). Peter's leadership is clarified pastorally as he is mandated as the new shepherd of the burgeoning flock of children of God. Peter indicated at the foot washing that he wanted to follow Jesus, but he was not ready. Jesus said then that Peter would indeed follow him but later. Now that he has been reconstituted, Peter's journey thus comes to an end *in* the story even as it begins anew *beyond* the story's boundaries. In a final poignant moment, Jesus demands Peter's obedience, suggests his role in authority, and implies his eventual crucifixion in parallel to Jesus's own, all in the succinct imperative, "Follow me" (vv. 18–19, 22).⁵⁰

---

48. Chennattu, *Johannine Discipleship*, 175.

49. David Shepherd, "'Do You Love Me?': A Narrative-Critical Reappraisal of ἀγαπάω and φιλέω in John 21:15–17," *JBL* 129 (2010): 777–92. I concur with this overview of these terms but do not agree with his exegetical conclusion of John's views of Peter's role and character.

50. On John 21 as the culmination of a series of physical and metaphorical journeys, see

Then what of the Beloved Disciple? The narrator indicates that there have been queries about the destiny of the disciple Jesus loved, who has journeyed alongside him throughout his mission. Peter gives voice to them, and the scene closes with Jesus describing that disciple's unique mandate (John 21:20–23). He is the paradigmatic disciple and witness. The relationship between Peter and the Beloved Disciple has come to the forefront across the second half of the gospel as they worked in tandem to understand their experience of Jesus. Here, Jesus's instruction to Peter that the Beloved Disciple's role is of no consequence for him confirms their mutual but distinctive roles. Peter is the one who must learn to follow so that he can lead, even to martyrdom (vv. 18–19; see 16:1–4), and the Beloved Disciple is the consummate follower who becomes the leading witness to this good news (21:24; see 19:35). Audience questions about believing and authority are resolved with the affirmation that Peter is their shepherd and they are part of the larger burgeoning church. Nonetheless, the Beloved Disciple remains their model for believing and witnessing, more so now that they must believe without seeing the physical signs and presence of Christ.

Conclusion: The Mandate for Mission in the Gospel of John

Peter Judge claims that, "Jesus' opening question, 'What are you seeking?' and the disciples' question in return, 'Where do you abide, Rabbi?' serve to open the quest for every reader. The quest will be fulfilled when one responds to the invitation: 'Come and see.'"[51] When the evangelist concludes his story by attesting to its limitless nature (John 21:25), he turns to the audience and speaks directly in the testimonial tradition of the Beloved Disciple. His final words send his audience into the world and their shared future as the new children of God, receiving and abiding with Christ with a mandate for mission that entails going out in believing and loving as Jesus did, which is sustained by participating in the indwelling relationship of God as Father, Son, and advocating Spirit. In John's Gospel Jesus challenges the prevailing religious, political, and ethical status quo of his day, and any day, and encourages the newly formed children of God to do the same. For this reason, the Johannine Elder can say,

---

Fernando Segovia, "The Journey(s) of the Word of God: A Reading of the Plot of the Fourth Gospel," *Semeia* 53 (1991): 23–54, esp. 50–51.

51. Peter Judge, "Come and See: The First Disciples and Christology in the Fourth Gospel," in *Studies in the Gospel of John and Its Christology*, 69.

> Little children let us love, not in word or speech, *but in truth and action*. And by this we will know that we are from the truth and will reassure our hearts before him whenever our hearts condemn us; for God is greater than our hearts, and he knows everything.... And this is his commandment, that we should believe in the name of his Son Jesus Christ and love one another, just he has commanded us. All who obey his commandment abide in him, and he abides in them. And by this we know that he abides in us, by the Spirit that he has given us. (1 John 3:18–20, 23–24)

And, thus, Michael Gorman can inspire disciples of all ages, "Abide, and *go!*"[52]

---

52. Emphasis in both 1 John and the reference to Gorman's profoundly moving work, *Abide and Go*, is mine.

························· *Chapter 11*

An Alternative Global Imaginary: Imperial Rome's *Pax Romana* and Luke's "Counter-Violent" *Missio Dei*

Drew J. Strait

My esteemed colleague Michael Gorman is among a handful of New Testament scholars who have devoted consistent energy to animating the theme of peace and peacemaking in early Christianity for the life of the church today.[1] The dearth of scholarship on the role of peace as a vital behavioral trait of Christian identity is striking given the centrality of peace to the life and teachings of Jesus, along with the early church's imitation of Jesus's messianic ethic in Luke's second volume—the Acts of the Apostles.[2] If the moment we find ourselves in is any indication, pastor-theologians need fresh reading strat-

---

1. See Michael J. Gorman, *Inhabiting the Cruciform God: Kenosis, Justification, and Theosis in Paul's Narrative Soteriology* (Grand Rapids: Eerdmans, 2009), 129–60; *Reading Revelation Responsibly: Uncivil Worship and Witness: Following the Lamb into the New Creation* (Eugene, OR: Cascade, 2011), 145–47, 183–84; "The Lord of Peace: Christ Our Peace in Pauline Theology," *JSPL* 3 (2013): 219–53; *The Death of the Messiah and the Birth of the New Covenant* (Eugene, OR: Cascade, 2014), 132–202; "Shalom in the Book of Revelation: God, Church, Judgment, New Creation," in *Struggles for Shalom: Peace and Violence across the Testaments*, ed. Laura L. Brenneman and Brad D. Schantz (Eugene, OR: Wipf and Stock, 2014), 279–90; *Becoming the Gospel: Paul, Participation, and Mission* (Grand Rapids: Eerdmans, 2015), 144–211; and *Peace in Paul and Luke* (Cambridge: Grove Books, 2015).

2. So Gorman, "It is perhaps equally odd how relatively little attention is paid by most people, including many scholars, to the theme of peace in the Bible, whether Old Testament or New, whether the Gospels or the letters of Paul" (*Death of the Messiah*, 133). Mennonite scholarship, however, has filled this void for decades. See especially the series *Studies in Peace and Scripture*, sponsored by the Institute of Mennonite Studies at Anabaptist Mennonite Biblical Seminary in Elkhart, IN.

egies to persuade the church that peace is not only the way of Jesus but also the way of Jesus's followers. Put more bluntly, if the zealot option of violent retaliation or its more modern equivalent in militarized Christian nationalism is compatible with the way of Jesus, then why does Luke portray the apostolic mission imitating Jesus's messianic ethic of nonviolence from Jerusalem to Rome?[3] And what does the early Christian distinctive of nonviolence tell us about unexplored questions related to Luke's attitude toward Roman imperialism—and more specifically, the *pax Romana*?

In this essay, I explore the relationship between the expansion of early Christian mission and the expansionist ambitions of Roman imperialism. More specifically, I compare what I call Luke's "counter-violent global imaginary" with the mechanics of Roman imperialism underlying the *pax Romana*.[4] To probe this topic, I first discuss classic approaches to Luke's attitude toward the *pax Romana*, showing that scholars have overlooked how fear of retaliation through Roman treason laws influenced strategies of discursive dissimulation in the Roman world. Second, I contextualize the language of Roman imperialism that legitimated the *pax Romana*, with a particular focus on how violent military domination, xenophobia/prejudice, and the metaphor of enslavement both justified and upheld Roman imperialism and its conception of peace and peacemaking. Finally, I pivot to critique the notion that Luke has a positive view of the *pax Romana* by investigating Peter's proclamation of "peace through Jesus Christ" in Cornelius's household in Acts 10:36. I argue that, in proclaiming peace through Israel's Messiah in the home of an agent of Rome's occupation of Judea, Luke does *not* characterize Cornelius as a "parabolic exemplum" of Christian discipleship as a part of "Luke's larger interest in promoting a positive view of the empire."[5] Rather, drawing on the arts of Hellenistic discursive resistance, Luke subsumes Cornelius's allegiances under

---

3. This is especially true of Paul, who is incarcerated or almost assassinated on at least eleven occasions in Acts without retaliating (see 9:23–25, 29; 13:50; 14:19; 16:19–24; 17:5–9, 13; 18:12–17; 19:23–40; 20:3; 21:27–40).

4. My emphasis in this essay on Luke's counter-imperial *and* "counter-violent" mission is inspired by Gorman's perceptive observation that "it has become commonplace (with some notable exceptions) in Pauline scholarship to speak of Paul's gospel of Christ's death and resurrection as counter-imperial, which, in my view, is quite true. But his gospel is also counter-violent, and that dimension has, surprisingly, received far less attention" (*Inhabiting the Cruciform God*, 139n47).

5. So Laurie Brink, *Soldiers in Luke-Acts: Engaging, Contradicting, and Transcending Stereotypes* (Tübingen: Mohr-Siebeck, 2014), 173–75. So also, Alexander Kyrychenko, *The Roman Army and the Expansion of the Gospel: The Role of the Centurion in Luke-Acts* (Berlin: Walter de Gruyter, 2014), 8, 189.

the supra-imperial power and benefaction of Israel's God, reorienting Roman notions of peace/peacemaking in the frontier around *another king*.[6]

The Cornelius episode cannot reconstruct an all-encompassing understanding of Luke's political-peace theology. However, I contend it is a crucial starting point for better understanding how Luke's alternative global imaginary invites the church to dismantle the language of imperialism within our own cultural metanarrative(s) and, ultimately, invites us to *participate* in and *become* God's counter-violent, inbreaking message of peace through the agency of the church's witness to Jesus's resurrection.

Acts, Empire, and the *Pax Romana*

The rise of post-colonial criticism and the publication of Simon Price's *Rituals and Power* in 1986 increased New Testament scholars' sensitivities to the conditions of subordinate Christian communities facing the stressors of imperial power, hegemony, and competing allegiances between Christ the king and the Roman imperial cults.[7] A deeper appreciation for this imperial reality has stimulated a seismic shift in scholarship on Luke-Acts, where the three-century scholarly consensus that Luke is the most pro-Roman author in the New Testament has been called into question over the past sixteen years.[8] In the ongoing aftermath of this shift, the relationship between the *pax Romana* and Christian mission remains a neglected point of entry for investigating Luke's attitude(s) toward imperial Rome.[9]

Luke's attitude toward the *pax Romana* is admittedly muddled by contra-

---

6. I borrow the descriptor "supra-imperial" from Karl Galinsky, "The Cult of the Roman Emperor: Uniter or Divider?," in *Rome and Religion: A Cross-Disciplinary Dialogue on the Imperial Cult*, ed. Jeffrey Brodd and Jonathan L. Reed (Atlanta: SBL Press, 2011), 222.

7. Simon Price, *Rituals and Power: The Roman Imperial Cult in Asia Minor* (Cambridge: Cambridge University Press, 1984).

8. For an overview, see Drew J. Strait, "The Gospel of Luke," in *The Face of New Testament Studies*, ed. Scot McKnight and Nijay Gupta (Grand Rapids: Baker Academic, 2019), 322–29; and Michael Kochenash, "Taking the Bad with the Good: Reconciling Images of Rome in Luke-Acts," *RelSRev* 41 (2015): 43–51.

9. To date, an imperial-critical investigation of mission in Luke-Acts remains largely lacking, but see Steve Walton, who largely relegates the discussion to bearing witness to Jesus before political authority and calling them to do justice ("What Does 'Mission' in Acts Mean in Relation to the 'Powers That Be'?," *JETS* 55 [2012]: 537–56). Rowe, on the other hand, focuses on the uniqueness of Christian mission and its relationship to the universal lordship of Jesus (C. Kavin Rowe, *World Upside Down: Reading Acts in the Graeco-Roman Age* [New York: Oxford University Press, 2009], 116–26).

dicting material. On the one hand, in Luke's first volume, Jesus proclaims an ethic that is incompatible with the violence underlying the *pax Romana*. On the other hand, Luke presents some Roman soldiers and officials positively, and Paul's repeated innocence in the Roman justice system insinuates that Christian mission benefits from the *pax Romana*. Material that purports to present Rome treating Christians favorably inspired multiple generations of scholars to believe, in one way or another, that Luke affirms imperial Rome.[10] This view is promoted by the Lukan scholarly giant Henry Cadbury, who quotes approvingly the Chief Justice of England, Lord Hewart:

> It is not often stated, yet perhaps it is the fact, that the best short general picture of the *pax Romana* and all that it meant—good roads and posting, good police, freedom from brigandage and piracy, freedom of movement, toleration and justice is to be found in the experiences written in Greek, of a Jew who happened to be a Roman citizen—that is, in the Acts of the Apostles.[11]

The "freedom of movement" approach is, somewhat surprisingly, supported by two classic studies devoted to peace and the New Testament by Klaus Wengst and Ulrich Mauser.[12] Both books recognize the system of violence underlying the *pax Romana*, but both believe that Luke affirms Roman benefits of peace nonetheless.[13] While it is hard to deny that Christian mission experienced *some* concrete benefits from the *pax Romana*, it is another thing to suggest that these benefits made Luke "treasure the Roman peace."[14] After

---

10. For research history, see Steve Walton, "The State They Were In," in *Reading Acts in the Discourse of Masculinity and Politics*, ed. Eric D. Barreto, Matthew L. Skinner, and Steve Walton (London: T & T Clark, 2017), 75–106.

11. Henry J. Cadbury, *The Book of Acts in History* (London: Adam and Charles Black 1955), 58. Elsewhere Cadbury argues for the *apologia pro ecclesia* approach: *The Making of Luke-Acts* (New York: Macmillan, 1927), 308–15.

12. Klaus Wengst, *Pax Romana and the Peace of Jesus Christ*, trans. John Bowden (Munich: SCM, 1987); Ulrich Mauser, *The Gospel of Peace: A Scriptural Message for Today's World* (Louisville: John Knox, 1992).

13. So Wengst writes that he finds "no negative statements about Rome and its representatives ... the extraordinarily positive way in which almost all the Roman soldiers are presented in Luke's accounts needs to be noted as a first characteristic of his perception of the Pax Romana" (*Pax Romana*, 89–90, 92). Mauser draws similar conclusions: "The Christian mission has nothing to fear from it [the *pax Romana*]; on the contrary, it serves as a means of protection for the messengers of the gospel and, indirectly, serves to spread the gospel" (*Gospel of Peace*, 96).

14. Wengst, *Pax Romana*, 105.

all, Jesus died on a *Roman* cross—a torture apparatus that symbolically represents the "*Pax Romana* [as an] instrument to protect the populace against dangerous criminals."[15] Either Luke's messianic-peace ethic is wholly inconsistent or we need a more sophisticated reading strategy for animating Luke's peace theology.

As I have argued in more detail elsewhere, the arts of discursive dissimulation in Greco-Roman antiquity affords us with such a reading strategy to understand *why* Luke writes between the lines with contradictory material.[16] Indeed, the perennial search for subversive speech in Luke-Acts often operates on the mistaken notion that if Luke is critical of the *pax Romana*, then he would say so explicitly. One can sense how such expectation for explicit, open criticism confounded Wengst, who acknowledges that, in Acts, "violence is not interrupted, but painted over."[17] Mauser, on the other hand, observes that Luke's concept of peace "is engaged in silent dialogue with the ideal of Roman peace (Pax Romana). Acts does not mention this ideal by name."[18] Why would Luke obfuscate explicit reference to the *pax Romana* in "silent dialogue" with realities that were incompatible with the way of Jesus? The answer, I contend, is that to criticize the *pax Romana* explicitly was to risk evoking Rome's power to retaliate and to lack rhetorical art.

To be sure, already by the time of Augustus, treason laws were expanded to include defection from the military, sedition, and any act that "diminishes the majesty of the people of Rome" (*maiestas populi Romani minuta*, Tacitus, *Ann.* 1.72).[19] But when Cassius Severus "defamed men and women of distinction through his insulting satires," Augustus expanded treason to include "legal inquiry to libelous writings" (Tacitus, *Ann.* 1.72).[20] "This development in Roman law, although not always consistent from one emperor to the next, stimulated a culture of suspense and unpredictability amid coded forms of

---

15. Martin Hengel, *Crucifixion: In the Ancient World and the Folly of the Message of the Cross*, trans. John Bowden (Philadelphia: Fortress, 1977), 50.

16. See Drew J. Strait, *Hidden Criticism of the Angry Tyrant in Early Judaism and the Acts of the Apostles* (Lanham, MD: Lexington/Fortress Academic, 2019), 2–4, 50–53, 121–22, 128–33, 143–51, 243–50.

17. Wengst, *Pax Romana*, 105.

18. Mauser, *Gospel of Peace*, 85.

19. For fuller discussion see especially Richard A. Bauman, *The Crimen Maiestatis in the Roman Republic and Augustan Principate* (Johannesburg: Witwatersrand University Press, 1967).

20. K. A. Raaflaub and L. J. Sammons II, "Opposition to Augustus," in *Between Republic and Empire: Interpretations of Augustus and his Principate*, ed. K. A. Raaflaub and M. Toher (Berkeley: University of California Press, 1990), 417–54.

character-assassination on the one hand, and a culture of career-decoders through paid informants (*delatores*) on the other."[21] The policing of discursive resistance was achieved through "the eyes and ears of the king," which included the emperor's vast "friends" (Xenophon, *Cyr.* 8.2.11–12; Dio Chrysostom, *Or.* 3.118), informants (Suetonius, *Nero* 32.2; *Dom.* 12.1), and, in rarer cases, plainclothes policing (Epictetus, *Diatr.* 4.13.5).[22] Fear of retaliation stimulated a new generation of literary sophisticates, who developed discursive strategies of anti-imperial innuendo to dissimulate one's object of resistance. As Vasily Rudich observes, "It was an uncanny world of illusion and delusion, of ambivalences and ambiguities on all levels of interaction."[23]

It is in this space of discursive ambiguity, I contend, that Luke's messianic global imaginary confronts Rome's claims to peace—without recourse to naming an object of resistance explicitly. Literary sophisticates knew well the dangers of employing blunt speech (παρρησία) before the angry tyrant (Aristotle, *Rhet.* 1382B; Quintilian, *Inst.* 9.2.66; Pseudo-Demetrius, *Eloc.* 294; Plutarch, *Adul. am.* 66B; Dio Chrysostom, *Or.* 3.12–13; Philo, *Somn.* 2.85; Pseudo-Hermogenes, *On Invention* 4.13). As Macrobius writes, "But I'll keep my peace: it's not easy to have a war of words with a man who can sign your death warrant" (*Sat.* II.4.1). To circumvent retaliation, sophisticates developed an allusive grammar called figured speech (*figurae*/σχήματα), where the dissident voice "shuns the deadly powerful, but first takes care not to seem to shun them" (Seneca, *Ep.* 8).[24] This oblique grammar primarily focused on ambiguous ways of speaking (Quintilian, *Inst. Or.* 9.2; Pseudo-Demetrius,

---

21. See Strait, *Hidden Criticism of the Angry Tyrant*, 139.

22. Jane McCarthy catalogues thirty-nine cases of defamation between 27 BCE and 117 CE, resulting in the declaimer's suicide, exile, execution, book burning, and sometimes *damnatio memoriae* ("Speech and Silence: Freedom of Speech and Processes of Censorship in Early Imperial Rome" [PhD diss.; King's College London, 2013], 285–97). On paid informants, see Bauman, *Human Rights*, 107. On the proliferation of soldiers working among civilians, see Christopher J. Fuhrmann, *Policing the Roman Empire: Soldiers, Administration, and Public Order* (Oxford: Oxford University Press, 2012), 100. Here I am in disagreement with Barclay, who argues that the "Roman empire was not a police state" and that "it did not take steps to monitor written communications" (John M. G. Barclay, "Why the Roman Empire Was Insignificant to Paul," in *Pauline Churches and Diaspora Jews*, WUNT 275 [Tübingen: Mohr Siebeck, 2011], 381). As evidence against Barclay's thesis, one should also not overlook Paul's impulse to intercept Christians' letters as a strategy to incarcerate them (Act 9:1–2).

23. Vasily Rudich, *Political Dissidence under Nero: The Price of Dissimulation* (London: Routledge, 1993), xvii.

24. On figured speech, see Frederick Ahl, "The Art of Safe Criticism in Greece and Rome," *AJP* 105 (1984): 174–208; Strait, *Hidden Criticism of the Angry Tyrant*, 138–50.

Eloc. 287–95; Philo, *Somn.* 2.81–92; Pseudo-Dionysius, *Ars rhetorica* 8–11; and Pseudo-Hermogenes, *On Invention* 4.13) but also suggests that the dissident voice can blame "others who have acted in a similar way" (Demetrius, *Eloc.* 292–295). So, for example, Plutarch frequently critiques dead Hellenistic kings without recourse to naming the point in fact that living Roman rulers were acting the same way (e.g., *Alex.* 28.1–2; 59.4; *Alex. fort.* 2.5; *Dem.* 10.4–11.1; 12.1; 13.1–3; 24.1–2; 30.4–5; 42.5, 8–11; *Ant.* 24.2–4; *Adul. am.* 56EF, 58A; 60D; 61A; 65E).[25] Conversely, post-Hellenistic kingship discourse developed a trope I call antithetical resistance, where praise/flattery could be infused with hidden polemic whereby the purported virtues of royal power evoke their semantic opposites.[26] As Pliny writes, "eulogy is best expressed through comparison" (*Pan.* 53.2).

This all-too-brief excursion into the world of discursive resistance problematizes a reading of Luke-Acts that takes Luke's purported positive presentations of Roman political authority at face value. Indeed, as the only author in the New Testament to narrate the expansion of Christianity into the Roman world, Luke is forced to thread a very narrow needle: to tell the truth about God's capacity to make peace between Jew and gentile through the *resurrection* of the Messiah, but to do so without stimulating Rome's ire. Toward that end, Luke is peerless among New Testament authors in terms of his literary sophistication and, as Ramsay MacMullen has argued, historiography was a common genre to disguise criticism in the Roman world.[27] At what point, then, does Luke dissimulate his objects of resistance—in this case the *pax Romana*—to articulate God's global imaginary embodied in the *pax Christi*? Before turning to the text of Acts, I will first define the relationship between Roman imperialism and the *pax Romana*, along with the ideological mechanisms of power that supported its proliferation through Rome's vast military apparatus.

The Global Imaginary of Roman Imperialism

The machinery of Roman imperialism found inspiration in the conquests of Alexander the Great (Cicero, *Phil.* 5.17.48). One Hellenistic Jewish author reflects on Alexander's thirst for expansion and personal enrichment off of subordinates in the periphery of the eastern Mediterranean in territorial and

---

25. See also Acts 12:20–23.
26. For further comment, see Strait, *Hidden Criticism of the Angry Tyrant*, 50–53.
27. Ramsay MacMullen, *Enemies of the Roman Order: Treason, Unrest, and Alienation in the Empire* (Cambridge: Harvard University Press, 1966), 35.

violent terms: "[Alexander] penetrated to the ends of the earth and took the spoils of a multitude of nations" (1 Macc 1:3 NETS). The influence of Alexander's typology of military conquest upon Caesar Augustus's militarized global imaginary is evident in a telling passage from Suetonius. After annexing Egypt in 30 BCE "to the empire of the Roman people,"[28] Augustus proceeded to honor Alexander's body with a golden crown and flowers at the *Sema* tomb in Alexandria. When asked if Augustus would also like to honor the bodies of the Ptolemaic kings, Augustus responds: "I wish to see a king, not dead men" (Suetonius, *Aug.* 18.1).

For Augustus, the spear-won "ends of the earth" ideology of Alexander's global expansion provided the kingship model worth imitating (the *imitatio Alexandri*). The *Diadochoi* bound to regional rule are merely "dead men." To represent the globalization of Roman power, authors and artists in the late Republic through the Julio-Claudian and Flavian eras depicted the "whole world" (*orbis terrarium*—οἰκουμένη) under Roman domination.[29] Augustus himself evokes this motif in the heading of his autobiographical aretology called the *Res gestae divi Augusti* (deeds of the divine Augustus), where he eulogizes himself for making "the world subject to the rule of the Roman people" (*orbem terrarum imperio populi Roman subiecet*, RGDA, heading, trans. Cooley). It is no accident, then, that the globe became an important accoutrement on iconographic and numismatic representations of Rome's global domination. Initially, the globe motif was employed with some moderation, associating the *Genius Populi Romani* with the wreath, globe, and rudder to indicate victory over land and sea (*RRC* 393.1a–b). After the conquests of Pompey in 61 BCE, the relationship between global domination and the ruling power became more explicit (see Cicero, *Pro Balb.* 16; *Cat.* 2.11; *de Imp.* 56). For example, Pompey's triumphal procession included "a trophy of the inhabited world" (οἰκουμένη, Dio Cassius, 37.21.2), and he was honored with a colossal statue depicting him holding the globe in his hand (Beard, fig. 6).[30]

The Pompeian propaganda of global domination was not lost on Julius Caesar. By 44 BCE, Rome issued coins with Venus holding Victory while resting on a shield propped on the globe; the obverse included Caesar's wreathed head with the inscription: CAESAR·DICT·IN·PERPETVO (Caesar, Dictator in Per-

---

28. Allison E. Cooley, *Res Gestae Divi Augusti: Text, Translation, and Commentary* (Cambridge: Cambridge University Press, 2009), 27. Hereafter cited as *RGDA*.

29. See especially Cicero, *Herenn.* 4.13; *Imp. Pomp.* 53; *Mur.* 22, *Cat.* 4.11, *Sull.* 33; Virgil, *Georg.* 3.16–33; *Aen.* 1.278–282; Horace, *Carm.* 4.15.13–16.

30. Mary Beard, *The Roman Triumph* (Cambridge: Harvard University Press, 2007), 27.

petuity, *RRC* 480.15-16).³¹ Lest we fail to understand the innuendo, Augustan media took the globe motif to a new level, minting coins of Octavian with foot propped on the globe or holding the globe to signal universal domination of the *orbis terrarum* (Zanker, Fig. 31a; 42; Giard, no. 5).³² The interrelationship between Augustus, divine power, and global domination is further evident on the reliefs of the famous Boscoreale Cups, where Augustus is seated with globe clasped in hand, flanked by divinities, with Venus holding animated Victory over the globe (Kuttner, pls. 1-3, 13).³³ The visual theology of Victory and Augustan domination is evident in other coin hoards, where she is represented sitting on the globe while the obverse represents Augustus's portrait with the inscription: AVGVSTVS DIVI F (Augustus, son of a god; *RIC* I, 185, 202-203, 213-218). In associating Augustus with Victory sitting on the globe—or representing Augustus standing on or holding the globe—subordinates were reminded of the universalizing claims of Roman global domination. In the words of Livy, "The expanse of the city of Rome and of the world is the same" (*Fast.* 2.684).

Roman material representation of the globe alongside Roman political authority communicated a clear message. Indeed, as Claude Nicolet writes, "the globe symbolizes . . . universal domination," a motif that is not difficult to unsurface from the Julio-Claudians through the time of Trajan.³⁴ What deserves further consideration is how the language of imperialism justified global domination, including the language of peace/peacemaking.

The Language of Imperium: Territoriality, Submission, Peacemaking

The material and literary cultures representing Augustus's global domination allow us to gaze at the growing compression of thought between territoriality and *imperium* (empire). As John Richardson has traced, Augustus's overwhelming concentration of power influenced the narrowing definition of *imperium* during Augustus's lifetime, transforming it from the shared "power"

---

31. On the globe motif, see especially Stefan Weinstock, *Divus Julius* (Oxford: Oxford University Press, 1971), 42-45, and Claude Nicolet, *Space, Geography, and Politics in the Early Roman Empire* (Ann Arbor: University of Michigan Press, 1991), 35-36.

32. Paul Zanker, *The Power of Images in the Age of Augustus* (Ann Arbor: University of Michigan Press, 1990), 41, 55; and J. B. Giard, *Monnaies de l'Empire Romain*, vol. 1: *Auguste* (Paris: Bibliothèque Nationale de France, 1976).

33. Ann L. Kuttner, *Dynasty and Empire in the Age of Augustus: The Case of the Boscoreale Cups* (Berkeley: University of California Press, 1995).

34. Nicolet, *Space, Geography, and Politics*, 36.

An Alternative Global Imaginary

of Roman magistrates and the power of the Roman people to "*imperium* as an extent of territory and as the power of the *princeps*."[35] Notwithstanding the evolving meaning of *imperium* to encapsulate the power of Augustus *and* global domination, Romans did not develop a singular word for imperialism, a concept that demands critical reflection since our modern terms of nationalism, internationalism, globalism, and colonialism remain somewhat elusive and sometimes anachronistic.[36]

To define imperialism, we do not need to reinvent the wheel. In Michael Doyle's monumental study on empires, imperialism is defined as "the process or policy of establishing or maintaining an empire."[37] By empire, Doyle means, "a relationship, formal or informal, in which one state controls the effective political sovereignty of another political society. It can be achieved by force, by political collaboration, by economic, social, or cultural dependence."[38] At the heart of Doyle's definition is the recognition that empires are funded by an urban *metropolis* that controls a *periphery*; this dichotomy, now widely acknowledged, affords us the conceptual clarity to analyze imperialism through three different optics: (1) the metrocentric (i.e., the ruling metropolis's tactics of domination, maintenance, and control); (2) the pericentric (i.e., the tactics of negotiation among those on the margins); and (3) the systematic (i.e., taking into account metrocentric and pericentric tactics of domination, control, and resistance).[39] The influence of Doyle's descriptive language of metropolis and periphery can be felt on the highly influential work of Edward Said, who defines imperialism as "the practice, the theories and the attitudes of a dominating metropolitan centre ruling a distant territory."[40] With these definitions in mind—especially of metropolis and distant periphery and of control and maintaining *imperium*—what is Roman imperialism, and what is its relationship to *pax*?

The relationship between Roman imperialism and the *pax Romana* is often acknowledged but rarely fleshed out among biblical scholars. Stefan Weinstock does not mince words on the interrelationship: "*Pax* . . . stood right from the

---

35. John Richardson, *The Language of Empire: Rome and the Idea of Empire from the Third Century BC to the Second Century AD* (Cambridge: Cambridge University Press, 2008), 185.

36. So Peter Edwell, "Definitions of Roman Imperialism," in *A Companion to Roman Imperialism*, ed. Dexter Hoyos (Leiden: Brill, 2013), 29.

37. Michael W. Doyle, *Empires* (Ithaca: Cornell University Press, 1986), 45.

38. Doyle, *Empires*, 45.

39. For Doyle's three models of imperial expansion, see *Empires*, 29, Table I.

40. Edward Said, *Culture and Imperialism* (New York: Vintage Books, 1993), 9.

beginning for Roman imperialism."[41] But how so? Notwithstanding classicists' acknowledgment of this relationship, as Hannah Cornwell has recently argued, "peace has taken a back seat in discussions in recent works on Roman imperialism."[42] Cornwell attempts to fill this gap, outlining Roman peace from the late Republic to the height of the *pax Augusta* to show how *pax* became a vehicle for Roman domination. Key to her thesis is the role of Augustus, whose rule politicized *pax* to mean peace over and pacification of the globe instead of reconciling agreements/pacts (*pactum*; *pactio*) between warring parties at the end of the Republic.[43] As Cornwell writes, "peace was established over the expanse of empire rather than in relation to an opponent.... This application of *pax* was expressed in terms of Roman *imperium* over the *orbis terrarum*."[44] Without an inimical opponent to come to terms with, the referent of peacemaking became subjects of the whole world—that is, the empire. Thus, *pax* functioned as a vehicle to articulate and justify Roman imperialism to subjects as a product of Augustus's victory, security, and generous benefaction; this representation was especially felt at Rome, where the Ara Pacis and the *Res Gestae* monumentalized *pax* to legitimate and explain the cosmology of the *imperium Romanum* as both power and territory under the Princeps to Roman subjects.[45] In Augustus's own words: "all land and sea was at peace under the Romans" (εἰρηνευομένης τῆς ὑπὸ Ῥωμα(ί)οις πάσης γῆς τε | καὶ θαλάσσης, *RGDA* 13, trans. Cooley).

If one only analyzes the *pax Romana* through the optics of the metropolis's bureaucrats, artists, and sophisticates, it would be possible to miscalculate its benefits for the periphery. Indeed, it is important to recognize that the security and benefits of the *pax Romana* were primarily aimed at maintaining power and justifying *imperium*—not helping "ordinary people."[46] A major innovation of Augustan Rome was the use of the military for policing purposes through imperial, gubernatorial, and freelance policing by soldiers detached

---

41. Stefan Weinstock, "Pax and the 'Ara Pacis,'" *JRS* 50 (1960): 45.

42. Hannah Cornwell, Pax *and the Politics of Peace: Republic to Principate* (Oxford: Oxford University Press, 2017), 3.

43. For the nuance, see Clifford Ando, "Pax Romana, Peace, Pacification and the Ethics of Empire," *C4eJournal: Perspectives on Ethics* 1 (2017).

44. Cornwell, Pax *and the Politics of Peace*, 81–154, here 197.

45. So Cornwell, Pax *and the Politics of Peace*, 126, 199. Augustus, of course, somewhat famously closed the gate of War (i.e., Janus) three times to signify peace over East and West (*RGDA* 13). On the role of *imperium* as power and territory in the *RGDA*, see Richardson, *The Language of Empire*, 117–20.

46. Fuhrmann, *Policing*, 91.

from their legion.⁴⁷ Soldiers functioned as the "eyes and ears" of the king through a mandate by Roman governors to keep provinces "pacified and quiet" (*pacata atque quieta*, Ulpian *Dig.* 1.18.13).⁴⁸ Thus, as Greg Woolf argues, "The emperors ruled not by abolishing violence but by channeling it."⁴⁹ To channel the energy of imperial ambition, Roman sophisticates employed the cognate verb pacify (*pacare*) and the past participle "pacified" (*pacatus*) to articulate subordinates' submission to Rome.⁵⁰ Myles Lavan has recently opened our eyes to the polysemy of this language of peacemaking, showing that the Latin is more expansive than our binary English equivalents by allowing for both means of peacemaking (to make peaceful through force) and ends of peacemaking (a peaceable people at peace with Rome).⁵¹ The ambiguity is intentionally hubristic: whether one is pacified by choice or by coercion, peacemaking in the Latin sense "expresses a remarkable confidence in Rome's ability to transform its conquered subjects—to make them peaceful."⁵² While Rome's peacemaking encoded Rome's coercive capacities for violence into the ethos of everyday life, an equally important (but often neglected) vehicle for rationalizing subjects' domination was the belief that distant peoples were ethnically and culturally inferior and therefore predisposed toward pacification through enslavement.

Rationalizing Imperial Domination: Inferior Peoples and Prejudice

The *Res gestae divi Augusti* provides us with a veritable catalog of peoples pacified by Augustus—fifty-five geographical names to be exact (*RGDA* 25–33). By comparison, the Acts of the Apostles references no less than ninety-nine geographical names and ethnic descriptors to signify the missional ambition of the apostles to extend salvation from Jerusalem to Rome. As John Moles observes, "*Luke-Acts* raises people *up*, Augustus' *Res Gestae* subjects them."⁵³

---

47. Fuhrmann, *Policing*, 89–122.
48. Quoted in Fuhrmann, *Policing*, 150.
49. Woolf, "Roman Peace," in *War and Society in the Roman World*, ed. John Rich and Graham Shipley (London: Routledge, 1993), 191.
50. For extensive examples, see Myles Lavan, "Peace and Empire: *Pacare, pacatus*, and the Language of Roman Imperialism," in *Peace and Reconciliation in the Classical World*, ed. E. P. Moloney and Michael Stuart Williams (London: Routledge 2017), 102–14.
51. See Lavan, "Peace and Empire," 111.
52. Lavan, "Peace and Empire," 112.
53. John Moles, "Accommodation, Opposition or Other? *Luke-Acts*' Stance towards Rome," in *Roman Rule in Greek and Latin Writing*, ed. Jesper Majbom Madsen and Roger Rees (Leiden: Brill, 2014), 88 (emphasis original).

What are we to make of this? Moles does not provide qualification for his terse comment, but we can fill in the gaps by probing the relationship between Roman imperialism and its mechanisms for classifying subordinates as inferior peoples.

As the *Res Gestae* and Roman iconography of the globe attests, geography was a crucial part of the machinery of Roman imperialism. It is also true that "geography has always been intimately bound to theories of race and ethnicity."[54] This point has been largely neglected by imperial-critical interpreters of the Bible (who too often leave imperialism undefined or reduce it to a militaristic venture apart from a racialized one). While concepts of race from Darwinian biological determinism cannot be imputed to antiquity, it is simply *not* true that Greco-Roman cultures were impervious to postures of racism, prejudice, and xenophobia. Benjamin Isaac calls these postures of prejudice "proto-racism" and has put forth a monumental effort to catalog their presence in Greek and Roman literature.[55] While violence provided an effective means to coerce subjects into submission, maintenance of *imperium* over the *orbis terrarum* demanded a coinciding ideology that emasculated subjects' ethnic autonomy and thereby justified their domination.

To rationalize global domination, Rome drew on proto-racist stigmas and Greek philosophers' idea of natural slavery to justify the imperialist vision. To paraphrase Pliny the Elder, the effects of the dominating metropolis on distant lands is to incorporate scattered peoples under the ruling metropolis, soften their customs, override cultural difference through common language, and civilize (*Nat.* 3.39). Toward such homogenizing ends, what sorts of theories and attitudes did Romans adopt in their perception of ethnic superiority? Isaac unearths three primary forms of racism in Greek and Latin literature: (1) environmental determinism (i.e., climate and geography shape collective characteristics of peoples, Isaac, 82–109); (2) the belief in the heritability of acquired characteristics (i.e., humans pass on from one generation to the next characteristics which they acquired during their lifetimes, 109–33); and (3) autochthony and pure lineage (i.e., the conviction that marriage between foreigners contaminates one's own culture, 134–63).[56] Taken together, proto-racist attitudes rationalized Roman superiority and legitimated the enslavement of

---

54. Rebecca Kennedy, C. Sydnor Roy, and Max L. Goodman, eds., *Race and Ethnicity in the Classical World: An Anthology of Primary Sources in Translation* (Indianapolis: Hackett, 2013), xvii.

55. Benjamin Isaac, *The Invention of Racism in Classical Antiquity* (Princeton: Princeton University Press, 2004). Hereafter, page references are given in parentheses in the text.

56. Isaac discusses two other forms of proto-racism, the cause and effect relationship

An Alternative Global Imaginary

distant peoples through master/servant metaphors and superior/inferior dichotomies.[57] So Hippocrates in the fifth century BCE suggests that Asians are weak and unable to rule themselves because their seasons are static (*Airs, Waters, Places* 16; Isaac, 62–63). Aristotle, on the other hand, argues that people in cold countries (Europe and Asia) lack intelligence to govern; the Greeks, conversely, "intermediate in geographical position . . . possess both spirit and intelligence . . . to show a capacity for *governing every other people*" (emphasis mine, *Pol.* 1327b, trans. Barker; see Isaac, 70–71).[58] The ancient Greek belief in ethnic superiority laid the intellectual groundwork for imperial Rome's expansionist ambitions by rooting the enslavement of distant peoples in natural law (indeed, "there are naturally ruling elements and elements naturally ruled" [Aristotle, *Pol.* 1260a, 7–9]; see Isaac, 170–94, esp. 175). But the metropolis's expansion toward the periphery, in Roman self-understanding, could also have the obverse effect of contamination of Roman purity by inferior peoples (Isaac, 239–47, 310–11).[59] Fear of contamination, however, reinforced boundaries of xenophobia, prejudice, and imperial impulses to conceptualize the cultural other as objects of mastery (Livy, 38.17.12; see Isaac, 90, 307).[60] Put another way, proto-racism justified enslavement, while enslavement fueled Roman imperialism—the process of establishing or maintaining an empire.

One of the perennial challenges of imperial-critical readings of the Bible is the often-neglected task of fleshing out resistance literature's objects of resistance. Indeed, what do we even mean by "imperial-critical"? And in employing this capacious descriptor, what *exactly* are the imperial referents that a text is critical of? In the preceding discussion, I have sought to put flesh on the mechanics of Roman global imaginary, especially the ways the *pax Romana* communicated Roman imperialism through military domination and metaphors of enslavement (along with proto-racist attitudes that justified domination). What remains for us to explore is the relationship between Roman imperial ambition and early Christianity's missional ambition. Indeed, with the above

---

between good government and human behavior (*Invention*, 92–93; 164–65) and physiognomics (*Invention*, 149–63).

57. On slave discourse as metonymy for imperialism, see especially Myles Lavan, *Slaves to Rome: Paradigms of Empire in Roman Culture* (Cambridge: Cambridge University Press, 2013), 14.

58. Among Roman authors who adopted this thinking, Isaac points to Vitruvius 6.1; Pliny, *Nat.* 2.80.190; and Vegetius 1.2.

59. In rare cases, it was possible for difference to be embraced as a positive influence; however, this is rare. See Isaac, *Invention*, 243.

60. On the language of mastery, see Lavan, *Slaves to Rome*, 74–97.

background in mind, what is the relationship between Roman imperialism and Peter's proclamation of peace in Cornelius's household? Lest we become tricked by Luke's rhetorical art, Cornelius is an agent of the *pax Romana*, a representative of Roman imperialism charged with the task of policing peace in Judea.

Alternative Global Imaginary: Peace through Jesus Christ

As the preceding discussion illustrates, the global imaginary of early Christian mission is not without precedent in the ancient Mediterranean.[61] The "spear-won" lands of Alexander the Great's conquests and the imperial drive of Augustus's divine mandate to rule "empire without end" (Virgil, *Aen.* 1.279), resulting in the *pax Romana*, are particularly striking parallels.[62] At the risk of sounding provocative, early Christianity and imperial Rome had at least two values in common. Both were concerned with geographical expansion, and both conceptualized their expansion through the lens of "peace" (Latin, *pax*; Greek, εἰρήνη). Notwithstanding the impressive geographical scope of these movements, the medium through which their global reach was achieved could not hinge on more different hardware. Rome expanded through the violence of military might and the systems of policing that uphold military domination. Christians, on the other hand, expanded through a nonmilitarized mission of universal salvation through preaching, table fellowship, healings, and a reorientation of divine and human power rooted in the new covenant of peace (Luke 22:20).[63]

The ethical implications of the new covenant of peace are immediately clear when Jesus's disciples break into a quarrel about greatness after the Lord's Supper (Luke 22:24-27). Jesus repudiates the disciples' thirst for imperial ambition by critically inverting Hellenistic/Roman royal ideology: "The kings of the Gentiles lord (κυριεύουσιν) it over them; and those in authority (οἱ ἐξουσιάζοντες) over them are called benefactors (εὐεργέται). But not so with you" (Luke 22:25-26). The implications of this new pattern of divesting power

---

61. I adopt the phrase "global imaginary" from Manfred B. Steger, *The Rise of the Global Imaginary: Political Ideologies from the French Revolution to the Global War on Terror* (Oxford: Oxford University Press, 2008).

62. On the Hellenistic trope of "spear-won" land, see Diodorus XVII.17.1-4; XIX 10.1-5; Arrian III.1.5-2.2; Polybius V.67; XVIII.49-51; 3 Macc 3:15; 6:5.

63. On the new covenant of peace, see Willard M. Swartley, *Covenant of Peace: The Missing Peace in New Testament Theology and Ethics* (Grand Rapids: Eerdmans, 2006), 177-88; and Gorman, *Death of the Messiah*, 132-69.

rather than accruing it are clear when, in Luke's second volume, the disciples ask Jesus when he will restore the kingdom to Israel (Acts 1:6). Here Jesus is confronted with the so-called zealot option—the impulse in early Judaism to "lord it over" Rome with violent retaliation. Instead of recognizing "the things that make for peace" (that is, the Messiah's embrace of all nations), the disciples are intoxicated with what Willie James Jennings calls the "nationalist fantasy"—a worldview that "places god-bound-to-our-nation over the God of all nations."[64] Jesus repudiates the disciples' nationalist fantasy by communicating how the kingdom will come—namely, through mission to the "ends of the earth" (Acts 1:8) and not sudden cosmic and/or physical retaliation. Jesus's repudiation of the zealot option grounds Christian mission in an alternative, counter-violent global imaginary, where "the ends of the earth" become an object of Israel's embrace and liberation (not domination).

It is in this Spirit-empowered space of missional ambition and gentile inclusion that Luke alludes to the political ethos of a world under the *imperium Romanum*. To be sure, Luke is alone among New Testament authors in mentioning a Roman emperor by name, acknowledging the presence of early Jewish resistance movements, and calling Simon a "zealot."[65] In juxtaposing the political perspectives of both metropolis *and* periphery in his narrative account, Luke invites his audience to interrogate the Jesus movement by comparing and contrasting the church's new covenant of peace with the nationalist fantasies of both imperial Rome and Jewish resistance movements.[66]

But amid such clashing ideologies of power, why does Luke portray Cornelius in positive hues? Wengst more or less captures the spirit of the history of interpretation when he writes: "Here [in Luke-Acts] we find virtually no negative statements about Rome and its representatives; rather, they are depicted in an explicitly favourable light."[67] In what follows I wish to problematize this reading, showing that terms of flattery toward imperial power could evoke

---

64. Willie James Jennings, *Acts*, Belief: A Theological Commentary on the Bible (Louisville: Westminster John Knox, 2017), 13–24.

65. See Augustus (Luke 2:1), Tiberius (Luke 3:1), and Claudius (Acts 11:28; 18:2). For resistance movements, see Theudas (Acts 5:36), Judas the Galilean (Acts 5:37), and the Egyptian who stirred up a revolt (Acts 21:38). On Simon as a zealot, see Luke 6:15 and Acts 1:13.

66. Notably, Paul himself is interrogated on trial for being "a pestilent fellow, an agitator among all the Jews throughout the world, and a ringleader of the sect of the Nazarenes" (Acts 24:5).

67. Wengst, *Pax Romana*, 90. Steve Walton has helpfully problematized this approach, drawing attention to Luke's subtle critique of Sosthenes (Acts 18:17), Lysias (23:26), Felix (24:26–27), and Festus (25:25). See Walton, "The State They Were In," 26–28.

ironic caricature and, in certain cases, the ideal ruler's semantic opposite: the angry tyrant and his sycophants.

Pax Christi *Meets* Pax Romana *in a Roman Centurion's Household*

Peter's proclamation of the gospel in a Roman centurion's household brings the *pax Romana* into direct contact with Christian mission (and not only because Peter employs the word εἰρήνη in Acts 10:36). Two recent exhaustive overviews of Roman soldiery in Greco-Roman and early Jewish literary sources draw similar conclusions about attitudes toward Roman centurions in antiquity—namely, centurions are represented in "predominantly negative" terms and, in "a very real sense, for the civilian population of the Empire the centurion was Rome."[68] Thus, if *pax* and imperialism are synonyms, then "centurion" is metonymy for *imperium Romanum* since the maintenance of empire was largely left up to centurions through judicial tasks and policing peace in the periphery. It is no exaggeration, then, to suggest that Cornelius is a composite character—a literary representation of Roman imperialism and its encroachment on Jewish subordinates.[69]

It would be easy to be tricked into thinking otherwise—that Luke's "extraordinarily positive" representation of Cornelius evokes "his perception of the Pax Romana."[70] After all, Luke portrays Cornelius and his household in flattering terms: a "devout man who feared God"; "he gave alms"; "prayed constantly"; "God-fearing man"; "well spoken of by the whole Jewish nation" (Acts 10:2, 22). What do we make of these terms of flattery, especially given the anomalous nature of representing centurions' character in positive terms in antiquity? Such flattery, as I have argued in more detail elsewhere, could also be construed as hidden criticism and ironic caricature.[71] To take one example, the "verbal slippage" of terms of praise/blame is acutely felt in Pliny's panegyrical speech to Trajan. Because of the pervasive presence of anti-imperial innuendo

---

68. Kyrychenko, *The Roman Army and the Expansion of the Gospel*, 186, 88. See also Brink, *Soldiers*, 28–91; and Justin R. Howell who argues that centurions were "notorious for using violent and unjust means to acquire wealth" ("Imperial Authority and Benefaction of Centurions and Acts 10:34–43: A Response to C. Kavin Rowe," *JSNT* 31 [2008]: 37–39, here 39).

69. See Frank Dicken, *Herod as a Composite Character in Luke-Acts* (Tübingen: Mohr Siebeck, 2014).

70. Wengst, *Pax Romana*, 92.

71. Strait, *Hidden Criticism of the Angry Tyrant*, 144–47. So also Howell, "Imperial Authority," 39–44.

through double speak in the Roman world, Pliny has to assure Trajan that his panegyrics are sincere. Pliny writes,

> There is no risk that when I speak of [Trajan's] civility, he thinks his arrogance is being reproached; his profligacy, when I talk of his frugality; his cruelty, when I speak of his clemency; his greed, when I speak of his generosity; his malice, when I speak of his kindness; his lust, when I speak of his self-control; his laziness, when I speak of his work; his cowardice, when I speak of his courage. (Pliny, *Pan.* 3.4)[72]

The point here is that terms of flattery can evoke their semantic opposites—a reading strategy that is tempting to adopt here. We also see this kind of double speak in Philo's *Embassy to Gaius*, where Philo eulogizes the benefits of the *pax Augusta* to criticize Gaius Caligula's encroachment on Jewish worship spaces (even though Augustus's annexation of Egypt had a profoundly negative impact on Jewish citizenship and autonomy [*Legat.* 143–153]). In other words, we cannot take Philo's eulogy of Augustus as sincerity; rather, Augustus serves Philo's rhetorical ends to manage the mad emperor in Gaius Caligula. The mistake interpreters make is to take such irony at face value (i.e., because Cornelius is pious, therefore Luke affirms the *pax Romana* and imperial Rome). Such logic misconstrues Luke's rhetorical artistry: Like the centurion of Luke 7, Cornelius's piety reflects his posture of subordination to *Israel's* God as *Soter* and *Euergetes*; this is not affirmation of the imperial apparatus—it is *criticism* (or what Anathea Portier-Young calls "critical inversion").[73] Whatever one makes of this reading, one cannot deny that Luke tips his hat to Cornelius's ultimate preconversion allegiances: "On Peter's arrival Cornelius met him, and falling at his feet, worshiped him" (Acts 10:25). We know centurions were partakers and proliferators of emperor worship and that Caesarea was a mini-Rome in Judea with colossal statues of Roma and Augustus side by side (Josephus, *J. W.* 1.414). For the attuned reader, Cornelius's impulse to worship Peter thus signals to Luke's audience that Cornelius's piety remains rooted in the religions of the Roman Empire. Indeed, Peter responds: "Stand up; I am only a mortal" (Acts 10:26).

The profundity of the unfolding confrontation between Peter's proclama-

---

72. Translation from Shadi Bartsch, "The Art of Sincerity: Pliny's Panegyricus," in *Oxford Readings in Classical Studies: Latin Panegyric*, ed. Roger Rees (Oxford: Oxford University Press, 2012), 174.

73. Anathea Portier-Young, *Apocalypse Against Empire: Theologies of Resistance in Early Judaism* (Grand Rapids: Eerdmans, 2011), 14.

tion of the gospel inside the home of an agent of Rome's occupation of Israel is not lost on recent interpreters. Kavin Rowe and Justin Howell have made a strong (albeit debatable) case that Acts 10:36 is a "point of exegetical entry" for understanding Luke's attitude toward the Roman imperial cults.[74] They both, however, focus on the latter half of v. 36—without recourse to discerning the role of peace within the larger narrative framework: "You know the message he sent to the people of Israel, proclaiming the good news of peace through Jesus Christ—this one is Lord of all" (τὸν λόγον [ὃν] ἀπέστειλεν τοῖς υἱοῖς Ἰσραὴλ εὐαγγελιζόμενος εἰρήνην διὰ Ἰησοῦ Χριστοῦ, οὗτός ἐστιν πάντων κύριος, Acts 10:36, my translation). Rowe is certainly correct to read the demonstrative not as a parenthetical remark ("he is Lord of all") but rather as polemical ("*this* one is Lord of all"). Howell nuances Rowe's thesis, showing that centurions were crucial representatives of the emperor's imperial authority and benefaction. Therefore, the referent of criticism is the emperor *and* his subordinate authorities.[75] But if the latter part of v. 36 represents Luke's attitude toward emperor worship, then Peter's proclamation of "peace through Jesus Christ" functions as an exegetical entry point for Luke's attitude toward the *pax Romana* and thereby Roman imperialism. Craig Keener alludes to this point when he writes, "Whatever 'preaching peace' might signify in other texts, it is highly significant when Peter addresses it to a military officer belonging to the occupying power."[76] Conversely, Rowe observes that "Luke's side of the conversation should be seen for what it is: a subversion and rearrangement of the very notion of peace."[77] While I agree with the general tenor of both statements, Keener does not provide qualification for what he means by "highly significant," and Rowe roots Luke's rearrangement of Roman peace in Jesus's redefinition of service in Luke 22:24–27. Certainly, this is good and true, but I contend we can go further: Peter's proclamation of "peace *through* Jesus Christ" contests the agency of the *pax Romana* (peace *through* salvation in Jesus—not *through* Rome's divine election and military might) and articulates an alternative cosmic hierarchy where Caesar and his bureaucrats are

---

74. Although 10:36 is important, I contend that Jesus's ascension to heaven represents a more programmatic point of entry for understanding Luke's attitude toward imperial Rome. See Strait, *Hidden Criticism of the Angry Tyrant*, 280–86.

75. Justin Howell, "Imperial Authority," 39.

76. Craig S. Keener, *Acts: An Exegetical Commentary*, vol. 2: *3:1–14:28* (Grand Rapids: Baker Academic, 2013), 1800.

77. Rowe, *World Upside Down*, 114. Later on, Rowe writes: "While I agree with Mauser about the necessity to read Luke-Acts in relation to the Pax Romana, I take Luke to be much more critical of this notion than Mauser does" (242n120).

An Alternative Global Imaginary

subordinate to the *Lord of all*. Luke thus intentionally juxtaposes messianic peace with a pious Roman centurion in order to critique the emperor cult and the *pax Romana* (i.e., Roman imperialism) without having to criticize a referent explicitly.

Luke's critique of Roman imperialism is further animated when we examine the narrative plot of Acts 10. To repeat: Luke's audience is, at this strategic point in the narrative, invited *inside* the home of the emperor's agent of *pax* over Judea. The representation of two distinctive global imaginaries converging in an imperial household challenges the racialized stigmas and prejudices upon which the imperialist vision is founded (including Jewish visions of gentile exclusion and/or destruction).[78] Indeed, it is a reminder that the project of Israel is not about segregating Jewish bodies from gentile bodies (or pacifying gentiles through military domination) but rather joining the two together in communion with God and one another. For Luke, the mission of the church is bound up with the mission of Israel: to desegregate the ends of the earth and empower humans to coexist amid difference in peace and life together with God—both in this world and the one to come. The scene therefore bolsters Luke's programmatic statement that "all flesh shall see the salvation of God" (Luke 3:6; Isa 40:5); this universal claim, as Luke has it, even encompasses Israel's enemies, reinforcing Jesus's teaching on enemy love in Luke's Gospel. As François Bovon writes, "The Lucan claim to reach all nations was an implicit polemic against Roman imperialism, much more discreet than the anti-Roman position of John's Revelation, but perceptible nevertheless."[79] Bovon correctly observes how Luke's universalism evokes an "implicit" and "discreet" polemic against Roman imperialism. However, Bovon fails to substantiate this reading by appeal to the *modus operandi* for conveying such discreet criticism in antiquity, especially figured speech (*emphasis*/σχῆμα) in the form of eulogy with double speak and antithetical resistance. The utility of this analytical tool is felt when applied to Luke's phrase "proclaiming goods news of peace" in Acts 10:36 (εὐαγγελιζόμενος εἰρήνην). By "peace" is Luke's referent politically innocuous or polemical? In favor of the latter, orators theorized that, to protect oneself from retaliation, "ambiguity of expression" (Quintilian *Inst. Or.* 9.2.64; Demetrius *Eloc.* 240) "packed into a few words is more forceful" when critiquing

---

78. For examples, see Scot McKnight, *A Light among the Gentiles: Jewish Missionary Activity in the Second Temple Period* (Minneapolis: Fortress, 1991), 22–25; and Mireille Hadas-Lebel, *Jerusalem against Rome* (Leuven: Brill, 2006), 22–29, 265–83, 455–76.

79. François Bovon, "Israel, the Church and the Gentiles in the Twofold Work of Luke," in *New Testament Traditions and Apocryphal Narratives*, trans. Jane Haapiseva-Hunger (Eugene, OR: Pickwick, 1995), 84.

imperial authority (Demetrius, *Eloc.* 241). We see this ambiguity in the Wisdom of Solomon's oblique criticism of the *pax Romana*, where ps.-Solomon embeds criticism of the cult of rulers in Hellenistic idol polemic, calling "such great evils peace" (τὰ τοσαῦτα κακὰ εἰρήνην προσαγορεύουσιν, Wis 14:22).

The arts of Hellenistic discursive resistance should caution us from taking Luke's positive presentation of Cornelius as innuendo for affirming the *pax Romana*. We know that Rome's imperial vision of peace was funded by military domination, racial prejudices, and enslavement of distant peoples. In a Roman centurion's house, the global domination of imperial Rome comes face to face with God's global imaginary incarnated in the resurrected Messiah of Israel and his followers. It is here that Luke is faced with a rhetorical problem: how to articulate the incompatibility of the gospel of peace with Roman idolatry, power and *pax* through coercion. To convey God's message of peace, Luke portrays Cornelius in pious terms while simultaneously flipping the script of Roman euergetism by contesting Roman agency (peace *through* Jesus Christ— not the *pax Romana*) and cosmology (*this one* is Lord of *all*—not Caesar and the gods). While our modern sensibilities see subtlety and discreet notes of contradictory criticism, the active reader in antiquity was trained to hear such innuendo as irony and thereby *criticism*—not *deferent eulogy.*

Live Your Exegesis: Global Imaginary and Christian Discipleship

Like Rome's imperialist iconography of the globe, Luke-Acts functions as a literary representation of God's global imaginary. What shape does this representation take? And what would it mean to embody this global iconography in a people? Notably, it is not motifs of standing on or mastering the globe in collaboration with the gods, nor is it images of "lording" divine and royal power over enslaved, distant subjects through military domination that captures the essence of Luke's portraiture. Rather, the Acts of the Apostles habituates the church into an alternative global imaginary: an alter-cultural community of disciples who think differently (*metanoia*) about divine identity, power, and human entanglements across cultural and racial lines to *become* agents of God's inbreaking, counter-violent message of peace that disrupts and reverses the violent grammar of imperialism (military domination, xenophobia, enslavement). The narrative of Acts, then, disorients nationalist fantasies by socializing disciples into allegiance to the crucified *Lord of all* and multicultural communities of fellowship that embrace human difference rather than fear it. Simply put: Luke's iconography of the globe is upside down: cruciform, counter-violent, and counter-imperial.

An Alternative Global Imaginary

The perennial danger of Christian mission is that, like the disciples in Acts 1, the church's conscience can become coopted by imperial ambition or assimilate the church's mission with the state's ambition for power. The Acts of Apostles is a narrative that disarms human impulses to concentrate power through nationalist fantasies and ethno-racial exceptionalism. In contrast to the metrocentric view of Roman imperialism, where the *other* in the frontier is emasculated and domesticated through a "booty raid on an epic scale" to invest benefits in the imperial metropolis, God's Spirit-empowered, counter-violent mission divests power and soteriological benefaction to "the ends of the earth" within an outward euergetic paradigm of peace, liberation, and forgiveness.[80] In missiological terms, the movement of soteriological benefaction is centrifugal rather than centripetal, but in imperial terms, Christian mission disrupts the flow of benefaction: it is from center to periphery (from Jerusalem to the gentile world) rather than periphery to center (the margins to Rome). For Rome, enslaving the periphery through militarized peace and violence were interrelated and overlapping strategies of economic enrichment through gift exchange; for Christians, peace and violence were incompatible modes of bearing witness to God's gift in Jesus's resurrection. The result, as Willie Jennings writes, is that the church's mission turns Israel's election "outward not inward" (a point Luke roots in the Scriptures of Israel [Luke 1:79; 2:32; Acts 13:47; 26:18, 23]).[81] The narratology of this outward movement is, in itself, critical of imperialism in that disciples' baptismal identity (and not weaponized ethnic allegiances) becomes the controlling narrative and agency through which God disarms and disrupts imperial and oppressive concentrations of power to bring about "universal restoration" (Acts 3:21).

Here in the United States, we live in an age where the nationalist fantasy has made many Christian circles believe that the state is the primary context for Christian mission. It is believed that if we have a Christian president, Christian supreme court, Christian police, Christian military, Christian laws, Christian foreign policies, Christian schools, and Christian monuments, then somehow God's kingdom will be established in the land. It is striking, though, that in the Lukan cosmology these institutions and their bureaucracies lie under the authority of Satan.[82] Here I am not suggesting that the state is an

---

80. Michel M. Austin, "Hellenistic Kings, War and the Economy," *ClQ* 36 (1986): 454.
81. Jennings, *Acts*, 115.
82. That is, the "kingdoms of the empire" that Luke places under the authority of Satan (πάσας τὰς βασιλείας τῆς οἰκουμένης, Luke 4:5). See also Acts 26:17–18. Barbara Rossing rightly argues that οἰκουμένη in Luke-Acts should be translated "empire" rather than "whole inhabited world" ("Turning Empire (οἰκουμένη) Upside Down: A Response," in *Reading*

205

illegitimate actor for the flourishing of human community; rather, I am suggesting that the proper Christian posture toward it is one of suspicion rather than trust. Indeed, for Luke, there is only one Christian nation and that nation is called the church—the nonmilitarized, borderless, multicultural people of God. What do we do with that? For Luke's Jesus, it is not Rome; it is not state and military power; it is not purity laws; it is not spatial segregation; it is not a weaponized or racialized church—none of this ushers in God's kingdom. Rather, it is weaponless disciples from all nations who bear witness to the reign of God through a message of *peace* through Jesus Christ and a radical ethic of *peacemaking* across lines of encrusted human difference. Indeed, as Gorman writes: "If violence and war is the way to peace, then Rome was right, and Christ died for nothing."[83]

Acts in the Discourses of Masculinity and Politics, ed. Eric D. Barreto, Matthew L. Skinner, and Steve Walton [London: Bloomsbury, 2017], 148–55).

83. Gorman, *Becoming the Gospel*, 161.

Chapter 12

The Past, Present, and Future of Bodily Resurrection as Salvation: Christ, Church, and Cosmos

Andy Johnson

Interpreters of Paul generally agree that Jesus's death and resurrection constitute one complex saving event and then readily appropriate explicit salvific functions to Jesus's death.[1] But even those not intending to downplay the salvific function of Christ's resurrection often only highlight the resurrection's (proper) epistemological role of *revealing* the salvific efficacy of Jesus's death rather than explicating its other direct soteriological effects for humanity and the cosmos.[2] Utilizing a participatory framework[3] for understanding

---

1. I use the word "appropriate" here in a similar way as when we say that the works of the Trinity in the world are indivisible but that one may "appropriate" certain functions to each trinitarian person within the divine economy. That is, while the saving events of Jesus's incarnation, life, death, resurrection, and exaltation/ascension are indivisible, we may appropriate certain saving functions to each within the single complex salvific trajectory of God's mission.

2. Cf. the claims of Clark Pinnock, "Salvation by Resurrection," *ExAud* 9 (1993): 1–2.

3. There is no current consensus on what "participation in Christ" means concretely. For a broad sample of approaches to the topic, see Michael J. Thate, Kevin J. Vanhoozer, and Constantine R. Campbell, eds., *"In Christ" in Paul: Explorations in Paul's Theology of Union and Participation* (Grand Rapids: Eerdmans, 2018); see also the recent survey of approaches in Grant Macaskill, *Union with Christ in the New Testament* (Oxford: Oxford University

---

It is difficult to overstate my indebtedness to Michael Gorman's scholarship, not just in the following essay, but in all my academic work. It is even more difficult, however, to overstate the grace and blessings God has channeled to me through Mike's friendship. In gratitude I offer this essay to my friend whose life has explicated the meaning of cruciformity as much as his academic work has.

Paul and salvation within an overall missional orientation toward Scripture,[4] I will attempt to *sketch* these direct soteriological effects in humanity's past, present, and future experience of salvation.[5] I emphasize the word "sketch" here because what follows is not a detailed exegetical treatment of particular passages in Paul but an attempt to connect some of the theological dots in Paul's occasional letters in a coherent way, dots that could perhaps also be connected in other coherent ways. The sketch of these salvific effects in the following argument may be succinctly summarized as follows: What God *has done* for the body of Jesus in microcosm in his resurrection, God *is doing* in the ecclesial body of Christ—the current locale of the new humanity and new creation/cosmos—and God *will do* for those in Christ and for the body of the cosmos in macrocosm at the parousia.

First, some working assumptions. Since the bulk of the chapter focuses on the *salvific* effects of Christ's resurrection in humanity's past, present, and future, I offer up front a working definition (in a missional key) of what I take to be "salvation" for humanity in its broadest and ultimate sense in Paul's letters. Salvation means that humans, by being incorporated into Christ's corporate

---

Press, 2013), 17–41. My understanding of participation is similar to that of Richard B. Hays ("What Is 'Real Participation in Christ'? A Dialogue with E. P. Sanders on Pauline Soteriology," in *Redefining First-Century Jewish and Christian Identities: Essays in Honor of Ed Parish Sanders*, ed. Fabian E. Udoh et al. [Notre Dame, IN: University of Notre Dame Press, 2008], 336–51) and Michael J. Gorman (*Participating in Christ: Explorations in Paul's Theology and Spirituality* [Grand Rapids: Baker Academic, 2019]). I take participation in Christ to mean that one is in a covenant relationship with the cruciform, risen Lord, sharing that covenant relationship with the members of his ecclesial body in which the narrative of his self-giving death and resurrected life is being embodied/re-presented, both individually and corporately. In this essay, when I use the language of being in the corporate body of Christ/the Truly Human One/the Last Adam, it is shorthand for this fuller articulation of participation in Christ.

4. What constitutes a "missional" interpretation of Scripture is the subject of a robust conversation. But for purposes of this essay focused on Paul, when I refer to a missional orientation toward Scripture, I mean that I am consciously interpreting his letters within what I perceive to be Scripture's overarching story of God's life-giving mission to bring creation to its intended destiny through the agency of humanity (on which, see my *1 and 2 Thessalonians*, THNTC [Grand Rapids: Eerdmans, 2016], 2–4). For a similar approach to Paul's letters using a participatory framework within an overall missional orientation to Scripture, see Michael J. Gorman, *Becoming the Gospel: Paul, Participation, and Mission* (Grand Rapids: Eerdmans, 2015), esp. 21–62.

5. My focus here is on identifying these salvific effects, *not on explaining the mechanics* of how these effects are achieved. I can no more explain the mechanics of the salvific effects that are more properly appropriated to Christ's saving resurrection than I can explain the mechanics of those more properly appropriated to Jesus's saving death.

body, forgiven, and conformed to the image of the cruciform, resurrected, truly Human One—Israel's messianic king—are restored to their rightful missional place as God's vice-regents, thereby sharing in/inheriting God's reign over a renewed creation permeated with the life-giving Spirit and filled with God's justice (δικαιοσύνη) and shalom (εἰρήνη).[6] Implicit in this definition is a necessary connection between anthropology and cosmology (i.e., between the soteriological effects for humanity and for creation itself) which will be fleshed out in the last section of the essay. For the sake of full disclosure, I will also state certain (contested) assumptions I will be making without argument: (1) "the righteousness/justice (δικαιοσύνη) of God" is primarily a pattern of *God's* own activity, not something to be "imputed" or "imparted";[7] (2) the Christocentric/subjective reading of πίστις [Ἰησοῦ] Χριστοῦ (the faith[fulness] of Jesus Christ) is probably correct; (3) πίστις in Paul's letters may connote not only belief and trust but also faithfulness/obedience.[8]

With these assumptions in place, the essay proceeds as follows. First, using 1 Cor 1:30 heuristically, I contend that Christ as "last Adam," the truly Human One and microcosm of the new cosmos, *experienced* resurrection salvifically as God's saving justice (δικαιοσύνη), as God's sanctifying action (ἁγιασμός), and as God's redemption from Death's power (ἀπολύτρωσις). Second, I argue that Paul depicts those who are participating "in Christ," in his new humanity, as *currently experiencing* analogous (not identical) salvific effects of the power that Christ's resurrection engenders, i.e., being justified, sanctified, and redeemed. In the last section, I argue that at the parousia of the "last Adam," who wields the resurrection power of the life-giving Spirit, those who belong to him *will experience* resurrection as salvific in that it completes their justification, sanctification, and redemption. Moreover, the salvific impact of Christ's bodily resurrection necessarily extends to the cosmos in macrocosm—itself a σῶμα[9]—as the life-giving Spirit "justifies" creation by setting it right, filling it with God's justice, and entirely sanctifies and redeems it. Hence—and

---

6. Cf. N. T. Wright's missionally oriented articulation of Paul's redefinition of salvation in *Paul and the Faithfulness of God* (Minneapolis: Fortress, 2013), 754–55.

7. For a recent argument challenging this assumption, see Charles Lee Irons, *The Righteousness of God: A Lexical Examination of the Covenant-Faithfulness Interpretation*, WUNT 2/386 (Tübingen: Mohr Siebeck, 2015). The jury remains out on whether Irons has demonstrated his case.

8. See now Nijay Gupta, *Paul and the Language of Faith* (Grand Rapids: Eerdmans, 2019).

9. "In the ancient world, the human body was not *like* a microcosm; it *was* a microcosm—a small version of the universe at large." Dale B. Martin, *The Corinthian Body* (New Haven: Yale University Press, 1995), 16.

this is critical—the essay shows that Christ's resurrection in Paul's letters is not simply a *sign* of the salvific efficacy of Jesus's death but is *constitutive of salvation itself*.

Resurrection as Salvation in (True) Humanity's Past

One might speak of humanity's past—at least *true* humanity's past—in terms of the past complex event of Jesus's incarnation, life, death, resurrection, and exaltation. This is because, for Paul, Christ is the "last Adam," the truly Human One as compared with "the first human, Adam" (1 Cor 15:45).[10] Whereas Death (as a power) comes through the first Adam, resurrection/life comes through the last Adam (1 Cor 15:20–23, 45; Rom 5:12–21). In 1 Cor 1:30, Paul claims that his Corinthian audience is "in Christ Jesus [the truly Human One] who has become (saving) wisdom from God for us, that is, saving justice (δικαιοσύνη), sanctification (ἁγιασμός), and redemption (ἀπολύτρωσις)."[11] Prior to becoming these things *for us*, Christ first experienced them himself as the truly Human One. In other words, this one who represents true humanity experienced God's salvation, *and this not through his own death per se*, as if he had died for his own sins, but through God's raising him from the dead. What might it mean that the one true human experienced resurrection salvifically as God's saving justice (δικαιοσύνη), God's sanctifying action (ἁγιασμός), and God's redemption from Death's power (ἀπολύτρωσις)? These terms describe salvific effects that overlap with one other, and each deserves a brief comment.

In Second Temple Judaism, "resurrection and divine justice came to be so intimately interconnected that they offered mutual, even inseparable, corroboration."[12] So when God raised Jesus, he experienced it as an act of *justification*, that is, an execution of God's saving justice that *vindicated* his faithful "obedience unto death" (cf. 1 Tim 3:16)[13] *and transformed* his crucified, dishonored

---

10. Pinnock rightly claims that "the fundamental category for understanding the soteriological role of the resurrection is Christ's solidarity with humanity as the last Adam" ("Salvation by Resurrection," 4). Not surprisingly, 1 Cor 15, Paul's most detailed treatment of the connection between Christ's resurrection and the future resurrection, is also one of two places where he explicitly uses the Adam/Christ typology (see also Rom 5), calling Christ "the last Adam" (1 Cor 15:45). 1 Corinthians 15 is also the only place Paul explicitly uses the language "in Adam" (1 Cor 15:22), describing a death-bound sphere ("in Adam all die").

11. All translations of Scripture are my own unless otherwise noted.

12. C. D. Elledge, *Resurrection of the Dead in Early Judaism 200 BCE–CE 200* (Oxford: Oxford University Press, 2017), 82.

13. Cf. N. T. Wright, *The Resurrection of the Son of God* (Minneapolis: Fortress, 2003), 248, 270–71.

body into a human body of δόξα (Phil 3:21; by implication 1 Cor 15:43). He experienced resurrection, to use a term coined by Peter Leithart, as God's "deliverdict," God's salvific act of *redemption* delivering him from Death's dominion (Rom 6:9), thereby enacting God's verdict that Jesus is the truly faithful human being who is creation's rightful Lord (Phil 2:9–11).[14]

Moreover, because in the OT and Second Temple Judaism, "holiness at its source is life itself—the antonym of death," and "the nature of the living God is in opposition to dead bodies,"[15] Christ experienced resurrection as God's sanctifying act, a cleansing from the impurity associated with death and burial.[16] While its meaning is disputed, Rom 1:3–4 may imply something of the sort if its sense is rendered as follows: "Jesus, [the truly Human One] from David's messianic line (τοῦ γενομένου ἐκ σπέρματος Δαυὶδ κατὰ σάρκα), was publicly declared to be the true Son-of-God-in-power (ὁρισθέντος υἱοῦ θεοῦ ἐν δυνάμει), [enthroned as] Israel's messianic king our Lord (Χριστοῦ τοῦ κυρίου ἡμῶν), and this according to the Spirit who sanctifies by raising the dead (κατὰ πνεῦμα ἁγιωσύνης ἐξ ἀναστάσεως νεκρῶν)."[17] This rendering of Rom 1:3–4, if viewed together with Phil 2:9–10, might also suggest that Christ experienced resurrection as "sanctifying" in a second sense. That is, the life-giving Spirit's raising him from the dead[18] is a public declaration that this truly Human One

---

14. Peter Leithart, "Justification as Verdict and Deliverance: A Biblical Perspective," *ProEccl* 16 (2007): 56–72. Leithart articulates the issue well: "The key point is that for Paul the paradigmatic justification, the justification of Jesus, is not a 'mere verdict,' a mere verbal/judicial declaration that Jesus is righteous. Had the Father pronounced Jesus to be in the right but left Him in the grave, the Father's promise would have been falsified. Jesus's justification takes the form of a resurrection, a transforming event that is also His deliverance from the realm of death. Justification for sinners is precisely the same, an 'enacted verdict' that both declares us in the right and delivers us from the dominion of sin and death" (67).

15. Hannah K. Harrington, *Holiness: Rabbinic Judaism and the Graeco-Roman World* (New York: Routledge, 2001), 179.

16. The confession that Christ was "raised on the third day" may imply that he had not yet begun the decomposition process itself (cf. Acts 2:27, 31; 13:35, 37; and see Martin Pickup, "'On the Third Day': The Time Frame of Jesus' Death and Resurrection," *JETS* 56 [2013]: 533–34). Even so, occupying a tomb as a corpse would certainly have made him impure, in need of cleansing.

17. This rendering of the verse assumes that: πνεῦμα refers to God's Spirit; ἁγιωσύνης refers to that Spirit's sanctifying activity, or is perhaps an objective genitive (i.e., "Spirit who engenders holiness"); ἐξ ἀναστάσεως νεκρῶν refers to God's raising Jesus from the dead through this Spirit. Although I differ with his conclusion on the meaning of κατὰ πνεῦμα ἁγιωσύνης, for the interpretive possibilities of the phrase, see Richard N. Longenecker, *The Epistle to the Romans*, NIGTC (Grand Rapids: Eerdmans, 2016), 69–75.

18. As Fee emphasizes, Paul never explicitly says that the Spirit is the agent of Jesus's

was also *set apart* ("sanctified") as one who embodies the character/holiness of his Father, Israel's God, as would be expected of a true Son/King who now shares in the Father's divine name (Phil 2:9-10).[19]

It is plausible, then, to say that the one who defines true humanity has become for us saving justice, sanctification, and redemption (so 1 Cor 1:30) because, in his representative truly human body, he first experienced God's salvation in the justifying, sanctifying, and redeeming act of resurrection. Obviously, all this presupposes his death, but it is his death, resulting from human injustice engendered by Sin's cosmic power, *from which resurrection saves him*. Thus, Christ's resurrection itself is constitutive of salvation in true humanity's past.

Resurrection as Salvation in Humanity's Present

The ecclesial body of Christ is the current locale of the last Adam's new humanity[20] and fittingly, the locale of the new creation/cosmos (2 Cor 5:17; cf.

---

resurrection (*God's Empowering Presence: The Holy Spirit in the Letters of Paul* [Peabody, MA: Hendrickson, 1994], 808-11). However, he comes very close to doing so in this Romans passage and in Rom 8:11. One might also argue, based on Paul's rhetoric in 1 Cor 15 in which he consistently argues for an analogy between Christ's resurrection and that of those who belong to him, Paul would say that Christ also had been raised with a "spiritual body," i.e., a body acted upon, transformed, and totally permeated by the life-giving Spirit, fitting it for the new creation (on which see my "Turning the World Upside Down in 1 Corinthians 15: Apocalyptic Epistemology, the Resurrected Body, and the New Creation," *EvQ* 75 [2003]: 291-309). Moreover, it is not surprising that Paul can say elsewhere that God the Father raised Jesus "through his glory/power" (Rom 6:4/1 Cor 6:14) since the body permeated by the Spirit is raised in "glory" and "power" (1 Cor 15:43). Cf. Wesley Hill, *Paul and the Trinity: Persons, Relations, and the Pauline Letters* (Grand Rapids: Eerdmans, 2014), 154-63.

19. While God's exaltation of Christ in Phil 2:9-10, in which Christ is given the privilege of sharing in the divine name (YHWH), is distinguishable from his resurrection, the two are not separable (as Rom 8:34 also implies). His exaltation/enthronement as Lord of creation (Phil 2:11) is dependent on, and inclusive of, the Spirit's raising him from the dead.

20. The language of "the new humanity" only occurs outside the undisputed letters (Eph 2:15 [καινὸν ἄνθρωπον]; Eph 4:22-24 and Col 3:9-11 juxtaposing the old and new humanity), making explicit what is implied in the undisputed letters. For example, since Paul explicitly depicts Christ as "the last Adam" (1 Cor 15:45) and forges the comparison between "the one human being," Adam, through whom Sin and Death entered the world, and "the one human being," Jesus Christ, who brings life (Rom 5:12-21), the implication is that a community depicted as Christ's body is the body of the new humanity. Moreover, Paul's language in Rom 6:6 of "our old humanity" (ὁ παλαιὸς ἡμῶν ἄνθρωπος, cf. Col 3:9; Eph 4:22) as having been co-crucified with Christ would imply our sharing in his "new humanity" after having been raised from the waters of baptism to walk in newness of life (cf. also Gal 3:27-28).

The Past, Present, and Future of Bodily Resurrection as Salvation

Gal 6:15) to which his resurrection gave birth. For those in this ecclesial body, God is currently doing something analogous to what God did for the body of the last Adam in his resurrection. Those participating in this new humanity/new cosmos, are *currently experiencing* analogous (not identical) salvific effects of the life-giving power that engendered Christ's resurrection and emanates from it (Phil 3:10).[21] This power—also known as the Holy Spirit ("the Lord and giver of life")—enables their simultaneous conformity to Christ crucified and their co-resurrection with him to new life within the corporate body of this new humanity. As a result, they are currently being justified, sanctified, and redeemed. These salvific effects overlap and are intimately connected with one another.[22]

Before the last Adam experienced God's saving justice (δικαιοσύνη) in his resurrection, he was its singular human embodiment in that God's δικαιοσύνη was revealed in his (cruciform) faithfulness (Rom 3:22). He was first God's primary instrument through which God's δικαιοσύνη is channeled to others, and after that he experienced his own resurrection as an enactment of divine saving justice (δικαιοσύνη). One might, then, extend and paraphrase Rom 4:25 as follows: "[Christ] was handed over because of our trespasses *in a cruciform act of faithfulness that was the human embodiment of divine saving justice*. He was raised, *thereby himself experiencing divine saving justice*, with a view to (διά)[23] our justification (δικαίωσιν), i.e., *our experiencing God's saving justice*." He has indeed become God's saving justice (δικαιοσύνη) for us (1 Cor 1:30) in that he is the one in whom both human δικαιοσύνη and God's own δικαιοσύνη come to their fullest expression. Using this paraphrase of Rom 4:25 as a starting point, I will focus for much of the rest of this section on Rom 5–6,

---

21. Taking ἀναστάσεως in the phrase, "τὴν δύναμιν τῆς ἀναστάσεως αὐτοῦ," as a plenary genitive. Arguably, this δύναμις is the life-giving power that enables him (ἐνέργειαν τοῦ δύνασθαι αὐτὸν) to conform us to his own body and subject all things to himself in Phil 3:21 (cf. 1 Cor 15:23–28), the same power by which God raised the Lord and will raise us (1 Cor 6:14).

22. While these three salvific effects are the heuristic focus of this essay, they do not exhaust the current experience of salvation in Paul's communities. Other overlapping metaphors might include being washed, being forgiven, being transferred into the Son's kingdom, etc.

23. Although he focuses more on the forensic aspect of justification than I do here, for a defense of this prospective translation of διά, see Michael Bird, "Justified by Christ's Resurrection: A Neglected Aspect of Paul's Doctrine of Justification," *Scottish Bulletin of Evangelical Theology* 22 (2004): 83–84. For the opposite view (i.e., the retrospective translation of διά, "because of"), see J. R. Daniel Kirk, *Unlocking Romans: Resurrection and the Justification of God* (Grand Rapids: Eerdmans, 2008), 77–81.

attempting to *distinguish but not separate* the current salvific effects of Christ's being handed over for our sins (i.e., his atoning death) from the salvific effects of his being raised for our justification.

Immediately after Rom 4:25, the specific aspect of currently experiencing God's saving justice (being justified) on which Paul focuses is restored peaceful relations with God by being reconciled to God *through Christ's death* (5:1, 6–8, 10a). However, Paul does affirm the general salvific impact of Christ's resurrection or current resurrected life in 5:10b: "How much more, since we have been reconciled, will we be saved (σωθησόμεθα) by means of his (resurrected) life." In addition, while Paul's language in 5:9 of "having been justified now by means of his blood," is usually read as the equivalent of "being reconciled to God through the death of his son" in 5:10, an alternative interpretation may be relevant for our purposes. Relying on the work of David Moffit regarding the sacrificial logic of Leviticus where the blood represents life not death,[24] Downs and Lappenga argue that "by means of his blood" in 5:9 is not a reference to Jesus's death but to his (continuing) resurrection life.[25] If this is the case, Paul is continuing to connect our justification with Christ's resurrection. The implication would be that, while reconciliation as one aspect of justification can rightly be appropriated to Christ's "being handed over for our trespasses," justification itself includes more than that and must be completed by the act of Christ being "raised with a view to our justification." The "more than that" will become apparent as we proceed.

In Paul's Adam/Christ typology in Rom 5:12–21, he does not *explicitly* mention the resurrection of the one man/last Adam. Rather, he focuses on the salvific impact of the last Adam's justice-bringing deed of faithful obedience (his δικαίωμα), consisting of his saving death for others, i.e., his willing act of being handed over for our trespasses (παραπτώματα). In contrast to Adam, whose trespass (παράπτωμα)/disobedience leads to the reign of Sin and Death (5:12–14, 17, 21) and to condemnation (5:16, 18), the last Adam's obedient deed leads to a reversal of that condemnation (5:16). It is, however, worth noting that this reversal of condemnation is only effective if this last Adam has been raised, since otherwise, as Paul says elsewhere, "you are still in your sins" (1 Cor 15:17). Hence, this reversal of condemnation, while explicitly appropriated to Christ's obedient deed/faithful death, is another aspect of our justification *for which Christ was raised*.

---

24. *Atonement and the Logic of the Resurrection in the Epistle to the Hebrews*, NovTSup 141 (Leiden: Brill, 2011); "Atonement at the Right Hand: The Sacrificial Significance of Jesus' Exaltation in Acts," *NTS* 62 (2016): 549–68.

25. David J. Downs and Benjamin J. Lappenga, *The Faithfulness of the Risen Christ: Pistis and the Exalted Lord in the Pauline Letters* (Waco: Baylor University Press, 2019), 125–29.

The Past, Present, and Future of Bodily Resurrection as Salvation

But we might be able to say more here. Certainly Paul's argument in 1 Cor 15 (see esp. vv. 17, 20–22) makes it clear that the full story of the death *and resurrection* of the last Adam is operative in bringing about the resurrected life of the new age (cf. 1 Thess 4:14), a salvific benefit that Paul does mention in Rom 5:21 (ζωὴν αἰώνιον, the resurrected life of the new age).[26] In addition, in 5:17, he claims that "the ones who receive the abundance of the grace whose content is the gift of God's saving justice (τῆς δικαιοσύνης)[27] will reign in life (ἐν ζωῇ) through the one [true] human, Jesus Christ." In this context with its Adamic background, the language of *reigning* in life probably refers to the restoration of humanity's original vocation of co-reigning as vice-regents with God over creation. As such, reigning *in life* could signal that their co-reigning begins with their future resurrection. Or, it could signal that even now, as they currently share the resurrected life of the truly Human One, they become God's *cruciform*[28] weapons of saving justice through which the reigning Risen King continues God's mission of restoring justice and shalom to the created order (see more on this below). In light of the discussion of 6:1–23 below, the latter alternative makes good sense. We might, then, recognize a subtle hint in 5:17 that Christ's resurrection, leading to his present resurrected life of reigning (1 Cor 15:25), is somehow effective in enabling those participating in the new humanity to currently "co-reign" with him through their cruciform suffering, which is an aspect of what salvation entails in the present.

In Rom 6:1–11 Paul forges a seamless connection between the salvific effect of sharing in Christ's death *in the present* and sharing in his resurrected life, not just in the future (6:5b, 8), but indeed *in the present* by "walking in newness of life" (6:4b; cf. the similar implications of Rom 7:4).[29] Dying and being

---

26. And also, in 5:18 if δικαίωσιν ζωῆς is understood as justification which engenders the resurrected life of the new age.

27. Note that the grace/gift of the obedient deed of the one is characterized in 5:17 as (or as consisting of) *the* saving justice (τῆς δικαιοσύνης), which I take to be the same saving justice that has been the subject of Paul's argument in Romans all along, viz., God's saving justice. Since the saving justice of God is revealed precisely in the faithfulness of Jesus Christ (3:22)—referred to by Paul in this context as the δικαίωμα of the one man—it makes sense to take *the* saving justice in 5:17 as God's saving justice. Cf. Leander Keck who argues along similar lines (*Romans*, ANTC [Nashville: Abingdon, 2005], 153–54).

28. On the importance of describing our present sharing in Christ's resurrected life as being "resurrection suffused but cruciform in shape" rather than as "resurrectiform" in shape, see Gorman, *Participating*, 53–76. Even more so should any talk of currently "co-reigning" with him be explicated in cruciform terms characterized by suffering resulting from participation in God's redemptive mission.

29. While some continue to insist that Paul restricts his resurrection language to the fu-

buried with Christ in baptism transfers one "into Christ Jesus" (6:3), i.e., into the corporate body of the last Adam in which our old humanity (ὁ παλαιὸς ἡμῶν ἄνθρωπος)—our humanity after the pattern of the first Adam—has been co-crucified with Christ (6:6a). The salvific effect of participating in Christ's death in these verses is so that "the body under the control of the cosmic power of Sin (τὸ σῶμα τῆς ἁμαρτίας) might be done away with so that we might no longer be enslaved to Sin" (6:6b). This last Adam's—this truly Human One's— one-time death to Sin's ability as a cosmic power to subject him to injustice (6:10)[30] kills the *inevitability* of our being enslaved to that cosmic power as its instruments of enacting injustice (cf. 6:2, 13). Hence, for those who participate in his death, this one man's obedient act of saving justice (δικαίωμα) releases/ justifies (δεδικαίωται) them from Sin's cosmic, enslaving power (6:7).[31] This being released from the slavery to Sin's cosmic power in order to be slaves/ weapons of God's saving justice (6:13, 18–19) is one of the salvific aspects of being justified (δεδικαίωται). It is also the first step of God's saving act of *redemption* for us in the present. But, as with reconciliation with God and the reversal of humanity's condemnation, since this release is explicitly a result of participating in Christ's *death*, it seems more closely related to Christ's being "handed over for our trespasses" (i.e., his saving death) than to his being "raised with a view to our justification."

These salvific effects of Christ's death, however, are incomplete by themselves to accomplish our justification and redemption in the present. We begin to see this in Rom 6:10–11 where Paul sets up a parallel pattern shared by Christ and those in Christ. To paraphrase both verses: "For the death that

---

ture, others have convincingly argued that Paul believes those who are "in Christ" participate in his resurrected life even now. For recent examples, see Frederick S. Tappenden, *Resurrection in Paul: Cognition, Metaphor, and Transformation*, ECL 19 (Atlanta: SBL Press, 2016), 135–227; Michael J. Gorman, *Inhabiting the Cruciform God: Kenosis, Justification, and Theosis in Paul's Narrative Soteriology* (Grand Rapids: Eerdmans, 2009), 73–75; Wright, *Resurrection*, 248–54; Kirk, *Unlocking Romans*, 107–17; Richard B. Gaffin, "Redemption and Resurrection: An Exercise in Biblical-Systematic Theology," *Themelios* 27 (2002): 16–31, esp. 26–27.

30. Christ was not at one time under Sin's power in the sense that he was himself a weapon of injustice in its hand. Rather, as God's paradigmatic weapon of saving justice, he was subject to the injustice performed by those under Sin's power. His death to Sin, then, was a death to Sin's power to subject him to injustice. In this sense, his death to Sin is not analogous to ours but rather its obverse. Similarly, Robert Jewett, *Romans*, Hermeneia (Minneapolis: Fortress, 2007), 407.

31. Since the whole context is about participating in the one man's death/crucifixion, whether 6:7 is read christologically or as referring generically to everyone "in Christ" matters little for the argument here.

The Past, Present, and Future of Bodily Resurrection as Salvation

Jesus died was a one-time *death to Sin*, and the *risen life* he is currently living (as he is reigning in power until all things are placed under his feet) *is for God*. So also, you all consider yourselves as *dead to Sin* but *alive for God* in the cruciform, corporate body of the now risen and reigning Christ." A similar pattern continues in 6:12–14 where Paul's prohibitions assume Christ's death has broken Sin's enslaving power so that those in Christ are no longer forced to present their members to Sin as weapons of injustice (ὅπλα ἀδικίας). His positive commands assume that Christ's resurrection has engendered the gift of an alternative power/agency for those in him to "present [themselves] to God as *alive from the dead* and [their] members as weapons of saving justice (ὅπλα δικαιοσύνης) to God" for use in his continuing saving mission (6:13b). Jesus's resurrection, then, appears to engender the power for freed humans to now present themselves as slaves to God as justified weapons of God's saving justice through whom God continues his rescue mission of reversing the chaos of life in Adam, i.e., humanity's enslaving, chaotic spiral of Rom 1:18–32.

We may say, then, that Christ *experienced God's saving justice* in his resurrection with a view to (or to engender) our justification, an aspect of which is our incorporation into a just community whose members practice justice by becoming channels of God's saving justice. The salvific impact of Christ's resurrection, therefore, is instrumental in enabling those who participate in it to embody—or even become!—the gospel in their life together.[32] The truly Human One *first* became the human instrument of God's saving justice in his cruciform obedience unto death and only *then* experienced resurrection as an act of God's saving justice. *In the present*, for those who are in the corporate body of the truly Human One, the order is reversed. They *first* experience being raised to walk in newness of life as a *transformative* act of God's saving justice in order to *then* become the cruciform human instruments of that saving justice. As Michael Gorman puts it, "Paul understands justification as participatory transformation in the justice of God in Christ that creates a just people."[33]

Hence, it is Christ's justifying resurrection that generates the gift of transformative, salvific power—also known as the "making-alive" Spirit—enabling those "in him" to experience an analogous act of God's saving justice in the present when they are raised to walk in newness of life by being given a new power/agency to present themselves to God as his cruciform,[34] human instru-

---

32. Cf. Gorman's claims in *Becoming the Gospel*.
33. Gorman, *Becoming the Gospel*, 228.
34. Gaffin's language in this regard is on target: "The imprint left in our lives by Christ's resurrection power is, in a word, the Cross" ("Redemption and Resurrection," 30).

ments of saving justice. Being "re-enslaved" to this gracious God constitutes the completing step of experiencing God's saving act of redemption in the present, fully incorporating us into "the redemption that is in Christ Jesus" (Rom 3:24, τῆς ἀπολυτρώσεως τῆς ἐν Χριστῷ Ἰησοῦ). We might refer to this as currently co-reigning with the risen Messiah/Lord and last Adam in life (Rom 5:17) in the sense that those "in Christ" share the kingly task that humans were given from the beginning and that the ideal king was supposed to exercise (e.g., Ps 72), i.e., being God's instrument(s) of shalom and justice.[35] Having their humanity restored by participating in the truly Human One as justified, cruciform weapons of God's saving justice (Rom 6:13), they are becoming the saving justice (δικαιοσύνη) of God (2 Cor 5:21) and therefore participants in God's rescue mission as a constitutive part of their "being saved" (1 Cor 1:18).

This cruciform pattern of life of enslavement to God/saving justice is also constitutive of holiness/sanctification (ἁγιασμός),[36] whose ultimate end is the resurrected life of the new age (Rom 6:22). Romans 6:18–19 (with my interpretive comments in brackets) is particularly instructive here:

> Now having been freed from Sin [by sharing in the death of the truly Human One], you all have been enslaved to [God's] saving justice (τῇ δικαιοσύνῃ) [by sharing in the resurrected life of the truly Human One]. . . . For just as you all presented your members as slaves to impurity (ἀκαθαρσίᾳ) resulting in lawlessness leading to more lawlessness, so now [by the enabling salvific power that emanates from the last Adam's resurrection] present yourselves as slaves to [God's] saving justice (τῇ δικαιοσύνῃ) leading to holiness/sanctification (εἰς ἁγιασμόν).

We noted in the last section that Christ experienced God's sanctifying power in his own resurrection as both a cleansing from the impurity associated with death and burial and as being *set apart* as one who embodies the

---

35. Haley Goranson Jacob's argument that the language of "being conformed to the image of his Son" (Rom 8:30) is vocational in nature (i.e., that those in Christ might share currently in his reign/glory) is helpful here (*Conformed to the Image of His Son: Reconsidering Paul's Theology of Glory in Romans* [Downers Grove, IL: IVP Academic], 264, passim). However, I remain unconvinced that: (1) this language is only vocational; (2) sharing in Christ's glory is only a transformation of status to that of "co-reigner" rather than also becoming more like God; (3) currently co-reigning with Christ is not itself constituted by cruciform suffering.

36. For a sustained development of this theme more widely in Scripture, see my *Holiness and the* Missio Dei (Eugene, OR: Cascade, 2016).

character/holiness of his Father. Those currently sharing in the resurrected life of that truly Human One as slaves of God's saving justice experience God's sanctifying power in analogous ways. First, they are being cleansed from their former ἀκαθαρσία (Rom 6:19), the ἀκαθαρσία of 1:24, the only other place in Romans where Paul uses this term. In that context (1:22–32) impurity is clearly connected with idolatry/idols, which Second Temple Jews typically associated with the realm of death.[37] Hence, not surprisingly, humanity's worship of *dead* idols leads to actions of impurity (sexual and otherwise), becoming the catalyst for the enslaving chaotic spiral into the "lawlessness leading to more lawlessness" characteristic of life "in Adam" (1:22–32). Those rescued from this chaotic spiral who are currently sharing in Christ's resurrected life are experiencing God's sanctifying power as they are cleansed "by means of [Christ's] blood" (cf. 5:9) from their impurity that came from their former worship of *dead* idols.[38]

Moreover, by means of the making-alive Holy Spirit currently at work among and in them, setting them apart "in Christ Jesus," the truly Human One, they are being empowered to act as cruciform channels of the holy God's δικαιοσύνη. Since this is "the Holy God [who] displays himself as holy by his [and his people's] צְדָקָה/δικαιοσύνη" (Isa 5:16b),[39] acting as cruciform weapons of God's saving justice simultaneously displays his holiness. In this way, those participating in the resurrection of the truly Human One are not only becoming truly human themselves, but are also being set apart and reshaped into the image of God, sharing in God's holiness/divine life.[40] Those, then, who are participating in the justified and redeemed new humanity, walking in the cruciform resurrected life of being instruments of God's saving justice, are also currently being sanctified as a result of the enabling salvific power that emanates from the last Adam's sanctifying resurrection.

---

37. Cf. the language of Mary Douglas: "God is living, life is his. Other gods belong to death and the contagion of decay" (*In the Wilderness: The Doctrine of Defilement in the Book of Numbers*, JSOTSup 158 [Oxford: Oxford University Press, 2001], 24 [quoted in Harrington, *Holiness*, 179]).

38. Recall that Moffitt's analysis of the sacrificial logic of Leviticus suggests that the offering of sacrificial blood represents life and is an act that pushes back against the corrupting power of death (*Atonement*, 219, 257–58).

39. On the implications of this, see R. W. L. Moberly, "Whose Justice? Which Righteousness? The Interpretation of Isaiah V 16," *VT* 51 (2001): 55–68, esp. 63.

40. The theme of *theosis* has not been the focus of this essay, but that is not to deny its importance for Pauline soteriology in general (see esp. Gorman, *Inhabiting*) or in Romans in particular (e.g., Michael J. Gorman, "Romans: The First Christian Treatise on Theosis," *JTI* 5 [2011]: 13–34).

We may, then, conclude this lengthy section by affirming that Christ's resurrection proper—the resurrection of the last Adam—is directly salvific in humanity's present in that those "in Christ Jesus" are currently experiencing its salvific effects in the form of justification, sanctification, and redemption.

Resurrection as Salvation in Both Humanity's and Creation's Future

We turn now to the way Christ's resurrection is salvific in both humanity's and creation's future. For Paul, Christ's resurrection is so organically connected to the future resurrection that he can argue that "if there is not going to be a future resurrection, then not even Christ has been raised" (1 Cor 15:13).[41] To deny the former is to deny the latter. Hence, to say that Christ has been raised from the dead as first fruits of those sleeping (15:20) is to assert that the resurrection of the truly Human One is itself the catalyst for humanity's salvific resurrection in the future. As a warrant for this assertion, in 1 Cor 15:21-22, Paul offers a pithy summary of his more detailed comparison of the first and last Adams in Rom 5:12-21:

> For since Death came through a human being,
> through a human being comes resurrection of the dead.
> For just as in Adam all are continuing to die,
> so also, in Messiah all will be made alive.

But Christ's resurrection is more than a catalyst; it is also the pattern of future resurrection. Aside from those alive at the parousia whose living bodies will also be conformed to Christ's resurrected body (1 Cor 15:51-52, 53b, 54b; Phil 3:21), the future bodily resurrection is the culminating salvific act that fully conforms those who participate in the new humanity to the risen body of the truly Human One (e.g., 1 Cor 15:20-28, 49; 6:14; Phil 3:21; Rom 8:11, 23). At the parousia of the last Adam, who wields the resurrection power of the making-alive Spirit, those who died participating in his corporate body *will experience* resurrection as justifying, sanctifying, and redeeming. Once again, each of these calls for further comment.

In 1 Thess 4:13-18 Paul draws on a loose pattern of cultural expectations from Greco-Roman parousia traditions to describe Christ's return.[42] Describ-

---

41. Taking the "to be" verbs in 1 Cor 15:12-19 as futuristic presents.
42. In some parts of this section, I have adapted material from my *1 and 2 Thessalonians*, 257-59.

The Past, Present, and Future of Bodily Resurrection as Salvation

ing Christ's coming as a parousia carries with it cultural images of a victorious king coming in great honor into a city, a royal victory parade in which those who go out to welcome him *share in the honor he receives*. These images highlight the *vindicating aspect of future resurrection* in that the resurrection of those who have died as a part of a cruciform people publicly reverses their ascribed shame and dishonor and they are the *first* to go into this royal welcoming parade (1 Thess 4:15-17). This imagery in 1 Thess 4:13-18 as well as Paul's language in 2 Thess 1:12 of the Thessalonians being "honored/glorified (ἐνδοξασθῇ) in him" at his coming depicts the whole royal event as the culmination of 1 Thess 2:12, i.e., God's calling the Thessalonians into his own kingdom and glory/honor (βασιλείαν καὶ δόξαν). This δόξα is at once both sociological and vocational in that, for those with their true humanity restored, it signifies the honor associated with their co-reigning with the truly Human One in his eschatological βασιλεία/new creation.[43] Hence, in their resurrection, the last Adam who wields the making-alive Spirit[44] *transforms* their bodies of cruciform humility (τὸ σῶμα τῆς ταπεινώσεως ἡμῶν, Phil 3:21)[45] into conformity with his body of δόξα (cf. "it is sown in dishonor, it is raised in δόξα," 1 Cor 15:43). This vindicating, transformative resurrection, whose catalyst and pattern is that of the resurrection of the truly Human One, is indeed their full and final justification.

Being conformed by the Spirit to Christ's body of δόξα in this saving resurrection is also a final act of sanctification, first as a sanctifying cleansing from the corruption associated with death (1 Cor 15:42: sown in corruption [φθορᾷ], raised in incorruption [ἀφθαρσίᾳ]). And second, since in Second Temple Judaism the δόξα of the Lord is a manifestation of his holiness made visible (Lev 10:3; Isa 6:3; Hab 3:3),[46] being raised and conformed to the body of the Lord's δόξα and being "honored/glorified (ἐνδοξασθῇ) in him" (2 Thess

---

43. On this vocational aspect of glory, see esp. Jacob, *Conformed to the Image of His Son*. See below for the ontological aspect of δόξα in association with holiness in eschatological contexts.

44. As I have argued elsewhere, Paul's language in 1 Thess 4:13-18 suggests that God the Father raises the dead through the actions of the risen Lord Jesus as he wields the life-giving Spirit in the parousia (*1 and 2 Thessalonians*, 126-30, 305-16).

45. I understand this phrase to refer to bodies that have become habituated to, even physically marked, by the pattern of Phil 2:8, i.e., self-lowering cruciform activity in faithfulness to God. This leads to their vindicating resurrection in 3:21 on analogy with the movement of 2:9-11 so that those bodies who have habitually experienced public shame because of their cruciform faithfulness to God are conformed fully to Christ's body of δόξα at his coming.

46. Harrington, *Holiness*, 30-31.

1:12) in his royal coming completes the sanctification of the whole ecclesia and the whole of every individual's body with which it is constituted (1 Thess 5:23). This is essentially the upshot of Paul's petitionary prayer in 1 Thess 5:23: "Now may the God of peace himself make your whole life together holy, that is, may the whole spirit, soul, and body of [each of] you be kept blameless [in holiness] in the royal coming of our Lord Jesus Christ." So, then, this saving resurrection (and eschatological transformation of the living) is also the culmination of the whole process of sanctification in which the corporate body of the truly Human One and those in it will fully reflect what their Spirit-empowered[47] life together has been in the process of becoming, viz., the holy character or image of the *living* God. They will be shown to be what they have become by grace, "blameless in holiness" and ontologically transformed to share in the living Lord's δόξα, incorruption, and life in the new age.

In God's salvific act of *redemption* (ἀπολύτρωσις) that delivered the last Adam from Death's power so that it no longer was able to exercise dominion over him (Rom 6:9), God dealt Death a death blow that will culminate when the truly Human One destroys Death as the last enemy at his royal coming (1 Cor 15:26). The resurrection of those who belong to the truly Human One that releases them from the clutches of Death constitutes Death's final destruction and is, therefore, the final redemption (ἀπολύτρωσις) of their bodies (Rom 8:23). This, the culminating salvific act of redemption for humanity in the future, is intimately related to creation's future.

When I said in the introduction that what God *has done* for the body of Jesus in microcosm in his resurrection, God *will do* for the cosmos in macrocosm at the parousia, I did not mean that the cosmos/creation will somehow die and be "resurrected" by God (although, with the recent grim reports regarding the increasing severity of human-induced climate change, this may not be off the mark). But since, in the Greco-Roman world, the cosmos was understood to be a σῶμα,[48] we might argue that it too will experience *similar* salvific effects at the parousia as did Jesus in his bodily resurrection and as do those "in him" in their resurrection. In Rom 8:21 Paul says that "the creation[49] itself will be set free from its slavery to corruption (δουλείας τῆς φθορᾶς) into the freedom that is engendered by the glory of the children of God."[50] When God's children are fully glorified by completely sharing in the true humanity

---

47. I.e., that power engendering, and emanating from, the Last Adam's sanctifying resurrection.
48. Martin, *The Corinthian Body*, 16.
49. With most recent interpreters, I take ἡ κτίσις to refer to the nonhuman created order.
50. I am following Jacob here in translating the genitive relationship between τὴν ἐλευ-

of the last Adam and are installed as vice-regents with him at their resurrection, creation itself is freed to become what God intended from the outset. It is freed to become filled with God's justice—"justified" in the sense of being set right—because it is now ruled over by the true King and his truly human vice-regents whose primary missional task was always to fill the kingdom of creation with justice so that there might be shalom (e.g., Ps 72).

In addition, creation's being "*set free* from its slavery *to corruption* (φθορᾷ)" is both a *redemptive* act of liberation and a *sanctifying* act of cleansing all creation from the decay and corruption associated with the trappings of Death. It is the life-giving power that engendered Christ's resurrection and emanates from it, the Holy Spirit, that is the active agent in all of this. The same Spirit who transforms the human body "sown in corruption (οθορᾷ)" in 1 Cor 15:42 by raising it "in incorruption (ἀφθαρσίᾳ)" will transform the σῶμα of the cosmos by freeing it from its corruption (φθορά) and making it incorruptible (Rom 8:21). This same Spirit, who completely permeates dead human bodies so that they become a "spiritual body (σῶμα πνευματικόν)" when they are raised (1 Cor 15:44), will do something similar for the σῶμα of the cosmos. That is, the life-giving Spirit will totally permeate the cosmos, entirely sanctifying it and making all of it God's cosmic sanctuary, resulting in God's becoming "all in all" (1 Cor 15:28).

To conclude this section, we may indeed say that Christ's resurrection is salvific in both humanity's and creation's future. That one can draw a parallel between the salvific effects of Christ's resurrection for both humanity and the nonhuman creation is not surprising given that humanity and the rest of God's creation have been inseparably joined by God's creative acts in Genesis. It is not possible to conceive of becoming "truly human" apart from the completion of God's mission of creation becoming what it was truly intended to be.

Conclusion

In this essay, I have offered a sketch from Paul's letters of the direct soteriological effects of Jesus's resurrection for humanity and the cosmos. Assuming a participatory framework within an overall missional orientation to Scripture, I have used 1 Cor 1:30 heuristically to argue that Christ's bodily resurrection is directly salvific in justifying, sanctifying, and redeeming true humanity in the past, present, and future and is analogously salvific for creation's future.

θερίαν and τῆς δόξης as one of means (*Conformed to the Image of His Son*, 241), although there is a similar effect if the latter is taken as a subjective genitive.

We may, then, say that what God *has done* for the body of Jesus in microcosm in his resurrection, God *is doing* in the ecclesial body of Christ—the current locale of the new humanity and new creation/cosmos—and God *will do* for those in Christ and for the body of the cosmos in macrocosm at the parousia. Hence, for Paul, Christ's resurrection is not simply a sign of the salvific efficacy of Jesus's death; it is *constitutive of salvation itself*.

Chapter 13

Mother Zion Rejoices:
Psalm 87 as a Missing Link in Galatians 4

N. T. Wright

Alfred North Whitehead is credited with saying that Western philosophy can be seen as footnotes to Plato. An overstatement, no doubt, but we get the point. In the same way, Western theology has sometimes appeared as a set of footnotes to Paul; and one of the reasons we need those footnotes is because Paul frequently writes more like Aristotle than Plato. His prose is dense, allusive, often cryptic, and we often want to stop him in mid-flow and say, "Wait! Were you actually referring to Isaiah?"—or, as it may be, Deuteronomy, the Psalms, Genesis, whatever—"and if so, what did you mean by it?" We need Paul's footnotes. Since he did not supply very many, we must fill in the blanks as best we can.

If that is true for our reading of Paul in general, it seems particularly so in Galatians; and, within that hasty and hot-headed harangue, perhaps the densest and most complex passage is the final paragraph of chapter 4, the "allegory" about Abraham's two wives and their respective sons. Many interpreters have effectively thrown up their hands in despair at the twists and turns of the argument—if it is an argument at all. Some have regarded the passage as a *jeu d'esprit*, a kind of fantasy-exegesis, meant more as a somewhat harsh tease, added on to the main argument of the letter to ward off an obvious rejoinder from his shadowy opponents, rather than belonging centrally to Paul's overall case.[1]

---

1. This was argued famously by C. K. Barrett in "The Allegory of Abraham, Sarah, and Hagar in the Argument of Galatians," in *Rechtfertigung: Festschrift für Ernst Käsemann*

In the last generation considerable advances have been made in reading this and similar passages through scholars who have followed the lead of Richard B. Hays in his ground-breaking *Echoes of Scripture in the Letters of Paul*.[2] Hays famously proposed a "metaleptic" reading of Paul's scriptural allusions and echoes: when we think we hear a passage of Scripture resonating in the argument, we should examine the larger context for previously unsuspected clues as to what Paul had in mind. Objections have of course been raised: how can we be sure, how did Paul expect his recent converts to catch on to what he was doing, and would it not be better to see him simply as trying to impress a less educated audience by being able to quote apparently authoritative sources? I have discussed these issues elsewhere, and I put them to one side for now—not least because one of the best vindications of Hays's proposal is to test it out on passages as yet unexamined and see whether or not there is an "aha," a proof-of-the-pudding moment.[3] My topic in the present essay—a congratulatory gift to celebrate a scholarly friendship of many decades—is, I submit, just such a case in point.[4]

Granted Hays's own lifelong fascination with Galatians, it is all the more surprising that neither he nor the many who have followed his lead have investigated what precisely Paul might be doing with the apparent allusion to Ps 87:5//Ps 86:5 LXX in Gal 4:26 ("the Jerusalem which is above is free—and she is our mother").[5] An important section of *Echoes* (111–21) was devoted to Gal 4:21–31, where Hays probed deeply and carefully into the Genesis story of

---

zum 70. Geburtstag, ed. J. Friedrich, W. Pöhlmann, and P. Stuhlmacher (Tübingen: Mohr Siebeck, 1976), 1–16.

2. R. B. Hays, *Echoes of Scripture in the Letters of Paul* (New Haven: Yale University Press, 1989). I am grateful to Richard Hays and Richard Bauckham for helpful comments on an earlier draft of this essay and to Simon Dürr for help in tracking down certain materials. NT quotations in what follows are from my *The Kingdom New Testament*, in the UK *The New Testament for Everyone* (San Francisco and London: HarperOne and SPCK, 2011).

3. See N. T. Wright, *Pauline Perspectives: Essays on Paul, 1978–2013* (London and Minneapolis: SPCK and Fortress, 2013), 547–53; *Paul and His Recent Interpreters* (London and Minneapolis: SPCK and Fortress, 2015), 98–101.

4. I was relieved, in planning this essay as a gift for Michael Gorman, to see that so far as I can tell he has not discussed the point at issue. It relates directly, however, to his long-standing concern with what I would call covenantal ecclesiology.

5. Similar points can be made about K. H. Jobes, who investigates the use of Isa 54:1 thoroughly but ignores the Psalm reference, assigning the echo in 4:26 instead to Isa 1:26 ("Jerusalem, Our Mother: Metalepsis and Intertextuality in Galatians 4:21–31," *WTJ* 55 [1993]: 310). C. M. Maier insists that Paul's image of the heavenly Zion as mother does indeed rest on his use of the Psalm but does not see the link with Isa 54 ("Psalm 87 as a Reappraisal of the Zion Tradition and its Reception in Galatians 4:26," *CBQ* 69 [2007]: 473–86).

Abraham and his wives and their sons on the one hand and into the substantial quotation of Isa 54:1 in Gal 4:27. Hays, and many following him, have drawn attention to the ways in which, both within the book of Isaiah itself and in much subsequent Jewish tradition, chapter 54 is seen as a simultaneous invocation of Sarah, Isaac's mother, and of Jerusalem, made barren by the Babylonian devastation but now to be restored to extraordinary fecundity.[6] Monographs and essays, alongside the never-ending flood of commentaries, have continued to dig deeper into the resonances set up by the Isaiah text in Paul's own day and subsequently, often drawing into the discussion the idea of "Jerusalem above" in 4:26, a theme quite well known in the so-called "apocalyptic" writings as well as later rabbinic works, from the latter of which it is clear that the barren woman now to be consoled in Isa 54 was regularly seen as Jerusalem.[7] But there in the midst of Paul's argument stands a text, Ps 87//Ps 86 LXX, which is often drowned out by its noisier neighbors (Genesis and Isaiah), but which, when allowed to make its own contribution, ties the whole argument much more tightly together and strengthens the case, which can be made on other grounds as well, for seeing Gal 4:21–5:1 not as an added extra but as the real argumentative climax of the letter.[8] I therefore propose that Ps 87//Ps 86

---

6. See, among many studies, J. J. Schmitt, "The Motherhood of God and Zion as Mother," *RB* 92 (1985): 557–69, e.g., 562: "Then in chapter 54, the once barren woman is, of course, Zion. Her children are abundant (54:1), widespreading (v. 2), and prosperous (v. 13). The wife and mother who had been abandoned is now restored to her uxorial status and maternal function." See too, e.g., A. D. Myers, "'For It Has Been Written': Paul's Use of Isa 54:1 in Gal 4:27 in Light of Gal 3:1–5:1," *PRSt* 37 (2010): 295–308. Myers (296) points out that the regular use of Isa 54 in contexts like this already refutes the suggestion of C. D. Stanley that 54:1 is "seemingly unrelated" to Paul's theme (*Arguing with Scripture: The Rhetoric of Quotations in the Letters of Paul* [New York: T & T Clark, 2004], 131); my present argument takes this refutation a stage further.

7. See H. L. Strack and P. Billerbeck, *Kommentar zum Neuen Testament aus Talmud und Midrasch* (Munich: C. H. Beck, 1926–61), 3:574–75. H. D. Betz notes some of these and adds Philo, *Praem.* 158–59, which predictably allegorizes the story in quite a different way to Paul, namely in terms of the soul (*Galatians: A Commentary on Paul's Letter to the Churches in Galatia*, Hermeneia [Minneapolis: Fortress, 1979], 248n102). See too R. N. Longenecker, *Galatians*, WBC (Dallas: Word Books, 1990), 215. For this theme at Qumran see e.g. CD 6.8; 4Q176 fr. 8 11–12. The jewels promised in Isa 54:11–12 are echoed in, e.g., Tob 13:16. The older but still important work of A. T. Lincoln (*Paradise Now and Not Yet: Studies in the Role of the Heavenly Dimension in Paul's Thought with Special Reference to His Eschatology* [Cambridge: Cambridge University Press, 1981]) merely notes that Ps 87:5 "may have been particularly influential" in the development of the idea of Jerusalem as "mother" (23), without seeing any further link with the line of thought in Gal 4.

8. For a list of those who discuss, or fail to discuss, the allusion, see Maier, "Psalm 87,"

LXX, read with full attention to its metaleptic potential, forms a vital link in the argument which has so far been missing from scholarly discussions.[9]

Psalm 87//Psalm 86 LXX within Paul's Argument

The point can be put succinctly. If Paul is indeed alluding to Ps 87//Ps 86 LXX in Gal 4:26, as some commentators (by no means all) suggest, though none follow up, he seems clearly to be doing so with the LXX in mind. It is the LXX, not the MT, that refers to Zion as "mother" in the first line of Ps 87:5// Ps 86:5 LXX.[10] But two verses later, at the close of the psalm, the LXX and the MT diverge quite drastically. The Hebrew speaks of the singers and the dancers saying together "all my fountains are in you," or words to that effect, a line normally interpreted as a metaphor for the life-giving joy of being in Jerusalem (and perhaps with an added dash of metonymy because of Jerusalem's actual water-springs, as in Ps 46:4).[11] But the LXX, perhaps reflecting a puzzlement

---

481. F. F. Bruce (*The Epistle to the Galatians: A Commentary on the Greek Text*, NIGTC [Grand Rapids: Eerdmans, 1982], 221) refers to C. Gore (*The Reconstruction of Belief* [London: John Murray, 1926], 770) and C. F. D. Moule (*The Birth of the New Testament*, 3rd ed. [London: A & C Black, 1981], 60) without saying that Gore, who discusses the passage as evidence for the "invisible church," says that Paul "appears to be quoting" the Psalm, and that Moule links the first verse of the Psalm (LXX 86:1: Οἱ θεμέλιοι αὐτοῦ ἐν τοῖς ὄρεσιν τοῖς ἁγίοις) with Heb 11:10, referring to "the city which has foundations" (τὴν τοὺς θεμελίους ἔχουσαν πόλιν), suggesting by implication that Ps 87//Ps 86 LXX was seen by others, not just Paul, as predicting a "new Jerusalem." Interestingly, the other LXX references to the θεμέλιοι of Jerusalem are in the eschatologically pregnant passages of Isa 28:16; 54:11; 58:12, with only Lam 4:11 being an exception.

9. In his Galatians commentary, Richard Hays, like many commentators, notes Ps 86:5 LXX as one instance of the metaphor of Jerusalem as "mother" but does not suggest that Paul has the Psalm specifically in mind in this text, and so does not investigate further its potential links with the rest of the passage ("Galatians," *NIB* 11 [Nashville: Abingdon, 2000], 304). Ben Witherington is typical of many when he simply appends Ps 87 to a list of texts referring to Jerusalem as mother (*Grace in Galatia: A Commentary on St Paul's Letter to the Galatians* [Edinburgh: T & T Clark, 1998], 335n48).

10. LXX: μήτηρ Σιων, ἐρεῖ ἄνθρωπος; the MT has no word corresponding to μήτηρ, simply stating וּלֲצִיּוֹן יֵאָמַר אִישׁ וְאִישׁ , "to Zion this one or that will say." Some LXX MSS, notably one version of Origen's text, read μη τη for μήτηρ. See A. Pietersma and B. G. Wright, *A New English Translation of the Septuagint* (New York: Oxford University Press, 2007), ad loc., translating "with regard to Sion, surely no person will say . . ." See further Schmitt, "The Motherhood of God," 564; Maier, "Psalm 87," 480.

11. Cf. too Ps 36:9: "with you is the fountain of life;" Ps 84:6; Isa 12:3; Ezek 47:1; Joel 3:18; Zech 14:8. Stuart Hall suggests to me that Ps 87:7 might have originally been a rubric, giving instructions to the singers and dancers, rather than part of the Psalm.

at the oblique water metaphor, cashes it out into an expression of rejoicing which ought to sound familiar to readers of Isa 54 or Gal 4: ὡς εὐφραινομένων πάντων ἡ κατοικία ἐν σοί, literally "the dwelling in you is as of many rejoicing," rendered somewhat woodenly by Pietersma and Wright as "Seeing that they are glad, the habitation of all is in you," and perhaps to be understood quite straightforwardly as "living in you, Zion, is like a great celebration."

Now at last we see—having unveiled the metaleptic point hidden by Paul's allusion to the Psalm—the direct link with Isa 54. The Psalm's ὡς εὐφραινομένων πάντων is at once answered triumphantly by Isa 54:1: Εὐφράνθητι, στεῖρα ἡ οὐ τίκτουσα, "Celebrate, barren one who did not bear." This is the kind of verbal link that some have associated with the rabbinic exegetical technique of *gezera shawah*.

It is just possible that this is a complete coincidence, unintended by Paul. But a moment's thought will suggest otherwise. There have been many studies of the "mother" theme in Isaiah, all agreeing that here in chapter 54 we have one clear expression of a theme which runs through Isa 40–66.[12] (It is found already in the LXX of Isa 1:26, which addresses Zion as μητρόπολις πιστή, "faithful mother city," in an interesting parallel to πόλις δικαιοσύνης, "city of righteousness."[13]) But the theme is, apart from this, fairly infrequent in Scripture, and Ps 87—especially in the LXX!—is one of the few outstanding examples.[14] If Paul wanted to provide further scriptural support for exactly the points he is making in this paragraph, he could hardly have done better.

Two further considerations add strength to this proposal. First, Ps 87:4// Ps 86:4 LXX is, on anyone's reading ancient or modern, quite a surprise. It appears to relish the fact that foreigners, not just any old foreigners either, but Egypt ("Rahab") and Babylon, the two great slave masters in Israel's long story, were to be regarded as having been born in Zion—along with David's enemies the Philistines (the LXX calls them ἀλλόφυλοι, "foreigners," but this is such a regular designation for "Philistines" that we cannot infer that the

---

12. See Isa 49:19–21; 50:1; 51:17–23; 61:10. What God did for Abraham and Sarah is what he will do for Zion: Isa 51:1–3. See esp. M. Callaway, *Sing, O Barren One: A Study in Comparative Midrash* (Atlanta: Scholars Press, 1980); and many others, e.g., S G. Eastman, *Recovering Paul's Mother Tongue: Language and Theology in Galatians* (Grand Rapids: Eerdmans, 2007), 127–60.

13. The LXX uses the title, μητρόπολις, for Gibeon, Kiriath-arba, and Hebron (Josh 10:2; 14:15; 21:11; 15:13); comp. Esth 9:19. In 2 Sam 20:19, Abel of Beth-Maacah is called "a city and a mother (πόλιν καὶ μητρόπολιν) in Israel." See further Maier, "Psalm 87," 479.

14. One might also draw in, e.g., Jer 31:2–22, where Israel as YHWH's bride is assured of the family's restoration. See Schmitt, "The Motherhood of God," 565–657.

translator was trying to broaden the reference) and the wicked city denounced by Ezekiel, Tyre.[15] "Cush," the last nation named here, is taken by the LXX to refer to far-off Ethiopia, not a traditional enemy but perhaps a representative of the southern ends of the known world.[16] Now we see what the apostle is doing with this apparently distant reference. *Paul's allusion to Ps 87//Ps 86 LXX provides one of the most dramatic possible scriptural indications that his gentile mission was the fulfillment, rather than the abrogation, of the original divine intention.* There are many scriptural passages in which some or most of these nations are regarded as hostile, dangerous, and polluting enemies; this psalm appears to offer a prophecy (who knows how many of Paul's contemporaries would have read it like that?) that the worst enemies imaginable will somehow become true-born citizens of Zion. Not just strangers brought in alongside, either, as in proselyte conversion: "These ones were born there."[17] The point would be strengthened further if we were to note that in Ps 87:4//Ps 86:4 LXX Rahab and Babylon, the great slave masters in Israel's traditions, are said to be "among those who know me." Once that has been said, there ought to be no problem about recognizing, as among the inhabitants of the "Jerusalem above," the uncircumcised gentiles who have come "to know God—or, better, to be known by God" (Gal 4:9).[18]

This allusion, read in this way, fits well with Paul's strategy earlier in the

---

15. Ezek 26–28. Ezekiel also denounces Egypt (29–32); Babylon is of course denounced in Isa 13–14 and 40–52, as well as in Jer 50–51; Philistia, in Jer 47 and elsewhere. In the LXX the Philistines refer to themselves as ἀλλόφυλοι, as in, e.g., 1 Kgdms 4:9. For the designation "Rahab" for Egypt—perhaps the old sea-monster, a personification of the Red Sea overcome in the exodus—see, e.g., Isa 30:7; 51:9; Zech 14:16–19; comp. Pss 74:13–14 and 89:11; Job 26:10. The strangeness of the Psalm in this respect, and the attempts of scholars to mitigate this, is noted by Maier, "Psalm 87," 477–78.

16. See further T. Longman, *Psalms*, TOTC (Downers Grove, IL: IVP Academic, 2014), 318. Ethiopia is the subject of oracles in Isa 18 and 20; Jer 46:9; Ezek 30:4, 5, 9; Nah 3:9.

17. One of the comparatively few commentaries to note this thematic implication, though without seeing the metaleptic links, is A. Vanhoye and P. S. Williamson, *Galatians*, Catholic Commentary on Sacred Scripture (Grand Rapids: Baker Academic, 2019), 164–65. For the idea of people being enrolled in the chosen people see, e.g., Ezek 13:9; and for the tracing of genealogical records after some exiles had returned from Babylon, see Ezra 2:59–63; Neh 7:5–65, where the same term, "document" (כתב), as in Ps 87:6, occurs (Ezra 2:62; Neh 7:64). The variant reading of πάντων in Gal 4:26 ("mother of us all"), though unlikely to be original, certainly indicates that some early scribes were recognizing this point; perhaps, even, that they were adding the word from the relevant line in the LXX of v. 7 (ὡς εὐφραινομένων πάντων).

18. "Knowing" YHWH seems to be one way of designating God's true people: e.g., Jer 9:24; 22:16; Ps 36:10—and of course the "knowing-YHWH" with which the world will be

letter. In chapter 1, defending himself against the (implicit but clear) charge of having learned his gospel from the central authorities in Jerusalem, he describes his original call, and its immediate aftermath, in terms which resonate with Israel's scriptural traditions. The call-description itself echoes Isa 49:1 and Jer 1:5. In neither case is this simply a matter of Paul using vaguely biblical language as though to say, "My experience has some scriptural precedent." Isa 49:1 invites the "coastlands" and "you peoples from far away" to listen to what is said, and the passage goes on (v. 6) to explain that Israel's covenant God has called the "servant" to be "a light to the nations" so that his salvation may reach to the ends of the earth. This is in any case a favorite passage for Paul. He clearly has the whole of it in mind in Gal 1, since he alludes to it again in 1:24, where "they glorified God because of me" echoes Isa 49:3, the servant as the one "in whom I will be glorified." Similarly, Jer 1:5 assures the prophet that God, having known him prior to his forming in the womb, had appointed him "a prophet to the nations." In both passages, then, Paul is not simply sprinkling some biblical flavoring into his autobiography. He is saying, for those with ears to hear, "My calling to be the apostle to the Gentiles is rooted quite specifically in Israel's Scriptures; so far from being disloyal to the Jewish traditions, as my opponents are suggesting, I can claim the high ground." So too, as I have argued in various places, he alludes to the traumatic experience of Elijah, who after his "extremely zealous" persecution of the prophets of Baal, went off south to Mount Sinai and was told to return to Damascus for a new phase of his work.[19] Paul is writing swiftly, gesturing, so it seems, to larger and deeper themes than he has time to explore, but well aware of the implications they bring with them. So, I suggest, it is with his use of Ps 87//Ps 86 LXX in Gal 4.

So the first point of strong support for seeing a deliberate allusion to the psalm here is that it provides one of the most remarkable statements anywhere in Israel's Scriptures of the divine intention to see foreigners—including the most hated of traditional enemies!—as sharing equally in the birthright of Jerusalem's own inhabitants. But this points on to the second supporting theme. Paul's invocation of this Psalm, far more than the implication of Isa 54, enables him to draw, in good Jewish style, the sharp distinction he requires between "the present Jerusalem" and "the Jerusalem above." Jerusalem is of course a major theme, geographical, political, theological and symbolic, throughout

---

full in Isa 11:9. I am grateful to Andy Johnson for pointing out this connection between Ps 87:4//Ps 86:4 LXX and Gal 4:9.

19. Gal 1:14–17 with 1 Kgs 19:10, 14, 15; see *Pauline Perspectives*, 152–59.

Scripture and post-biblical Jewish thought and writing.[20] This psalm brings one aspect of that into sharp focus.

Psalm 87//Psalm 86 LXX is indeed remarkable, deeply counterintuitive within the world of the Hebrew Scriptures where Egypt, Babylon, and the rest are more or less stock villains rather than newborn citizens of Zion.[21] That makes it all the more natural to read the psalm prophetically or eschatologically, perhaps in line with (though still going further than) such prophecies as Isa 2:2–4; Mic 4:1–3; Zech 8:20–23 and the perhaps equally remarkable Isa 19:18–25 which (sandwiched between oracles of judgment against Egypt!) includes Egypt and Assyria in the blessings promised to Israel and declares "blessed be Egypt my people, and Assyria the work of my hands, and Israel my heritage" (19:25).[22]

If, then, Ps 87//Ps 86 LXX is taken to refer to the age to come, which "Zion" is being referred to? Clearly not the present Jerusalem, which is on the one hand in a continuing form of slavery under pagan overlords, and on the other hand a seething hotbed of zealous Torah observance, for which any compromise with gentiles would be anathema. It concerns, rather, a new city altogether, one not built by regular human builders but established by "the Most High himself" (αὐτὸς ἐθεμελίωσεν αὐτὴν ὁ ὕψιστος, 86:5 LXX). This can only be the city at the heart of the new creation.[23] Here therefore, as so often, Paul is standing at the overlap of the ages. Through the Messiah's self-giving to death

---

20. See esp. A. Y. Collins, "The Dream of a New Jerusalem at Qumran," in *The Bible and the Dead Sea Scrolls*, vol. 3, *The Scrolls and Christian Origins*, ed. J. H. Charlesworth (Waco: Baylor University Press, 2006), 231–37. Collins's survey does not, sadly, include Gal 4:26.

21. As J. W. H. Bos points out ("Psalm 87," *Interpretation* 47 [1993]: 284), psalms that highlight Zion see the nations either doing homage, or raging against God and his city, or being subdued before it (29:1–2; 46:4; 47:2–3; 60:10; 108:10). This psalm, uniquely, sees the nations as sharing the birthright of Israel.

22. One might also bring in Amos 9:7, where the prophet cuts Israel down to size by suggesting a parallel between the exodus from Egypt and YHWH's acts in bringing the Philistines from Caphtor and the Syrians from Kir. See too, e.g., *Pss. Sol.* 17:30–31 (not 17:33 as Longenecker, *Galatians*, 214), where Gentiles will be brought from the ends of the earth to serve the Lord, to see his glory, and "to bring as gifts her children who had been driven out" (*OTP*, 2:667).

23. For similar arguments in relation to Ezekiel's prediction of a new temple, see Collins, "The Dream of a New Jerusalem," 233–34. She divides the theme at Qumran into three: the community itself as "Jerusalem" or "temple" (238); a new temple that they themselves would build (239–44), as in the *Temple Scroll* (though this is subject to many different interpretations); and—directly relevant to Ps 87:5//Ps 86:5 LXX—a new temple created by God himself and lasting forever (244–48), as arguably in 4QFlor = 4Q174 1.1–13 and elsewhere, including the fragmentary *Description of the New Jerusalem*, where the city to be built is the fulfillment

for sins, God has rescued his people "from the present evil age" (Gal 1:4) so that now all the Messiah's family are citizens, not of an earthly city, but of the heavenly one. This fits precisely with the famous passage in Phil 3:20 ("we are citizens of heaven . . . and we're eagerly waiting for the saviour, the Lord, King Jesus, who is going to come from there"); though there the "citizens of heaven" are contrasted, by implication, not with citizens of the present Jerusalem but with the citizens of Rome.[24]

This is the point at which so much Western interpretation has reached for Plato instead of the Jewish hinterland: "citizens of heaven" does not mean "so that we are looking forward to leaving earth and returning to our true home in heaven." That takes us straight into the world not of Paul but of Plutarch.[25] The "heavenly Jerusalem" or the "New Jerusalem," as we shall see in a moment, formed part of the overall Jewish expectation of what Israel's God, the creator, would do in the end: in the present time the future purposes to put all things right were stored up in "heaven," God's domain, but in the "age to come" they would be revealed "on earth as in heaven." For Paul, the "age to come" has been inaugurated, so it makes perfect sense that he would take "new Jerusalem" passages—precisely texts like Ps 87//Ps 86 LXX and Isa 54!—and declare that they were already operative. Thus, exactly in line with his overall claim of the inauguration of the new age through Messiah Jesus, Paul indicates with this Psalm and with Isa 54 that the promised time of blessing is here. *And the ingathering of surprised and surprising gentiles is not only something with scriptural warrant behind it; it is itself the sign that the creator God has established his promised New Jerusalem, completely upstaging the present one.* And this serves not only as a further vindication of Paul's inclusion of uncircumcised gentiles within Abraham's family. It makes it clear that any appeal to "the present Jerusalem," as though that might trump Paul's own apostolic authority, is itself part of the step back into slavery against which Paul is warning. By contrast, Paul insists that this "Jerusalem" is "free"—presumably because, having already set out the terms of his "allegory" with Sarah as the "free woman," he is about to back up the Psalm reference with the verbally linked Isa 54:1, which was already widely taken to refer to Jerusalem in terms of Sarah.

Those who have noted the other Jewish and Christian texts which speak of

---

of the bejewelled city of Isa 54:11–12. Since that text speaks of God himself "making" the city, Collins argues that it refers to the eschatological city created by God himself (247).

24. On the political implications of Phil 3 see my *Paul and the Faithfulness of God*, vol. 4 of Christian Origins and the Question of God (London and Minneapolis: SPCK and Fortress, 2013), 1292–94.

25. See, e.g., Plutarch, *Exile* (*Moralia* 607D).

a heavenly Jerusalem, or a "new Jerusalem," have often gestured toward such passages as though they were detached *topoi*, part of a general stock-in-trade of miscellaneous Jewish ideas, a rag-bag from which one might pick vaguely related themes at random.[26] But they are not. They form part of a regularly invoked narrative in which God's promised new city—the place where God himself will be at home and will, in the end, welcome his family to be with him—is the reality for which the cities of the present world, whether Jerusalem or Rome or anywhere else, are at best advance signposts and at worst ghastly parodies. The positive side of this goes back all the way to Exodus, where Moses was shown the heavenly tabernacle and told to make an earthly copy of it.[27] Thus Heb 12:22–24 (with which we should associate 8:2 and 11:14–16) indicates that the followers of Jesus belong to the true "Mount Zion" rather than the present Jerusalem; and Rev 21–22 (with which we should link 3:12) emphasizes that Jesus's people are indeed citizens of the "New Jerusalem," which will come down from heaven to earth as the "bride," contrasted with the "whore" of Babylon. The larger story provides the clue to the meaning.

So it is with the well-known antecedent Jewish texts. Baruch 4 and 5, closely dependent on themes from Isa 40–66, invites Jerusalem to take off the garment of sorrow and affliction and put on forever the beauty of the glory of God (5:1). Five times in this passage the word εὐφροσύνη occurs, the same word that, as we saw, links LXX Ps 86:7 and Isa 54:1: once for the initial rejoicing of God over his people before their catastrophe (4:11), three times for the future celebration which is coming from God (4:23, 29, 36), and once, in the final verse of the book (5:9), for the rejoicing at their ultimate restoration, when God "will lead Israel μετ' εὐφροσύνης into the light of his glory with his own mercy and righteousness" (my translation). All this takes place in the context of Israel's ongoing slavery, the αἰχμαλωσία of continuing exile.[28] First Enoch 53:6, within a scene of cosmic judgment, likewise echoes Isa 40 in the notion of the glorious divine appearing and declares that the Messiah will "reveal the house of his congregation," in other words, the ultimate temple. The construction of this new temple is described more fully in 90:28–29, again within a larger picture of the coming messianic age. The symbolic language is fully consistent with an interpretation in which the temple is being rebuilt in the ordinary way.[29] This seems not to be the case, however, with 2 Enoch 55:2, where the "highest

---

26. Cf., e.g., Betz, *Galatians*, 246.
27. Exod 25:40; 26:30; 27:8; cf. Num 8:4; Wis 9:8; see Heb 8:1–7.
28. E.g., Bar 4:10; comp. Rom 7:23.
29. See, more fully, Collins, "The Dream of a New Jerusalem," 248–50.

Jerusalem" is located in the "highest heaven"; but this is a later text whose relevance for the first century is in any case dubious. The *Sibylline Oracles* offer a picture similar to that in *1 Enoch*, in which a savior figure will create the new city and adorn it with great size and beauty.[30]

More directly germane for our purposes are *2 Baruch* and *4 Ezra*, both normally dated in the period after the destruction of Jerusalem in AD 70. In *2 Baruch* 4, which assumes the fictive scenario of the Babylonian destruction in order to address the real situation of the Roman destruction, the seer is firmly told that the city which presently appears is not the one of which God had said "on the palms of my hands I have carved you."[31] Rather, the true Jerusalem was prepared before God made Paradise and was revealed to Adam, to Abraham and to Moses.[32] Here, then, as in various isolated sayings in the period, we have the idea of a "Jerusalem above," or a temple in the heavens — the two are more or less interchangeable — with the implication that this present heavenly reality, as in Rev 3 and 21, is ready to be revealed, brought down to earth, at the proper time, and that one must not mistake the present Jerusalem and temple for this future one.

Finally, we have *4 Ezra*, likewise mourning the destruction of the present Jerusalem by the Romans and wrestling with the question of how this can possibly fit within the righteous purposes of Israel's God. In the third vision (6:35–9:25) the seer is assured that in fact "Paradise is opened, the tree of life is planted, the age to come is prepared, plenty is provided, a city is built, rest is appointed, goodness is established and wisdom perfected beforehand" (8:52; *OTP*, 1:544). The fourth vision, which like other "new Jerusalem" texts appears to be drawing in part on Isa 40–55, sees "Ezra" trying to console a weeping mother who suddenly turns into a great city (10:25–27). Zion has indeed been desolate, he is told, but something dramatic and new, not made by human hands, is to appear. In the field where the seer must wait, there is no foundation for a building, "for no work of man's building could endure in a place where the city of the Most High was to be revealed" (10:54; *OTP*, 1:548).

A similar viewpoint emerges from the various "new Jerusalem" texts found at Qumran. In line with the normal perception of the scroll writers, the present Jerusalem regime is seen as hopelessly corrupt, so that the only alternative left is to abolish the present city with its rulers and for a new city to replace it.[33]

---

30. *Sibylline Oracles* 5:286–433, esp. 5:420–427.

31. A reference to Isa 49:16.

32. *2 Baruch* 4:3–5. A later rabbinic saying, in bPes 54a, suggests that the Temple was one of the seven things which God made before the foundation of the world.

33. See e.g. 11QT; 4QFlor.; 4Q554 2.2.14–16; and the song of Zion in 11QPs Zion, 22.1–15; 4Q504 1–2.4.

No single coherent picture emerges from these Jewish and early Christian texts. But the underlying implicit narrative is clear. An overall impression is given of the sharp contrast between the city that has been destroyed—or that is to be destroyed—and the new city that is to be built. The latter is presently prepared in the heavenly realms, against the day when it will be brought out, not by a regular restoration programme (one thinks of the Maccabees cleansing the shrine, or of Herod the Great rebuilding it) but by a sovereign divine act. And what is important for our purposes is that these passages thus provide more than just a floating *topos*, a strange or vague idea of a "heavenly Jerusalem" which writers like Paul could drop into an argument as extra embellishment. They provide some kind of implicit narrative, which has telltale resonances with the lament, and then the promise, of Isa 40–66.

Two things then begin to fall into place. First, where we find talk of a new or a heavenly Jerusalem, this is in explicit contrast to a city which has sinned and is under judgment, or at the very least is now, as in Heb 8:13, "ready to disappear." In Revelation, the condemned city is "Babylon"; in the other texts, it appears to be the Jerusalem which has reaped, or is about to reap, the rewards of its own corruption and rebellion. This fits exactly with Paul's purpose in Galatians, however cryptically it is expressed. The Galatians seem to have been told that they can appeal over Paul's head to Jerusalem and its resident apostles, as though they possessed some special authority by reason of their geographical location. Paul is at pains to suggest that "the present Jerusalem" is still "in slavery with her children," whereas the gospel he proclaims carries with it the power and authority of the "Jerusalem above." Second, where we find Paul proposing such a contrast, the parallels in the other Jewish literature we have glanced at suggest that we might expect a reference to some key part of the lament-and-consolation theme from Isa 40–55. This is, of course, exactly what we find in Gal 4:27, where Paul quotes Isa 54:1.

This contrast between the present and the New Jerusalem—the earthly and the heavenly, not in a Platonic sense but in the biblical sense of heaven as the storage house for God's future purposes—thus serves Paul's strongly polemical purpose.[34] As we read between the lines of Gal 1:6–2:10, as we reflect on the "people who came from James" in 2:12, and as we put two and two together in the closing polemic of 6:11–16, Paul appears to be sending out the strong message: do not trust people who claim to be telling you what the Jerusalem leaders are saying. The fact that they are based in historic Jerusalem says nothing about their supposed authoritative status, or about any sug-

---

34. See, e.g., Lincoln, *Paradise*, 16–18, referring to earlier literature.

gested superiority over Paul himself. Paul's mission is about the new creation, launched with the Messiah's resurrection after the overcoming of the powers of the "present evil age." As we should expect from the Jewish context, this suddenly inbreaking new creation was rooted in the promises of Israel's Scriptures themselves, and in the combination of those Scriptures into a powerful web of Messiah-shaped meaning.[35]

The Climax of Galatians: Torah, Prophets, and Writings

Once we allow for a full and intended allusion to Ps 87//Ps 86 LXX in Gal 4:26, the paragraph 4:21–5:1 displays, as in one or two other Pauline summaries, all the signs that this is indeed where Paul thinks his argument is going. It is not, that is, an addendum, a fanciful or playful bit of "allegory," meant as a tease, tacked on to the real argument which had finished earlier (e.g., at 4:11).[36] Paul has assembled Torah (Gen 16 and 21), Prophets (Isa 54), and Writings (Ps 87// Ps 86 LXX). This corresponds to at least three clearly climactic passages in Romans. In Rom 8:31–39 he alludes to Gen 22; he echoes Isa 50; and he quotes directly from Ps 44. In Rom 10 (arguably the deliberate centerpiece of Rom 9–11)[37] he quotes from Leviticus and Deuteronomy, from Isaiah and Joel, and from Ps 19. Then, in the final summary in 15:7–13, he quotes from Deut 32, from Isa 11, and from Pss 18 and 117. I do not think any of this is accidental. In drawing to a head his argument that his mission is the truly Jewish—because truly messianic—fulfillment of Israel's Scriptures, over against those who claim to speak for the Jewish way and to accuse him of being a "people-pleaser,"[38] Paul assembles a classic Jewish argument from every part of Scripture.

This solidifies, to my mind, the sense that it is here in Gal 4:21–5:1, rather than in 4:1–11, that the ultimate thrust of Galatians lies. To be sure, there is more to come in chapters 5–6. But with 4:21–5:1 his foundational argument

---

35. For a critique of present "apocalyptic" theories, see my *Paul and His Recent Interpreters*, Part II, 135–218. At this point, of course, my case does indeed overlap with part of the argument of J. L. Martyn, *Galatians*, AB33A (New York: Doubleday, 1997), 463. Martyn cites *Pesikta Rab. Kah.* 22.1 for a rabbinic reading of the Sarah story in Genesis, coupled with, e.g., Isa 61:10, as prophesying the extension of salvation to Gentiles.

36. As suggested by, e.g., E. de W. Burton, *A Critical and Exegetical Commentary on the Epistle to the Galatians*, ICC (Edinburgh: T & T Clark, 1921), 251: "a supplementary argument ... apparently as an after-thought."

37. See my *Paul and the Faithfulness of God*, ch. 11, esp. 1156–1258.

38. See the charge in 1:10; for the background, see the polemic against the "people-pleasers" in *Psalms of Solomon* 4.

is complete, and the primary imperative is stated: those who are causing the trouble, and threatening to lead the Galatians back into a form of slavery, must be put out of the congregation (4:30, citing Gen 21:10).[39] That, however, raises a whole other set of questions which are beyond the scope of this article to investigate.

It might appear that the present study has little to do with the themes which Michael Gorman has made his own over recent decades, particularly the notions of "cruciformity" and the indwelling of the living Messiah Jesus within believers corporately and individually. (Certainly, that contribution has been wonderfully fresh and invigorating both personally and academically, and the present essay is offered in thankfulness for it.) But on closer inspection we might suggest that this study has everything to do with these themes. The challenge Paul faces here, just as in the earlier climactic passage of Gal 2:15–21, is that of the radical reshaping of God's people through the death and resurrection of Israel's Messiah. "Through the law I died to the law, so that I might live to God" (2:19): the point of Paul's first-person language there was never, after all, to hold up his own "experience" for its own sake, but to say, in effect, "this is what it looks like when Israel's Messiah, crucified and risen, reshapes the chosen people, including the most zealous." Perhaps, in fact, that cryptic statement was always waiting for the fuller statement in 4:21: "So, you want to live under the law, do you? All right, tell me this: are you prepared to hear what the law says?" "And what does the Bible say? 'Throw out the slave-girl and her son'" (4:30, quoting Gen 21:10). The "dying to the law" of 2:19, and the "crucifying of the flesh" in 5:24, have their ecclesial correlate in a "no tolerance" policy for those who offer "another gospel," as we already see in the repeated "anathema" of 1:6–9. Within this overall argument, the allusion to Ps 87//Ps 86 LXX in Gal 4:26 functions as the corporate application not only of "so that I might live to God" in 2:19 but of the fuller statement in 2:20–21: "the life I

---

39. With, e.g., Martyn, *Galatians*, 445–46. It should go without saying that this is not about "the exclusion of the Jews" (so, e.g., Jobes, "Jerusalem, Our Mother," 301). It is about the distinction between Messiah-believing Jews and gentiles on the one hand and, on the other hand, any, whether Jews or gentiles, who do not believe in the crucified and risen Jesus as Israel's Messiah. In relation to alternative proposals, see the comments of R. B. Hays, "Hope for What We Do Not Yet See: The Salvation of All Israel in Romans 11.25–27," in *One God, One People, One Future: Essays in Honour of N. T. Wright*, ed. John Anthony Dunne, Eric Lewellen (London and Minneapolis: SPCK and Fortress, 2018), 549–50. Attempts to mollify Paul's sharp command (e.g., Eastman, *Recovering Paul's Mother Tongue*, 132–33) are unconvincing: the fact that the key word Ἔκβαλε in 4:30 is in the singular, not plural, is due to the fact that Paul is directly quoting Sarah's command to Abraham in Gen 21:10.

do still live in the flesh, I live within the faithfulness of the son of God, who loved me and gave himself for me," thereby attaining the status of "righteousness" which the law could not give. The corporate life of the Messiah's family is precisely the life of *cruciform faithfulness*, with no room for compromise. As, again, in Isa 1:26, the "righteous city" is also the "faithful city," in the LXX the μητρόπολις πιστὴ Σιων, the "faithful mother city Zion"—contrasted, as we now see to be normal within the relevant literature, with the faithless and wicked city (Isa 1:21–25). To belong to the "Jerusalem above," the Sarah-city of Isa 54, requires the putting to death of all that still focuses on the "flesh," and in ecclesial terms this means the expulsion of those who are advocating circumcision. When we understand Paul's allusion to Ps 87//Ps 86 LXX, with its close metaleptic link with Isa 54:1, within the larger world of ancient Jewish and early Christian narrative, we see that he has thereby highlighted the urgent challenge of cruciformity, which the gospel of the crucified and risen Messiah presented to the churches of Galatia.

... Chapter 14

Citizenship and Empire:
A Missional Engagement with Ephesians

Sylvia C. Keesmaat

I was teaching an introductory seminar on the whole of the biblical story, and a couple of doctoral students had joined us for our discussion of Paul. As we finished our overview of the epistles, the conversation turned to the implications of Paul's teachings for today. What were the political implications of what he had said? The environmental implications? The economic implications? As the conversation became more animated, one of the visiting doctoral students became more and more agitated.

> Finally, she blurted out, "But you can't *do* that!"
> "Do what?" I asked.
> "You can't ask those questions of Paul. That's not allowed!" she said.
> "Not allowed by *whom*?" I asked.
> "It's just not allowed. Questions like that aren't really . . . *academic*," she replied. "We aren't supposed to ask about implications."

This conversation happened around twenty years ago. Thankfully there has been a shift in the guild of biblical studies since then, a shift that has been evident in the work of scholars like Michael Gorman. Academic rigor and scholarly depth meet theological richness and contemporary context in his writings so that the missional character of our lives and the embodiment of the gospel become visible as he writes of them. Not many biblical scholars discuss the latest scholarship and the work of Christian Peacemaker Teams, the tragedy in Nickel Mines, and the rebirth of Sandtown in Baltimore as a seamless whole. It is a privilege, therefore, to have the opportunity to contribute an essay to this volume in honor of Michael and to attempt to carry forward into my own readings of Ephesians some of the lessons I have learned from him about a missional reading of the text.

Citizens of the Kingdom?

Before delving into the text of Ephesians, however, I would like to situate my topic in the context of a query raised by a friend as we discussed the increasing problems around citizenship, refugees, and immigration in our contemporary world. Given escalating environmental degradation and the resultant poverty in Asia, Africa, and Central and South America, alongside the growing reluctance of those in wealthier countries, such as the United States, to welcome those in need from other countries, he began to speculate about our responsibility as Christians. As Christians we confess that our primary citizenship is the kingdom of God. Why, then, do Christians appeal to their state citizenship as their fundamental allegiance, rather than their citizenship in the kingdom of God? And he suggested that if Christians were to consider their citizenship in God's kingdom to be foundational to every other part of their identity, wouldn't this impact their willingness to welcome the refugee and immigrant into "their" countries and communities? In fact, he pushed this even further: why couldn't churches claim their citizenship in the kingdom of God in such a way that they could grant that citizenship to people from other countries who are in need? What would it look like if the commonwealth of the kingdom were to supersede any mere political construct that humanity has created for ordering society?[1]

Such questions have become even more critical in the current political ethos in North America. The increasing intolerance of those in leadership in the United States has contributed to a climate of overt racism and prejudice, with incidents of racial profiling, racial slurs, and racist harassment becoming common not only in the United States but also in places where multiculturalism is celebrated, such as Canada. This coincides with the rise of nationalism in various countries around the world, such as Hungary, Turkey,

---

1. My thanks to James Padilla-deBorst for first raising these questions and for facilitating a context for their discussion. On the state as a construct that has become ubiquitous only recently in human history, see James C. Scott, *Against the Grain* (New Haven: Yale University Press, 2017). Also illuminating is his *Seeing Like a State* (New Haven: Yale University Press, 1998).

and Brazil, including the increasingly vocal white nationalist movement in North America.

What would it look like if we were to explore some of these questions in light of Paul's startling claim in Ephesians: "So then you are no longer strangers and aliens, but you are citizens with the saints and also members of the household of God" (Eph 2:19). What are the implications of being *citizens with the saints* and might this stand in tension with any other citizenship or allegiance that we have? Perhaps an exploration of this verse in Paul's wider political context, the larger biblical story, and the whole of the letter to the Ephesians will provide some insight into how Paul's words can speak into our own troubling context.[2]

The Peoples in Ancient Rome

Some of the difficulty in discerning what Paul is saying in Eph 2:19 has to do with our lack of understanding of how people groups were viewed in the ancient world. For instance, as Paul's layered argument builds, it is clear that he is revealing God's plan for all time, a plan where the good news of the riches of Jesus the Messiah reveals that "the peoples" are now heirs of God's promises (3:6). Many of our translations obscure Paul's reference to "the peoples" here by translating τὰ ἔθνη as "the gentiles." For most of those who were listening to this letter—whether in Ephesus, or Laodicea, or any other city in Asia Minor—τὰ ἔθνη would not have denoted "gentiles" as a homogenous group comprised of everyone who was not Jewish but would rather have referred to "the peoples," all of the diverse peoples who made up the known world.

At the time that Ephesians was written, moreover, the perception of "the peoples" was a construct that came to be overwhelmingly shaped by Rome so that τὰ ἔθνη came to mean those who were non-Roman.[3] In the ancient world, most people's allegiance was primarily to their city, and the kind of cultural and linguistic cohesion that characterizes nation-states today was unknown. Hence provinces were portrayed by Rome using the most prominent ethnic group as a handy way of identifying those geographic areas that

---

2. The more I have worked on the Epistle to the Ephesians in an imperial context, the more firmly I am convinced that Paul wrote this letter. For a brief outline of my reasons see Sylvia C. Keesmaat, "Ephesians and Colossians," in *The New Cambridge Companion to Paul*, ed. Bruce Longenecker (Cambridge: Cambridge University Press, 2020).

3. Davina C. Lopez, *Apostle to the Conquered: Reimagining Paul's Mission* (Minneapolis: Fortress, 2010), 26.

Citizenship and Empire

they had conquered. Often these groups were depicted as having unusual and uncivilized characteristics that could distinguish them from the norm of Roman civilization.[4]

Examples of this were common in Asia Minor. For instance, in the city of Aphrodisias, just over the hill from Colossae, there is evidence of a great causeway, filled with images three stories high. On one side of the causeway are images of the gods and the emperors; on the other side are images of τὰ ἔθνη, the peoples. Representing a wide spectrum of peoples, these images depict the scope of Roman conquest, for all of the peoples represented have been conquered by Rome and brought into the empire.[5] The peoples are represented in each case by a draped woman who has a distinctive pose and clothing that indicates the degree of "civility" or "barbarism" of that people. A demure well-coiffed and well-draped woman represents a civilized or Hellenized people; a woman with warlike attributes represents a "barbarian" people, as does a woman with loose and wild hair. One woman, whose clothing is slipping off her shoulders and whose arms are crossed in front of her, is reminiscent of victory reliefs of captive women with chained hands. As one scholar has pointed out, even without inscriptions it would be possible to place these women in varying degrees of proximity to Rome and the far reaches of the empire.[6] Each statue would have stood on a base that consisted of an inscription of the ethnic group being depicted and a male head that was representative of that group. These heads also had a wide degree of characterization: short hair, long hair, unshaven, big beards, trimmed beards, menacing expressions, benign expressions, all intended to reveal the characteristics of the people so depicted. In total, fifty statues of different ethnic groups from across the entire empire could be accommodated in the colonnade. This collection of images of τὰ ἔθνη was likely modeled on the series by Augustus in Rome and was copied in more than one place across the empire.[7]

---

4. See R. R. R. Smith, "*Simulacra Gentium*: The *Ethnē* from the Sebasteion at Aphrodisias," *JRS* 78 (1988), 57. On the linguistic variety in an area as small as the Lycus Valley, see Rick Strelan, "The Languages of the Lycus Valley," in *Colossae in Space and Time: Linking to an Ancient City*, ed. Alan H. Cadwallader and Michael Trainor, NTOA 94 (Göttingen: Vandenhoeck & Ruprecht, 2011), 77–103.

5. Smith indicates that "all the *ethnē* certainly included here seem to have one of three qualifications in Augustan imperial thinking. They have been either simply defeated, or defeated and added to the empire, or brought back into the empire after unwilling secession" ("*Simulacra Gentium*," 59).

6. Smith, "*Simulacra Gentium*," 60.

7. Smith, "*Simulacra Gentium*," 75; Lopez, *Apostle*, 52.

However, this is not the only type of image that would be brought to mind when Paul referred to τὰ ἔθνη in Ephesians. Even more ubiquitous than collections of τὰ ἔθνη was the iconography of victory on coins, altars, and statues which portrayed those peoples that Rome had defeated in various postures of submission and humility. Of the images that are still somewhat intact at Aphrodisias, there are five such depictions of humiliated and defeated peoples. These were not unusual. Coins minted to celebrate the victories of the empire regularly depicted the people they had conquered in standard poses, usually as women with clothing and hair in disarray and with bound hands.[8]

Such images, of course, were rooted in reality. When parades were held in honor of military victories, the procession included those who had been captured, bound in chains and heading for death or slavery.[9] The message was clear: these are the peoples who opposed us, whom we have now vanquished and subjected to our imperial rule.

What are the implications of such depictions for Paul's audience? In light of these portrayals of τὰ ἔθνη, how would the Ephesians have interpreted Paul's assurance that the hostility and dividing wall between the "uncircumcised" and Israel had been broken down (Eph 2:14)? Might they have understood that this also implied that all other dividing walls among τὰ ἔθνη themselves had been broken down (2:14)? How would they have envisioned the peace that Paul described? How would they have heard Paul's assurances that they are no longer aliens and strangers but citizens with the saints and members of the household of God?

It is possible to imagine that Paul's audiences would have heard echoes of imperial promises here. Rome also promised peace to those who were far off and peace to those who were near (cf. Eph 2:17). Rome was also interested in unity, in concord between peoples, and in harmony among those who were traditionally enemies.[10] How was Paul's gospel to the peoples different from the good news of military victory brought by Rome? I suggest five ways in which Paul challenged Roman ideals of unity, harmony, and concord. Taken together, these reinforce one another to provide a challenge not only to ancient Rome but also to the way that we construct national and ethnic identity in our own time.

---

8. On the gendered character of such images, see Lopez, *Apostle*, 19–55.
9. Lopez, *Apostle*, 115.
10. See Harry O. Maier, *Picturing Paul in Empire: Imperial Image, Text and Persuasion in Colossians, Ephesians and the Pastoral Epistles* (London: T & T Clark, 2013), 110–18, on the celebration of concord between the cities of Asia Minor.

Paul, a Prisoner in Chains

Paul describes himself twice in this letter as a "prisoner" (Eph 3:1; 4:1) and once as an "ambassador in chains" (6:20). Numerous scholars have pointed out that the latter phrase is an oxymoron since an ambassador would usually be granted diplomatic immunity.[11] However, perhaps we are assuming an overly diplomatic milieu for Paul's language here. In the context of a victory march, military and political leaders were the first to be paraded in chains. This would have included ambassadors. Rather than being an ambassador on a diplomatic mission, Paul is evoking an image of Rome leading victims with shackled hands in humiliation and shame.[12]

Such images were also common on the victory statues and coins that celebrated Roman conquest and often included a prisoner (symbolizing a conquered people) crouching at the feet of Caesar with chained hands. Helpful for our purposes are the surviving panels from the Sebastion of Aphrodisias, which give us an idea of how these images were portrayed in Asia Minor. The reliefs from Aphrodisias contain five such images. Two are images of men with bound hands: one is of Augustus with the goddess Nike, a prisoner, and a trophy; the second is of Germanicus with a captive and a trophy. In both images the male prisoner has chained hands and is depicted as much smaller than the emperor.

Even more evocative are the three reliefs depicting women. The first is Claudius vanquishing Britannia, who is bare-breasted with loose hair, and about to be killed. She is not bound, but that is only because she is still being subdued. The second is a depiction of Nero victorious over Armenia, who is also naked and appears to be unconscious. Given her comatose state, she is not bound. While it appears that Nero is raising her up, it is unclear whether this is benign or not. Her limp, unconscious state suggests that her subjection has already been complete. The final image of the three is of Claudius being crowned by the Senate with a captive woman at his feet. As Maier points out, "The classical serenity of Claudius crowned by a properly coiffed and dressed matron who represents Rome contrasts with the terror of the subjugated female depicted in Hellenistic style, who kneels, with bare breast and

---

11. E.g., Andrew T. Lincoln, *Ephesians*, WBC 42 (Dallas: Word, 1990), 454; John Muddiman, *The Epistle to the Ephesians*, BNTC (New York: Continuum, 2001), 296; Margaret Y. MacDonald, *Colossians and Ephesians*, SP (Collegeville, MN: Liturgical Press, 2000), 347–48.

12. So also, Lopez, *Apostle*, 138.

falling hair."[13] Her hands are bound behind her back. The message is clear: the conquest of foreign peoples is the basis for the emperor's authority. The fact that in many of these images the emperor is naked evokes not only divinity but also the threat of sexual violence toward the women. These were captive peoples depicted with immodest clothing and wild hair because they were themselves immodest and wild, unable to control their passions and in need of Roman culture and civilization. Portraying them as women emphasized not only their weakness but also their emotional, irrational nature. They are *meant* to be subjugated. The emperor, on the other hand, is calm and rational, and his naked body reveals his authoritative male character. It is because he is male and rational that the emperor is entitled to be dominant and expected to conquer.[14]

Such images were not unique in the ancient world but were a common trope for depicting the triumph of Rome over her enemies. When Paul, therefore, describes himself as a prisoner in chains (cf. Col 4:18), he is identifying himself with those who have been defeated and humiliated by the empire. He is taking on the identity of those who have been shamefully captured by Rome.

Of course, for many of those hearing this letter, the fact that Paul was a Jew already created an identification with a conquered people. As Lopez puts it, "The Jews belong to the underside of a Romans/nations hierarchy as one of the many defeated and incorporated peoples and Paul's self-presentation and mission . . . should be seen in that light."[15] It is no surprise that the gospel Paul proclaims is the gospel of a disgraced Messiah, who himself was captured, imprisoned, and finally killed by the powers of the empire. However, Paul turns the trope of defeat and humiliation on its head. For he indicates that his suffering is for the sake of those Jesus followers to whom he is writing (Eph 3:1, 13). Rather than being defeated, Paul's imprisonment is the result of the *success* of his proclamation of the mystery of the gospel and of Christ (6:19–20). In the same way, the blood of Jesus's cross has resulted not in imprisonment but in release for those in Ephesus (1:7), and the cross has not brought shame but an end to hostility and distance (2:13, 16). As a result, rather than proclaiming a good news that celebrates a military basis as the foundation for the citizenship of τὰ ἔθνη, the peoples, in the household of God, Paul is identifying both himself and the Messiah that he proclaims with those who have been conquered.

---

13. Maier, *Picturing Paul*, 88.
14. For more on the gendered nature of this imagery, see Lopez, *Apostle*, 19–55.
15. Lopez, *Apostle*, 25.

Citizenship and Empire

The effect of such an identification on the recipients of the letter should not be underestimated. The purpose of imperial depictions of τὰ ἔθνη was twofold. On the one hand such images created distance between those who were defeated and paraded by Rome and those who had already accepted Roman culture and civilization. By suggesting that those who were defeated by Rome "deserved" such conquest, the empire was able to justify its never-ending agenda of continual conquest.[16] Such conquest was essential for both economic and environmental reasons. As the empire used up the available forests and land necessary for mining, and as environmental degradation increased as a result of deforestation, new land was needed to provide timber for ships and resource extraction, as well as more arable land for the grain and other exotic items demanded by Rome's increasing population.[17] Economically, the capture and selling of slaves was essential for the functioning of the Roman economy, and warfare provided access to an unlimited source of human beings for slaves. By identifying both Jesus and himself with those who are considered the barbaric "other," Paul is undermining the visual rhetoric that sought to depict other peoples as worthy of enmity or conquest.

On the other hand, such images were an important warning to those who would dare to resist Roman rule. In Aphrodisias, as elsewhere in the empire, depictions of terrorized war captives are closely linked to depictions of the emperor either as one of the gods, or as being granted victory by the gods. These depictions, therefore, functioned much like modern rhetoric from political leaders that depicts middle eastern people as terrorists, or Latinx people as rapists and drug smugglers in order to justify the building of a wall to keep them out. The violence and humiliation of these images also function like the threat of deportation does today. Do not protest against the violent and inhumane practices of the empire or you will find yourself a prisoner, apprehended and cuffed by an ICE officer who will do all that he needs to in order to "subdue" you.[18]

---

16. Lopez describes such depictions as naturalizing the place of the nations in the social order and thereby justifying Roman conquest (*Apostle*, 100).

17. See Sylvia C. Keesmaat and Brian J. Walsh, *Romans Disarmed: Resisting Empire, Demanding Justice* (Grand Rapids: Brazos, 2019), 170–79; and J. Donald Hughes, *Environmental Problems of the Greeks and Romans: Ecology in the Ancient Mediterranean*, 2nd ed. (Baltimore: John Hopkins University Press, 2014), 68–70.

18. ICE stands for Immigration and Customs Enforcement, the United States agency that aggressively seeks out and arrests those who are considered to be in the United States illegitimately. They also arrest a large number of legitimate residents who happen to be ethnic minorities.

In identifying himself with those who are defeated, and in telling the story of a Messiah whose blood brings peace (2:13), Paul challenges this story line. He himself has entered into solidarity with the defeated and identified with their humiliation, and in so doing he has added a layer to his challenge of the dominant narrative.[19] That challenge is also found in the language of inheritance.

From Aliens and Strangers to Heirs

Whereas in the story of Rome, τὰ ἔθνη are depicted as gaining the Roman attributes of civilization and culture when they begin to worship the gods of Rome, Paul portrays allegiance to such gods as the root of hostility and enmity in their lives.[20] Paul describes those in the Ephesian community as previously having followed "the age of this world, the ruler who belongs to the power of the air, the spirit that is now at work among those who are disobedient" (Eph 2:1-3; my translation). Fredrick J. Long has convincingly demonstrated that the ruler of the age of this world was perceived to be Caesar, who was associated with the gods, "especially Jupiter/Zeus, who granted human kings their rule."[21] Although there are many examples of images and coins that portray the identification of Jupiter with the Caesars, perhaps the most well-known is the *Gemma Augustea*. This relief, carved out of onyx, has two tiers. On the top, Augustus is enthroned. At his feet is the eagle, symbolizing Jupiter, and he is partially unclothed, signifying divinity, leading scholars to believe that he is being identified as the divine Jupiter. The goddess Roma sits on his right, surrounded by military weapons. He is being crowned by Oikoumene, the inhabited world. Below him, on the lower tier, is a scene of Roman soldiers and conquered peoples, some bound and all with the long hair and immodest clothing of barbarians. This cameo demonstrates the close association between the emperor and Jupiter/Zeus and the indisputable connection between the approval of Zeus and the capture and submission of τὰ ἔθνη.

Closer to home for the Ephesians, both geographically and temporally, is

---

19. The phrase "solidarity with the defeated" is from Lopez, *Apostle*, 151, 168.

20. Frederick J. Long, "Roman Imperial Rule under the Authority of Jupiter-Zeus: Political-Religious Contexts and the Interpretation of 'The Ruler of the Authority of the Air' in Ephesians 2:2," in *The Language of the New Testament: Context, History, Development*, ed. Stanley E. Porter (Leiden: Brill, 2013), 147-52.

21. Long, "Roman Imperial Rule," 139. The eagle used on Roman coins and the Roman standard was also associated with Jupiter. Jupiter was the Roman name for the Greek god Zeus. See also Maier, *Apostle*, 72-73.

the Marble Stele in Acraephia in Boeotia where Nero is referred to as "Zeus the Deliverer" or "Zeus Savior," with the words "To Zeus the deliverer, Nero, forever" on an adjacent altar.[22]

The association with Zeus is also suggested by Paul's reference to "the ruler who belongs to the power of the air," since Zeus was the god traditionally associated with lightning and the skies (or the air).[23] Given the way that Zeus was associated with the military might that enabled Rome to defeat her enemies, Paul is indicating not only that the emperor is in service to Zeus but also how the gods that the Ephesians formerly worshiped contributed to the breakdown of peace between the various peoples.

However, unlike Zeus, who raises up the emperor to join him in the pantheon, Paul proclaims that God, out of his great love and mercy, raises up those who are part of the community of believers to be seated with him in the heavenly places in Messiah Jesus (Eph 2:6).[24] This is a God who does not reward the practitioners of violence and warfare but rather elevates the peoples who have traditionally been the conquered (2:11). The Pauline equivalent of the *Gemma Augustea* would have placed the conquered peoples, τὰ ἔθνη, on the top tier with Jesus and God. Given Paul's message of reconciliation, perhaps the bottom tier would be an image of welcome between former enemies, maybe sharing food around a table.

Paul then refers to the recipients of the letter as "τὰ ἔθνη by birth" and "the uncircumcision" (Eph 2:11), who were aliens from the commonwealth of Israel and strangers to the covenant of promise, having no hope and being without God in the world (2:12). There is no doubt that Paul is here describing the community using Jewish constructs by referring to "the circumcision" and "the uncircumcision"—along with aliens to the commonwealth of Israel and strangers to the covenants of promise (vv. 11–12). Given that Paul's imprisonment is a result of his inclusion of τὰ ἔθνη, those whom Jews would have called the gentiles (3:1), this is not surprising.[25] And while his Jewish hearers might have heard Paul describing the tearing down of the wall dividing Jews and gentiles in the temple as well as an abrogation of the Torah when Paul mentions the "dividing wall" and "the law with its commandments and ordinances," his

---

22. Long, "Roman Imperial Rule," 142.

23. Long, "Roman Imperial Rule," 115–16, 136–38. I owe this translation to Andy Johnson, in personal correspondence.

24. See also Fredrick J. Long, "Ephesians: Paul's Political Theology in Greco-Roman Context," in *Christian Origins and Greco-Roman Culture: Social and Literary Contexts for the New Testament*, vol. 1, ed. Stanley E. Porter and Andrew W. Pitts (Leiden: Brill, 2013), 284.

25. So also, Long, "Roman Imperial Rule," 121.

"uncircumcised" hearers were more likely to hear a broader reference to the divisions that existed more generally between ethnic groups in the ancient world. John Muddiman puts it this way:

> Perhaps then, the "dividing wall" of partition is not exclusively either the barrier in the Temple or the palisade of Jewish Law. It is rather constituted by *all* the expressions of social enmity, familiar to any Jew or Gentile in the Hellenistic world, the differences in place of residence, manner of worship, food and dress, politics and ethics, and above all the blank wall of mutual incomprehension, fear and contempt between the two groups. And this apartheid between Jews and Gentiles is understood here not as a legitimate peace-keeping measure, but on the contrary as the institutionalization of mutual antipathy. For real peace involves the abolition of such barriers.[26]

Muddiman leaves out the differences in language that would also have created a dynamic of superiority and inferiority in a mixed ethnic group, some of whom would not speak Greek as a first language.[27] While the good news or gospel of Rome requires the victory over and *subjection* of all peoples, the good news of the gospel that Paul proclaims is the *reconciliation* of all peoples. Although Ephesians emphasizes the reconciliation of all things as the culmination of the story of Jesus and the world, Paul here focuses specifically on the reconciliation of the ἔθνη, the peoples of the world who are welcomed into the Jewish story now fulfilled in Jesus. As we saw above, Roman iconography portrayed imperial interaction with the nations in terms of violence and conquest. The power and rule of God (as seen in the rule of Jesus over all rulers, thrones, powers, and authorities; Eph 1:20–21) is one where peace and reconciliation ensure that instead of enemies being destroyed, what is put to death is the *hostility* between peoples, not through subjugation but by becoming one humanity who make home together, becoming the place where God dwells (2:13–21).

This one humanity is also emphasized in Eph 3:14, where Paul says that he bows his "knees before the Father, from whom every family in heaven and on

---

26. Muddiman, *Ephesians*, 128; James R. Harrison also suggests that this verse refers to wider cultural and ethnic divisions ("An Epigraphic Portrait of Ephesus and Its Villages," in *The First Urban Churches*, vol. 3, *Ephesus*, ed. James R. Harrison and L. L. Welborn [Atlanta: SBL Press, 2018], 15). In a similar vein, Michael J. Gorman interprets this passage to refer to the overcoming of all binaries that are constructed by human beings (*Becoming the Gospel: Paul, Participation and Mission* [Grand Rapids: Eerdmans, 2015], 192).

27. See Strelan, "The Languages," 77–103.

earth takes its name" (3:14–15). Literally this could be translated, "I bow my knees before the *Father*, from whom every *fatherland* in heaven and on earth takes its name." In a world where the Roman emperor was known as "Father of the Fatherland" (*Patria Patriae*), Paul's assertion is a challenge both to the realm of the gods (in heaven) and the realm of Roman Empire (on earth)—all are subject to God as Father. If one were to picture that long three-story-high colonnade in Aphrodisias once more, with images of the gods and the emperors on one side and the nations of the world on the other, it is as if Paul has swept his arms along the whole lot and said that they are all—nations, gods, and rulers alike—subject to the one God and Father of Jesus Christ (see also 1:20–21).

Why is it that Paul is bowing his knees before the Father of all? He is doing so because τὰ ἔθνη, the peoples, are now heirs. Throughout Ephesians, redemption and forgiveness are described in terms of obtaining and sharing in an inheritance (Eph 1:11, 14, 18; 3:6). Such language had powerful resonance for both gentile and Jewish hearers of these letters. Those who were welcomed into an inheritance by adoption in the first century received the legal rights of the family (along with land grants and, if necessary, citizenship) and, moreover, for security a pillar or statue was engraved with the honor and placed in a temple.[28] In this context, Paul's description of believers as growing into a temple, a dwelling place for God, is quite evocative. Long puts it this way: "the letter's recipients might understand, in addition to their official adoption with full inheritance rights, that they themselves are likened to the inscribed pillars and statues that testified to the transaction, especially as they themselves are built into a temple of God."[29] The members of the Ephesian community are themselves the record of their own adoption, just as the Corinthians are themselves the letter of recommendation written by the Holy Spirit on living flesh rather than stone tablets (2 Cor 3:1–3). Instead of needing proof of their adoption on stone pillars in pagan temples, the Ephesians are themselves a living temple, proof of their own membership in the household and of their own citizenship in the people of God (Eph 2:19–22).

While these resonances might have been present for gentile hearers of the letters, for those Jewish followers of Jesus in Colossae and Ephesus, there would have been another layer of meaning arising out of the story of Israel, a story Paul is alluding to throughout both letters. In the story of Israel, the language of adoption and being welcomed into an inheritance is rooted in

28. Long, "Ephesians," 278.
29. Long, "Ephesians," 279.

the exodus tradition, where Israel is adopted by God and redeemed in order to inherit the land (Exod 4:22-23; Hos 11:1). This language is picked up by Paul in places such as Rom 8:14 (cf. 8:29) and Gal 4:1-4 and becomes a powerful and evocative image for the inclusion of all peoples in the family of God.

The effect of Paul's imagery in this part of Ephesians undermined all assumptions of Roman superiority. Although Rome was eager to welcome τὰ ἔθνη into the empire as loyal subjects who would pay tribute and contribute children and slaves to the continuation and benefit of Roman society, there is never any suggestion that these peoples would have shared in the divine story line or descent of the Roman people.[30] By describing God as the Father of every nation, Paul is asserting that no nation is more "chosen" or more divine than any other, and that all peoples are now welcome—as heirs—in the household of God.

Oddly enough, such an assertion is becoming just as startling today as it was in the ancient world. As white supremacists ironically lay claim to the United States as "their" country, those in political leadership engage in rhetoric that suggests that those who are of white European descent "deserve" to enjoy the North American way of life, and as evangelical Christians continually assert their own white privilege in the eyes of God over against Christians of other ethnicities and those of other religious traditions, such as Islam, Paul's words seem more urgent than ever. All peoples, who in the ancient world worshiped many gods, find themselves under the care of the Father God who roots them and grounds them in love (Eph 3:17).

Leading Captivity Captive

The depth of Paul's argument in Ephesians gains volume and resonance in the scriptural allusions he employs throughout the letter. This not only includes the language of inheritance in the prophetic texts that Paul echoes but is also grounded in prophetic hope for the inclusion of the peoples as part of God's restoration of all things.

The first of such echoes is found in Eph 2:17: "So he came and proclaimed peace to you who were far off and peace to those who were near." We find in this verse an allusion to Isa 57:19. In the context of attacking the unfaithful idolatry of the people, the prophet turns from condemnation to hope: "Build up, build up, prepare the way, remove every obstruction from my people's way"

---

30. Lopez, *Apostle*, 135.

(Isa 57:14). Prepare the way for what? "Peace, peace, to the far and the near, says the Lord; and I will heal them" (Isa 57:19).[31]

The overtones of Isa 57, with its emphasis on idolatry, could not be stronger for those Ephesian Christians whose former life is described later precisely using the prophetic terminology of idolatry (Eph 4:17-23). However, they now worship a ruler who is part of a different story line. While the imperial narrative of the Pax Romana achieves peace by means of violent death to the stranger, Paul tells the story of a different Messiah, who himself dies that there may be peace.

In addition, this passage also echoes Isa 52:7 where a messenger brings the good news of peace. In both Eph 2:17 and Isa 52:7, peace becomes the object of the proclamation. Isaiah 52 proclaims a word of freedom in the midst of a recollection of captivity. The empires of Egypt and Assyria and the oppression that they inflicted (v. 4) are now challenged by a new gospel, a word of salvation that says to Zion, "your God reigns."

Peace, good news, salvation—all of these are used by the empire to describe the story of Rome. But the gospel of peace that Paul proclaims is one that challenges that of Rome. In evoking Isa 52, itself a challenge to Egypt and Assyria, Paul is reminding the Ephesian Christians that their God is one who has a history of challenging oppressive empires with a different peace and another kind of salvation. The world of Isa 52, like the world of the first century, might seem to be dominated by an all-powerful empire, but both Paul and Isaiah bring another word and proclaim another reality: "our God reigns!"

Like Isa 52, Eph 2 is concerned with allegiance. In a world where allegiance to Rome was ultimate, Paul turns the categories on their head by describing a misplaced allegiance in terms of being aliens and strangers not to Rome but to the πολιτείας of *Israel*. However, whereas Rome severely judged those who were unfaithful to her πολιτείας—and did so by subjecting them to death on a cross—Paul describes a Messiah who makes peace with those who are alien, and who does so by offering himself on such a cross.

This story line is reinforced in two subsequent allusions in Ephesians. The first is a passage which is concerned with the issue of unity in the community. In Eph 4:8, Paul strikingly paraphrases Psalm 68:18:

---

31. This and the following paragraphs are dependent on my "In the Face of Empire: Paul's Use of Scripture in the Shorter Epistles," in *Hearing the Old Testament in the New Testament*, ed. Stanley E. Porter (Grand Rapids: Eerdmans, 2006), 189-92.

> When he ascended on high
> he made captivity itself a captive;
> he gave gifts to his people. (Eph 4:8)

> You ascended the high mount
> leading captives in your train
> and receiving gifts from people,
> even from those who rebel against the LORD God's abiding there.
> (Ps 68:18)

Psalm 68 is a psalm of conquest. The captives being led are those kings whom God has scattered (vv. 11–14) and as the psalm continues to describe the tribute that kings bring to God, it also describes God's salvation in terms of increasingly violent battle imagery. Ironically, the story line of this psalm is not that far removed from the story line of Rome, who rejoiced in precisely this kind of festival, where humiliated captives were led in a victory parade while glory and honor was given to Caesar by those subject peoples who had formerly rebelled.

Paul's (mis)quotation of this psalm overturns all such ways of being empire, whether Jewish or Roman, and describes a different Lord and Messiah who made *captivity* a captive (Eph 4:8). That is, no more is captivity the way that enemies are to be treated, no more is servile subjection the order of the day. This Messiah overturns captivity and instead of receiving tribute as gifts, he *gives* gifts (4:8). These gifts are later described this way: "that some would be apostles, some prophets, some evangelists, some pastors and teachers, to equip saints for the work of ministry, for building up the body of Christ" (vv. 11–12). That is, unlike the empire, which seeks to fragment the body with its humiliating festivals, this ruler, this Messiah, is one whose gifts work for unity, for upbuilding, for peace.

Psalm 68 had also been interpreted extensively in rabbinic tradition, becoming associated with Moses's ascension to heaven to receive the Torah and other heavenly secrets. As a result, Ps 68 came to be closely associated with Pentecost, which increasingly was the feast that commemorated the law-giving at Sinai. If this is the case, then Paul's citation of Ps 68 also undermines the law, replacing the gift of Torah, which set Israel apart as a special people before God, with a new set of gifts, which builds up a new body, made up of Jew and gentile, those near and those far off.

Paul's evocation of Ps 68, therefore, creates a number of resonances for his listeners. On the one hand, they are resonances of God's power and rule over other peoples. But these resonances are undermined by Paul's change of quotation. This results in a subversion of any authority and rule that violently deals in death rather than in building up a new body rooted in peace. On the other hand, Paul's evocation of Ps 68 creates resonances of the giving of Torah. But again, the storyline of the Torah is undermined, for the gifts of this Messiah are those that create a new humanity drawn from beyond the boundaries of the law.

Renewed in the Image of a Suffering God

Since there is not space in this essay for a complete exploration of the way in which the last three chapters of Ephesians speak to the way that Paul is including the peoples as "citizens with the saints," I will focus on two remaining passages. The first is Eph 4:17–5:2, which begins with language that echoes Rom 1:21–22: "Now this I affirm and insist on in the Lord: you must no longer live as τὰ ἔθνη, in the futility of their minds. They are darkened in their understanding, alienated from the life of God because of their ignorance and hardness of heart. They have lost all sensitivity and have abandoned themselves to licentiousness, greedy to practice every kind of impurity. That is not the way you learned Christ!" (4:17–20). This passage evokes the futility that is a result of idolatry described in Rom 1:21. Such idolatry was particularly evident in the lives of the emperors, which by the time that Ephesians was written had become full of excessive sexual decadence and lavish extravagance.[32] Paul is calling this community away from their allegiance to such rulers ("You were taught to put away your former way of life, your old self, corrupt and deluded by greed," 4:22, my translation), and into a new identity, "[clothed] . . . with the new self, created according to the likeness of God in true righteousness and holiness" (v. 24).

It could be argued that Paul is expecting a change similar to the change that the empire expected of τὰ ἔθνη. As the images of Aphrodisias show, the change from the wild immoderation of "barbarian" identity is symbolized by the donning of demure clothing in line with the clothes worn by the elite and the imperial family. In this case, however, Paul continues with a description of the behavior of this community that is in direct opposition to the social expectations that are required to become part of the hierarchical status-seeking society that Rome fostered. As the argument unfolds in 4:25–5:2, Paul writes that, rather than engaging in the flattery necessary for the maintenance of the

---

32. Long, "Roman Imperial Rule," 152; Keesmaat and Walsh, *Romans Disarmed*, 22, 334–38.

patronage system, they are to speak the truth to their neighbors; rather than households in competition, they are members of one another; rather than allowing difference to feed offense, they should not let the sun go down on their anger; rather than behaving like the elite who depend upon and look down on the labor of their slaves and freedpersons, they are encouraged to labor and work honestly with their hands; rather than engaging in the language of division and suspicion that reinforces social division, they should only build up; all of the anger, wrangling, and slander that differences create and that tear a community apart should be replaced with kindness and tenderhearted forgiveness. Such forgiveness and kindness are necessary in a diverse community where different social mores can create unintentional hurt and misunderstanding. All of this should be rooted in love, as Christ loved and gave himself up for them. The counter-cultural character of these virtues is summed up in the last verse. Rather than modeling themselves on a ruler whose power is in strength, military might, and cold-blooded subjection of the enemy (the most striking feature of the reliefs of Aphrodisias is the *lack of expression* on the faces of the emperors when faced with the terror of their captives), followers of Jesus are to be renewed in the image of a savior who gave himself up for them in love. This is a new identity, yes, but one that is fundamentally different from anything the empire has on offer.

The Armor of God

Such fundamental difference is reinforced by Paul's description of the armor of God in Eph 6:10–17. This is, paradoxically, a description of weapons that themselves undermine enmity. The recipients of this letter would have been familiar with the many ways in which armor was used in imperial iconography. The goddess Roma, depicted with Caesar on coins and reliefs, was often surrounded by weaponry.[33] Caesar himself was depicted in full armor, and the focal point of his Forum in Rome was a temple to the war god, Mars Ultor.[34]

However, this depiction of armor also contains a rich set of allusions to Isaiah, the prophetic book that most clearly emphasized the inclusion of the gentiles into God's hopes for a new heaven and a new earth. As a result, this is the passage that brings to a climax Paul's assertions throughout the letter that the inclusion of the peoples is the mysterious plan that God has been working on all along, that the promises will only be fulfilled when all the peoples of the

---

33. Long, "Ephesians," 303.
34. Lopez, *Apostle*, 62.

world are included in the inheritance of the saints, and that the importance of this mission explains Paul's willingness to suffer for it.

Using verb forms that indicate that he is talking to the community as a whole and not to individuals, Paul echoes the baptismal language of "putting on" found earlier in the letter. Echoing the Greek form of Isa 11:5, he describes the belt of truth and the breastplate of justice.[35] In Isaiah, the shoot from the stump of Jesse is the one who, wearing this truth and justice, will act for the poor and judge the wicked (11:3-4). His rule, like that of Jesus in Ephesians, will be a sign to other peoples that God is glorious and has redeemed his people from their captivity (11:10-16).

Echoing again the beautiful feet of those who announce peace in Isa 52:7, Paul describes shoes that will equip the missional community to proclaim the gospel of peace (Eph 6:15). For, as Gorman puts it, the gospel must not be taken to the world but *walked* into the world, incarnationally, as we might say.[36] And, as in Isaiah, this peace of the gospel that Paul proclaims in Ephesians is rooted in an alternative sovereignty. In spite of all appearances to the contrary, God is the one who reigns. This, of course, is the central message of hope in Ephesians.

Paul also echoes Isa 59:17. In a context that laments Israel's inability to practice justice or righteousness, Isaiah describes God's decision to intervene by putting on justice like a breastplate and the helmet of salvation on his head. Paul's language in Eph 6, however, is consistent with the rest of the epistle. Whereas in Isaiah God comes clothed not only in justice and salvation but also in vengeance and fury, the community in Ephesus is to foreground the peacemaking work of Christ on the cross. Their only weapon is God's word of restoration, nourishment, and forgiveness (see Isa 55:10-13). In short, it is a word that bears the fruit of good works, truth, and justice (Eph 5:9).

Paul, however, does not merely echo Isaiah; he radically recontextualizes these verses. For in addition to Isaianic texts which celebrate the welcoming of the peoples into the community of Israel, there are other texts which speak of God's judgment on unfaithful nations. Two of the texts we addressed above occur in the context of such vengeance. In Isa 11, God's people will swoop down on the Philistines, plunder the people of the east and put forth their hands against Edom, Moab, and the Ammonites (11:14). In Isa 59, God will deal out wrath and requital to his enemies (59:18). It is striking therefore that, while Paul borrows the terminology of these passages, he does so in a way

---

35. On justice as a more faithful translation of δικαιοσύνη, see Keesmaat and Walsh, *Romans Disarmed*, 12.

36. Gorman, *Becoming*, 206.

which rejects such violent judgment on behalf of God's people. Rather than appropriating the imagery of Isa 59:17 in its entirety, Paul stops short. Vengeance and fury are *not* part of the armor of this community. As we have seen, in Ephesians, those who follow Jesus are living out a different story, one that challenges the parameters and assumptions not only of the Roman Empire, but also of Israel when she acts like empire.

Not everyone in the community would have caught these allusions to the story of Israel. However, for τὰ ἔθνη in the Ephesian community, achingly familiar with the prevalence of armor on coins, statues, in temples, and on reliefs, the image of a community whose identity is given strength not by weapons of destruction but by truth, justice, peace, faithfulness, salvation, and the life-giving Word of God would have been deeply liberating and hopeful.

As these allusions show, Paul's conviction that in Jesus all are citizens with the saints is rooted in a grand narrative about God's hopes for all the peoples of the world. The tearing down of the wall of enmity is not merely a side issue in the story of salvation that Paul is telling; it is the crux of the narrative, a central outcome, the evidence that Jesus's death has been a reconciling force for all peoples, and through them for all of creation (although this latter emphasis is not explored in Ephesians).[37] In short, the missional center of the gospel is rooted in the welcome of the peoples, τὰ ἔθνη, into the household of God. Or, to put it another way, without the inclusion of the peoples, that household is missing some of the pillars that make it a temple and a home for God.

Citizens of the Kingdom

As we return to our question from the outset of this chapter, we realize that the world in which the letter to the Ephesians was written and our own are not that far apart. And it is clear that in participating in the rhetoric of exclusion and fear, many Christians are not just diminishing the gospel, they are failing to embody the gospel in the life of their community.

So, what would it look like if those who followed Jesus really sought to embody the new community that they are called to be? What might it look like to make citizenship in the household of God a reality for those excluded by the national constructs of empire that surround us?

---

37. I consider this to be another way of describing Gorman's placing of peacemaking at the heart of both Ephesians and the gospel. The peacemaking that Christ's death effects is seen in this breaking down of enmity between various people groups. See Gorman, *Becoming*, 206–7.

At the very least, it might mean being more intentional about how we as a community define ethnicity and political allegiance. Perhaps that will mean deliberately holding small groups in our churches that together watch films with subtitles, set in the countries with which our country is at war. Perhaps it will mean reading the literature of the countries whose peoples our governments are trying to exclude. Perhaps it will mean trying to enter into their stories so that we can see how they resonate with our own.

Or perhaps it will mean following the lead of churches such as Augustana Lutheran in Portland, which provides sanctuary for those who are facing deportation.[38] Perhaps it will mean joining an organization such as the Interfaith Movement for Immigrant Justice, which accompanies immigrants facing detention and deportation and engages in political advocacy.[39] Perhaps it will mean becoming a part of a community that welcomes refugees such as Romero House in Toronto or the Sisters of St. Joseph, who wait at the border between Canada and the United States in order to provide assistance and shelter to refugees entering Canada.[40]

By engaging in these kinds of activities and entering into the lives of those whom our culture considers a threat or uncivilized, perhaps we too will begin to reconfigure ethnicity and national identity. Perhaps we too will begin to realize that we were once aliens and strangers and have now been welcomed into a new household. Perhaps we too will realize that by inviting other peoples into the story, we are finally entering into it ourselves.

---

38. For the full story see Steve Duin, "Sanctuary and Justice at Augustana Lutheran Church," *OregonLive/The Oregonian*, Sept. 23, 2014. https://www.oregonlive.com/news/oregonian/steve_duin/2014/09/steve_duin_sanctuary_and_justi.html.

39. For more information on the Interfaith Movement for Immigrant Justice, see imirj.org.

40. For more information on Romero House, see romerohouse.org. The Sisters of St. Joseph house refugees at Casa Maria Homes in Peterborough, Ontario. https://www.csjcanada.org/new-canadians-and-refugees.

.... Chapter 15

Following the Lamb Wherever He Goes: Missional Ecclesiology in Revelation 7 and 14:1–5

Dean Flemming

The two-part vision of the people of God in Rev 7:1–17, along with its counterpart in 14:1–5, have shaped the imagination of Christian communities in numerous ways. Few ecclesial images in the New Testament have elicited such a range of interpretive perspectives as the 144,000 who are sealed from the tribes of Israel (7:4–8), the white-robed multinational multitude (7:9–17), or the 144,000-strong company of virgins "who have not defiled themselves with women" (14:1–5). Any attempt to interpret these texts theologically must wrestle, not only with the role of these ecclesial visions within the unfolding story of God's triumph over evil in Revelation, but also with how they might shape the identity and mission of the church in its various historical and global contexts.

This essay argues that undertaking a missional reading of these texts can help to address both these issues. On one hand, reading these passages missionally can lead to a richer, more faithful understanding of John's vision of God's people in Revelation. On the other hand, it offers the church resources for living out its present calling as a missional community. Missional interpre-

---

It is an extraordinary privilege to dedicate this essay to my friend Michael Gorman. I have learned from his writings how to read Scripture more faithfully in view of God's mission. I have seen in his life of faithfulness an example of "becoming the gospel" in character and practice.

tation has gained considerable traction in recent years,[1] but it has seldom been applied to the book of Revelation.[2] What if, however, we read the Apocalypse as a whole, and John's ecclesial visions in chapters 7 and 14 in particular, as *missional texts*? How might these visions bear witness to the sweeping narrative of God's mission in the world, and how might they energize and equip God's people to participate in that divine mission within their local settings?

This study explores John's missional ecclesiology in Rev 7:1–17 and 14:1–5. First, I focus on the identity of the 144,000 Israelites and the multinational multitude, including some ways they have been understood in reception history. Second, I explore how these visions unveil a character sketch of the church in mission, one that helps shape ecclesial communities in John's day and our own.

Future Visions and John's Audience

Before undertaking a closer look at Revelation's visions of the church in 7:1–17 and 14:1–5, I will address two preliminary questions: first, where are they located within the overall story that the Apocalypse tells; and second, how do these pictures of God's people relate to the Christian communities John addresses in chapters 2 and 3?

Both texts fall within the long series of strange and often terrifying judgments in Rev 6–20. Within these central chapters of the book, the seer pictures the future destiny of God's people in the form of three strategically placed visions.[3] The first comprises an interlude between the sixth and seventh seals— John's picture of the 144,000 sealed Israelites, immediately followed by the immeasurable multitude of worshipers (7:1–17). Second, John narrates the story of the "two witnesses" (11:1–13), during an interlude between the sixth and seventh trumpets. These dramatic figures represent the church as a whole in its

---

1. See, especially, the seminal work of Christopher J. H. Wright, *The Mission of God: Unlocking the Bible's Grand Narrative* (Downers Grove, IL: IVP Academic, 2006) and the essays in Michael W. Goheen, ed., *Reading the Bible Missionally* (Grand Rapids: Eerdmans, 2016).

2. See, however, Dean Flemming, "Revelation and the *Missio Dei*: Toward a Missional Reading of the Apocalypse," *JTI* 6 (2012): 161–78; Michael J. Gorman, *Reading Revelation Responsibly: Uncivil Worship and Witness: Following the Lamb into the New Creation* (Eugene, OR: Cascade, 2011).

3. Joseph L. Mangina, "God, Israel, and Ecclesia in the Apocalypse," in *Revelation and the Politics of Apocalyptic Interpretation*, ed. Richard B. Hays and Stefan Alkier (Waco: Baylor University Press, 2012), 95.

witnessing role.[4] A third interlude offers a reprise of the 144,000, now appearing on Mount Zion with the Lamb (14:1–5). This pause in the action continues with three angelic messages (14:6–13) and two visions of the harvest (14:14–20), before giving way to the "last" series of judgments in Revelation, the seven plagues/bowls (15:1; 16:1). Due to space constraints and the specific concerns of this essay, I will focus on the first and third of these visionary texts.

What, then, is the connection between these pictures of the eschatological people of God (Rev 7:1–17; 14:1–5) and John's audience, whether the ἐκκλησίαι in places like Smyrna and Sardis (2–3) or readers today? As Joseph L. Mangina wisely notes, ἐκκλησία—a term that drops from sight between the end of the messages to the churches (3:22) and John's epilogue (22:16)—represents who John's readers *are*. In contrast, the visions in chapters 7 and 14 reveal "what they must *become*."[5] More precisely, what the church "becomes" operates in two senses. On one level, the visions of God's people unveil the church's future destiny, as God exercises judgment on all powers of evil and ultimately brings forth a new heaven and a new earth. On another level, however, these visions reveal what the ἐκκλησίαι must "become" in their present life in the world. Negatively, John's future visions give these churches the imaginative resources to resist the kinds of compromises with the idolatrous empire that Christ's messages expose. Positively, Revelation's pictures of the church's future energize local congregations to live as communities who bear witness to God's truth and faithfully follow the Lamb. How, then, should we read the symbolic language in these compelling visions of the people of God? I begin with an overview of each vision.

The Sealed 144,000 (Rev 7:1–8)

Revelation 6, which describes the opening of the first six seals of divine judgment, ends with a question: in view of the wrath of God and the Lamb, "who is able to stand?" (6:17). The answer comes in part with a vision of four angels,

---

4. John makes this connection clear when he identifies the witnesses as lampstands (11:4), a symbol that in chapter 1 represents the seven churches (1:12, 20).

5. Mangina, "God, Israel, and Ecclesia," 95; italics original. The term "church" (ἐκκλησία) occurs twenty times in Revelation, all but once in chapters 1–3. Popular dispensationalism holds that the reason for this linguistic disappearing act is that the church has been "raptured" out of the world at the beginning of chapter four. Consequently, the visions that follow have little to do with the church's existence in the world. But such a reading renders Revelation into "an escapist fantasy with strongly gnostic overtones" (Mangina, "God, Israel, and Ecclesia," 94), in which both the church and its mission are "left behind."

"standing" at the earth's four corners to hold back the mighty winds of judgment on the earth (7:1). This allows another angel to seal 144,000 servants of God, drawn from "every tribe of the people of Israel" (7:2–4). The fuller answer to the question in 6:17 unfolds in the picture of a great, multinational multitude "standing before the throne and before the Lamb" (7:9). Whom do these two groups represent, and what is their relationship to one another?

John's picture of the sealed 144,000 spotlights two key aspects of their identity. First, they are members of the tribes of Israel (Rev 7:4–8). Some interpreters, both ancient and modern, take this identification literally, signifying ethnic Jews or Jewish Christians.[6] Popular dispensationalism, for example, typically reads 144,000 as the number of the Jewish evangelists who will preach the gospel to those who have been left behind on earth after the church has been "raptured" to heaven. But a literal reading is unlikely, given that the 144,000 are called "servants" (δοῦλοι, 7:3), a term that throughout Revelation refers to the whole people of God, Jews and gentiles alike.[7] Indeed, nowhere does Revelation's portrait of God's people distinguish between Jewish and gentile Christians.

At the same time, the identification of the sealed 144,000 with Israel in Rev 7:4–8 is far from incidental. John imagines God's people as the restored Israel in the Messianic age. The number 144,000 is clearly symbolic. It is the product of 12 x 12, representing the fullness of the twelve tribes of Israel, times one thousand, which, biblically, signifies a vast number. The number 144,000, then, symbolizes an unimaginably large people of God.[8] It stands for fullness and completion, announcing that Jewish hopes for eschatological restoration *are* fulfilled in the redeemed followers of the Lamb.[9]

---

6. E.g., Irenaeus, *Against the Heresies* 5.30.2, cited in Judith Kovacs and Christopher Rowland, *Revelation: The Apocalypse of Jesus Christ* (Malden, MA: Blackwell, 2004), 102; Victorinus, *Commentary on the Apocalypse* 7.2, in *Revelation*, ACCS NT 12, ed. William C. Weinrich (Downers Grove, IL: IVP Academic, 2014), 104; Oecumenius, *Commentary on the Apocalypse* 7.1–8, ACCS NT 12:105; John Wesley, *Explanatory Notes upon the New Testament*, repr. (Salem, OH: Schmul, n.d.), 676; Margaret Barker, *The Revelation of Jesus Christ* (Edinburgh: T & T Clark, 2000), 158; Tim LaHaye, *Revelation Unveiled* (Grand Rapids: Zondervan, 1999), 149–52.

7. The word δοῦλοι, literally, "slaves," can designate John's audience (1:1; 22:6), the "prophets and saints" (11:18; cf. 10:7), or the redeemed in heaven (19:5; 22:3).

8. Andy Johnson, *Holiness and the Missio Dei* (Eugene, OR: Cascade, 2016), 167. Ancient interpreters who take the 144,000 to refer to the whole people of God include Bede, *Explanation of the Apocalypse* 7.4, ACCS NT 12:102, and Primasius, *Commentary on the Apocalypse* 7.9, ACCS NT 12:110–11.

9. Stephen S. Smalley, *The Revelation to John: A Commentary on the Greek Text of the Apocalypse* (Downers Grove, IL: IVP Academic, 2005), 185.

Moreover, as Richard Bauckham demonstrates, the tribal census in Rev 7:4–8 suggests that the 144,000 are pictured as an army of holy warriors. Prepared for holy war, they follow the Davidic Messiah, the Lion of the tribe of Judah (5:5; 7:5).[10] This Lion, however, turns out to be a Lamb (5:6), and the messianic army fights and conquers by their own faithful witness and by the poured out "blood of the Lamb" (12:11).

A second crucial characteristic of the 144,000 involves their bearing the seal of God on their foreheads (Rev 7:3, 4). This visible seal denotes God's protection. Even as God's mark on the forehead shielded the faithful in Israel from destruction in Ezekiel's ancient prophecy (Ezek 9:3–10; cf. Exod 12:22–28), so John assures Christians that the sealed 144,000 will be protected from God's wrath (Rev 6:17; 7:1–3; 9:4), although not from all suffering. Further, the seal conveys identity and ownership. The 144,000 belong to God alone, in contrast to followers of the beast, who brandish the beast's mark on their foreheads (13:16–18; 14:9–11). Ultimately, the sealing of God's people evokes God's promise of salvation and membership in the people of God.

Do the sealed 144,000 represent the *whole* people of God? Some interpreters think that their numbering *out of* the tribes of Israel indicates that they comprise a special group *within* God's people, whether specifically martyrs (see Rev 6:9–11),[11] or a remnant group of Jewish and gentile Christians.[12] It is better, however, to take the sealed 144,000 as a symbol for *all* faithful Lamb followers. This fits the broader term "servant" in 7:3 (cf. 1:1; 22:6). What is more, in chapter 14, the 144,000 signify the "redeemed" by the Lamb (14:3, 4), whom John earlier identified as those ransomed from every tribe and nation (5:9).

These servants of God represent the church on earth (Rev 7:1), "situated in the midst of the tribulation associated with the seven seals of judgment."[13] Although John envisions end-time apocalyptic realities, this picture of God's people speaks with a clarion voice to his audience in Roman Asia. *They are*

---

10. For arguments supporting this identification, see Richard Bauckham, *The Theology of the Book of Revelation* (Cambridge: Cambridge University Press, 1993), 76–80; Richard Bauckham, *The Climax of Prophecy: Studies on the Book of Revelation* (Edinburgh: T & T Clark, 1993), 210–37.

11. E.g., G. B. Caird, *The Revelation of St. John the Divine*, HNTC (New York: Harper and Row, 1996), 96–97; Mitchell G. Reddish, *Revelation*, SHBC (Macon, GA: Smyth and Helwys, 2001), 152; Bauckham, *Theology*, 77–79.

12. Brian K. Blount, *Revelation: A Commentary*, NTL (Louisville: Westminster John Knox, 2009), 140, 145–46; G. K. Beale, *The Book of Revelation: A Commentary on the Greek Text*, NIGTC (Grand Rapids: Eerdmans, 1999), 423; David E. Aune, *Revelation 6–16*, WBC (Nashville: Thomas Nelson, 1998), 444–45.

13. Gorman, *Reading Revelation Responsibly*, 133.

the restored Israel, who receive the promise that God's seal of ownership will protect them through the suffering they must face.

The Multinational Multitude (Rev 7:9–17)

The second part of chapter 7 pictures a countless, multinational multitude in heaven, "standing before the throne and before the Lamb" (Rev 7:9). Their portrait is striking: they wear white robes, symbolizing purity and triumph; they hold palm branches, signaling victory and celebration; and they trumpet the salvation of God and the Lamb (7:9–10). Because they have "come out of the great ordeal" and have washed their robes in the Lamb's blood (7:14), many interpreters, from the church fathers on, have identified them as martyrs.[14] Other early commentators limit this crowd to believing gentiles, in contrast to Jewish believers in the first part of chapter 7.[15] But the text leads us to recognize them as the same group as in 7:1–8—all the Lamb's followers—seen from a different perspective.[16]

Here the pattern resembles that in chapter 5, when John first *hears* the elder speak of the Lion of the tribe of Judah but then immediately *sees* a slaughtered Lamb (Rev 5:5–6). In chapter 7, John *hears* the number of those sealed from the tribes of Israel (7:4), but he *sees* an unnumbered assembly from all nations (7:9). Like a two-paneled altarpiece in which the scenes are hinged together, chapter 7 paints a dual vision of the church. The first scene envisions the afflicted church on earth, sealed in the face of tribulation; the second shows the victorious church in heaven, which already experiences some of the blessings of God's new creation (7:15–17; cf. 21–22). To use another analogy, narratively, they function like "before" and "after" photos of the same people, posted on the same screen. But these are not simply eschatological realities. Although both visions picture aspects of the church's future, both represent what God's people must embody now. For John, the ἐκκλησίαι live as a foretaste of what is to come. The church is simultaneously the restored Israel, mustered for battle against the evil powers that oppose them, *and* the multinational community of the redeemed, engaging in perpetual worship of God and the Lamb (7:15).

---

14. E.g., Andrew of Caesarea, *Commentary on the Apocalypse* 7.9–10, ACCS NT 12:111; Tertullian, *Scorpiace* 12, ACCS NT 12:114; Bauckham, *Climax of Prophecy*, 226–29; Gordon D. Fee, *Revelation*, New Covenant Commentary Series (Eugene, OR: Cascade, 2011), 114–15.

15. Oecumenius, *Apocalypse* 7.9–17, ACCS NT 12:106, 110; Hippolytus, in Kovacs and Rowland, *Revelation*, 103.

16. See, e.g., Primasius, *Apocalypse* 7.9, ACCS NT 12:110–11; Caesarius of Arles, *Exposition on the Apocalypse* 7.9, *Homily* 6, ACCS NT 12:111, and most modern commentators.

The Redeemed "Virgins" (Rev 14:1-5)

Revelation 14:1-5 recasts the 144,000, now standing with the Lamb on Mount Zion (14:1). Like chapter 7, Rev 14 forms a pause in John's eschatological drama. It offers a stunning contrast to chapter 13, in which an unholy trinity of the dragon and the two beasts unleash their fury on God's people and demand universal worship from those who dwell on earth. Chapter 14 reassures John's readers, giving them an advance screening of the outcome of the conflict against the powers of evil. The redeemed stand victorious on the holy mountain, and God judges those who persist in worshiping the beast.

Our primary concern rests with Rev 14:1-5 and its picture of the church. How does this company of 144,000 Lamb followers relate to the sealed 144,000 from Israel in 7:1-8 and the multinational throng of worshipers in 7:9-17? Although some interpreters see the redeemed in 14:1-5 as a different group from either of those in chapter 7,[17] the connections between 7:1-17 and 14:1-5 in structure, language, and imagery are striking.[18] John here reintroduces us to the 144,000 who were sealed for God in 7:1-8 and sharpens the focus of their image. The seal on the foreheads of God's servants (7:3) is now revealed as the divine name, emblazoned on the foreheads of the redeemed (14:1). At the same time, this community represents the "anti-image" of the beast's followers, whose name is marked on their foreheads (13:16-17).[19] In other ways, the redeemed 144,000 resemble the multinational multitude in 7:9-17. Both companies, for example, stand before the throne in the Lamb's presence (7:9, 11; 14:1, 3), voicing songs of praise to God and the Lamb (7:10; 14:3). All three passages, then, offer different perspectives on the identity and mission of the whole people of God.

The vision in 14:1-5 locates the 144,000 on Mount Zion, standing with the Lamb (14:1). In the biblical tradition, Mount Zion symbolizes not only God's eschatological kingdom but also his security, victory, and presence.[20] Like the

---

17. For Victorinus (*Apocalypse* 20.1, ACCS NT 12:214) and Oecumenicus (*Apocalypse* 14:1-5, ACCS NT 12:215), the 144,000 in 14:1-5 represent Jewish Christians, who are converted in the last days. Modern dispensationalist author Tim LaHaye suggests that, in contrast to the Jewish evangelists in 7:4-8, these are "probably the most outstanding 144,000 saints of the Church from the early days of the spread of the gospel to the Rapture of the Church" (*Revelation Unveiled*, 232).

18. See David Aune, who observes a parallel three-part structure in both passages (*Revelation 6-16*, 796).

19. Elisabeth Schüssler Fiorenza, *The Book of Revelation: Justice and Judgment* (Philadelphia: Fortress, 1985), 182.

20. Reddish, *Revelation*, 273.

vision of the great multitude in 7:9-17, this scene shows the church participating in the salvation and triumph of the Lamb. It anticipates the church's triumph over the beast and the powers of evil.

We cannot read 14:1-5, however, without encountering some rough sledding. In verse 4, John famously describes the redeemed 144,000 as "these who have not defiled themselves with women, for they are virgins." Many church fathers take the term παρθένοι ("virgins") at face value. Methodius, for example, concluded from this passage that those who would be like God must "aspire to the virginity of Christ."[21] Augustine, in turn, urged his unmarried readers not to lose the good of their virginity, for only virgins can "follow the Lamb wherever he goes" (14:4).[22]

At the same time, some modern interpreters read these words as poison arrows, targeted at both sexuality and women. For Tina Pippin, women are stunningly absent from Rev 14:4: "The 144,000 represent the whole number of the faithful, and they are all men." What is more, she observes a negative portrayal of women's bodies, which are capable of defiling men. "The apocalypse," she concludes, "is not a safe space for women."[23]

We cannot dismiss such readings with the flick of a hand. The language of Rev 14:4a is difficult. Nevertheless, this text need not be read as a denigration of either women or human sexuality. As in Rev 7:4-8, here the military background is important. The point of John's imagery seems to be this: even as Israel's warriors practiced ritual purity by abstaining from sexual relations during battle (Deut 23:9-10; 1 Sam 21:5), so the church is called to *moral* purity in order to overcome the Lamb's enemies.[24] Likewise, the masculine term παρθένοι—as a hyperbole—may refer to the same holy warriors, who temporarily refrain from sexual relations while on duty.[25] Once again, the language in 14:4

---

21. Methodius, *Symposium* 1.5, ACCS NT 12:217.

22. Augustine, *Holy Virginity* 12, 14.26-29, ACCS NT 12:219-21. See also Cyprian, *The Dress of Virgins* 4-5, ACCS NT 12:217; Jerome, *Against Jovinian* 1.40, ACCS NT 12:218.

23. Tina Pippin, *Death and Desire: The Rhetoric of Gender in the Apocalypse of John* (Louisville: Westminster/John Knox, 1992), 70, 80. See also Hanna Stenström, "'They Have Not Defiled Themselves With Women...'; Christian Identity According to the Book of Revelation," in *A Feminist Companion to the Apocalypse of John*, ed. Amy-Jill Levine (London: T & T Clark, 2009), 33-54.

24. Bauckham, *Theology*, 77-78; Marianne Meye Thompson, "Reading What Is Written in the Book of Life: Theological Interpretation of the Book of Revelation Today," in *Revelation and the Politics of Apocalyptic Interpretation*, 167.

25. Mangina, "God, Israel, and Ecclesia," 96. Craig R. Koester, however, points out that the use of παρθένοι for *male* virgins is almost unprecedented in the first century (but see *Jos. As.* 4:7 and 8:1). Instead, Koester takes virgin as a female image, which anticipates the

is symbolic, not literal. It cannot be restricted to the celibate or the married, males or females. This community of holy warriors and virgins embraces all who follow the Lamb (14:4b), all who are redeemed for God (14:4c; cf. 5:9), all who stand with the Lamb on Mount Zion (14:1). John's churches, then, see an advance picture of their future, one that calls them to follow the Lamb "wherever he goes" (14:4).

The Missional Character of the Church in Revelation 7:1-17 and 14:1-5

How, then, do the visions of God's people in Rev 7 and 14 shape and energize the church's participation in the mission of God? These passages offer a rich, multidimensional portrait of the church in mission.

A Redeemed Church

Revelation as a whole, and the visions in 7:1-17 and 14:1-5 in particular, bear witness to God's sweeping mission to redeem all people and to bring the whole creation to its intended goal, as well as the church's active role in that mission. In response to God's gracious, life-giving purpose for the world, the multiethnic multitude thunders its praise,

> Salvation belongs to our God
> who is seated on the throne,
> and to the Lamb! (7:10)

In the context, "salvation" (σωτηρία; cf. Rev 12:10; 19:1) surely includes victory and deliverance for God's faithful. Stamped with the seal of God's ownership and protection, they have emerged triumphant out of tribulation (7:3, 4, 14). But this "salvation" likely reaches beyond deliverance from God's enemies alone. It also embraces the kind of wholeness and well-being for which God's people offer praise in 7:15-17. This salvation "belongs" to God; it defines God's identity.[26] In the words of the Psalmist, "Our God is a God of salvation" (Ps 68:20). At the same time, John's audience must understand that salvation belongs to *our* God, *not* to Rome, or the emperor, or any other god or savior.

---

church's role as bride of the Lamb (19:7; 21:2, 9) in *Revelation: A New Translation with Introduction and Commentary*, AB (New Haven: Yale University Press, 2014), 610-11, 618-19.

26. Wright, *Mission of God*, 118.

Following the Lamb Wherever He Goes

In the empire, politics and religion are intertwined, and Rome touted its role as the dispenser of peace, well-being, and salvation. Here God's people stand before the throne, boldly announcing that Rome's pretenses amount to a mere puff of smoke; only God and the Lamb can save.

Furthermore, "our God" is the God of Israel. Revelation 7:9–17 creatively reworks the story of God and Israel, particularly God's great act of deliverance in the exodus. David Barr notes that the images of palm branches, white clothing, and proclaiming salvation recall the Feast of Tabernacles, which celebrated God's victory over the Egyptians and Israel's safe passage to the promised land.[27] Exodus imagery also looms large in 7:15–17: God will "tabernacle" (σκηνόω) with his people (7:15; cf. Ezek 37:27–28) and give them food, water, and protection (7:16–17). In Revelation's narrative, "the 144,000 from the tribes of Israel . . . find their way through the wilderness trials of the latter days to the New Jerusalem."[28]

Salvation, however, also belongs to the Lamb (Rev 7:10). The story of the slaughtered Lamb forms the master narrative in Revelation, one that gives meaning to all of history. Twice in chapter 14, John calls God's faithful the "redeemed" (ἀγοράζω, 14:3, 4). This language evokes the hymn in chapter 5, in which the slain Lamb redeemed for God people from every tribe and nation by his blood, making them a kingdom and priests (5:9–10). In chapter 14, the redeemed church stands in closest relationship with the Lamb. They bear the Lamb's name on their foreheads and follow him "wherever he goes" (14:1, 4). Following the Lamb includes participating in the Lamb's story—his faithful witness, death, resurrection, and exaltation. Prior to chapter 14, the beast wages war against God's people, conquers them, and kills them (13:7, 9, 15). Now, however, they stand with the Lamb on Mount Zion, raised and vindicated by God (14:1).[29]

A similar pattern of death and vindication appears in chapter 7. The first scene spotlights the sealed holy warriors, prepared for persecution and possible martyrdom (Rev 7:1–8). In the second scene, we catch sight of the victorious people of God, raised from tribulation through washing their robes in the Lamb's blood (7:9–17). The church shares both in Christ's suffering and his victory over evil. In 7:14, the faithful "have washed their robes," paradoxically making them "white in the blood of the Lamb." Here the Lamb's blood signifies Christ's costly, sacrificial death for others. Although, as we have seen,

---

27. David L. Barr, *Tales of the End: A Narrative Commentary on the Book of Revelation* (Santa Rosa, CA: Polebridge, 1998), 74.

28. John Christopher Thomas and Frank D. Macchia, *Revelation*, THNTC (Grand Rapids: Eerdmans, 2016), 506.

29. Johnson, *Holiness and the Missio Dei*, 166.

some interpreters take this as a reference to martyrdom, the focus here rests on the blood of *Christ*, not that of his followers. What, then, does it mean for God's people to "do their own laundry?" This is likely a striking image for the persevering faith and costly allegiance that enables God's people to participate in the cleansing, redeeming work of Christ (1:6; 5:9).[30]

A Multinational Church

John's ecclesial vision in Rev 7:9–17 focuses on "a great multitude that no one could count," drawn from every nation, tribe, people, and language (7:9). This multiethnic throng of worshipers fulfills God's covenant promise that through Abraham "all the families of the earth shall be blessed" (Gen 12:3). God's missional promise to Abraham in Gen 12:1–3 arrives in the context of, and as a response to, God's dealing with all nations in Gen 10–11.[31] These nations "spread abroad on the earth" in chapter 10 (see Gen 10:32). But when they try to join forces against God and make a name for themselves in chapter 11, God "spreads" them across the face of the earth (Gen 11:1–9). Christopher J. H. Wright spots "a great trajectory—from the 'tribes, languages and nations' of Gen 10, who stood in need of redemptive blessing, to that 'great multitude that no one could count, from every nation, tribe, people and language', who will constitute the redeemed humanity in the new creation (Rev. 7:9)."[32]

The church, then, remains both the restored Israel (Rev 7:4–8) and the ethnically diverse people of God (7:9). In addition to finally realizing what God promised to Abraham, the vision of the great multitude fulfills Israel's servant role as a "light to the nations" (Isa 42:6; 49:6). In Revelation, this happens through the Lamb's spilling his own blood to ransom for God a servant people from every tribe, language, people, and nation (Rev 5:9–10).

The same four terms show up again in chapter 14 (see Rev 14:6). Hard on the heels of the vision of the 144,000 redeemed "from the earth" (14:3), John sees an angel proclaiming "an eternal gospel" to the earth-dwellers of every nation (14:6). The message is unambiguous: "Fear God and give him glory" (14:7)— or face God's judgment. Although this vision forms the first of three angelic messages to the unbelieving nations, it provides "a kind of commentary" on

---

30. Beale, *Book of Revelation*, 436–38; Felise Tavo, *Woman, Mother and Bride: An Exegetical Investigation into the 'Ecclesial' Notions of the Apocalypse*, BTS 3 (Leuven: Peters, 2007), 167–68.

31. Christopher J. H. Wright, *The Mission of God's People: A Biblical Theology of the Church's Mission* (Grand Rapids: Zondervan, 2010), 70–71.

32. Wright, *Mission of God's People*, 71.

14:1-5.³³ As Joseph Mangina recognizes, we see a similar pattern here as that in chapter 7; in both, a more limited group (144,000) is followed by a global depiction of all peoples and nations. However, whereas in 7:9-17, the multicultural multitude represents those who are *already* followers of the Lamb, those who hear the gospel in 14:6-7 must *become* worshipers of God.³⁴

Later, in Rev 15:3-4, those who have conquered the beast sing their confident hope that "all nations" will fear God, glorify his name, and worship before him. The actions of fearing, glorifying, and worshiping God represent genuine repentance and trust, not a forced confession.³⁵ Such visions of the nations turning to God not only reveal the character of God's seeking love for all people, but they also invite John's audience to get caught up in that transforming mission to the nations.

John's vision of the uncountable multitude standing before the throne in heaven in Rev 7:9-17 surely offered hope and encouragement to the marginalized Christian communities in Asia. Not only the sheer size of the community of worshipers but also its composition of people from every tribe and nation would stretch their imaginations almost to the breaking point. It would assure them that their costly, prophetic witness *will* produce a harvest. This vision, however, is not simply a snapshot of the church's heavenly future. It also shapes the identity and mission of God's people in the present, both for John's context and that of the church today. It continues to call God's people to *be* a consciously multiethnic, multicultural, multiracial people of God in a world teeming with ethnic divisions, religious animosities, and racial biases. Amid all their differences, God's people unite in the one song that proclaims: "Salvation belongs to our God . . . and to the Lamb" (7:10).

A Witnessing Church

From Revelation's perspective, the church's participation in the *missio Dei* involves bearing faithful witness to God and the Lamb. That witness happens in the public square. God's seal and the name of the Lamb and the Father are emblazoned on the foreheads of God's servants, the most visible place possible (Rev 7:3; 14:1). The seal enables God's people to fly their colors of allegiance to God and the Lamb. The faithful stand in brazen antithesis to the earth-dwellers, whose

---

33. Joseph L. Mangina, *Revelation*, Brazos Theological Commentary on the Bible (Grand Rapids: Brazos, 2010), 174.
34. Mangina, *Revelation*, 174.
35. Dean Flemming, *Why Mission?* (Nashville: Abingdon, 2015), 115.

foreheads bear the number and name of the beast (13:16–18). John's audience faces a stark choice—either publicly display the beast's mark or God's name.

The church's witness involves proclaiming the truth that salvation resides in our God (Rev 7:10), against the idols of the empire, which are no-gods. Furthermore, the statement, "in their mouth no lie was found" (14:5) in part reflects Revelation's concern for faithful witness to the truth, in contrast to the lies and falsehood of Satan and the beast (cf. 1:2, 9; 6:9; 11:3–13; 12:11; 13:14; 19:20).[36] But those who share in God's mission not only *proclaim* the truth; they also *embody* it. God's witnesses "follow the Lamb wherever he goes" (14:4), which entails a costly witness of both word and poured-out life. Even as Jesus bore sacrificial witness to God's truth at the hands of the earthly powers (see "the testimony of Jesus," 12:17; 19:10), Lamb followers must be ready to speak and embody the truth when confronted with the power of the beast.[37]

Yet, Revelation once again assures God's people that this faithful and demanding witness *will* bear fruit. The seer pictures the redeemed community as "the first fruits (ἀπαρχή) of God and the Lamb" (Rev 14:4). "First fruits" constituted the first parts of the harvest offered to God, which demonstrated God's claim over the full harvest to come (Exod 23:19). In Revelation, the first fruits represent not a limited group but the whole people of God. First fruits point to "a far greater harvest to come from among the mass of human beings from whom the 144,000 have been redeemed."[38] John envisions a great ingathering of people for God, when the risen Christ comes to reap the harvest of the earth (Rev 14:14–16). In Rev 14:14–16, reaping the harvest constitutes a positive image, symbolizing that God will graciously gather an abundant harvest from all nations into his kingdom in the end (cf. Matt 9:37–38; Mark 4:29; John 4:35–38).[39]

A Suffering Church

From John's perspective, the church's faithful witness inevitably involves suffering. John affirms that God's holy warriors "follow the Lamb *wherever* he goes" (Rev 14:4, italics added). Where is the Lamb going? As the *slaughtered* Lamb, he goes to the cross. Resisting the idolatry and deceptive narratives of the empire comes with a cost attached. The way of the Lamb is "the way of conquering through suffering, victory through defeat, overcoming through

---

36. Bauckham, *Theology*, 78.
37. See Johnson, *Holiness and the* Missio Dei, 167.
38. Johnson, *Holiness and the* Missio Dei, 167.
39. See Bauckham, *Climax of Prophecy*, 290–96.

Following the Lamb Wherever He Goes

cruciform love."[40] For Christians in Asia, such cross-shaped discipleship may require sacrificing their social status, their livelihoods, their security, even their lives (2:13).[41] Yet this loving and sacrificial witness carries a missional effect. It magnetically will draw some from the world's nations to worship the God "who made heaven and earth" (14:7; see 14:6–7; 15:2–4; cf. 11:3–13).

Returning to chapter seven, the 144,000 servants of God are sealed *through*, not *from*, the trials and persecution to come (Rev 7:3–4). Later, a wise elder informs John that the great multitude from all nations are "they who have come out of the great ordeal" (7:14). The picture of the "great tribulation" (θλῖψις) finds its roots in Daniel's vision of a time of great anguish for God's people prior to the final coming of God's kingdom (Dan 12:1–4; cf. Matt 24:21; 2 *Baruch* 25:4). Accordingly, some interpreters read Revelation's "great ordeal" as an imminent event, still in the future.[42] Dispensationalist readings position the "great tribulation" *after* the "rapture" of the church. Consequently, the great multitude of Rev 7:9–17 must represent "Tribulation saints" who are saved during the tribulation period.[43] Nowhere, however, in either Revelation or the entire New Testament, do we find the notion that the church is guaranteed an *escape* from persecution and suffering. For John, the final tribulation is *already* underway (1:9; 2:9, 10). Indeed, θλῖψις ("tribulation") remains the "normal" experience of those who follow the Lamb.[44] The white-clad, palm-waving crowd in Rev 7 assures the church in history that God will sustain and protect them *in the midst of* suffering, not exempt them from it.

A Holy Church

John's portrait of the church in Rev 7 and 14 also spotlights its holiness. In 7:9–17, those who have come through tribulation wear white robes (7:9, 14). A wardrobe of white garments symbolizes both victory and purity in the Apocalypse (3:4–5, 18; 6:11). Earlier we noted the striking image of the tri-

---

40. Dean Flemming, "'On Earth as It Is in Heaven': Holiness and the People of God in Revelation," in *Holiness and Ecclesiology in the New Testament*, ed. Kent E. Brower and Andy Johnson (Grand Rapids: Eerdmans, 2007), 355.

41. Although some interpreters take "follow[ing] the Lamb wherever he goes" (Rev 14:4) as a metaphor for martyrdom (e.g., Aune, *Revelation 6–16*, 813–14; Reddish, *Revelation*, 274–75), this is too narrow. The emphasis falls on costly witness and discipleship, which *may* ultimately entail martyrdom.

42. E.g., G. R. Beasley-Murray, *Revelation*, NCB (Grand Rapids: Eerdmans, 1974), 146–47.

43. Lahaye, *Revelation Unveiled*, 161.

44. Mangina, "God, Israel, and Ecclesia," 98.

umphant church washing their robes with the only cleansing agent that can make them white—"the blood of the Lamb" (7:14).[45] Here the blessings that result from Christ's sacrificial death include moral purity. Forsaking "the sins of the idolatrous culture," they have "attached themselves to the Lamb in his holiness."[46] Later, clean robes become the mandatory "dress code" for entering New Jerusalem, the holy city (22:14). The church as the Lamb's bride adorns herself in pure, bright linen, woven from the righteous deeds of the "holy ones" (19:7–8).[47] In Revelation, what God's people wear on the outside symbolizes the holiness of their character and actions.

Chapter 14 pictures Lamb followers as holy warriors and a holy, priestly people. Like the high priest Aaron, who wears the name of his holy Lord on the turban that rests on his forehead (Exod 28:36–38), the foreheads of the redeemed publicly bear the name of God and the Lamb (Rev 14:1).[48] As we have seen, John likely pictures the saints as holy warriors, "who have not defiled themselves with women" (14:4). Israel's soldiers forsook the ritual defilement associated with sexual intercourse as they prepared for holy war. But here the church represents an even higher standard of holiness. As "virgins," they have *never* been defiled.[49] They are morally pure and holy ("blameless," v. 5), like the God they serve. It is also possible that this language evokes priests, who needed to avoid ritual defilement, in preparation for temple service.[50] This would fit Revelation's picture of the church as a community of priests (1:6; 5:10; 20:6).

Both images—holy warriors and priests—carry missional implications. This holy army, as Andy Johnson perceives, "have been missionally faithful in their costly battle with the beast, actively participating in the saving, reconciling, life-giving purposes of the missional God."[51] Likewise, as God set apart Israel to be a holy and priestly nation, conveying God's light to the surrounding nations (Exod 19:5–6; Isa 42:6; 49:6), so God's new priestly community mediates God's presence to the world's peoples, by its distinctive, Lamb-like witness (Rev 5:9–10; 7:9; 14:6–7; 15:3–4).

John's picture of the redeemed as "virgins" in Rev 14:4 may also anticipate the church's character as the faithful and pure bride of the Lamb (19:7–8;

---

45. Tavo, *Woman, Mother and Bride*, 167.
46. David A. deSilva, *Honor, Patronage, Kinship and Purity: Unlocking New Testament Culture* (Downers Grove, IL: IVP Academic, 2000), 303.
47. Flemming, "On Earth as It Is in Heaven," 351.
48. Johnson, *Holiness and the* Missio Dei, 167.
49. Thompson, "Reading What Is Written," 167.
50. Koester, *Revelation*, 610.
51. Johnson, *Holiness and the* Missio Dei, 167.

Following the Lamb Wherever He Goes

21:2, 9).⁵² What is more, the saints are free from lies and deceit (14:5). This entails, not only a truthful witness, but also moral integrity. Such integrity of word and life stands in glaring antithesis to Revelation's cast of deceptive characters, which includes Jezebel (2:20), fake apostles (2:2; cf. 3:9), Satan (12:9; 20:3, 8, 10), the false prophet (13:14; 19:20), and the harlot Babylon (18:23). John then adds an exclamation point to his description of God's people in 14:1–5: "they are blameless" (ἄμωμοι 14:5). Used in the Old Testament for the character of Israel's sacrificial offerings, here being "blameless" represents the moral purity of the redeemed. In short, they are like the Lamb they follow (14:4)—holy (3:7) and driven by cruciform love (12:11).

A Worshiping Church

John's visions of the church in Rev 7 and 14 reverberate with the sounds of jubilant worship. In a compelling worship scene, the unnumbered multitude stands in the very presence of God, clasping palms of victory and resounding their praise to God and the Lamb (7:9–10). Suddenly the worship choir swells with the addition of *all* the angels, the elders, and the living creatures. These worshipers prostrate themselves and sing a sevenfold doxology, symbolizing perfect worship (7:11–12). Because of God's redemptive and sanctifying mission in Christ, the Lamb's choir worships (λατρεύω) God "day and night within his temple" (7:15). The word λατρεύω is used in Scripture for both worship and service to God (e.g., Deut 6:13; Josh 24:15; Heb 8:5). As a priestly people (Rev 1:6; 5:10), the redeemed serve unceasingly in God's temple. But the temple is the place of the divine presence, and in the New Jerusalem, the only "temple" to be found is God and the Lamb (21:22). For John's audience, this picture of unbroken service to God and the Lamb means that all of life must be lived in God's presence and for God's glory.

In chapter 14, the seer *sees* God's people standing on Mount Zion, traditionally the center of Israelite worship (14:1). But he *hears* the sound of music from heaven—a thunderous resonance of singers singing and harpists playing (14:2; cf. 5:8). The 144,000 then join the heavenly "worship band" with a "new song" (14:3), one that only those purchased by the Lamb's blood can learn (5:9).

Those who worship the beast sing a different song. The wider context of

---

52. Koester, *Revelation*, 610–11; Stephen Pattemore, *The People of God in the Apocalypse: Discourse, Structure and Exegesis*, SNTSMS 128 (Cambridge: Cambridge University Press, 2008), 187. Since symbolic language can operate on multiple levels, associating these "virgins" with the feminine image of the chaste bride of the Lamb is not incompatible with the masculine picture of undefiled holy warriors.

this worship scene highlights the idolatrous worship of the beast by the inhabitants of the earth (Rev 13:4, 8, 12, 15; 14:9, 11; cf. 16:2; 19:20). For the churches in Asia, worship becomes a political as well as a religious act. John's world was drenched with the worship of Caesar and praise for the power of Rome. "Coins announced Caesar's deity, poets extolled Rome's invincibility, and choral societies shouted the emperor's praise."[53] Worship requires John's readers to publicly announce where their allegiance lies. When the community sings the "new song" before the throne of Almighty God, it declares that the emperor "has no clothes" and the idols of the empire are false.

Worship is also missional.[54] When John pictures a vast multinational choir of worshipers shouting their praises to God and the Lamb (Rev 7:9–10), he offers the church a snapshot of the goal and purpose of God's loving, reconciling mission in the world—universal worship of the one true God.

At the same time, worship itself becomes an instrument for fulfilling God's mission to the nations. In chapter 14, no sooner have the redeemed lifted their new song of worship to God and the Lamb, when an angel invites people from every nation, tribe, language, and people on earth to fear God and give him glory. These beast-worshipers are called to switch sides and join those who worship the maker of heaven and earth (Rev 14:6–7). In 15:1–4, which forms a sequel to 14:1–5, the victorious community sings its assurance that, because God is holy, "all nations will come and worship before [him]" (15:4). The church's worship is not for the church alone but seeks to teach others the song of the redeemed.

A Healing Church

In Rev 7:15–17, an elder gives John a sneak preview of the church's future. In the second half of v. 15, the text shifts from the present to the future tense ("will shelter them," σκηνώσει), which continues through the end of the passage. The provision of food, water, protection, comfort, and God's presence echoes both the Israelites' experience in the wilderness and the prophetic promises to the exiles in Babylon (Ezek 37:27; Isa 49:10; 25:8). Even more significantly, they anticipate God's care for his people in the new Jerusalem. The blessings of the new creation include a lavish abundance of food and water for everyone (Rev 21:6; 22:1–2). What is more, the new Jerusalem will bring an end to human

---

53. Flemming, *Why Mission?*, 123. On the political implications of Revelation's worship scenes, see Wes Howard-Brook and Anthony Gwyther, *Unveiling Empire: Reading Revelation Then and Now* (Maryknoll, NY: Orbis, 2001), 202–7.

54. See Flemming, "Toward a Missional Reading of the Apocalypse," 174–75.

suffering, mourning, and pain. Like a tender parent, God "will wipe away every tear from their eyes" (21:4; cf. 7:17; 21:7).

How do these eschatological blessings relate to John's audience? On one level, the promises in Rev 7:15-17 speak directly into the life circumstances of the churches in Asia, which surely need God's provision, protection, and comfort. They assure God's faithful that human suffering is not a permanent condition, that God will triumph over all the powers of death and evil in the end. On another level, however, these promises help to set an agenda for the church in mission. The mission of the new Jerusalem is no less than the "healing of the nations" (22:2; cf. 21:24, 26).[55] This points toward God's healing, restoring work in every human relationship and every dimension of human need. John's vision of God's future in 7:15-17 and in chapters 21-22 energizes God's people to live as a foretaste of God's ultimate purpose for humanity and all creation. Although the vision of Rev 7:15-17 will not be fully realized until God makes everything new (21:5), it calls the church to participate in God's restoring mission *now*. It invites Christian communities to love and serve the hungry, the homeless, the defenseless, and the sorrowful.

Conclusion

How does this exploration into missional ecclesiology in John's visions in Rev 7 and 14 help to shape communities of worship and witness today? Let me spotlight several implications.

First, the church's missional identity must flow out of the defining vision of God seated on the throne and the story of God's saving, restoring purposes for all humans and the entire creation. In one sense, we cannot speak ultimately of the *church's* mission—at least not if we think of it as something the church possesses. The church only *has* a mission insofar as it participates in the mission of the God "who made heaven and earth" (14:7) and desires to bring that creation to its goal in the *new* heaven and earth.

Second, the church's witness in the world is shaped by and conforms to the mission of the slaughtered Lamb. God's people "follow the Lamb wherever he goes" (14:4). Revelation's alternative vision of the world enables Christians to resist today's beastly powers in favor of Lamb-power—the power of self-giving love. Churches that challenge the idols, injustice, and immorality of their cultures may find themselves ridiculed and marginalized. They may suffer. But this has always been the way of the slain Lamb.

55. Flemming, "Toward a Missional Reading of the Apocalypse," 176.

Third, the worship scenes in chapters 7 and 14 remind us that worship is inseparable from mission. Worship shapes the church's common life as a faithful, missional people who belong to God alone. As that worship overflows into the lives of unbelievers, others will be drawn into the choir of worshipers. At the same time, in worship, the gathered community publicly declares that "salvation belongs to *our God*" and not the idols of the culture—whether economic power, political parties, or popular celebrities. The community's worship teaches God's people to counter-imagine the way things are in the world.

Fourth, John's vision of the innumerable throng from every people and nation (7:9-17) shapes both the church's identity and its mission. In a time when many Christian communities find themselves in contexts where fear and mistrust of the "other"—other races, other nations, other religions, refugees and immigrants—abound, this vision reminds God's people of who we *are*. The church encounters "the other" with open arms, not closed fists. Revelation's untold multitude also energizes the church to participate in a mission to all peoples and language groups. What is more, it assures God's people that such a mission, empowered by the Spirit, will ultimately lead to an unthinkable harvest of those who will stand in the presence of God and the Lamb.

Fifth, these visions call the church to become a holy community that speaks and embodies God's truth. What does that mean in settings where public truth appears increasingly unreliable or where postmodern sensibilities reduce truth to a matter of personal preference? There is no "one-size-fits-all" response. Yet surely the church's witness to the truth must be coupled with humble integrity of character and conduct. When God's people live in the likeness of the slain Lamb, that very difference and authenticity has the potential to draw others into the fellowship of the redeemed.

Revelation's visions of the victorious church gathered before the throne, then, call God's people not only to eagerly anticipate God's future but to *embody* it. Whenever the church prays with conviction, "Your kingdom come, your will be done, on earth as it is in heaven," the future breaks into the present world.[56] God's people share in the restoring, life-giving purposes of a missional God, in the hovels and high rises of the earth.

---

56. J. Nelson Kraybill, *Imperial Cult and Commerce in John's Apocalypse*, JSNTSup 127 (Sheffield: Sheffield Academic Press, 1996), 221.

.... **Epilogue**

Like all children welcomed by loving parents and raised in a healthy family, we are thrilled whenever we see our parents honored or recognized as widely as possible for their achievements. We know as well as anyone that Dad should be celebrated. And yet, our perspective is perhaps doubly unique, for we also have been his students. Each of us has taken graduate courses where his texts were on the syllabus. Two of us (Amy and Brian) have taken, and one (Mark) has co-taught, classes with him. It is as Dad's children and students that we offer this epilogue.

Brian Gorman:

The word "apostle" has largely departed from the language of most church traditions, but when it comes to Dad, I can think of no better appellation. Indeed, the title of one of his books feels most accurate: apostle of the crucified Lord. As Dad's children and students—sometimes formally—we have witnessed an embodied commitment to the message of the cross in our father, an impassioned, disciplined, and self-sacrificial abandonment to the calling which he received early in his lifetime. Whether it was manifest in the prestigious posts at academic institutions that he turned down so that we could remain stable and near other family, the years of humble service as an adult Sunday School teacher at his local church, or the simple practice of Friday night Bible study with friends for more than three decades, the study of Paul, the gospel, and the cross has never been merely an academic exercise for our Dad. He has truly been sent with the kerygma of the gospel to young and old, highly and lowly educated, Catholics, Protestants, evangelicals, and especially, his own children.

EPILOGUE

Amy Caruso:

One thing that I have learned from my father over the years has been that the lifestyle of cruciformity is often quiet.

I discovered a secret when I grew older—my parents are special. When I later discussed my childhood with friends from Eastern University, I felt like I had won the lottery. No violent or explicit movies? An elementary school where I learned to love to read the Bible? Resisting empire in our own way by, for example, not saying the pledge? Theological debates at meals? Parents who saw their family as a sacred gift? I never knew anything different.

In a world where people love to display their accomplishments, Christians struggle to relinquish the desire for fame and fortune in favor of—in whatever manner, be it quietly or loudly—returning thanks to God. My father is a person with immeasurable gifts. But he does not think a lot of himself, and I can't help but think that's in part because he knows so well the ins and outs of the work of Paul as he witnesses to Christlikeness.

Mark Gorman:

Scholarly excellence need not come at the expense of family or personal relationships. Major events in my life turned out also to be significant markers in Dad's life of scholarship. I was born in 1982, when Dad published his first book, *Abortion and the Early Church*. Eighteen years later, I graduated from high school, following which Dad was granted his first sabbatical, when he wrote his second book, *Elements of Biblical Exegesis*. The timing was not a coincidence: work did not trump family. And it paid off. Eight years later, when I began seminary, Dad was renowned for his work on the apostle Paul, so much so that professors and fellow students alike regularly asked if we were related. I was and remain proud to answer yes.

We are grateful to the editors and contributors for honoring Dad's scholarship with this volume, and we thank Eerdmans for publishing many of Dad's books and for supporting this project. We hope readers will come away with a greater appreciation for his work and a desire to participate more fully in the cruciform lordship of Jesus Christ.

.... **Dr. Michael J. Gorman**: *Cursus Vitae*

Education and Academic Appointments

1955	Born in Fort Meade, Maryland (near Baltimore)
1973	Graduated from Glen Burnie High School (Glen Burnie, Maryland)
1977	Earned BA from Gordon College with a major in French and a double minor in New Testament/Greek and Education
1982	Earned MDiv from Princeton Theological Seminary with an emphasis in New Testament studies
1989	Earned PhD (with distinction) from Princeton Theological Seminary in New Testament studies with a dissertation titled "The Self, the Lord, and the Other: The Significance of Reflexive Pronoun Constructions in the Letters of Paul, with a Comparison to the Discourses of Epictetus"
1989	Appointed Assistant Director of the Council for Religion in Independent Schools (CRIS)
1991	Began teaching at the Ecumenical Institute of Theology, St. Mary's Seminary & University (Baltimore, Maryland)
1993	Appointed Associate Professor of New Testament and Early Church History, The School of Theology and the Ecumenical Institute of Theology, St. Mary's Seminary & University
1993	Appointed Extraordinary Member of the Pontifical Faculty, St. Mary's Seminary & University
1993	Appointed Associate Dean of the Ecumenical Institute of Theology, St. Mary's Seminary & University
1994	Appointed Acting Dean of the Ecumenical Institute of Theology, St. Mary's Seminary & University
1995	Appointed Dean of the Ecumenical Institute of Theology, St. Mary's Seminary & University; held the position until 2012
1998	Promoted to Professor of New Testament and Early Church History,

	The School of Theology and the Ecumenical Institute of Theology, St. Mary's Seminary & University
2002	Appointed Professor of Sacred Scripture, The School of Theology and the Ecumenical Institute of Theology at St. Mary's Seminary & University
2012	Named Raymond E. Brown Chair in Biblical Studies and Theology, St. Mary's Seminary & University

Other Academic Appointments

2006	Mars Hill Graduate School (Bothell, Washington), Visiting Professor
2009	Wesley Theological Seminary (Washington, DC), Guest Professor of New Testament
2009	Grand Séminaire Notre Dame de l'Espérance (Bertoua, Cameroon), Visiting Professor of New Testament
2009	Duke Divinity School (Durham, NC), Visiting Professor of New Testament
2016	Shalom University (Bunia, Democratic Republic of the Congo), Adjunct Professor of New Testament; appointment continued through 2018
2017	Regent College (Vancouver, BC, Canada), Visiting Lecturer (reappointed for 2021)
2019	Carey Baptist College Graduate School (Auckland, New Zealand), Visiting Professor

Publications

Below is a list of the academic and professional publications of Dr. Michael J. Gorman from the fall of 1982 to the end of 2019, a period spanning nearly four decades. Among this impressive list of publications are twelve authored books, one co-authored book, two edited books, two booklets, twenty-seven articles, thirty-five book chapters, six encyclopedia entries, forty-three book reviews, five sermons, and study notes for two different study Bibles. The subject matter represented here includes early Christian views on abortion, NT ethics, theological interpretation of the NT, the Johannine literature, the interpretation of Revelation, and Gorman's most influential and widely known work on the life and letters of Paul. Several of his works have been translated into Korean, Portuguese, and Lithuanian. This list is a testimony to the breadth of Gorman's expertise and the consistency with which he has produced substantive research for both academy and church.

1982

Abortion and the Early Church: Christian, Jewish and Pagan Attitudes in the Greco-Roman World. Downers Grove, IL: InterVarsity; Mahwah, NJ: Paulist, 1982; reprinted by Wipf and Stock, 1998.

1984

Review of *Shorter Lexicon of the Greek New Testament*, by F. Wilbur Gingrich and Frederick W. Danker. *RelSRev* 10 (1984): 177.

1985

Review of *A New Testament Greek Morpheme Lexicon*, by J. Harold Greenlee. *RelSRev* 11 (1985): 192.

1986

Review of *Pro-Life/Pro-Peace: Life-Affirming Alternatives to Abortion, War, Mercy Killing, and the Death Penalty*, by Lowell Erdahl. *Christianity Today* 30 (November 7, 1986): 38–40.
"Shalom and the Unborn." *Transformation* 3 (1986): 26–33.

1990

"Historical Perspectives [400 B. C.–A. D. 1900]." Pages 124–43 in *Bioethics and the Beginning of Life: An Anabaptist Perspective*. Edited by Roman J. Miller and Beryl H. Brubaker. Harrisonburg, VA: Herald, 1990.
Review of *The Kindness of Strangers: The Abandonment of Children in Western Europe from Late Antiquity to the Renaissance*, by John Boswell. *Christianity Today* 34 (April 6, 1990): 33.
Texts and Contexts: A Guide to Careful Thinking and Writing about the Bible. The Council for Religion, 1990; revised edition distributed by the Ecumenical Institute of Theology, 1994; published by Wipf and Stock, 1998.
Translation of Oscar Cullmann, "Pluralisme et Unité dans le Nouveau Testament." Pages 335–51 in *Faith and History: Essays in Honor of Paul W. Meyer*, ed. John T. Carroll, Charles H. Cogrove, and E. Elizabeth Johnson. Atlanta: Scholars Press, 1990.

1991

"The Church's Changing Mind [on birth control]." *Christianity Today* 35 (November 11, 1991): 42–43.

"The Pagan World." Pages 164–67 in *Ethics and Life: An Interdisciplinary Approach to Moral Problems*. Edited by Elaine E. Englehardt and Donald D. Schmeltekopf. New York: McGraw Hill, 1991.

1992

"Divorce and Remarriage from Augustine to Zwingli." *Christianity Today* 36 (December 14, 1992): 32.

"The Sounds of Silence: Abortion and the New Testament Canon." *Life and Learning II: UFL Proceedings 1992*. Washington, DC: University Faculty for Life, 1992.

1993

"Ahead to Our Past: Abortion and Christian Texts." Pages 25–43 in *The Church and Abortion: In Search of New Ground for Response*. Edited by Paul Stallsworth. Nashville: Abingdon, 1993. Reprint: Pages 917–24 in *On Moral Medicine: Theological Perspectives on Medical Ethics*, 3rd ed. Edited by M. Therese Lysaught and Joseph A. Kotva. Grand Rapids: Eerdmans, 2012.

"Why Is the New Testament Silent about Abortion?" *Christianity Today* 37 (January 11, 1993): 27–29.

1994

"Abortion and the Biblical 'Divine Feminine.'" Pages 253–70 in *Life and Learning IV: UFL Proceedings 1994*. Washington, DC: University Faculty for Life, 1994.

1995

Review of *Ut Unum Sin [That They May Be One]*, by Pope John Paul II. *The Catholic Review* 60 (September 6, 1995): 11.

"The New Testament Canon Condemns Abortion." Pages 33–38 in *The Abortion Controversy*. Edited by Charles Cozic and Jonathan Petrikin. San Diego: Greenhaven, 1995.

"The Use and Abuse of the Bible in the Abortion Debate." Pages 140–84 in *Life* and *Learning V: UFL Proceedings 1995*. Washington, DC: University Faculty for Life, 1995.

1996

Review of *Not My Own: Abortion and the Marks of the Church*, by Terry Schlossberg and Elizabeth Achtemeier. *Int* 50 (1996): 218-20.

"Scripture, History, and Authority in a Christian View of Abortion: A Response to Paul Simmons." *Christian Bioethics* 2 (1996): 83-96.

1997

Review of *The Crucified Jew: Twenty Centuries of Christian Anti-Semitism*, by Dan Cohn-Sherbok. *Bridges: An Interdisciplinary Journal of Theology, Philosophy, History, and Science* 4 (1997): 308-10.

Review of *Images of Personal Value*, by Philip Mooney. *Bridges: An Interdisciplinary Journal of Theology, Philosophy, History, and Science* 4 (1997): 183-84.

Review of *Life's Living Toward Dying*, by Vigen Guroian. *Bridges: An Interdisciplinary Journal of Theology, Philosophy, History, and Science* 4 (1997): 167-69.

Review of *Scripture and Discernment: Decision Making in the Church*, by Luke Timothy Johnson. *Int* 51 (1997): 208-9.

"Who Is My Neighbor? The Right Answer to the Wrong Question." Pages 57-60 in *The Right Choice: Pro-Life Sermons*. Edited by Paul T. Stallsworth. Nashville: Abingdon, 1997.

1998

Review of *Christianity and Culture in the Crossfire*, by David A. Hoekema and Bobby Fong, eds., and *Fact, Value, and God*, by Arthur F. Holmes. *Bridges: An Interdisciplinary Journal of Theology, Philosophy, History, and Science* 5 (1998): 100-103.

Review of *Introduction to the New Testament*, by Raymond E. Brown. *Christianity Today* 42 (September 7, 1998): 94-99.

1999

"Encountering the 'Chalcedonian' Word: Ecumenical Perspectives on the Reading and Teaching of Scripture." *Bulletin de Saint-Sulpice* 24 (1999): 168-89.

2000

"Irreconcilable Differences: The Church Should Divorce the Military." *Christianity Today* 44 (March 6, 2000): 77–78.

Review of *Consequences: Morality, Ethics, and the Future*, by James H. Burtness. *Bridges: An Interdisciplinary Journal of Theology, Philosophy, History, and Science* 7 (2000): 297–99.

Review of *The Paul Quest: The Renewed Search for the Jew of Tarsus*, by Ben Witherington III. *Int* 54 (2000): 77–78.

Three Sermons on "Stewardship." Pages 137–39 in *Sixty Second Stewardship Sermons*. Edited by Charles Cloughen Jr. Collegeville, MN: Liturgical Press, 2000.

2001

Cruciformity: Paul's Narrative Spirituality of the Cross. Grand Rapids: Eerdmans, 2001.

Elements of Biblical Exegesis: A Basic Guide for Students and Ministers. Peabody, MA: Hendrickson, 2001; revised and expanded edition, 2009.

Review of *Calvin's Institutes* Abridged Edition, by Donald McKim, ed. *Bridges: An Interdisciplinary Journal of Theology, Philosophy, History, and Science* 8 (2001): 312–14.

2002

Review of *The Bible in Translation: Ancient and English Versions*, by Bruce M. Metzger. *PSB* 23 (2002): 224–25.

Review of *Paul: Apostle of the Living God: Kerygma and Conversion in 2 Corinthians*, by Mark J. Goodwin. *Int* 56 (2002): 216.

Review of *Sacred Choices: The Right to Contraception and Abortion in Ten World Religions*, by Daniel Maguire. *Bridges: An Interdisciplinary Journal of Theology, Philosophy, History, and Science* 9 (2002): 131–33.

2003

Holy Abortion? A Theological Critique of the Religious Coalition for Reproductive Choice. Coauthored with Ann Loar Brooks. Eugene, OR: Wipf and Stock, 2003.

Review of *Broken Yet Beloved: A Pastoral Theology of the Cross*, by Sharon G. Thornton. *ThTo* 60 (2003): 245.

Review of *Handbook of Early Christianity: Social Science Approaches*, by Anthony J. Blasi, Jean Duhaime, Paul-André Turcotte, eds. *Bridges: An Interdisciplinary Journal of Theology, Philosophy, History, and Science* 10 (2003): 305–6.

Review of *Jesus and Empire: The Kingdom of God and the New World Disorder*, by Richard A. Horsley. *Bridges: An Interdisciplinary Journal of Theology, Philosophy, History, and Science* 10 (2003): 319–21.

Review of *The Message and the Kingdom: How Jesus and Paul Ignited a Revolution and Transformed the Ancient World*, by Richard A. Horsley and Neil Asher Silberman. *Bridges: An Interdisciplinary Journal of Theology, Philosophy, History, and Science* 10 (2003): 178–82.

Review of *Remembering Jesus: Christian Community, Scripture, and the Moral Life*, by Allen Verhey. *Int* 57 (2003): 434–37.

2004

Apostle of the Crucified Lord: A Theological Introduction to Paul and His Letters. Grand Rapids: Eerdmans, 2004; 2nd ed. 2017.

2005

"The Bible and Spiritual Growth." Coauthored with Pat Fosarelli. Pages 229–38 in *Scripture: An Ecumenical Introduction to the Bible and Its Interpretation*. Edited by Michael J. Gorman. Peabody, MA: Hendrickson, 2005.

"The Character and Composition of the Books of the New Testament." Pages 71–90 in *Scripture: An Ecumenical Introduction to the Bible and Its Interpretation*. Edited by Michael J. Gorman. Peabody, MA: Hendrickson, 2005.

"The Healthy Church: Embodying the Cross in Perilous Times." *Catalyst* (2005): https://www.catalystresources.org/the-healthy-church-embodying-the-cross-in-perilous-times/.

"The Interpretation of the Bible in Protestant Churches." Pages 177–94 in *Scripture: An Ecumenical Introduction to the Bible and its Interpretation*. Edited by Michael J. Gorman. Peabody, MA: Hendrickson, 2005.

"Introduction." Pages vii–ix in *Scripture: An Ecumenical Introduction to the Bible and Its Interpretation*. Edited by Michael J. Gorman. Peabody, MA: Hendrickson, 2005.

Review of *Colossians Remixed: Subverting the Empire*, by Sylvia Keesmaat and Brian J. Walsh, and *In Search of Paul: How Jesus' Apostle Opposed Rome's Empire with God's Kingdom*, by John Dominic Crossan and Jonathan Reed. *ChrCent* 122 (June 28, 2005): 36–38.

Review of *The Word in This World: Essays in New Testament Exegesis and Theology*, by Paul W. Meyer. *Int* 59 (2005): 90.

Scripture: An Ecumenical Introduction to the Bible. Peabody, MA: Hendrickson, 2005.

2006

"Cross." Pages 80–85 in vol. 1 of *New Interpreter's Dictionary of the Bible*. Edited by Katharine Doob Sakenfeld. Nashville: Abingdon, 2006.

Review of *Contemporary Issues in Bioethics: A Catholic Perspective*, by James J. Walter and Thomas A. Shannon. *Bridges: An Interdisciplinary Journal of Theology, Philosophy, History, and Science* 13 (2006): 410–13.

Review of *The Soul of the Embryo: An Enquiry into the Status of the Human Embryo in the Christian Tradition*, by David Jones. *Studies in Christian Ethics* 19 (2006): 125–28.

2007

"'Although/Because He Was in the Form of God': The Theological Significance of Paul's Master Story (Philippians 2:6–11)." *JTI* 1 (2007): 147–69.

"A 'Seamless Garment' Approach to Biblical Interpretation?" *JTI* 1 (2007): 117–28.

Review of *Paul: In Fresh Perspective*, by N. T. Wright. *Int* 61 (2007): 232.

"'You Shall Be Cruciform for I Am Cruciform': Paul's Trinitarian Reconstruction of Holiness." Pages 148–66 in *Holiness and Ecclesiology in the New Testament*. Edited by Kent E. Brower and Andy Johnson. Grand Rapids: Eerdmans, 2007.

2008

Reading Paul. Eugene, OR: Cascade and Milton Keynes, U. K.: Paternoster, 2008.

"Romans 13:8–14: From Text to Sermon." *Int* 62 (2008): 170–72.

2009

"Abortion: Christianity: Patristic and Medieval." Pages 143–45 in vol. 1 of *Encyclopedia of the Reception of the Bible*. Edited by Constance Furey, Steven L. McKenzie, Thomas Römer, Jens Schröter, Barry D. Walfish, Eric Ziolkowski. Berlin: Walter deGruyter, 2009.

"The Gospel of John: Introduction and Notes." In the *Wesley Study Bible*. Edited by Joel B. Green and William H. Willimon. Nashville: Abingdon, 2009.

Inhabiting the Cruciform God: Kenosis, Justification, and Theosis in Paul's Narrative Soteriology. Grand Rapids: Eerdmans, 2009.

"Response to Bockmuehl." *ExAud* 25 (2009): 61–66.

"Saint." Pages 41–43 in vol. 5 of *New Interpreter's Dictionary of the Bible*. Edited by Katharine Doob Sakenfield. Nashville: Abingdon, 2009.

"Salvation." Coauthored with Richard Middleton. Pages 45–61 in vol. 5 of *New Interpreter's Dictionary of the Bible*. Edited by Katharine Doob Sakenfield. Nashville: Abingdon, 2009.

"St. Paul and the Resurrection." *The Priest/Our Sunday Visitor Weekly* (April 2009). https://www.osv.com/OSVNewsweekly/ByIssue/Article/TabId/735/Art MID/13636/ArticleID/9011/St-Paul-and-the-Resurrection.aspx.

2010

"Effecting the New Covenant: A (Not So) New, New Testament Model for the Atonement." *ExAud* 26 (2010): 26–59.

Review of *Apocalypse and Allegiance: Worship, Politics, and Devotion in the Book of Revelation*, by J. Nelson Kraybill. *ChrCent* 127 (July 27, 2010): 37–40.

Review of *Beginning from Jerusalem: Christianity in the Making*, vol. 2, by James D. G. Dunn. *Int* 64 (2010): 302–4.

Review of *World Upside Down: Reading Acts in the Graeco-Roman Age*, by C. Kavin Rowe. *Divinity Magazine* 9 (Spring 2010): 32–33.

2011

"Abortion." Page 35–37 in *The Dictionary of Scripture and Ethics*. Edited by Joel B. Green, Jacqueline Lapsley, Rebekah Miles, and Allen Verhey. Grand Rapids: Baker Academic, 2011.

"Cruciformity." Page 197–98 in *The Dictionary of Scripture and Ethics*. Edited by Joel B. Green, Jacqueline Lapsley, Rebekah Miles, and Allen Verhey. Grand Rapids: Baker Academic, 2011.

"Douglas Campbell's *The Deliverance of God*: A Review by a Friendly Critic." *JSPL* 1 (2011): 99–108.

"Justification and Justice in Paul, with Special Reference to the Corinthians." *JSPL* 1 (2011): 23–40.

"Missional Musings on Paul." *Catalyst* (2011). https://www.catalystresources.org/missional-musings-on-paul/.

Reading Revelation Responsibly: Uncivil Worship and Witness: Following the Lamb into the New Creation. Eugene, OR: Cascade, 2011.

"Romans: The First Christian Treatise on Theosis." *JTI* 5 (2011): 13–34.

2012

"Cruciformity according to Jesus and Paul." Pages 173–201 in *Unity and Diversity in the Gospels and Paul: Essays in Honor of Frank J. Matera.* Early Christianity and Its Literature 7. Edited by Christopher W. Skinner and Kelly R. Iverson. Atlanta: Society of Biblical Literature, 2012.

"Preaching and Living the Resurrection Today." *The Living Pulpit* (2012). https://www.pulpit.org/2012/04/preaching-and-living-the-resurrection-today/.

Review of *Remember the Poor: Paul, Poverty, and the Greco-Roman World*, by Bruce W. Longenecker. *Int* 66 (2012): 217.

"What Has the Spirit Been Saying? Theological Reflections on the Reception/Impact History of the Book of Revelation." Pages 12–30 in *Revelation and the Politics of Apocalyptic Interpretation.* Edited by Richard B. Hays and Stefan Alkier. Waco: Baylor University Press, 2012.

2013

"The Lord of Peace: Christ our Peace in Pauline Theology." *JSPL* 3 (2013): 219–53.

"Paul and the Cruciform Way of God in Christ." *JMTh* 2 (2013): 64–83.

Review of *Practicing Theological Interpretation: Engaging Biblical Texts for Faith and Formation*, by Joel B. Green. *Int* 67 (2013): 93–94.

"Romans: Introduction and Notes." In the *CEB Study Bible.* Edited by Joel B. Green. Nashville: Abingdon, 2013.

"The This-Worldliness of the New Testament's Other-Worldly Spirituality." Pages 151–70 in *The Bible and Spirituality: Exploratory Essays in Reading Scripture Spiritually.* Edited by Andrew T. Lincoln, J. Gordon McConville, and Lloyd K. Pietersen. Eugene, OR: Cascade, 2013.

2014

"Birth, Death, and Becoming Like God: Reflections on a New Testament Theme." *The Living Pulpit* (2014). https://www.pulpit.org/2014/11/birth-death-and-becoming-like-god-reflections-on-a-new-testament-theme/.

The Death of the Messiah and the Birth of the New Covenant: A (Not So) New Model of the Atonement. Eugene, OR: Cascade, 2014.

"Paul's Corporate, Cruciform, Missional Theosis in Second Corinthians." Pages 181–208 in *"In Christ" in Paul: Explorations in Paul's Theology of Union and Participation*. WUNT 2/384. Edited by Kevin J. Vanhoozer, Constantine R. Campbell, and Michael J. Thate. Tübingen: Mohr Siebeck, 2014.

Review of *God's Saving Grace: A Pauline Theology*, by Frank Matera. *Int* 68 (2014): 438–40.

Review of *Reading Paul's Letter to the Romans*, by Jerry L. Sumney. *Int* 68 (2014): 218–19.

"Shalom in the Book of Revelation: God, Church, Judgment, New Creation." Pages 279–90 in *Struggles for Shalom: Peace and Violence Across the Testaments*. Edited by Laura L. Brenneman and Brad D. Schantz. Eugene, OR: Wipf and Stock, 2014.

"Spirituality and the Book of Revelation." *Transmission* (2014): 20–22.

"Wright about Much, but Questions about Justification: A Review of N. T. Wright, *Paul and the Faithfulness of God*." *JSPL* 4 (2014): 27–36.

2015

Becoming the Gospel: Paul, Participation, and Mission. Grand Rapids: Eerdmans, 2015.

"Being 'In Christ' Today: Paul's Letter to the Contemporary Church in North America." *Canadian-American Theological Review* 4 (2015): 69–85.

"A New Translation of Phil 2:5 and Its Significance for Paul's Theology and Spirituality." Pages 101–21 in *Conception, Reception and the Spirit: Essays in Honor of Andrew T. Lincoln*. Edited by J. Gordon McConville and Lloyd K. Pietersen. Eugene, OR: Cascade, 2015.

Peace in Paul. Grove Booklet. Cambridge: Grove, 2015.

Review of *Apocalyptic Paul: Cosmos and Anthropos in Romans 5–8*, by Beverly Roberts Gaventa, ed. *Int* 69 (2015): 224–26.

Review of *Peace and Peacemaking in Paul and the Greco-Roman World*, by Edward M. Keazirian. *ExpTim* 126 (2015): 457–58.

"The Work of Christ in the New Testament." Pages 72–86 in *The Oxford Handbook of Christology*. Edited by Francesca Aran Murphy. Oxford: Oxford University Press, 2015.

2016

"The Apocalyptic New Covenant and the Shape of Life in the Spirit according to Galatians." Pages 317–37 in *Paul and the Apocalyptic Imagination*. Edited by Ben C. Blackwell, John K. Goodrich, and Jason Maston. Minneapolis: Fortress, 2016.

"The Cross in Paul: Christophany, Theophany, Ecclesiophany." Pages 21–40 in *Ecclesia and Ethics: Moral Formation and the Church*. Edited by E. Allen Jones III, John Frederick, John Anthony Dunne, Eric Lewellen, and Janghoon Park. London: T & T Clark, 2016.

Review of *Paul: An Outline of His Theology*, by Michael Wolter. *Int* 70 (2016): 481–83.

2017

"The Bible: A Book, a Library, a Story, an Invitation." Coauthored with Paul P. Zilonka. Pages 3–22 in *Scripture and Its Interpretation: A Global, Ecumenical Introduction to the Bible*. Edited by Michael J. Gorman. Grand Rapids: Baker Academic, 2017.

"The Bible and Spirituality." Coauthored with Patricia Fosarelli. Pages 339–52 in *Scripture and Its Interpretation: A Global, Ecumenical Introduction to the Bible*. Edited by Michael J. Gorman. Grand Rapids: Baker Academic, 2017.

"Cruciform or Resurrectiform? Paul's Paradoxical Practice of Participation." *ExAud* 33 (2017): 60–83.

"Participation and Ministerial Integrity in the Letters of Paul." Pages 1–14 in *Practicing with Paul: Reflections on Paul and the Practices of Ministry in Honor of Susan G. Eastman*. Edited by Presian Burroughs. Eugene, OR: Cascade, 2017.

"Protestant Biblical Interpretation." Pages 220–39 in *Scripture and Its Interpretation: A Global, Ecumenical Introduction to the Bible*. Edited by Michael J. Gorman. Grand Rapids: Baker Academic, 2017.

"Reading Gal 2:15–21 Theologically: Beyond Old and New, Beyond West and East." Pages 321–47 in *Participation, Justification and Conversion: Eastern Orthodox Interpretation of Paul and the Debate between Old and New Perspectives on Paul*. WUNT 2/442. Edited by Athanasios Despotis. Tübingen: Mohr Siebeck, 2017.

Review of *Paul: The Apostle's Life, Letters, and Thought*, by E. P. Sanders. *SCJR* 11 (2017): 1–3.

Review of *Why Mission?*, by Dean Fleming. *International Bulletin of Mission Research* 41 (2017): 85–86.

(Editor) *Scripture and Its Interpretation: A Global, Ecumenical Introduction to the Bible*. Grand Rapids: Baker Academic, 2017.

"The Writings of the New Covenant (The New Testament)." Pages 72–96 in *Scripture and Its Interpretation: A Global, Ecumenical Introduction to the Bible.* Edited by Michael J. Gorman. Grand Rapids: Baker Academic, 2017.

2018

Abide and Go: Missional Theosis in the Gospel of John. Eugene, OR: Cascade, 2018.
"First Corinthians and the Marks of God's *Ekklēsia*: One, Holy, Catholic, and Apostolic." Pages 167–90 in *One God, One People, One Future: Essays in Honor of N. T. Wright*. Edited by John Anthony Dunne and Eric Lewellen. Minneapolis: Fortress, 2018.
"The Holy Spirit and Cruciformity." Pages 177–84 in *Holy Spirit: Spokesperson, Scripture, Sermon, Society*. Edited by Johnson T. K. Lim. Singapore: Armour Publishing and Word & Works, 2018.
Participation: Paul's Vision of Life in Christ. Grove Booklet. Cambridge: Grove, 2018.
Review of *Christosis: Engaging Paul's Soteriology with His Patristic Interpreters*, by Ben C. Blackwell. *Int* 72 (2018): 439–41.
"The Spirit, the Prophets, and the End of the 'Johannine Jesus.'" *JTI* 12 (2018): 1–23.

2019

Participating in Christ: Explorations in Paul's Theology and Spirituality. Grand Rapids: Baker Academic, 2019.
Review of *The Mind of the Spirit: Paul's Approach to Transformed Thinking*, by Craig S. Keener. *Int* 73 (2019): 80–81.
"Romans from the Participationist Perspective." Pages 59–79 in *Preaching Romans: Four Perspectives*. Edited by Scot McKnight and Joseph B. Modica. Grand Rapids: Eerdmans, 2019.

Works in Translation

Apostle of the Crucified Lord: A Theological Introduction to Paul and His Letters. Published in Korean by Christian Literature Society of Korea, 2014.
Becoming the Gospel: Paul, Participation, and Mission. Published in Korean by Holy Wave Publishing, 2019.
"The Church's Changing Mind." Reprinted from *Christianity Today*, November 11, 1991, and published in the Lithuanian journal *PRIZME* 3 (1997).
Cruciformity: Paul's Narrative Spirituality of the Cross. Published in Korean by Holy Wave Publishing, 2010.

DR. MICHAEL J. GORMAN

The Death of the Messiah and the Birth of the New Covenant: A (Not So) New Model of the Atonement. Published in Korean by Ekklesia Publications, 2016.
Elements of Biblical Exegesis: A Basic Guide for Students and Ministers as Opening the Sacred Text. Published in Korean by Holy Wave, 2006; published in Portuguese by Vida Melhor Editora, 2019.
Reading Revelation Responsibly: Uncivil Worship and Witness: Following the Lamb into the New Creation. Published in Korean by Holy Wave Publishing, 2014.

Contributors

Ben C. Blackwell is associate professor of theology at Houston Baptist University in Houston, Texas.

Sherri Brown is associate professor of New Testament at Creighton University in Omaha, Nebraska.

Frank E. Dicken is associate professor of New Testament at Lincoln Christian University in Lincoln, Illinois.

Dennis R. Edwards is associate professor of New Testament at North Park Theological Seminary in Chicago, Illinois.

Rebekah Eklund is associate professor of theology at Loyola University Maryland in Baltimore, Maryland.

Dean Flemming is professor of New Testament and missions at MidAmerica Nazarene University in Olathe, Kansas.

Patricia Fosarelli is associate dean of instruction and professor of spirituality and practical theology at St. Mary's Ecumenical Institute, Baltimore, Maryland.

Stephen E. Fowl is professor of theology at Loyola University Maryland in Baltimore, Maryland.

Nijay K. Gupta is professor of New Testament at Northern Seminary in Lisle, Illinois.

Richard B. Hays is George Washington Ivey Professor Emeritus of New Testament at Duke Divinity School in Durham, North Carolina.

Andy Johnson is professor of New Testament at Nazarene Theological Seminary in Kansas City, Missouri.

Sylvia C. Keesmaat is an adjunct professor at the Institute for Christian Studies, as well as Trinity and Wycliffe Colleges at the University of Toronto.

CONTRIBUTORS

Brent Laytham is dean and professor of theology at St. Mary's Ecumenical Institute, Baltimore, Maryland.

Christopher W. Skinner is associate professor of New Testament and Early Christianity at Loyola University Chicago in Chicago, Illinois.

Klyne R. Snodgrass is professor emeritus of New Testament Studies at North Park Theological Seminary in Chicago, Illinois.

Drew J. Strait is assistant professor of New Testament and Christian origins at Anabaptist Mennonite Biblical Seminary in Elkhart, Indiana.

N. T. Wright is professor in the School of Divinity at the University of St. Andrews in Scotland.

Index of Modern Authors

Achtemeier, Paul, 147, 149n22
Adams, Sean A., 54n78
Aguilar, José E., 139n62, 141n66
Ahl, Frederick, 189n24
Allison, Dale, 12
Ando, Clifford, 194n43
Ashton, John, 61n15
Attridge, Harold, 163, 164nn4–5, 174n28
Aune, David, 264n12, 266n18, 273n41
Austin, Michel, 205n80

Barbu, Liviu, 18n37
Barclay, John M. G., 89–105, 128n27, 189n22
Barker, Margaret, 263n6
Barr, David, 269
Barr, James, 75n7, 77n10
Barrett, C. K., 65n22, 66, 68n30, 225n1
Barrett, George, 13, 14, 19
Barth, Karl, 18, 112
Bartsch, Shadi, 201n72
Bauckham, Richard, 145n4, 150, 151n26, 264, 265n14, 267n24, 272n36, 272n39
Bauman, Richard A., 188n19, 189n22
Bauman-Martin, Betsy, 157
Beale, G. K., 140n63, 264n12, 270n30
Beard, Mary, 191n30

Beare, Francis W., 146–47
Beasley-Murray, G. R., 108n8, 111n21, 116nn40–41, 273n42
Beers, Holly, 41n13, 50n57
Belle, Gilbert van, 58
Bennema, C., 163n3, 173n24
Betz, H. D., 113n28, 119n57, 227n7, 234n26
Beutler, Johannes, 172n22
Bickerman, Elias J., 152n30
Billerbeck, P., 227n6
Bird, Michael, 213n23
Blackwell, Benjamin, 126n13, 144n3, 144n5
Blomberg, Craig, 116n43
Blount, Brian K., 53n66, 53n70, 264n12
Boakye, Andrew K., 123n2, 140n65
Bock, Darrell L., 38n5
Bockmuehl, Markus, 98n11
Bøe, Sverre, 41n13, 42n18, 43nn23–24, 43n28, 48nn47–48, 48n51, 49nn54–55, 53n67, 53n69, 53n72
Boer, Martinus de, 126, 127
Boismard, Marie-Émile, 59n9
Bond, Helen K., 54n78
Bonhoeffer, Dietrich, 15, 16, 34n15, 37, 55, 149
Booth, Wayne C., 166n12
Bos, J. W. H., 232n21

Bovon, François, 203
Boyarin, Daniel, 168n18
Brink, Laurie, 185n5
Brown, Alexandra, 74n5
Brown, Raymond E., 40n11, 45n33, 51n63, 65n22, 166n9, 166n11, 168n17, 169n19, 177n34, 178n35
Brown, Sherri, 67n28, 163n1, 166n13
Bruce, F. F., 228n8
Bultmann, Rudolf, 56, 57, 162n7
Burroughs, Jeremiah, 15n29
Burton, E. de W., 237n36

Cabasilas, Nicholas, 18n37
Cadbury, Henry, 187
Caird, G. B., 264n11
Callaway, M., 229n12
Calvin, John, 6nn8–9, 14, 15, 125, 130n32, 142
Campbell, Constantine R., 117n50, 207n3
Campbell, Douglas, 11, 126n15
Carroll, John T., 46n38
Carson, D. A., 177n34
Charlesworth, J. H., 232n20
Chennattu, Rekha M., 174n26, 180n46, 181n48
Chester, Stephen J., 124n6, 125n8
Chilton, Bruce, 109n11
Cohen, S. J. D., 108nn8–9, 109n10
Collins, Paul, 145n4, 155
Conzelmann, Hans, 39n9
Cook, John Granger, 25n4
Cooley, Allison E., 191n28
Cornish, Cheryl, 8n13
Cornwell, Hannah, 194
Cosgrove, Charles H., 139n62
Cowan, J. Andrew, 132n39
Cranfield, C. E. B., 115, 117n49, 119n55
Crosby, Michael, 18n37

Crowder, Stephanie B., 53n68, 53n73
Culpepper, R. Alan, 65n22, 67n29, 166n13, 168n17, 180n45

Davis, Ellen F., 3n2
Dennis, John, 57n3
Derrett, J. Duncan M., 43n24
deSilva, David A., 128, 129n28, 132n40, 145n7, 274n46
Dicken, Frank, 45n34, 200n69
Doble, Peter, 37n2
Dodd, C. H., 168n18
Donfried, Karl P., 140n62
Douglas, Mary, 219n37
Dowd, Sharyn, 42n18, 43n24, 43n29, 48n47, 48n49
Downing, F. Gerald, 131
Downs, David, 214n25
Doyle, Michael, 193
Dschulnigg, Peter, 53n67, 53n71, 54n78
Duin, Steve, 259n38
Dunn, J. D. G., 109n13, 111n22, 113n28, 117–18, 120, 126n16, 140n63
Dunne, John Anthony, 135n50

Eastman, S. G., 229n12, 238n39
Edwards, Dennis R., 146n9, 153nn35–36
Edwell, Peter, 193n36
Eklund, Rebekah, 16n34
Elledge, C. D., 210n12
Elliott, John H., 147, 149n22, 156

Fee, Gordon, 74n3, 130n33, 136n56, 211n18, 265n14
Ferguson, Everett, 108nn8–9, 109n10, 110n20
Fewster, G., 80n23
Fitzmyer, Joseph A., 38nn4–5, 41n13,

41n15, 43n27, 45n35, 52, 53n74, 54n77, 89
Flemming, Dean, 261n2, 271n35, 273n40, 274n47, 276nn53–54, 277n55
Forestell, J. Terrance, 57
Fowl, Stephen, 75n7, 97nn9–10
Frey, Jörg, 145n4, 145n8
Fridrichsen, Anton, 43n26, 43n29
Fuhrmann, Christopher J., 189n22, 194n46, 195n48
Fung, Ronald Y. K., 133n44, 137n58

Gaffin, Richard B., 216n29, 217n34
Galinsky, Karl, 186n6
Gaventa, Beverly R., 127n18, 130–31n35, 139n59
Genette, Gerard, 58n8, 59
Giard, J. B., 192n32
Goheen, Michael, 159n57, 261n1
Gordley, Matthew E., 73–74n2
Gorman, Heather M., 51n63
Gorman, Michael J., 3n1, 4, 6–8, 10–11, 15n30, 17, 20–21, 23n1, 35n16, 39n8, 58, 68–72, 84n25, 95n7, 102n12, 106, 123, 127, 130, 134n48, 143n70, 144, 146n10, 149, 151n27, 153n36, 155, 156n50, 157n53, 158n54, 159n56, 164, 165n8, 174n29, 175n30, 176n31, 184, 185n4, 198n63, 206n83, 208nn3–4, 215n28, 216n29, 217n33, 219n40, 238, 250n26, 257n36, 258n37, 261n2, 264n13
Green, Joel B., 38nn4–5, 40n12, 42n17, 43n23, 43n25, 46n39, 46n42, 47n45, 49n56, 50n58, 52n64, 53n67, 153n34
Green, Michael P., 43n24
Gupta, Nijay K., 82n24, 209n8
Guroian, Vigen, 16
Gwyther, Anthony, 276n53

Hadas-Lebel, Mireille, 203n78
Hall, Stuart, 228n11
Harrington, Hannah K., 211n15, 221n46
Harris, Murray J., 114n32
Harrison, James R., 250n26
Hartman, Lars, 108n8, 109n12, 115n33
Harvey, W. J., 166n12
Hastings, Ross, 159n57
Hays, Christopher M., 48n50
Hays, Richard B., 3n2, 24n3, 26n6, 27n10, 28n11, 74n5, 208n3, 226, 227, 228n9, 238n39
Headlam, Arthur, 112
Healy, Mary, 74n5
Heitmüller, Wilhelm, 116n41
Hellerman, Joseph, 74n4, 78n11
Hengel, Martin, 25n4, 188n15
Hill, Wesley, 212n18
Hooker, Morna, 112n26, 149, 156, 177n33, 178, 179n40
Horrell, David G., 148, 152, 158n55
Hoskyns, Edwin C., 177n32
Howard-Brook, Wes, 276n53
Howell, Justin R., 200n68, 202
Hughes, Donald J., 247n17
Hultgren, Arland J., 118n54
Hunsinger, George, 18n37
Hylen, Susan, 62, 63n18

Irons, Charles Lee, 209n7
Isaac, Benjamin, 196, 197n59

Jacobs, Haley Goranson, 218n35, 221n43, 223n50
Jennings, Willie James, 199, 205
Jensen, Robin M., 122nn66–67
Jewett, Robert, 216n30
Jobes, K. H., 226n5
Johnson, Andy, 157n51, 208n4, 218n36,

221n44, 262n8, 269n29, 272n38, 274n48, 274n51
Judge, Peter, 182
Just, Arthur A., 54n78

Käsemann, Ernst, 168n18
Keck, Leander, 215n27
Keener, Craig S., 61n16, 74n5, 75n6, 155n41, 202
Keesmaat, Sylvia C., 242n2, 247n17, 253n31, 257n35
Kirk, Daniel, 213n23, 216n29
Kochenash, Michael, 186n8
Koester, Craig, 267n25, 274n50, 275n52
Kraybill, J. Nelson, 278n56
Kümmel, Werner Georg, 38n5
Kuttner, Ann L., 192n33
Kyrychenko, Alexander, 185n5, 200

Labahn, Michael, 163n2
Lagrange, M. J., 177n32
LaHaye, Tim, 262n6, 266n17, 273n43
Lange, John Peter, 18
Lappenga, Benjamin J., 214n25
Lavan, Myles, 195, 197n60
Lawrence, J. D., 108n6, 110n17
Lee, Chee-Chiew, 133n42, 133n45, 135n51
Lee, Dorothy, 164, 170n21, 172
Leithart, Peter, 143n71, 211
Levine, Amy-Jill, 267n23
Lincoln, Andrew T., 164, 178n35, 227n7, 236n34, 245n11
Litwa, M. David, 122n69
Loader, William, 57n3
Long, Frederick J., 248, 249nn22–25, 251, 255n32, 256n33
Longenecker, Richard N., 211n17, 227n7, 232n22
Longman, T., 230n16

Lopez, Davina C., 242n3, 243n7, 244n9, 246, 247n16, 252n30, 256n34
Luther, Martin, 112, 124–25, 132n41

Macaskill, Grant, 207n3
Macchia, Frank D., 143n72, 269n28
MacDonald, Margaret Y., 245n11
MacMullen, Ramsay, 190
Maier, C. M., 226n5, 228n10, 229n13, 230n15
Maier, Harry O., 244n10, 245, 248n21
Mangina, Joseph L., 261n3, 262, 267n25, 271nn33–34, 273n44
Mann, Joshua L., 54n76
Marcus, Joel, 3n3, 26n6
Marshall, I. Howard, 38n6, 43n29, 45n32, 46n40, 120
Martin, Dale B., 209n9, 222n48
Martyn, J. Louis, 74n5, 237n35, 238n39
Matera, Frank J., 69
Mauser, Ulrich, 187, 188
McCarthy, Jane, 189n22
McGrath, Alister, 125n9
McKay, K. L., 180n44
McKnight, Scot, 156, 203n78
Meeks, Wayne A., 74n5, 75n6
Metzger, Bruce, 178n38
Meyer, Paul W., 141n67
Michaels, J. Ramsey, 62n7, 66n26, 152n30
Milbank, John, 70
Miller, Donald E., 41n13, 42n18, 43n25
Milligan, G., 76n9
Moberly, R. W. L., 219n39
Moessner, David P., 45n33, 45n36, 46n40, 46n42
Moffit, David, 214, 219n38
Moles, John, 195, 196
Moloney, Francis J., 67n27, 68n31,

166n13, 167n13, 177n32, 178nn35–36, 179n41
Moo, Douglas J., 120n57
Morales, Rodrigo J., 135n50
Morgan-Wynne, John, 57n3
Moule, C. F. D., 228n8
Moulton, J. H., 76n9
Muddiman, John, 245n11, 250
Myers, A. D., 227n6

Nicolet, Claude, 192
Nolland, John, 42n18, 43n26, 43n28, 44n30, 45n32, 46n39, 47n44, 48n49, 50n60

Oberman, A., 178n36
Okure, Teresa, 164, 174n26

Painter, John, 167n16
Pattermore, Stephen, 275n52
Pickup, Martin, 211n16
Pietersma, A., 228n10, 229
Pinnock, Clark, 207n2, 210n10
Pippen, Tina, 267n23
Plessis, Isak J. du, 38n4
Portier-Young, Anathea, 201
Powers, Daniel G., 146, 147n14
Price, Simon, 186n7
Prothro, James B., 124n3, 126n13, 128n27, 129n29, 131, 140n64
Pryor, John W., 169n20

Quaintance, Chad, 14n27, 15n28

Raaflaub, K. A., 188n20
Rabens, Volker, 143n69
Ramelli, Ilaria, 180
Reasoner, Mark, 107n4
Reddish, Mitchell G., 264n11, 266n20, 273n41

Reinhartz, Adele, 59
Reumann, John, 73n2, 125n10
Richardson, John, 192, 193
Riesenfeld, H., 178n37
Rimmon-Kenan, Shlomith, 58n8
Robertson, A. T., 58n8
Rossing, Barbara, 205n82
Rowe, C. Kavin, 186n9, 202
Rudich, Vasily, 189
Rutledge, Fleming, 25n5

Sabou, Sorin, 119n56
Said, Edward, 193
Sammons, L. J., II, 188n20
Samuelsson, Gunnar, 25n4
Sanday, William, 112
Sanders, E. P., 108n6, 116–17, 118n53, 137n57
Sänger, Dieter, 109n10
Schmitt, J. J., 227n6, 228n10, 229n14
Schnackenburg, Rudolf, 116n40, 117, 120, 178n35
Schneiders, Sandra M., 164, 166n10
Schulz, Siegried, 57n3
Schüssler Fiorenza, Elisabeth, 266n19
Schweitzer, Albert, 117
Scott, Ian W., 74n5
Segovia, Fernando F., 177n32, 182n50
Seifrid, Mark, 140
Shauf, Scott, 129–30
Sheen, Fulton, 13–14, 19
Shepherd, David, 181
Siikavirta, Samuli, 110n18
Skinner, Christopher W., 64n19, 67n28, 163nn1–3
Smalley, Stephen S., 263n9
Smith, D. Moody, 163n2
Smith, R. R. R., 243nn4–6
Smith, Shively T. J., 152, 154
Snodgrass, Klyne, 106

INDEX OF MODERN AUTHORS

Soards, Marion L., 52n65
Spencer, Patrick, 180n42
Sprinkle, Preston M., 135n53
Stanley, Christopher D., 134n46, 227n6
Starr, James M., 145n4, 145n6
Stegemann, Hartmut, 112n26
Steger, Manfred B., 198n61
Stenström, Hanna, 267n23
Stoll, Brigitta, 13n22
Strack, H. L., 227n7
Strait, Drew J., 186n8, 188n16, 189n21, 190n26, 200n71, 202n74
Strelan, Rick, 243n4, 250n27
Swartley, Willard, 198n63
Sweetland, Dennis M., 39n10, 40n12

Talbert, Charles H., 38n3, 38n5, 39n9, 44n3, 167n14
Tannehill, Robert C., 118n52, 148–49
Tappenden, Frederick S., 216n29
Tavo, Felise, 270n30, 274n45
Thatcher, Tom, 166n12
Thate, Michael J., 207n3
Thiessen, Matthew, 135n55
Thomas, John Christopher, 269n28
Thompson, Marianne Meye, 162n7, 267n24, 274n49
Tovey, Derek, 166n9
Trozzo, Lindsey M., 163n2
Turner, M. M. B., 142n68

Untergassmair, Franz Georg, 53n71, 53n73

Vanhoozer, Kevin J., 207n3
Vanhoye, A., 230n17
Vellanickal, Matthew, 155n41

Wallace, Daniel, 177n34, 178n37
Walsh, Brian, 247n17, 257n35
Walsh, Joseph, 7n12
Walton, Steve, 186n9, 199n67
Wansink, Craig S., 75n7
Webb, Robert L., 109n12
Weinstock, Stefan, 192n31, 193
Wengst, Klaus, 187–88, 199, 200n70
Wesley, John, 262n6
Westerholm, Stephen, 124n5, 126–27, 140n63
Whitehead, Alfred North, 225
Wiarda, Timothy, 180
Wikenhauser, Alfred, 57n3, 117, 121–22
Wilckens, Ulrich, 113n28
Williams, Sam K., 134n49
Williamson, P. S., 230n17
Wilson, Benjamin R., 38n2, 41n14, 41n16, 42n17, 46n39, 46n42, 51n61, 54n75
Wilson, Carol Bakker, 6n7
Wirt, Sherwood E., 19
Witherington, Ben, III, 228n9
Woolf, Greg, 195
Wrede, William, 149
Wright, B. G., 228n10, 229
Wright, Christopher J. H., 261n1, 268n26, 270
Wright, N. T., 107, 126–27, 131n35, 209n6, 210n13, 216n29, 226n3, 231n19, 233n24, 237n35, 237n37

Yarbro Collins, Adela, 73n2, 109n10, 232n20, 232n23, 234n29
Ysebaert, J., 112n26

Zanker, Paul, 192n32
Zerwick, Maximillian, 59n9

Index of Scripture and Other Ancient Texts

Old Testament

Genesis
10–11	270
10:32	270
11:1–9	270
12:1–3	270
12:3	270
16	237
18:4	174
19:2	174
21	237
21:10	238, 238n39
22	237
24:32	174
26:26–30	179
31:43–54	179
35:16–17	98n11
43:24	174
46:31–34	83
49	76
49:10	76

Exodus
4:8	177
4:9	177
4:17	177
4:22–23	252
4:28	177
4:30	177
7:3	177
10:1	177
10:2	177
12:22–28	264
19:5–6	274
23:19	272
24:5–11	180
25:40	234n27
26:30	234n27
27:8	234n27
28:36–38	274
29:45–46	175

Leviticus
10:3	221
11:44	155
11:45	155
19:2	155
20:7	155
20:26	155
26:11–12	175

Numbers
8:4	234n27
14:11	178
14:22	178
21:6–9	61

Deuteronomy
4:34	178
6:5	180
6:13	275
6:22	178
7:9	180
7:19	178
10:12	180
11:1	180
11:3	178
13:3	180
16:38	178
20:11	78
23:9–10	267
26:8	178
27:6–7	180
29:3	178
30:36	180
31:13	178
31:17	178
32	237
34:11	178

Joshua
17:13	78
22:5	181
24:15	275

INDEX OF SCRIPTURE AND OTHER ANCIENT TEXTS

Judges
12:3 — 62
19:21 — 174

1 Samuel
19:5 — 62
21:5 — 267
25:41 — 174
28:21 — 62
29:10 — 65n22

2 Samuel
20:19 — 229n13

1 Kings
19:10 — 231n19
19:14–15 — 231n19

2 Kings
5:14 — 110, 111

Ezra
2:59–63 — 230n17
2:62 — 230n17

Nehemiah
7:5–65 — 230n17
7:64 — 230n17

Job
9:31 — 110n14
22:22 — 65n22

Psalms
29:1–2 — 232n21
36:9 — 228n11
36:10 — 230n18
44 — 237
46:4 — 228, 232n21
47:2–3 — 232n21
60:10 — 232n21
67:28 — 76
68 — 254, 255
68:11–14 — 254
68:18 — 253, 254
68:20 — 268
72 — 218, 223
84:6 — 228n11
86:4 — 229
86:5 — 228, 232
86:7 — 234
87 — 227–33, 237, 238, 239
87:4 — 230, 231
87:5 — 226, 232n23
87:6 — 230n17
108:10 — 232n21
117:28 — 61n14
118:22 — 29
143:2 — 128

Proverbs
4:3 — 78

Isaiah
1:2 — 175
1:21–25 — 239
1:26 — 239
2:2–4 — 232
4:2–4 — 109n12
5:16b — 219
6:3 — 221
11 — 257
11:3–4 — 257
11:9 — 231
11:10–16 — 257
11:14 — 257
12:3 — 228n11
13–14 — 230n15
18 — 230n16
19:18–25 — 232
19:25 — 232
20 — 230n16
21:4 — 111
25:8 — 276
30:7 — 230n15
40–52 — 230n15
40–55 — 235, 236
40–66 — 229, 234, 236
40:5 — 203
42:6 — 270, 274
45:7 — 10
49:1 — 231
49:3 — 231
49:6 — 231, 270, 274
49:10 — 276
49:16 — 235n31
49:19–21 — 229n12
50 — 237
50:1 — 229n12
51:1–3 — 229n12
51:9 — 230n15
51:17–23 — 229n12
52 — 253
52:7 — 253
53:4–6 — 146
53:5 — 150
54 — 229, 239
54:1 — 226, 229, 234, 236
54:11–12 — 233n23
55:10–13 — 257
57:14 — 253
57:19 — 252, 253
59 — 257
59:17 — 257, 258
59:18 — 257
61:10 — 229n12

Index of Scripture and Other Ancient Texts

Jeremiah
1:15	231
4:22	76
9:24	175, 230n18
22:16	20n188
31:2–22	229n14
31:15	4
31:33–34	5
38:15	4
46:9	230n16
47	230n15
50–51	230

Ezekiel
9:3–10	264
13:9	230n17
26–28	230n15
26:35–36	109n12
29–32	230n15
30:4–5	230n16
30:9	230n16
34:25	175
37:26	175
37:27	276
37:27–28	269
47:1	228n11

Daniel
2:48	76
12:1–4	273

Hosea
11:1	252

Joel
2:28–32	113, 115
3:18	228n11

Micah
2:6	76

3:9	76
3:11	76
4:1–3	232
5:1	76
5:2	76

Habakkuk
2:4	135, 139
3:3	221

Zechariah
8:20–23	232
9:9	63
13:1	109n12
13:7	29
14:8	228n11
14:16–19	230n15

New Testament

Matthew
1:1	11
1:23	3
2:18	4
3:6	114
3:11	114
4:1–11	5
4:17	17
4:23–25	12
5–7	21
5:1	15
5:1–12	12
5:3	17
5:10	8, 17
5:10–12	6, 12
5:16–20	11
5:17–48	5
5:34–35	114n32
5:43–44	12
5:48	11

6:1–18	11
6:2–18	5
7:17–20	11
7:24–27	11
8:18–22	7, 15
8:20	8
9:6	9
9:37–38	97n9, 272
10:22	6
10:23	9
10:37–39	7, 15
10:38	39n7
10:41	115
11:30	7
12:40	8
13:24–30	10
13:36–43	10
13:41	9
13:45–46	85
13:47–50	10
15:24	5
16:17–19	23
16:21–23	9
16:24	39n7
16:24–26	7, 15
16:27–28	9
17:12	8
17:22	8
17:22–23	9
18:1–7	8
18:20	115
18:28	42n18
19:3–9	5
19:16–22	5
19:16–30	7, 15
19:27–30	33
19:28	9
20:17–23	9
20:18	8
20:19	38n6, 42n18

305

INDEX OF SCRIPTURE AND OTHER ANCIENT TEXTS

20:25–28	11	2:20	26	12:12	29		
20:28	8, 9	3:6	27	12:13–17	27n8		
21:33–46	10	3:19	27	13:9–13	34		
22:34–40	5	4:29	272	14:1	29		
23:4	7	6:14–29	26	14:8	29		
23:11–12	9	6:17–29	30	14:10	31		
23:24–33	77	6:30–32	26	14:10–11	29, 31		
24:21	273	8:15	27n8	14:11	31		
24:27	9	8:22	27	14:17–21	29		
24:29–31	9	8:22–26	27	14:18	32		
24:37–44	9	8:27–30	20	14:21	32		
24:42–51	20	8:29	23	14:22–25	25, 29		
25:1–13	10	8:31	27, 33, 42n18	14:27	29		
25:1–30	20	8:31–33	23	14:32–41	32		
25:31	9	8:34	22, 24, 33, 34, 39n7	14:36	28		
25:31–46	10, 11			14:41–42	32		
26:2	38n6, 42n18	8:34–35	23	14:43	32		
26:53	5	8:34–9:1	27	14:44	32		
26:56	53n74	9:7	28n11	14:50	53n74		
27:27–31	9	9:11–13	28	15:1	32		
27:32	39n7	9:31	27, 31, 42n18	15:10	32		
27:40	39n7	9:33–37	27	15:12–32	22, 25		
27:42	39n7	9:38	28	15:13–15	25		
27:45	17	10:21	23n2	15:15	32		
27:51–53	17	10:23–27	33	15:20	25		
28:2	17	10:28–31	33	15:21	22, 24, 39n7		
28:5–7	10	10:32–34	27, 33	15:24–25	25		
28:6	20	10:33–34	27, 31, 42n18	15:27	25		
28:18	9	10:35–45	27, 34	15:30	22, 24, 39n7		
28:19	10, 114, 115	10:38	111, 112	15:32	22, 24, 25, 39n7		
28:20	3, 10	10:42–45	25	16:5–6	36		
		10:45	22, 27	16:6	22, 35		
Mark		10:46–52	27				
1:8	114n31	10:52	27	**Luke**			
1:9	114	11:18	28	1:1–4:13	39n9		
1:14	26, 30	11:27	29	1:32–33	40		
1:16–20	33	12:1	29	2:1	199n65		
2:1–3:6	26	12:1–12	28	2:11	40		
2:14	33	12:7–8	28	2:49	42n17		

306

3:1	199n65	9:28–36	41	18:32	51n62
3:6	203	9:35	41	18:32–33	50
3:16	114n31	9:37–43	42, 53	18:33	45n35, 51n62
4:1–13	41	9:44	40, 41, 44, 50, 51n62	18:34	53
4:14–30	41			18:35	46
4:14–9:50	39, 40, 41	9:45–50	53	19:8	48
4:18	41	9:51	41	19:28	39n9
4:43	42n17	9:51–19:27	39, 40	19:28–24:53	39, 40
5:11	42	9:57–62	48n47	19:38	45
5:12	41	11:37–54	44, 45, 49	19:45	39n9
5:24	41	11:45–54	40	19:47–48	50
5:28	42	11:47–48	45	20:1–2	50
6:1–11	41	11:47–52	46	20:9–18	50
6:5	41	11:49	51n62	20:14–15	51n62
6:9	41	11:49–52	45	20:16	51n62
6:13	49	12:33	48	20:17	51n62
6:28	12	12:49–56	45n36	20:19	50
6:32	12	12:50	111, 112	20:20	50
6:36	12	13:31–32	45	21:9	42n17
7:6	41	13:32	45	22:3–6	50
7:13	41	13:32–33	45	22:4	51n62
7:19	41	13:33	45, 51n62	22:6	51n62
7:34	41	13:33–35	40, 44, 45	22:14	49
7:50	41	13:34	45, 51n62	22:15	51n62
8:1–3	42	13:35	45	22:19–20	38, 50
9:7–9	45	14:25–33	43, 47	22:20	198
9:10	49	14:26	47	22:21–22	51n62
9:18–50	40	14:27	39n7, 40, 47, 49, 53	22:22	50
9:20	41			22:24–27	198, 202
9:21–22	40, 41, 42n18, 44, 50	14:28–32	48	22:25–26	198
		14:33	47, 48	22:37	42n17
9:22	41, 42n17, 45n35, 46, 51n62	17:5	49	22:48	51n62
		17:20–21	46	22:54	50
9:23	39n7, 49, 53	17:22–37	45	22:63–65	50
9:23–27	40, 43, 49	17:25	40, 42n17, 44, 46	22:63–23:31	46
9:24	42, 47, 48			23:1–49	46
9:25	43n28	18:28–30	33, 48n47	23:14	51
9:26	43	18:31–33	46	23:15	51
9:27	43	18:31–34	40, 44	23:21	38n6

INDEX OF SCRIPTURE AND OTHER ANCIENT TEXTS

23:22	51	1:29	170	5:28	64n21
23:23	38n6	1:29–36	170	5:42	59n9
23:26	39n7, 40, 50, 53	1:34	170	6:3	180
23:32–46	51	1:36	170	6:7	180
23:32–24:53	40	1:38	165, 170	6:11	180
23:33	38n6	1:38–39	165, 170, 173	6:15–22	180
23:47	51	1:42	180	6:29–51	171
24:7	38n6, 42n17, 45n35, 51	1:46	170	6:30–58	170
		1:50–51	170	6:59–71	171
24:20	38n6, 51	1:51	170	6:70	65
24:21	45n35	2:1–11	170	7:1–9	61
24:26	42n17, 51n62, 52	2:4	64n21, 173	7:6–8	173
24:26–27	46	2:19–22	60, 63, 177	7:10–24	61
24:44	42n17	2:22	170	7:23	169
24:44–46	54	2:23–25	171	7:25–31	61
24:46	45n35, 46, 51n62, 52	3:1–21	166, 170, 171	7:27	59n9
		3:10–12	60	7:30	64n21, 173
		3:14	173, 177	7:31–52	171
John		3:14–15	60, 63	7:39	61n16, 169
1:1–11	167	3:16–17	172	7:40–44	61
1:1–18	56, 166	3:16–18	171	7:45–52	61
1:5	56	3:22	110	8:12–20	61
1:7	170	3:22–36	170	8:12–59	171
1:7–8	170	3:23	114	8:20	64n21, 173
1:8	168	3:27	169	8:21	62
1:9–10	167, 169	3:28–36	169	8:21–30	60, 61, 63
1:10	168	4:1–2	110	8:22	62
1:10–11	56	4:1–29	170, 171	8:22–26	62
1:10–14	165	4:1–42	166	8:27	62
1:11	168	4:21	59n11, 64n21	8:28	62, 173, 177
1:12	165, 168, 169, 170, 176	4:23	64n21	8:50–59	170
		4:29	170	9:1–41	170
1:14	56, 67, 169, 170	4:35	59n9	9:8	59n9
1:15	170	4:35–38	272	9:29	59n9
1:16–17	169	4:36	169	10:7	63
1:18	56, 169, 170	4:39–44	171	10:11	62, 63, 65
1:19–28	170	4:45–54	171	10:11–18	60, 62, 63, 65
1:19–12:50	166	5:10–47	171	10:14	63
1:26	114	5:25	64n21	10:15	62, 63, 65

10:17	62, 63, 65	13:12–17	66	16:13	70
10:18	62, 63, 65, 169	13:14b	66	16:14	61n16
10:24–41	171	13:15	64, 173	16:14–15	70
10:42	171	13:18–30	68	15:16	177
11:1–17	171	13:19	171	15:23–33	171
11:1–44	166	13:20	170	15:24	170
11:20–30	171	13:26–27	174	16:25–26a	175
11:28–40	171	13:31–32	61n16	16:26–27	70
11:31	59n9	13:34–35	68, 165, 173, 174	16:26b–28	175
11:34	170			16:29–30	175
12:1–8	171	13:37	63	16:32–33	175
12:12–13a	63	14:1	171, 175	17:1	61n16
12:12–30	60, 63	14:1–31	173	17:1–5	176
12:13b	63	14:2–29	171	17:1–26	171, 173, 176
12:14–15	63	14:3	175	17:4	61n16
12:16	63	14:7	175	17:5	61n16
12:23	61n16, 64n21, 171, 173	14:7–20	170	17:6–19	176
		14:15	175	17:18	176
12:27	64n21	14:16	59n11	17:21–26	176
12:28	61n16	14:17	59n9, 175	18:15–27	179
12:32	173, 177	14:18–19	177	18:37–38	165
12:33	173	14:20–21	175	19:17	38n6
12:36–50	171	14:21	175	19:30	177
12:45–50	170	14:23–24	175	19:35	171, 181
13:1	65, 68, 172	14:26	59n11, 175	20:1–29	177
13:1a	64	14:27	175	20:8	171
13:1d	64	14:29	171	20:24–29	172
13:1–17	64, 68	15:1	63	20:25–29	170
13:1–38	173	15:1–17	175	20:29	172, 179
13:1–17:26	64n20, 171, 176	15:1–16:3	173	20:30–31	165, 172, 176, 177, 179
		15:13	174		
13:2	65, 174	15:18–27	175	21:2–14	179
13:3	65	15:26	59n11	21:9–13	179
13:4–20	174	15:26–27	175	21:15–17	181
13:5	66	16:1–4	175, 182	21:18–19	181, 182
13:6	66	16:4	59n9	21:19	179
13:6–9	66	16:4–24	175	21:20–23	181
13:8a	66	16:4–33	173	21:22	165, 179, 181
13:11	179	16:8–11	70	21:24	181

INDEX OF SCRIPTURE AND OTHER ANCIENT TEXTS

21:24–25	179	20:3	185	6:1–14	93
21:25	181	20:21	121n64	6:1–23	215
		21:27–40	185	6:2	106, 216
Acts		21:38	199	6:2–6	121
1:5	114n32	22:16	115	6:3	113, 115, 119, 121, 216
1:8	199	23–24	77		
1:13	199	23:26	199n67	6:3–4	113, 116–17, 118, 119
2:17–21	115n38	24:5	199n65		
2:38	114, 115, 141	24:24	121n64	6:4	212n18, 215
5:36–37	199n65	24:26–27	199n67	6:4–5	113
7:55–60	55	25:25	199n67	6:5	118, 214
8:16	115	26:28	152	6:6	25n4, 113, 119
9:14	115n38			6:6a	216
9:21	115n38	**Romans**		6:6b	216
9:23–25	185	1:3–4	211	6:7	216, 216n31
9:29	185	1:5	12	6:8	215
10:25	201	1:18–32	217	6:8–9	113
10:26	201	1:21	255	6:9	222
10:36	200, 202, 202n74	1:21–22	255	6:10–11	216
		1:22–32	219	6:12–14	217
10:43	121n64	1:24	219	6:13	216
10:48	114, 115	3:22	213	6:13b	217
11:16	114n31	3:23–24	129	6:14	118
11:26	152	3:24	218	6:18–19	216, 218
11:28	199n65	4:3–8	138	6:19	219
12:20–23	190	4:18	121n64	6:22	218
13:50	185	4:25	213, 214	7:1–6	119
14:19	185	5–6	213	7:4	121, 215
14:23	121n64	5:1	213	7:14	93, 95
15:17	115n38	5:6–8	213	7:23	234n28
16:19–24	185	5:9	213, 219	8:1–13	93, 95
17:5–9	185	5:10	213	8:3	148
17:13	185	5:12–14	214	8:6–7	75
18:2	199n65	5:12–21	118, 138, 210, 212n20, 214, 220	8:10	93
18:12–17	185			8:11	121n61
18:17	199n67	5:17	214, 215, 215n27	8:11–13	113n30
19:3–5	115	5:21	214, 215	8:14	252
19:5	114	6:1–10	120	8:15	155
19:23–40	185	6:1–11	107, 215	8:17	7

310

Index of Scripture and Other Ancient Texts

8:21	222, 223	15:20–23	210	2:16	121, 128–29, 133
8:23	141, 155	15:20–28	220	2:19	25n4, 238
8:29	252	15:21–22	220	2:19–20	113n30, 119, 130
8:31–39	237	15:23–28	213n21	2:20–21	238
9–11	237	15:25	215	2:21	130
9:4	155	15:26	222	3:1–6	124
10	237	15:28	223	3:1–14	132–37
10:13	115n38	15:42	221, 223	3:11	129
12	21	15:43	211, 212n18	3:14	115n36, 127
12:1–2	75	15:44	223	3:21	127, 137–38
12:8	77	15:45	210, 212n20	3:22	137
13:14	113, 114	15:49	220	3:26–29	113, 141
14:17	128	15:51–52	220	3:27	113, 115, 118
15:7–13	237	15:53b	220	3:28	113, 115n36
16:26	12	15:54b	220	4	231
				4:1–4	252
1 Corinthians		**2 Corinthians**		4:3	129
1:2	115n38	1:21	115	4:4	82
1:13	113, 114, 115, 116	1:22	141	4:4–5	149
1:13–17	108	2:9	81	4:4–6	134
1:15	115, 116	3:1–3	251	4:5	155
1:30	209, 210, 212, 213, 223	4:10–12	113n30	4:7	113
		5:5	141	4:9	129, 230, 231
3:10–15	118	5:17	212	4:11	237
4	21	5:21	218	4:21–31	226
4:8–13	12	8:9	149	4:21–5:1	133, 227, 237
5:4	115	11:13	97n9	4:26	226, 232n20, 237, 238
6:11	112, 115n35, 128	11:15	97n9	4:27	226, 236
6:14	212n18, 213n21, 220	**Galatians**		4:30	238, 238n39
7:7–24	113n29	1	231	5:4–5	137–38
10:2	115, 121	1:4	129, 233	5:6	12
12:12–13	113	1:6–9	238	5:24	238
12:13	115, 118	1:6–2:10	236	5:25	124, 136
15	10	1:14–17	231n19	6:7–8	129n30
15:3–4	119	1:24	231	6:8	124, 136
15:9	100	2:11–21	128–32	6:11–16	236
15:13	220	2:12	236	6:15	213
15:17	214	2:15–21	123, 124		

311

Ephesians

1:5	155
1:7	246
1:11	251
1:14	141, 251
1:18	251
1:20–21	250, 251
2	253
2:1–3	248
2:6	249
2:11	249
2:12	249
2:13	246, 248
2:13–21	250
2:14	244
2:15	212n20
2:16	246
2:17	244, 252, 253
2:19	242
2:19–22	251
3:1	245, 246, 249
3:6	242, 251
3:13	246
3:14	250
3:14–15	251
3:17	252
4:1	245
4:8	253, 254
4:17–20	255
4:17–23	253
4:17–5:2	255
4:22	255
4:22–24	113, 212n20
4:24	255
4:25–5:2	255
5:9	257
6	257
6:10–17	256
6:15	257
6:19–20	246
6:20	245

Philippians

1–3	84
1:6	104
1:12–13	85
1:12–17	82
1:27–30	99
1:29	121n64
2:1–2	73
2:3	18, 75, 82
2:3–4	73
2:5	73, 85, 101
2:5–11	97, 99
2:6	75, 82, 84, 85
2:6–8	19, 74, 82
2:6–11	18, 73, 77, 80, 146, 150, 151
2:7	81
2:7–8	149
2:8	81, 82, 221n45
2:9	82
2:9–10	211, 212
2:9–11	82, 211, 221n45
2:10–11	10
2:11	84
2:12	78
2:12–13	12
2:25	75, 82
3	233n24
3:1–11	98
3:2	96
3:4–6	97, 98, 99
3:5	98n11
3:6	100
3:7	75
3:7–8	82
3:8	75
3:8–9	74
3:8–12	102
3:9–11	113n30
3:10	213
3:10–14	102
3:12	89
3:13	12
3:13–14	103
3:15	74
3:18	97
3:18–19	74, 75
3:19	101
3:20	233
3:21	101, 211, 221, 221n45
4:4–8	74

Colossians

2:5	121n64
2:12	119
2:12–13	113
2:20	113
3:1	113
3:1–5	113
3:9–11	113, 212n20
3:11	113
4:18	246

1 Thessalonians

2:12	221
4:13–18	221, 221n44
4:14	215
4:15–17	221
5:12	77
5:23	222

2 Thessalonians

1:12	221, 222

1 Timothy
3:16	210

Titus
3:5–7	141

Hebrews
3:1–5	113
8:1–7	234
8:2	234
8:5	275
8:13	236
10:29	77
11:11	77
11:14–16	234
11:26	77
12:22–24	234
13:7	77
13:17	77
13:24	77

James
2:7	115n38

1 Peter
1:1	154, 156
1:2	155
1:3	146, 153, 155, 158
1:4	152
1:6–7	154
1:11	149–50
1:14	115, 156
1:15	156
1:15–16	154
1:16	155
1:17	155
1:18	155
1:19	156
1:21	121n64, 151
1:22	156
1:23	146, 155, 158
2:4	154
2:9	156
2:15	151
2:17	151
2:20	158
2:21	146, 151
2:21–24	158
2:21–25	150, 151
3:8	151
3:12	146
3:16	146
3:18	146, 150
3:18–22	153
3:21	121n63, 159
4:1	150
4:2–4	157
4:8	151
4:12	154
4:13	150, 151, 158
4:16	152
4:17	155
4:18	146
5:1	150, 151, 153
5:2–13	153
5:10	146, 153, 156
5:14	146, 151

2 Peter
1:4	145

1 John
3:18–20	183
3:23–24	183

Revelation
1:1	263n7, 264
1:2	272
1:6	270, 274, 275
1:9	272, 273
1:12	262n4
1:20	262n4
2:2	275
2:9	273
2:10	273
2:13	273
2:20	275
3	235
3:4–5	273
3:7	275
3:9	275
3:12	234
3:18	273
3:22	262
5:5	264
5:5–6	265
5:8	275
5:9	264, 268, 270, 275
5:9–10	269, 270, 274
5:10	274, 275
6–20	261
6:9	272
6:9–11	264
6:11	273
6:17	262, 264
7	17, 273, 277
7:1	263, 264
7:1–3	264
7:1–8	262, 265, 269
7:1–17	260, 261, 266, 268
7:2–4	263
7:3	263, 264, 268, 271
7:3–4	273
7:4	265, 268

INDEX OF SCRIPTURE AND OTHER ANCIENT TEXTS

7:4–8	260, 263, 264, 267, 270	13:16–18	264, 272	20:8	275
		14	277	20:10	275
7:5	264	14:1	266, 269, 271, 274, 275	21–22	234
7:9	263, 265, 266, 270, 273, 274			21:2	268n25, 275
		14:1–5	260, 261, 262, 266, 267, 268, 271, 275, 276	21:4	277
7:9–10	265, 275, 276			21:5	277
7:9–17	260, 265, 266, 267, 269, 270, 271, 273, 278			21:6	276
		14:2	275	21:7	277
		14:3	264, 266, 269, 270, 275	21:9	268n25, 275
7:10	268, 269, 271, 272			21:22	275
		14:4	264, 267, 268, 269, 272, 274, 275, 277	21:24	277
7:11	266			21:26	277
7:11–12	275			22:1–2	276
7:14	265, 268, 273, 274	14:5	272, 274, 275	22:2	277
		14:6	270	22:3	263n7
7:15	269, 275, 276	14:6–7	271, 273, 274, 276	22:6	263n7, 264
7:15–17	265, 268, 276, 277			22:14	274
		14:6–13	261	22:16	262
7:16–17	269	14:7	273, 277		
7:17	277	14:9	276	**DEUTERO-**	
7:21–22	265	14:9–11	264	**CANONICAL BOOKS**	
9:4	264	14:11	276		
10:7	263n7	14:14–16	272	**Judith**	
11:1–13	261	15:1	262	7:8	76
11:3–13	272, 273	15:1–4	276	12:7	111
11:4	262	15:2–4	273	14:10	108
11:18	263n7	15:3–4	271, 274		
12:9	275	15:4	276	**Wisdom of Solomon**	
12:10	268	16:1	262	9:8	234
12:11	264, 272, 275	16:2	276	14:22	204
12:17	272	18:23	275		
13:4	276	19:1	268	**Sirach**	
13:7	269	19:5	263n7	10:2	76
13:8	276	19:7	268n25	34:25	111
13:9	269	19:7–8	274	41:17	76
13:12	276	19:10	272	44:16	67n29
13:14	272, 275	19:20	272, 275, 276	46:18	76
13:15	269, 276	20:3	275		
13:16–17	266	20:6	274		

Index of Scripture and Other Ancient Texts

Baruch
4   234
4:10   234
4:11   234
4:23   234
4:29   234
4:36   234
5   234
5:1   234
5:9   234

1 Maccabees
1:3   191
9:30   76

2 Maccabees
6:28   67n29

1 Esdras
6:27   79n16

Old Testament Pseudepigrapha

2 Baruch
4   235
4:3–5   235n32
25:4   273

1 Enoch
53:6   234
90:28–29   234

2 Enoch
55:2   234

4 Ezra
6:35–9:25   235
8:52   235

10:25–27   235
10:54   235

Joseph and Aseneth
4:7   267n25
8:1   267n25
24:15   79n15

Letter of Aristeas
44   79n20
253   79n20

4 Maccabees
17:22–23   67n29

Psalms of Solomon
4   237n38
17:30–31   232n21

Sibylline Oracles
4:162–165   110
5:286–433   235n30
5:420–427   235n30
8:111   79n17

Dead Sea Scrolls

1QS
II, 25–III, 8   110
V, 13–15   110

3Q15
I, 11–12   111n15

4QFlor.   235n33

4Q255
f.2, 1–5   110

4Q257
f.3, 6–14   110

4Q274
2i, 4–5   111n15

4Q414
f.2, ii, 3–4   110

4Q504
1–2.4   235n33

4Q512
f.2 ii, 3–4   110

4Q554
2.2.14–16   235n33

11QPs Zion
2 2.1–15   235n33
11QT   235n33

11Q19
XLV, 15–16   108n7

Ancient Jewish Writers

Josephus

Antiquities
2.212   79n20
5.248   79n16
9.212   111n23
10.3   81
10.169   111n23
14.84   79n14
14.484   81
15.55   111n23

20.34–46	108	*De sacrificiis Abelis et Caini*		**EARLY CHRISTIAN WRITINGS**	
20.47	79n17	9	79n21		
Jewish War		*De somniis*		**Ambrose**	
1.355	81	1.162	79n14	*The Sacraments*	
1.414	201	2.81–92	190	2.23	122n68
2.457	81	2.85	189		
2.476	111	*De specialibus legibus*		**Cyril of Jerusalem**	
2.97	79n20	2.48	79n21	*On the Mysteries*	
3.196	111n24	*Legatio ad Gaium*		2.4	122n67
3.423	111n23	143–153	201	**Gregory of Nyssa**	
Philo		*Legum allegoriae*		*Life of Moses*	
De agricultura		3.88	79n15, 79n21	225–226	103–4
57–59	83	*Quod omnis probus liber sit*		**GRECO-ROMAN LITERATURE**	
65	83				
66	83	154	79n14		
De cherubim		**RABBINIC WORKS**		**Appian**	
83	79n21, 80, 82			*Civil War*	
De confusione linguarum		**b. Kerithot**		1.35	79n20
54	79n14	9a	109n10	*Foreign Wars*	
De decalogo		**b. Yebamot**		10.56	79n14
166	79n14	46a	109	**Aristotle**	
De ebrietate		**m. Pesahim**		*Politics*	
198	79n19	8:8	108	1260A 7–9	197
De gigantibus		**m. Miqwa'ot**		1327B	197
46	79n14, 79n18	1:7–2:2	108n7	*Rhetoric*	
De migratione Abrahami		8:5–9:3	108n7	1382B	189
8	79n14	**m. Tebul Yom**	110n16	**Athenaeus**	
De opificio mundi		**Sifre on Numbers**		*Deipnosophistae*	
142	79n14	108	109	1.9b	79n17
165	79n21, 80				

Index of Scripture and Other Ancient Texts

Augustus

Res gestae Divi Augusti
13	194
25–33	195

Chariton

De Chaerea et Callirhoe
3.4.6.3	111n24

Cicero

De imperio Cn. Pompeii
53	191n29
56	191

In Catalinam
2.11	191
4.11	191

Orationes philippicae
5.17.48	190

Pro Balbo
16	191

Pro Murena
22	191

Pro Sulla
33	191

Rhetorica ad Herennium
4.13	191

Dio Cassius
37.21.2	191

Dio Chrysostom

Orations
3.12–13	189
3.118	189
64.6	79n21

Diodorus Siculus

Library
16.80	111n24

Epictetus

Diatribai
2.9.19–21	108
4.13.5	189

Horace

Carmina
4.15.13–16	191

Livy

Fasti
2.684	192

Lucian

Timon
44	111

Macrobius

Saturnalia
II.4.1	189

Plato

Symposium
176b	111n24

Pliny the Elder

Naturalis historia
3.39	196

Pliny the Younger

Panegyricus
3.4	200
53.2	190

Plutarch

Alexander
28.1–2	190

Antonius
61.1	79n17

De adulatore et amico
56EF	190
58A	190
60D	190
61A	190
65E	190
66B	189

De Alexandri magni fortuna aut virtute
2.5	190

Demosthenes
10.4–11.1	190
12.1	190
13.1–3	190
24.1–2	190
30.4–5	190
42.5	190
42.8–11	190

De superstitione
3	112

Exile
607D	233n25

Marriage Advice
3	79n20

Ps.-Demetrius

De elocutione
240	203
241	204
287–295	190
294	189

Ps.-Dionysius

Ars rhetorica
8–11	190

Ps.-Hermogenes

On Invention
4.12	190
4.13	189

Quintilian

Institutio oratoria
9.2.64	203
9.2.66	189

Seneca

Epistulae morales
8	189

Soranus

Gynecology
2.63	111n24

Suetonius

Augustus
18.1	191

Domitian
12.1	189

Nero
32.2	189

Ulpian

Digest
1.18.13	195

Virgil

Aeneid
1.278–292	191
1.279	198

Georgica
3.16–33	191

Xenophon

Cyropaedia
8.2.11–12	189

www.ingramcontent.com/pod-product-compliance
Lightning Source LLC
Chambersburg PA
CBHW032000220426
43664CB00005B/92